London Churches
& Olde Celebrities

Vol. II: Environs - A Compleat Guide and Perambulation

John Blythe Smart

Published by Blythe Smart Publications in 2012

A CIP catalogue record for this book is available from the British Library.

ISBN: 978 - 0 - 9545017 - 7 - 8

Cover, Type: Blythe Smart Publications
Printers: Berforts Group Ltd.

Blythe Smart Publications
Kingsbridge - England

Contents

London City (see Volume I)

About the Author

John Smart was born at Farnborough, Kent in 1960 and educated at Alleyn's School in South London and Nottingham University. His main academic interests were historical geography and the history of architecture.

In addition his forebears included E.G. Blythe and E.H. Niemann, 19th century artists, and Colin Blythe the famous cricketer leading to a further interest in matters historical. Consequently, he undertook genealogical study at home and abroad over many years, as well as indulging in local history research.

His family supported Millwall F.C. from the 1920s and it was this sporting experience which provided the initial inspiration for a writing career. After visiting most historic football grounds located in Britain, he determined to write about them and researched soccer history, and thus became interested in the lives and genealogies of the founders. The result was *The Wow Factor - How Soccer Evolved* with two editions in 2003-05, whilst as a diversion he wrote an historical allegory *The Wizards of Wight*.

More recently he published a seminal work on the first F.A. president, *Arthur Pember's Great Adventures*, a biography of the Victorian polymorph and undercover reporter over two continents. This was followed by a concise version *The Founders of Soccer* revealing the founders were connected to every aspect of British history.

His most recent work *The Real Colin Blythe* provided a detailed biography of the Kent and England spin-bowler, re-examining his origins and other related historical issues. The latter three books were published during the period 2007-09.

Introduction

Edward Stanford (cartographer)

All the changes to London's fabric detailed in the first volume were soon recorded by a cartographer of note. Edward Stanford was born at Holborn in 1827 and educated at the City of London School, then worked as an assistant to Trelawney Saunders stationer and map-seller at 6 Charing Cross from 1848. Meanwhile he received training from Augustus Petermann a geographical draughtsman who worked next door.

Stanford became a partner by 1852 and the next year sole proprietor and a fellow of the Royal Geographical Society. In addition he established the business as a *Map Specialist* on a firm basis, purchasing neighbouring properties and a printing works at Trinity Lane. Initially he commissioned Dr. Alexander K. Johnston to construct and engrave a series of library maps of *Great Continents*, the finest series of maps since the grand series of wall maps by Aaron Arrowsmith in the late 18th century.

Further to this, he employed his former boss Mr. Saunders to oversee the construction of a *Library Map of London*. At this time the sole official survey was a skeleton map with main roads, done by the R.E. for the "Commissioners of Sewers of the Metropolis," on a scale: 12 inches to a mile. Using this as a framework, surveyors were then employed to fill in any significant omissions. As fast as the sheets came in they were reduced to a scale of 6 inches to a mile, then engraved with infinite pains on steel plates.

This map was completed and published in 1862 bringing Stanford to prominence, and the R.G.S. then announced, "This is the most perfect map of London that has ever been issued." In 1873, after the death of John Arrowsmith (founder of the R.G.S.), the copper plates forming his *London Atlas* were purchased, and Stanford moved the business to 55 Charing Cross and then to 12 Long Acre near Covent Garden.

He married Mary Nesbitt Baker at Hendon in 1855 and had a son Edward at Charing Cross, who became his assistant, and married secondly to Constant Mary Hewer in 1871. His residence was then in Streatham although he moved to 81 Widmore Road, Bromley by 1881 and had sons William and Arthur. He was recorded as *a publisher of books and maps* but retired to Sidmouth, Devon in 1884 and his son Edward took over - selling the stationery business, with William a map compiler. Suffering from chronic asthma he died at Sidmouth on 3 November 1904 whilst his wife died in 1926. [1]

Regarding religion the Victorian apotheosis of worship was less of a pinnacle and more of a slippery slope, whereas the London of Johnson and Dickens encapsulated in these maps was dramatically altered over the next 150 years.

One significant change was carried out by the Metropolitan Board of Works to ease the severe traffic problems, especially on the toll bridges. They purchased 11 bridges at a cost of £1.4 million in 1878-80 and the Prince and Princess of Wales drove across them *for free* to celebrate Victoria's birthday, while Tower Bridge arrived in 1894.

---

[1] The Long Acre premises were expanded from 1900 and O.S. Maps sold there but the property was destroyed in the war. It became part of George Philip & Son from 1947-2001 but is now a separate company, again called "Stanford's," and remains at Covent Garden.

Wren's churches were on prime city locations and many were closed and demolished from the 1830s, the start of a practice that continued into the next century. This saw the loss of a number of masterpieces in the capital as well as more nondescript Victorian edifices built from the 1860s. A survey of 1890 revealed that Marylebone had 26 parishes and St. Pancras 33 yet a hundred years earlier "they were in the country."

However the greatest changes came in the 20th century and after the blitz many were left in ruins. Some were repaired especially those by Wren, whilst St. Anne's Soho and St. George's Camberwell were converted to flats and others went to new denominations or faiths. The wider issues of Christianity and State remain pertinent if these churches are not to become a relic of a bygone age, although many remain active thus Holy Trinity, Brompton founded and operated the very successful Alpha Courses.

Church of England attendance declined to as low as 5% of the population, a situation that could never have been envisaged in the 19th century, although evangelical groups from the Nonconformist sector experienced a rise. There has been a loss of moral input by religion which existed for a millennium, replaced by the influence of State control as clearly predicted by H.G. Wells, Aldous Huxley, and George Orwell.

The pivotal role of religion was thus removed from the social equation to produce an industrial dystopia, and this is mirrored in the skyline as *Canaletto's spires* are submerged amongst the *halls of finance*. Despite this many still work to keep the surviving churches and their architectural heritage ongoing, vibrant and alive.

In the remainder of this book there is a detailed discussion of all the major churches found within the boundaries of Stanford's map. In particular the historic parishes, since the Victorian Gothic of the suburbs came and went without major influence. This covers Poplar, Bow, Hackney and Islington, westwards to Paddington and Kensington, south to Chelsea and Battersea and east to Clapham, Camberwell and Greenwich.

London East

Our survey of London begins with the euphemistic East End an area of immigrants down through the centuries, poor sojourners who hoped to find part of the City rubbing off on their shirt sleeves. In olden times they came from Europe displaced by famine, religious persecution and war looking for a brighter future in a land of democratic opportunity.

Initially this area beyond the city limits was just a single parish abutting with the river, but the Renaissance brought to these burgeoning dockland haunts classical churches of immense stature. In Rome these edifices might have graced the latest *Baedeker*, but here they were often out of place among the crumbling terraces, wharves and warehouses.

Few succeeded from such a situation hence those of note are generally the architects who visited and took their profits to more sunny climes. Thus we consider Dance, Hawksmoor, Soane and Vulliamy added to some maritime celebrities such as Captain Cook and John Hunter.

Other names in the locality are Pater author and aesthete, Steevens a literary editor, Cass the philanthropist, James Parkinson the doctor, Jane Randolph mother of the president, the Burbages all thespians, Perkin the chemist and perhaps on an ill-wind blows the Beaufort scale. Whereas of the churches St. Katharine, amongst others, has a fascinating story to tell.

St. George in the East

A name with an oriental flavour - points towards the origins of its parishioners, but with a hidden secret behind its western door?

The East End

Passing out of the city environs through Aldgate one came to an area that was already built up by the 16th century, and it was here that Stow decried the loss of sweet fields for recreation. Regarding this, two historical events of major significance took place.

In the first instance the Revocation of the Edict of Nantes by Louis XIV of France in 1685, resulted in the closure of Calvinist or French Protestant churches and persecution of those who practiced the faith. As a result large numbers migrated to the neighbouring countries and in England they settled at Spitalfields and the adjacent districts. Here they became established mainly as weavers, in particular weavers of silk.

The second monumental event also had religious motives at its core and related to the succession to the throne after William & Mary and her sister Anne. With no Protestant heir apparent the *Act of Settlement* was passed in 1701 excluding Catholics (and those married to them) from taking the throne, thus denying any claims of James Stuart and his sister Louisa. The line passed to Electress Sophia of Hanover granddaughter of James I and matters were cemented with the *Act of Union* in 1707. [1]

After Queen Anne died in 1714 members of the Whig Party who supported the act rose to power, and George I son of Sophia acceded to the throne despite the fact he did not speak English. Back in his homeland there was church reform regarding both Calvin and Luther although such reforms did not generally extend to the wider society.

A provincial system existed in the towns that protected those in trade (like a "closed shop"), and excluded movement from the countryside. Land was then inherited under primogeniture and younger siblings were dispossessed and termed *Heuermann* or *Heuerling*. These hired men or "slaves" literally owned nothing, had nowhere to live and therefore had no prospects of marriage. Often taking up residence in a tumbledown barn owned by their elder brothers, this was not a recipe for social contentment, and under further pressure during wars many immigrated to the New World.

Hanover was in the north of Germany between Holstein and the emerging Prussian states, and many of its subjects left the rolling hillsides of their birthplace and followed their ruler to London - to look for work and a brighter future. In fact, large numbers of Hanoverians and Prussians occupied the East End, working in the extensive sugar baking and tobacco industries supplied through the nearby docks.

At the time of Rocque's map, the main thoroughfare of Whitechapel Road led east to Mile End Old Town with ribbon housing on each side, while Brick Lane and Spitalfields were completely built-up. However Stepney and its church remained rural, and Bethnal Green and its environs were dominated by market gardens and weaving.

Change was soon in the air and further development took place at Mile End New Town to the north, whilst Commercial Road was built by the East India Company in the early 19th century. Such developments attracted Irish and Jewish immigrants, but by that time there were no *sweet fields* left, much of the housing stock reduced to slums.

---

[1] Sophia daughter of Frederick V of the Rhine palatinate married Ernest Augustus at Heidelberg in 1658 and had seven children including George I in 1660. His father became the first ruler of Brunswick-Lüneburg or the Hanover (Hannover) Electorate in 1692.

St. Mary, Spital Square - The area of Lollesworth Fields was a swampy site beyond the walls, but Walter and Rosia Brune started St. Mary's priory hospital there in 1197 and it was called Spittle Fields. Some land to the south was given to the new Hon. Artillery Co. in 1537 and named the Old Artillery Ground, whereas the priory was dissolved two years later. The company went to Bunhill Fields during 1641-58 and the site was replaced with housing from 1682 - now demarked by Artillery Lane and Brushfield Street.

The other priory lands became the liberty of Norton Folgate, and Sir George Wheler established a chapel or tabernacle at Spital Square on the ruins during 1670-80. A short time afterwards Spitalfields Market was inaugurated nearby. In the years that followed the Huguenots occupied rows of houses, with lofts for spinning silk, and built nine French churches including one at Wheler Street. However, the former served the spiritual needs of the district including Norton Folgate and the Old Artillery Ground.

Rev. Josiah Pratt was minister at the "Wheler Chapel" in 1810-26 and it was made into the parish of St. Mary Spital in 1845 - covering the adjacent streets and Norton Folgate. However it was closed down as early as 1911 the parish going to Christchurch.

Christchurch, Spitalfields

Spitalfields, part of Stepney, was a highly populated area with about 20,000 inhabitants and was promptly designated under the Fifty Churches Act as needing two new parishes. A site was identified at Red Lyon Street in September 1712 and the following year the surveyors Hawksmoor and Gibbs marked out the ground, but it was Hawksmoor who provided a design costing £9,129 in April 1714. Shortly afterwards the footings were laid and it was determined that there should be a two tier gallery.

Christchurch, Spitalfields

One of three monumental churches designed by Hawksmoor in the East End - this being a part of the "Fifty Churches" remit.

The elongated façade has a theatrical or Baroque composition, while the similarity to **Diocletian's Palace** at Spalatro is definitely striking.

Hawksmoor never travelled to Italy but was inspired during his time with Vanbrugh and Wren, and the writings of Palladio who wrote *I Quattro Libri dell' Architettura* (Four Books) at Venice in 1570 - a treatise on pure classical design with many illustrations. In addition his scheme at Spitalfields looked to the Baroque of Borromini and incorporated elements from the ruins of Diocletian's Palace at Spalatro. [2]

The monumental construction had a three stage tower with Tuscan columns, arch and entablatures at the lower levels, and a somewhat Gothic spire at the apex. The interior consisted of a box-nave with a richly carved flat ceiling lit by clerestory windows, while the aisles had transverse barrel vaults supported on ornate composite columns. It was a great undertaking and the structure was completed in the years 1714-29.

However the original creation was radically altered after a restoration by Ewan Christian in 1850, the galleries being removed and windows lowered; then Commercial Street was built in front during the mid-19th century. From that time both the fabric and locality declined and the impressive ceiling was declared unsafe in 1960, forcing the parishioners to move into the church hall - a former Huguenot chapel.

Demolition was muted by the Bishop of Stepney but money was raised from the sale of St. John's, Smith Square for repairs, and extensive restoration took place in 1986-2004. This work revealed the beauty of the Portland stone and the interior was refurbished to Hawksmoor's design including reinstatement of the galleries and large windows.

The church was then re-opened for a variety of uses including orchestral concerts, and plans were made to repair the massive Richard Bridge organ (1735). There was a decline in the silk industry after the *Spitalfields Riot* in 1769 and the area became slums, but today the market (rebuilt on Victoria's Jubilee) and artisans' housing are worth a visit. To the east is the Truman, Hanbury & Co. brewery on Brick Lane, with a plaque to Thomas F. Buxton abolitionist and reformer who lived in the director's house there.

Local Residents - Several notables lived in this vibrant parish and of these Nicholas Culpeper (1616-54) was born in Red Lyon Street when it was still semi-rural. However he was baptized at Ockley, Surrey his father a clergyman and after a profitable marriage set up a pharmacy in Spitalfields - also working as an astronomer and herbalist.

In addition Obadiah Shuttleworth (d.1734) composer and organist was born there and first held a post at St. Mary's, Whitechapel before playing organ at St. Michael's, Cornhill and the Temple. Other births were Jack Sheppard highwayman and escapee of Newgate at Fashion Street, Jeremy Bentham philosopher and prison designer at Church Lane (see Aldgate) and Mary Wollstonecraft possibly born at 21 Hanbury Street. [3]

---

[2] Diocletian's Palace at Spalatro or Split in modern Croatia is now a World Heritage Site and the ruined interior with columns and pediment is a carbon copy of the Christchurch façade. This is despite the fact that it only became familiar after Robert Adam surveyed the ruins in Dalmatia and published his drawings and findings in London in 1764.

[3] Mary Wollstonecraft was born on 27 April 1759 the daughter of Edward John and Elizabeth (née Dixon) - baptized St. Botolph's, Bishopsgate. Her father was a trader and speculator but she improved her position as a governess and wrote influential works namely *A Vindication of the Rights of Women*. She married philosopher William Godwin and died in 1797 (see St. Pancras).

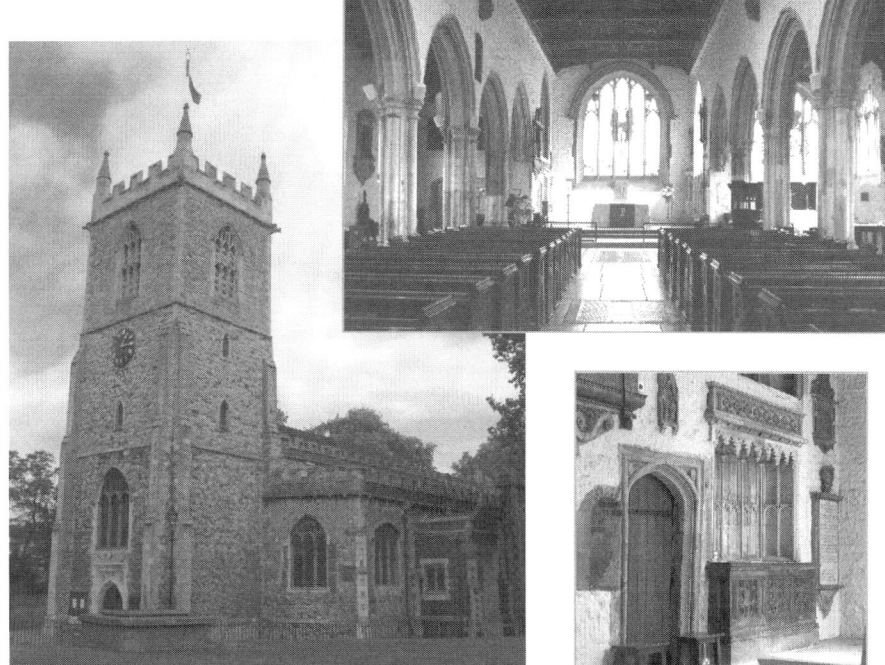

St. Dunstan's with detail from the chancel

St. Dunstan and All Saints, Stepney

When discussing the East End this is of great significance and was the "mother church" from Saxon times covering an area from the City to the River Lea, with hamlets at Mile End, Ratcliffe, Limehouse and Poplar plus the Isle of Dogs. It was located on Stepney Green below Mile End Road and despite its land-locked location was called the *Church of the High Seas* due to links with Ratcliffe to the south and the Port of London.

Dunstan, Bishop of London and Lord of the Manor, replaced the wooden church of All Saints with a stone building in 952. He was the Archbishop of Canterbury soon after and crowned King Edgar in 973, whilst his remains became a place of pilgrimage as with Thomas à Becket. His high status as a monk, scholar, reformer and statesman meant he was canonised in 1029 and the church dedication was altered to St. Dunstan's.

Today's building was the third on the site and the chancel dates to the 13th century, but the nave of Kentish ragstone was added in perpendicular style two centuries later. The parish had chapels at Stratford Bow and Whitechapel from the 1300s, and its ten bells were cast at Whitechapel Bell Foundry - the oldest (recast) dating to 1385.

A number of large houses were located nearby and Richard Fox vicar in 1488 was later a bishop and baptized Henry VIII. There is a canopied tomb in the chancel to Henry Colet (d.1505) mayor whose son John was vicar of St. Dunstan's, dean of St. Paul's and school founder and a friend of Erasmus. Opposite is that of Sir Thomas Spert (d.1541) comptroller of the Navy and the founder and master of Trinity House. At one time there was a rood screen thus the old rood cross survives, but it became a Puritan stronghold with box pews, a double-decker pulpit, galleries and panelling.

William Greenhill was vicar in 1654 but was ejected and went to the meeting house, while there was a rector/vicar until 1710 and Wesley preached in 1785. The porches and parish room were added in 1872 and the pews were restored using original wood. There is a memorial to John Charrington d.1815 and a window to Col. Cunningham, Admiral of the Fleet dedicated by the Bishop of Portsmouth in 1951. Indeed it is *a country parish church* by antiquity and design albeit now in a highly urbanised, concrete location.

Walter H. Pater (1839-94) wrote many works on the Renaissance and the aesthetic ideals it evoked.

St. Dunstan's parish records

C. 19 May 1736 George son of George Stevens of Poplar mariner and Mary [his wife, born] 9 May
2 October 1839 Walter Horatio son of Richard and Maria Pater M.E.O.T. [Mile End Old Town] surgeon born 4 August

B. 14 September 1680 Roger Crabb of Bethnal Green gentleman

Famous Parishioners - *Roger Crab* born c.1621 was a soldier in Cromwell's Army and a haberdasher in Chesham, but turned to ascetic ways and came to Bethnal Green as a herbal doctor in 1657. He adopted a strict vegetarian diet and challenged the Church authorities over the Sabbath, whilst producing a number of publications.

George Steevens was born at Poplar in 1736 - before a parish church was built. His father was a sea captain, vestryman, and director of the E.I.C. thus he went to Eton and King's, Cambridge, then was a bookseller and publisher leading a retiring life in Hampstead. He produced volumes of Shakespeare with Dr. Johnson from 1766, and Rev. T. Birch wrote to Lord Hardwicke commending his efforts. But his literary criticism was poor and he was bemoaned for his hoaxes viz. the *Java Upas Tree* for E. Darwin and an engraving of *Hardicanute's Tomb* at Kennington for the Society of Antiquaries. He died at Hampstead on 22 January 1800 and a memorial by Flaxman was erected at St. Matthias.

Walter Pater was born at 1 Honduras Terrace, Commercial Road in 1839 the son of a doctor who attended the poor in Stepney, then went to Canterbury and Oxford where he was taught by Benjamin Jowett. As a writer and critic he was influenced towards the arts by Ruskin, but lost faith in Christianity and was a friend of the Pre-Raphaelites. He had much influence especially with the Aesthetic Movement and died at Oxford in 1894.

Stepney Meeting House (Bull Lane Ind.) - This was started up by Rev. Greenhill in 1644 and a chapel was built above Stepney Way in 1674. A second building on the site dating to 1863 was destroyed in the war, and demolished in 1950. It then moved to the south beside Copley Street, but united with the John Knox church when the U.R.C. was formed, and it became a chapel for the John Cass foundation school in 1976.

Of its attendants Thomas Brown of Edinburgh married Amelia Haig a lady of Berwick but became poor, thus their son William was sponsored to attend Christ's Hospital and Pembroke. He excelled in the Classics and married Annie Marion daughter of Rev. E.E. Rowsell of Brinkley, whose sister Rosalind Grace married J.W. Barry - and was H.M. of Kensington (1857-63) and Charterhouse (1863-97) but died at Holborn in 1907.

C. 16 January 1824 William Haig Brown s. of Thomas and Amelia b. Bromley 3 Dec.

St. Philip's, Stepney Way - A number of parishes had separated by the 18th century but this was built as a chapel of ease by John Walters in 1818-23. It comprised a Gothic hall with pinnacles from the era of Henry VII - being one of the best in the country. A large edifice by Arthur Cawston replaced it in 1888-92 with red brick, vaults, ambulatory and apse although an intended tower was never built. It combined with St. Augustine's but closed in 1979 and became a library for nearby London Hospital in 1988.

St. Mary's, Whitechapel

The first detachment from the original Stepney parish came with the building of "a white chapel of ease" for the residents beyond Aldgate in the late 13th century. This was first recorded as the *parish* of St. Mary Matfelon under its rector Hugh de Fulbourne in 1329 although it did not officially have that status. Consequently the incumbent of Stebenhithe (Stepney) who held the living presented a clerk to be parson in 1336.

Regarding the unusual dedication its origins are unclear and Stow suggested it referred to a felon who failed to find sanctuary, but more likely *Matfel* a Hebrew or Syriac word meaning "babe in arms" after an icon that stood in the church or outside. Meanwhile, the name Whitechapel eventually came to denote the entire region, situated besides the mile long road leading up to Mile End (and its milestone).

During the earlier period there were prominent and well-to-do residents in the locality with many good houses for country retirement sitting on the Mile End Road. Amongst them were the Bishops of London, Henry Wallis mayor 1299 and Henry and John Colet. In addition, there was St. Mary Magdalene a Lazar hospital and almshouses belonging to several livery companies - one pertaining to Trinity House with its own chapel.

St. Mary Matfelon, Whitechapel

The mediaeval church fell into a ruinous state and was replaced with this new edifice in the late 17th century.

Due to the presence of wealthy parishioners the mediaeval church was repaired with a new south aisle in 1591. Then in the next century an inscription stated, "In thankfulness for the safe return of Prince Charles from the dangers of his Spanish journey the gallery was erected in 1623, the 7th year of Rev. William Crawshawe's pastorship."

Other beautifying repairs were undertaken although only superficial at a cost of £300 in 1633, and several handsome monuments existed both inside and outside the church. The edifice was then completely rebuilt in the Jacobean style in 1673, and a memorial was erected to the main benefactor William Beggs (d.1678) by his nephew Sir William Goulston. In addition, Rev. Ralph Davenant the rector established a free school in the parish in 1680, whose foundation is still in existence (at Loughton).

However, from the 17th century the fine houses were replaced by breweries, foundries and tanneries, and this became the epitome of the darker side of *Dickensian London*. But despite this the (Royal) London Hospital for the poor founded by John Harrison in 1740 came to Whitechapel Road in 1757 (Joseph Meyrick a patient); whereas William Booth began his Christian revival and mission locally from a tent in 1865, then established the Salvation Army at 272 Whitechapel Road on 7 August 1878.

The early immigrants came from Europe and there was a German Lutheran church in the vicinity (see p. 311), but by the later 19th century the area was occupied by poor Irish and Jewish residents with alleyways, courts, slum housing, and a proliferation of brothels. As a result the writer Jack London came there, donned ragged clothes and resided in a lowly boarding-house, then wrote of his experiences in *The People of the Abyss*.[4]

The church was rebuilt by Ernest C. Lee in lofty Victorian Gothic with tower and spire for 1,300 people in 1882, being quite a landmark, but like the surrounding housing was destroyed in the blitz in December 1940. Today, just a wall and green space remains of all this history. However St. Mary Whitechapel an Episcopal church at Lively, Lancaster, Virginia was founded in 1669 and named after its London counterpart.[5]

C. 5 Feb. 1694/95 Robert Studley s. of [Capt.] Robert and Ann in Chamber Street (The father had links to George of Denmark - also five daughters incl. Mary)

B. 15 July 1718 Sir John Cass alderman from Grove Street in Hackney (see Aldgate)
4 July 1797 Richard Parker of Sheerness 33 d. HMS Sandwich [ref. mutiny at the Nore]

Whitechapel Bell Foundry - The foundry was first established in 1570 and remains in operation today, whilst they moved to 32 Whitechapel Road a coaching inn in 1670. The master founders in the 18th century included Richard Phelps, Thomas Lester, Thomas Pack, William Mears and Thomas Mears (see Kath Cree Vol. 1), whereas output included the *Liberty Bell*, *Big Ben* and numerous City churches. Just to the north was Toynbee Hall, Commercial Street founded by reformers Samuel and Henrietta Barnett in 1884, and opposite the church was Whitechapel Gallery built by C.H. Townsend in 1901.

Whitechapel Bell Foundry, and the slums of **Dorset Street** (1902) to the north in Spitalfields. As recorded by Charles Booth in his London surveys during 1891.

---

[4] Jack London (1876-1916) author of *Call of the Wild* and *White Fang* produced his social survey of the East End in 1903 in response to a photographic work by Jacob Riis about New York entitled *How the Other Half Lives* of 1890. However, the originator of such schemes was Arthur Pember (first president of the F.A. and journalist) who dressed as a beggar on the streets of New York in the 1870s and produced *The Mysteries & Miseries of the Great Metropolis* (1874). After boarding in damp cellar lodging-houses he coined the phrase "how the other half lives" (see Brixton).

[5] Mary Ball Washington (mother of George) was born in the parish of St. Mary's, Lively in 1708.

St. Matthew's, Bethnal Green

This rural district was once part of Stepney, but due to the large weaving community a site was purchased in 1725. However, the church was only built by George Dance the elder in 1742-46.

Bethnal Green

The name of this district of Stepney seems to be derived from *Blithe* and *Heal* which were Saxon terms for a personal or descriptive name and a corner. In the 18th century the area (north of Whitechapel Road) was covered by fields with a hamlet on the green, the latter including a belt of common-land with some opulent residences nearby.

Bethnal House to the east was a fine property occupied by Sir Hugh Platt (1552-1608) a writer on gardens and was visited by Samuel Pepys, but was an asylum from 1727 and its inmates included Alexander Cruden who produced a bible concordance and the poet Christopher Smart from Wrotham. A new building was erected there in 1896 in place of the original "White House" and this later became Bethnal Green Library.

The area in particular attracted weavers and the population trebled from 1801 to 1831, thus Globe Town was developed to the east to take the overflow population. Indeed, by Victorian times the market gardens were replaced by dense housing but there were only two churches. As a result C.J. Blomfield, Bishop of London, set up a fund to construct ten more named after the remaining apostles with St. Matthias (replacing Judas Iscariot) from 1839-50. A number of these were built by prominent architects (see below).

St. Matthew's, Bethnal Green

There were plans for a separate parish at Bethnal Green as early as 1690 and a site was earmarked by the Commissioners in 1711. This was on some fields to the north of Hare (Cheshire) Street and £400 was agreed for the site. Hawksmoor then produced plans for a basilica-style church. However there were several objections including from the vicar of Stepney and a nearby location at Schlater's Ground was considered in 1714.

Eventually the land at Hare Street was purchased in 1725, this being a commercial area of weavers some distance from the original green (to the east). However, by then no more churches were being sanctioned consequently the plans were abandoned.

Authorisation to build finally came through in 1742 and a less adventurous design was put forward by George Dance the elder which was completed in July 1746. It was hoped that the arrival of the church would lift the morals of the area (and morale); but records confirm that baiting took place in the churchyard on Sundays from that time, and Rev. William Loxham the rector (appointed 1766) never actually came to the parish.

His successor Rev. Joshua King arrived in 1809 and set about cleaning up the district, and found Joseph Mercer churchwarden was manipulating funds and operating licensed premises and brothels. The latter was eventually imprisoned but ironically his memorial (of 1861), stating he was most honourable, is located in the churchyard.

A fire destroyed the interior of the building during 1859 and it was rebuilt with cupola, reredos and some stained glass. Stewart Headlam was a curate in 1873-78 and started a socialist guild there, but was barred by Church authorities for inflammatory opinions on several occasions! Meanwhile, he championed the downtrodden, supported less irksome pastimes and was a compatriot of Bernard Shaw and other radicals.

The church was destroyed in 1940 and a temporary structure was erected in its walls in 1954, but the original building was eventually redesigned by Anthony Lewis in 1961. This incorporated a number of furnishings from other bombed churches including St. Philip and St. Matthias, and from St. James the Great which became flats in 1984.

C. 24 October 1819 Charles Morton s. of Charles and Mary of Elizabeth Street tinplate worker born 15 August [a theatre manager and Father of the Music Halls]

M. 26 April 1869 John Wood & Matilda Mary Caroline Archer [parents of Marie Lloyd]

St. John's, Bethnal Green

This edifice resulted from the second great period of church-building after the *Battle of Waterloo*, as St. Matthew's became inadequate to the needs of the area. The Commission approached Sir John Soane who had designed Dulwich Picture Gallery in 1817 and also two churches viz. Holy Trinity, Marylebone (1820) and St. Peter's, Walworth (1822). In fact this to be his third such work in the capital and was erected from 1826-28.

The main body of the church was of brick with Bath and Portland stone detail and the vestibule, staircase and crypt had elegant style. However it lacked the classical aspiration seen elsewhere and was less impressive than his design at Marylebone, although was still reminiscent of his blueprint at Dulwich. A fire destroyed the interior in February 1870 and local architect William Mundy restored it with wooden galleries and a hammer-beam roof. Meanwhile, G.F. Bodley extended the chancel (to a great length) in 1887.

From the time of the Boer War it was the regimental church of the R.E. East London and there are brass plaques in the south aisle, whilst it combined with St. Bartholomew's in 1978. Just beyond is the Green, Roman Road and its markets, and the underground where a disaster took place in the war (a plaque commemorates the event).

St. John's was built by Sir John Soane the acclaimed architect and curator.

Blomfield's Twelve Apostles

The ten churches proposed by Bishop Blomfield in 1839 were situated in an area one mile long, and centred on Bethnal Green Road. This was a district desolate of Anglican provision and each church had a school and endowment of £200. But the sum was found to be inadequate, the vicars being poor and isolated from middle class society.

Blomfield's project was the forerunner of other philanthropic schemes in the East End and all the churches were completed by 1850. Of these St. James the Less and St. Peter's opened good schools and remain open. However, six of them have now gone without a trace, apart from one vicarage, and two others have been converted into flats.

St. James the Great and its neighbour **St. Peter's** were built by famous architects, and two of the apostles that graced Bethnal Green.

St. Peter's (1841) which was located on a square at St. Peter's Avenue off Warner Place was designed by architect Lewis Vulliamy, who had important churches at Highgate and Kensington. This example of his work with its attractive central tower and spire, in leafy surrounds, reminds one of the country parishes of old.

St. James the Less (1842) was built just above Old Ford Road near to Victoria Park and was also by Lewis Vulliamy. With its tall galleried tower it was reminiscent of later work by the Gothic Revival architect George Edmund Street.

St. James the Great (1843) at the corner of Bethnal Green Road and Pollard Row was designed by the architect Edward Blore. He became famous for completing the façade of Buckingham Palace in 1847 and was influenced by friend Sir Walter Scott, thus his designs displayed elements of the Scottish baronial. The church is now flats.

St. Bartholomew's (1844) was designed by William Railton on some back streets, just off Cambridge Heath Road below the Green. He trained under W. Inwood and worked on country houses but his church designs were less popular (also flats).

Other Churches now gone: St. Andrew's, Dunbridge St. (T.H. Wyatt); St. Jude's, Old Bethnal Gr. Rd. (H. Clutton); St. Matthias, Hare/Cheshire St. (T.H. Wyatt); St. Philip's, Mount/Swanfield St. (T.L. Walker); St. Simon Zelotes, Morpeth St. (B. Ferrey) vicarage survives; and St. Thomas's, Columbia Sq./Baroness Rd. (L. Vulliamy).

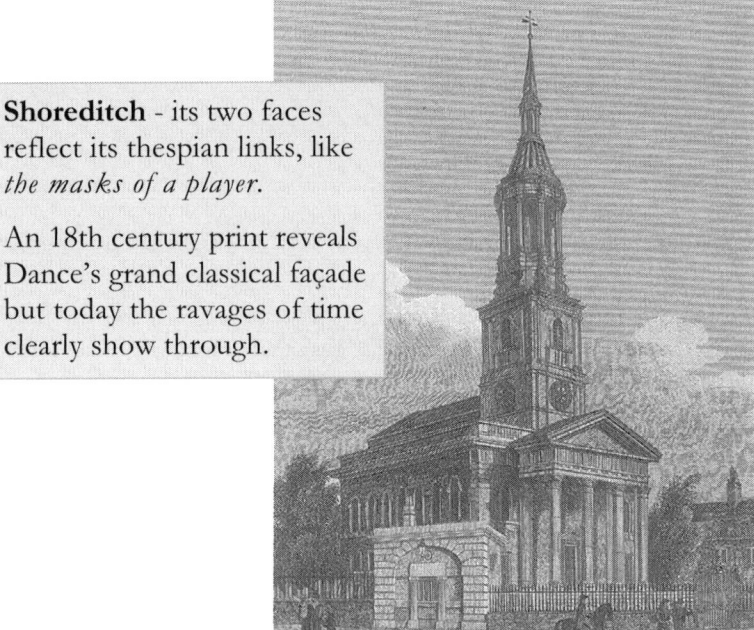

Shoreditch - its two faces reflect its thespian links, like *the masks of a player*.

An 18th century print reveals Dance's grand classical façade but today the ravages of time clearly show through.

St. Leonard's, Shoreditch

There was a Saxon church on the site of this important thoroughfare which went north from Bishopsgate to Stoke Newington, Tottenham, Edmonton and eventually Cambridge however it was first mentioned in the 12th century. According to Stow the Archdeacon of London was always the parson and the cure was operated by a vicar.

The importance of the church was indicated by the large number of memorials which included Sir Thomas Seymour mayor d.1535 and relatives of the Duke of Buckingham and Earl of Westmoreland in the 16th century. But its main association was thespian and inside the church is a memorial plaque to Tudor actors who were buried there:

Richard Tarlton a comedian of the pre-Shakespearean stage
James Burbage who built The Theatre the first successful playhouse in Curtain Road in 1576 and helped with The Curtain and Blackfriars theatres
Cuthbert Burbage (born 1566) who built The Globe in 1599 and was long term agent of the Lord Chamberlain's or King's Men to whom Shakespeare belonged
Richard Burbage (born 1568) who played the lead in the first performance of many of Shakespeare's plays including Hamlet, Othello, Richard III and King Lear

Meanwhile, there was a partial collapse of the tower in 1716 and the church was rebuilt by George Dance the elder (like nearby St. Matthew's) during 1736-40. The main features were its grand Tuscan portico, a steeple copied from Wren's St. Mary le Bow and interior of Doric columns. In fact many of the fittings from that time still remain. However, this was generally a poor area reaching up to Hoxton except for some more opulent housing situated on Hoxton Square and the Kingsland Road.

Regarding the residents two have tablets inside and James Parkinson was born there in 1755, and succeeded his father as an apothecary at 1 Hoxton Square (a plaque marks the site). In addition to his work he was most prolific and published political pamphlets opposing the Pitt Government, whilst he studied the history of geology and fossils.

Consequently he was at the first meeting of the Geological Society with Sir Humphrey Davy and others at the Freemasons Tavern in November 1807, and a number of fossils were named after him (including *Parkinsonia*). However, he was best known in the public sphere for *An Essay on the Shaking Palsy* in 1817, although the term Parkinson's disease was not used until sixty years later by Dr. Jean Charcot in France.

In the second instance John George Appold was born at 23 Wilson Street by Finsbury Square in 1800, and had little education but joined his immigrant father as a fur dyer. He married Maria Illman at Rusper, Sussex in 1825 and amassed a fortune by the 1840s, then concentrated on inventing and his centrifugal pump was shown at the Great Exhibition. Brunel and W. Cubitt sponsored him for the Royal Society and his cable-brake was used for the *Atlantic Telegraph* in 1857, but he died at Clifton, Gloucester in 1865.

Other churches were St. James's, Curtain Road on a theatre site in 1841 with a window to Shakespeare; St. Mark's, Old Street by B. Ferrey in 1848 (both gone); and All Saints, Haggerston Road by P.C. Hardwick in 1856. These were followed by High Church brick edifices by James Brooks: St. Michael's Mark Street an architectural salvage merchants, St. Chad's Nichol's Square and St. Columba's Kingsland Road. The old church remains on the High Street but Holywell Street is much altered from its famous theatrical past.

C. 29 April 1755 James s. of John and Mary Parkinson of Hoxton Square b. 11 April
31 May 1800 John George s. of Christian & Hannah Appold, White Cross Alley 14 April
30 October 1801 Thomas son of Thomas de la Garde Grissell and Ann [née Peto] of Hoxton Square born 4 October - five other children from 1803-13 [6]
20 March 1870 Matilda Alice Victoria Wood d. of John and Matilda M.A. Caroline of 3 John St. artificial florist b. 12 Feb [Marie Lloyd music hall singer re *Lloyd's Weekly*]

M. 12 May 1781 James Parkinson and Mary Dale b.o.t.p. by licence by me Alexander Kilgour curate pres. Wakelin Welch jun., John and Mary Parkinson, Jane Dale
21 December 1801 William Godwin widr. and Mary Clairmont wid. b.o.t.p. by banns by Joseph Rose curate pres. James Marshall, George Limming (see St. Pancras)

B. 3 September 1588 Richard Tarrelton was buryed of Haliwell Street
2 February 1596/97 James Burbedge was buryed of Halliwell
XVI th Marche 1618/19 Richard Burbadge a player was bur Hollywell Street
XVII th September 1636 Cuthbert Burbadge was buryed
7 January 1696/97 Samuel Annesley was buryed ye ------ [7]
29 December 1824 James Parkinson of Kingsland Road, 70 B. Crosby

---

[6] Samuel M. Peto was partner to his cousin Thomas de la Garde Grissell (junior) from 1830-46 and worked on Hungerford Market, Nelson's Column, railways (with Brunel), London clubs and docks. A sister Mary Grissell was born at Tyson Place on 29 July 1808 and baptized at the church and he married her at Lambeth in 1831 but she died in 1842. He was then partner to Edward Ladd Betts brother-in-law by his sister Ann Peto and worked on further railway projects.

[7] Samuel Annesley was a Puritan minister and chaplain to the Earl of Warwick then a lecturer at St. Paul's and vicar of St. Giles, Cripplegate (ejected 1662). His daughter Susanna married Samuel Wesley a poet and minister and their children were John and Charles (see Wesley's Chapel).

St. Mary's, Haggerston
(below) was designed by
John Nash, in the Gothic
style, in the 1820s.

St. John the Baptist (left)
was built by F. Edwards in
1826, its patrons being the
Haberdashers Comp. Their
school (above) was built at
this time, but they removed
to Hampstead in 1898 and
had another at Hatcham.

St. John the Baptist, Hoxton - This historic area was clearly delineated lying between City and Kingsland Roads, as well as Old Street and the Regent's Canal. It was originally a rural locality within Shoreditch parish beside the remains of Ermine Street, and had a number of houses with gardens providing retreat from the city.

Hoxton House on the High Street was owned by the Miles family but was an asylum in the late 17th century, and housed well-to-do inmates including Charles Lamb the writer. Robert Aske founded almshouses for twenty poor haberdashers on Pitfield Street in 1689 (by Hooke), while a school by D.R. Roper replaced them in 1826 and was enlarged in 1874. There were also some houses for the gentry at Charles and Hoxton Squares.

Over time, especially after the arrival of the canal, the area became working class. As a result the parish church of St. John the Baptist was built by the Commissioners in Greek Revival style, with Ionic portico, in 1825-26. The architect was Francis Edwards, and it was at the north end of Pitfield Street where the road diverged to the left and right.

St. Mary's, Haggerston - Just beyond Shoreditch church was Hackney Road leading to the northeast and above was the hamlet of Agostone or Haggerston. One of the principal residents was Edmond Halley, astronomer, son of a soap maker born there in 1656.

In this neighbourhood east of Kingsland Road was Nichol's Square named for Mr. John Nichols F.S.A. antiquary, who usually resided in Islington but also had a house there. He published several books and for many years was editor of the *Gentleman's Magazine* d.1826, while his son John Bowyer Nichols inherited the property and followed him as editor. The latter was the official printer to both Houses of Parliament.

St. Mary's, Brunswick Square was designed by John Nash in 1822-26 and had a striking west tower reminiscent of Wren's own design for St. Dunstan in the East. Nash had been working on the Regent's Park scheme just before and nearby was the Haggerston Basin of the canal and two large gas works. The church was greatly altered in 1862 and had a Father Schmidt organ from St. George's Chapel, Windsor, but was destroyed in the war and the site is now covered by flats on Thurtle and Whiston Roads.

Poplar

This was another rural hamlet of Stepney and according to Stow was so named for the prolific number of poplar trees growing on its moist soil. John de Poultney, four times mayor and founder of the college at St. Laurence, was the lord of the manor; and just to the east was the Black Wall - a harbour for ships by a wall of the Thames.

Generally this was a bleak expanse with the marshes of the Isle of Dogs to the south. In the latter there was a ruined-chapel and remains of fishermen's houses, although the fishermen had long since departed to more hospitable environs. However its bleakness and moisture was a decided asset producing large sheep and oxen, whilst it housed the kennels of Royal hunting dogs for Greenwich just across the water.

There was a large copperas works on the road leading from Poplar towards Bromley, but the principal industry was maritime and Sir Henry Johnson both father and son had a prominent shipyard at Blackwall - the forerunner of Thames Ironworks. [8]

St. Matthias (E.I.C. Chapel)

The manor of Poplar and Blackwall fell to the Crown and its land passed to the large Cistercian Abbey of St. Mary de Graces at East Smithfield (one of the Tower Hamlets). However the manor and lands transferred to private hands after the Dissolution and the new owners included William Benson and Thomas Middleton. The East India Company (formed in 1600) then set up their main shipyard at Blackwall in 1614, and established a hospital for its retired or injured seamen on Poplar High Street soon after.

Most of the residents were employees of the company and resented the long walk to Stepney for services thus they requested their own chapel. Gilbert Dethick a descendant of the principal of *The College of Arms* held the manor and left £100 for this purpose in his will, and there were benefactions from Maurice Thompson and Thomas Tomlins. As a result a chapel was built by John Tanner in the hospital grounds in 1653-54, its design probably based on the Broadway Chapel erected just before at Westminster.

This was one of the few churches initiated at the time of the Commonwealth and the E.I.C also provided a school with an annual sum of £20 to the minister. It was described as a commodious building and the barrel-vaulted roof (with coat of arms) was supported on eight Tuscan columns of oak/stone with entablatures. Outside there were red brick walls enveloped by stone quoins at the corners, the cost in the region of £2,000.

There were a number of benefactors including Sir Henry Johnson who left money to paint *the Dutch-style chapel* and for an almshouse for shipwrights, while the Rev. Josiah Woodward of Stepney assisted Strype with detailed facts regarding its foundation. But in general this remained a separate hamlet with maritime links and prayers were said in the church before undertaking difficult voyages.

---

[8] The element copper a reddish malleable metal created bronze, but copperas a sulphate of iron (green vitriol) was used from the 12th century to make purple iron gall ink applied to paper and vellum, and as a mordant in wool dyeing. In the 19th century it was used to create indigo dye and in the photographic process but became less common due to new products. Brunel built the *Great Eastern* at Millwall Ironworks to the south in 1858 and the slipway still remains.

St. Matthias (H.E.I.C. Chapel) - a Puritan church clad in Anglican garb.

In the early 18th century a tower and triple-decker pulpit were added, whilst Richard Jupp the company surveyor enlarged the building and altered the windows in 1776. One of the most significant additions was a *sculpture relief* of local resident George Steevens by John Flaxman in 1800, his family being merchants with links to the company. This showed him in reclining pose reading a book as in the Sistine Chapel, with an inscription regarding his Shakespearean work (now at the Fitzwilliam Museum, Cambridge).

After the Indian Mutiny in 1857 the E.I.C. were taken over by the Government and the chapel became the parish church of St. Matthias in 1866. Due to its origins the edifice had a centralised plan in the form of a cross with Puritan pulpit to hear the word of God, but this was all dramatically changed during the later 19th century.

William Milford Teulon (1823-1900) a younger brother of Samuel undertook alteration work, to provide an Anglican edifice with liturgical arrangement. Thus the box pews and galleries were removed and a modern pulpit, font and organ were installed in 1867-68. Likewise, the exterior was refaced with rag and Bath stone, a small spire was added and an extension to the eastern chancel was inserted in 1870-76.

Despite surviving the blitz there were declining attendances and the church was closed in 1976 causing it to be redundant, followed by a long period of decay and vandalism. However English Heritage and the *L.D.D.C.* initiated a restoration programme in 1990 and it was decided to conserve it in its present form, rather than attempting to reinstate the original Puritan chapel (due to poor condition of the brickwork). Operated by a trust it is now used as a community centre and a park with Poplar DLR nearby.

All Saints, Poplar

By the late 18th century there was increasing pressure on the Pool of London and the architect Willey Reveley proposed a scheme to straighten the Thames. The new channel was to go right through the Isle of Dogs and would have created three new islands and docks in the resulting ox-bow lakes. This proved far too costly and difficult but if it had gone ahead the whole geography of the region would have been transformed. [9]

---

[9] Willey Reveley (1760-99) designed the Panopticon for Jeremy Bentham and his drawings went to the Sir John Soane Museum, while his wife Maria James nursed Mary Godwin as a child. She declined a marriage proposal from William Godwin and went to Italy with her new husband John Gisborne being acquainted with Percy and Mary Shelley. The poet backed a scheme by her son Henry Willey (1788-1875) to operate a steamboat service from Leghorn (Livorno) to Marseilles. Shelley also wrote *Letter to Maria Gisborne* at Leghorn while H.W. Reveley was an engineer at Cape Town and at Fremantle near Perth where he designed the Round Gaol.

As it was the area was much altered. West India Dock was dug out between Poplar High Street and the Isle of Dogs, whereas the E.I.C. built Commercial Road and East India Dock Road above St. Matthias in 1803. Likewise, the East India Docks opened at Blackwall in 1806. Initially many were displaced but there was rapid population growth including wealthy merchants, followed by the Millwall Docks later that century.

Poplar remained without a parish church but an Act of Parliament was passed in 1817 to remedy matters. This included a caveat stating the vicar could close East India Dock Road during services! A parcel of land was bestowed by Mrs. Ann Newby and the design of Charles Hollis was chosen - he being clerk to a prominent parishioner.

All Saints was a relatively expensive church at £33,000 paid for by loans from George Green, John Stock and the West India Co., and it was constructed by Thomas Morris an engineer in Portland stone and granite during 1821-23. Rectangular in shape, it had an entrance portico of four Ionic columns with pediment surmounted by an elegant tower and spire, whereas the interior had galleries on all sides and a cranked pulpit. The latter could be raised and lowered according to the size of the congregation.

In 1866 there was a cholera epidemic and a City banking collapse which closed many shipyards, and Rev. Thomas Nowell worked tirelessly to help impoverished parishioners (a plaque commemorates his gallant efforts). Then in the 1890s the Rev. Arthur Chandler adopted the precepts of the Oxford Movement and grand steps were built up to the new carved altar, the latter commissioned from Oberammergau in Germany.

The east end and roof were destroyed during the war, while the restored church housed an organ from Clapham Congregational and the high altar received a canopy. The parish became the first team ministry in London in the 1970s and there is a community centre in the crypt, the church situated on Newby Place by East India Dock Road.

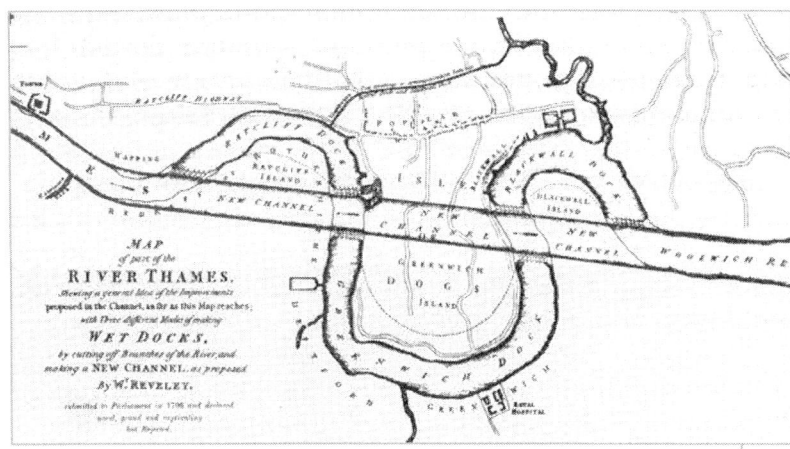

"Docklands" - The map shows an audacious plan by Willey Reveley to straighten the Thames in 1796.

All Saints, Poplar - Built at the expense of wealthy parishioners by Charles Hollis from 1821-23.

The Docklands

Another district within the parish of Stepney this was developed at a very early date. Its housing was concentrated east of the Tower, by the riverbank of the Thames, and to the north on The Highway which joined East Smithfield to Ratcliffe. The latter hamlet was on a bend of the river with dry docks and wharves, but is now largely gone - being remembered in a few street names between Limehouse and Shadwell Basins.

However, there were no Anglican churches until the arrival of St. John's and St. Paul's in the early 17th century. These were followed by the *Danish Church* at Wellclose Square south of Whitechapel built by Caius G. Cibber the Danish sculptor in 1696. This was put up at the expense of Christian V of Denmark, and both Cibber and his wife Jane Colley were buried there (with a memorial). It had a significant role in missions (see later), and the *Swedish Church* was also erected nearby at Princes Square in 1728. [10]

Clearly there was a need for new churches in docklands to supplement their dissenting brethren and the Commissioners provided two venues. In fact Hawksmoor and his peers were ahead of the game and St. Anne's and St. George's were erected on virgin plots in the 18th century. But in the next hundred years, as new docks were built, the remaining fields and market gardens were covered by dense housing, and many new churches were added to supplement the existing parishes.

St. Anne's, Limehouse

The epithet of *Lime House* referred to lime kilns and potteries by the river using chalk from Kent, and there was a dock present from mediaeval times. This part of Stepney had almost 1,000 houses and was earmarked by the Commissioners for a new church from 1711, although there was considerable argument about the site. The preferred location was at Westfield but the residents also put forward Rigby's Gardens, however a sum of £400 was paid to John West for his land in May 1714.

Soon after there was a petition from the residents for the speedy erection of a church and the designs of Hawksmoor were promptly approved. The monumental construction was built north of the main settlement in a completely rural area by 1730, and although it clearly dominated the location it must have looked strangely out of place.

The main features of the design were the austere rectangular nave with round-headed windows, the semi-circular entrance vestibule with grand staircase, and three tiered tower with pilasters about an opening - crowned by an offset cupola. However, it might all have been different. The tower blueprint was originally destined for St. Alfege's, Greenwich but problems of costing meant Hawksmoor reallocated it to Limehouse. In addition, a pyramid intended for the apex was left sitting in the churchyard.

---

[10] Caius Gabriel Cibber married Jane Colley at St. Giles in the Fields in 1670 and worked with Wren and W. Talman, sculpting the relief on the Monument. His son Colley Cibber (1671-1757) an actor and playwright at Drury Lane was controversially made the *Poet Laureate* by George II in 1730. The church at Wellclose Square closed in 1869 and was replaced by a school, whilst Wilton's Music Hall in Grace's Alley was characteristic of the era and still remains.

St. Anne's, Limehouse a *Grand Design* by Hawksmoor in 1714-30.

Clearly the architect was given free rein on a greenfield site and initially this was how it remained. His grand façade retained an uninterrupted view for nearly half a mile across the fields to Ratcliffe - a jewel awaiting a setting that would make it shine.

However, without associated street planning the church was gradually overcome by its situation, as Commercial Road was wrapped around the north side in 1803 and Limehouse Basin (Regent's Canal Dock) and the Lea Canal were inserted to the front in 1820. By the 1850s the Blackwall Railway had risen up on the south side and the church was encased in narrow streets and alleyways, as if it were captured in a spider's web.

Consequently, Hawksmoor's fine façade was only visible down a narrow street between terraced housing and the main approach was now behind. Matters initially got worse after a severe fire on Good Friday 1850, although its pipe organ won first prize at the Great Exhibition and it was restored by Philip Hardwick in the next four years. Two churches were also added to the district: St. James's, Ratcliffe by E. Lapidge in 1833 and St. John's, Limehouse east of Stepney Church by H. Clutton in 1853 (both now gone).

A distinctive war memorial was erected outside St. Anne's in 1918 and it was listed with the adjacent town hall and library, receiving further restoration and steel supports during 1983-93. It remains as an architectural gem but in a misguided location and can now be accessed from the attractively restored Limehouse Basin.

Limehouse Blues

The edifice was a tribute to design rather than function. It had a steeple brought "from Greenwich" and grand staircase reached up a small alley. The pyramid for the tower was thought to be a Masonic symbol by some.

St. George in the East

The parish of Shadwell covered an area around its basin, whereas Wapping was mainly by the river plus a small section east of St. Katharine's Dock. To the north was the area of Upper Wapping (or Wapping Stepney) which included housing and market gardens reaching up to Whitechapel - but still within the parish of St. Dunstan's.

This was the second region identified by the Commissioners as needing a new church and a site by Ratcliffe Highway and Cannon Street was identified in November 1711. A sum of £400 was agreed although this was only paid to the owner Bridges Watts in 1714 and a design by Hawksmoor was accepted. This was another monumental structure like those found at Limehouse and Spitalfields and it was completed by 1729.

Ample space was available to build the church which had a large churchyard and it was lined up with St. Paul's, Shadwell to the east, like the leading colour in a flotilla of ships. The main architectural features were the nave with round-headed windows, four turret domes (or pepper pots), a soaring west tower with four levels of coursing, and octagonal cupola with projecting pilasters. Internally, the layout was a Greek cross, with a mixed style of Doric columns and Dutch-oak ornamentation. In fact, the nave was designed to rise above the row of houses which were then present on The Highway.

One of the main promoters was Henry Raine who was born in 1679 and married Sarah Petrie of Mile End. He was a brewer at New Crane Wharf and started a charity school on Old Gravel Lane in 1719 (located on Raine Street with statues), and was buried at St. George's in 1738. His large memorial is also present behind the church.

There were still open fields to the north in the mid-18th century, but they were built on soon after and the principal occupations were rigging and rope-making. However, there were also some wealthy parishioners, and the survey by Daniel Lyson in 1795 noted the large number of captains and naval people who had memorials there. The London Docks designed by John Rennie opened to the south in January 1805 and many of the residents were Germans employed in sugar baking and tobacco preparation.

Later on in the 19th century the cemetery was turned into a public park, whereas the edifice was left a ruin after the bombing in 1941 with only the tower and walls remaining. Instead of demolition, the architect Arthur Bailey designed a new church inside the walls, which was consecrated by the Bishop of London on 26 April 1964. Originally it could be seen from the nearby docks but these were mostly filled in for housing.

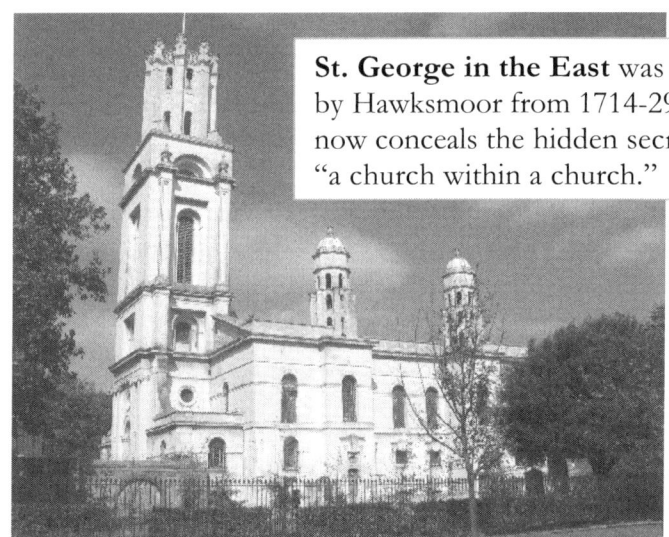

St. George in the East was built by Hawksmoor from 1714-29. It now conceals the hidden secret of "a church within a church."

St. John the Baptist, Wapping was built as a chapel of ease for Whitechapel in 1616. It was located close to the river and replaced by a larger church in 1756.

St. John's, Wapping

Regarding its ancient origins the area was once inhabited by the people of *Waeppa* but it was only in the late 16th century that the river wall was finally made secure. There were a number of public watergates and the buildings stretched out along the High Street, which Stow vividly described as, "A continual street or filthy strait passage, with alleys of small tenements of cottages, inhabited by sailors or victuallers."

A chapel to St. John the Baptist was established under the jurisdiction of Whitechapel at the partial costs of the residents in 1616. The first minister was Rev. Richard Sedgwick under the Rev. Richard Gardener rector of Whitechapel, who had a window there, and the gallery was paid for by local mariners (the total cost being £1,600).

This occupied *one third* of Whitechapel and received proportionate tithes, while there were several monuments and benefactors notably: Sir John Fenner of Inner Temple, Sir Samuel Sterling alderman, Sir Henry Saville of the Admiralty and King's household who gave £50 for coal in 1683, and Dudley Lewis a Swede who died in *The Great Storm* of December 1703 and left by nuncupative will his wages of £39 4s to the poor.

The original chapel was situated opposite Wapping Old Stairs in a large churchyard at the west end of Green Bank beside Cock, Milk and Peartree Alleys. It was an unusual structure of Continental flavour with large gable windows and a wooden tower, but was inadequate to the excessive number of residents. A parish was created in 1694 reaching in a belt along the High Street and inland at Hermitage Basin to the west.

Parochial returns showed that 18,000 people were crammed in the tenements near the Thames, and the Commissioners recommended a new church for the hamlet although it was never built. However the decaying chapel was demolished and Joel Johnson designed a new church of St. John the Evangelist, across the road to the east, in 1756. The living belonged to Brasenose, Oxford and inside was a fine monument by Roubiliac.

The business of the area was chiefly maritime, whilst the building of the London and Tobacco Docks contributed to its growth. Other events saw a free school established in 1695, and a building was erected beside the new church in 1756. Samuel Troutbeck of Madras also left a substantial bequest of £5,000 to this institution in 1822. [11]

However, after the bombing only the red brick tower (with quoins) of the church was left standing and this was recently developed as flats. Next door on Scandrett Street is the old school with statues in dress and opposite is the old churchyard (now a park).

---

[11] Rev. Thomas Dilworth was a master at Wapping School and was author of *A New Guide to the English Tongue* in 1761 which was widely used in England and America. A portrait of Dilworth in the frontispiece was mentioned by Dickens in *Sketches by Boz*, and Oliver Goldsmith quoted it as an example of good teaching in *The Rising Village* based in Nova Scotia.

St Peter's, London Docks - Charles Fuge Lowder (1820-99) attended King's College School and Oxford where he was influenced by Newman at St. Mary's. He thus joined the Oxford Movement and after a few curacies went to St. Barnabas, Pimlico for more Catholic worship, then helped found the *Society of the Holy Cross* at Soho in 1855. Three of the founders converted and this was part of the Anglo-Catholic revival.

Lowder was appointed head of missions at St. George in the East the next year and two of his curates Mackonochie and Wainwright were both later vicars of St. Peter's. Initially an iron chapel was erected at Wapping, but they moved into St. Saviour's Danish church at Wellclose Square in 1857 and worked with the poor, destitute and criminal. [12]

Despite veritable aims there was much controversy over the use of vestments etc. and Rev. Bryan King of St. George's used *Catholic forms of worship* causing a large riot in 1859. Lowder then obtained land in Old Gravel Lane (Wapping Lane) and the new church of St. Peter's was consecrated in June 1866. He was made perpetual curate and immediately helped with a large cholera epidemic earning him the epithet "The Father of Wapping." His funeral took place there in 1880 and he was buried at Chislehurst.

After the demise of St. John's this became the main parish for Wapping and the clergy house remains with the red-brick church - reached through a double-arched passage. At the front is a plaque to Father Lincoln Stanhope Wainwright (1847-1929) who was vicar from 1873, and lived in the clergy house from 1884. He worked tirelessly in the area for over fifty years even giving away his own clothes to help the poor.

St. Peter's, London Docks (right) which was founded by Lowder in 1866, was nearer to Oxford than many believed....

.... and arched entrance with a plaque to Father Wainwright.

St. John's, Wapping - the surviving tower beside the school famous for its "Dilworth."

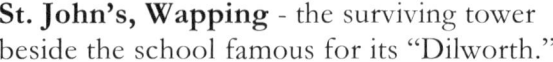

---

[12] Alexander Heriot Mackonochie (1825-87) came to St. George's in 1858 and witnessed the anti-Ritualist riots. He was then the long term vicar of St. Alban's, Holborn from 1863 in a similar poverty stricken environment, but after many battles with the authorities was forced to resign in 1882. He then spent a brief period at St. Peter's before returning to Holborn.

Thomas Telford built **St. Katharine's Dock** in 1827-28, but it was P. Hardwick who designed the warehouses and later developed Euston Arch and Albert Dock, Liverpool.

St. Katharine's by the Tower

Queen Matilda, the daughter of Henry I and wife of the Holy Roman Emperor and of Geoffrey Plantagenet, was briefly on the throne of England in 1141. She was removed by her cousin Stephen who returned to his former role, and began the hospital and college of St. Katharine in memory of two infant sons, east of the Tower, in 1148.

This had six brethren and sisters under a master and further endowments were made by Eleanor of Castile (wife of Edward I) and Philippa of Hainhault (wife of Edward III). It was then created a liberty outside the City jurisdictions in 1442 and a large shanty town of artisans developed there. Just to the north and east was the locality of East Smithfield which was a part of Aldgate parish and evolved in tandem with it.

The hospital was quite wealthy and had a fair church, whereas its Royal status meant it continued in Protestant form after the Dissolution and the parish records dated to 1564. The church itself was near the river with cloisters and gardens behind, but to the north was a warren of alleyways and courts with about one thousand houses. Stow described it as, "of homely cottages and tenements with both English and Strangers."

However, an Act of Parliament was passed and both the unsanitary housing and ancient hospital of St. Katharine were demolished in 1827. They were replaced by the relatively small development of St. Katharine's Dock designed by Thomas Telford, with its water level controlled by Boulton & Watt engines. This was just below East Smithfield and to the east was the Red Lion Brewery of Hoare & Co. beside Hermitage Basin.

The *St. Katharine's Foundation* then moved to Cumberland Terrace, Regent's Park and a new church and almshouses were built (later the Danish church). As a postscript some 11,000 people were displaced, and Walter Besant then decried the loss which included an income of over £10,000 per annum to the poor of the East End.

A campaign to recover the funds began in 1865 - but failed, and the foundation was eventually re-established in the vicarage of the destroyed St. James's, Ratcliffe after the Second War. The docks were the first to close in 1968 and were re-developed for leisure with a few warehouses retained, and today they sit beside the Thames Path.

St. Paul's, Shadwell

The second dockland area of Stepney to receive a church was Shadwell in 1656. Initially this was a chapel of ease but it was rebuilt as a parish church in 1669, and dedicated to St. Paul because the Dean and Chapter of St. Paul's were its patrons. This was the last of five London churches started after the Restoration. It was located south of The Highway the main thoroughfare and just beyond was a mixture of housing, market gardens, a food market, timber yard, coopers' premises and various wharves.

Constructed of brick with a fair steeple there was a north gallery added at the cost of Capt. Thomas Brian of Wapping Wall d.1681. In addition, a south gallery was erected by parishioners two years later and the west gallery displayed a record of its repair in 1691. There were a number of memorials and benefactions noted by Strype and that of most interest was to Captain James Cook d.1690 (and his family). He died in the East Indies leaving £50 to seamen's apprentices and his son had a chancel memorial of 1699, while his cognomen was simply one of those strange quirks of history.

There were several maritime links and Jane Randolph was born at Shakespeare's Walk a tree-lined avenue in 1721 - then returned to Virginia with her family four years later. Her father was a planter, merchant and ship-owner, but she married Peter Jefferson a surveyor who named his land "Shadwell" and their son Thomas was the third president.

Likewise, the other James Cook was born at Marton, Yorkshire in 1728 and enlisted in the Navy at Wapping in 1755. He married Elizabeth Batts at St. Margaret's, Barking on 21 December 1762 and lived at Shadwell when not at sea - thus his son was baptized there. His first voyage to Tahiti, New Zealand and Botany Bay took place in 1768-71 and amongst the crew was Joseph Banks (president of the Royal Society 1778-1820).

There were then two more voyages to the Pacific and Southern Oceans and on the last occasion Cook commanded the *Resolution* with Capt. William Bligh as his sailing master. The latter lived at Broad (Reardon) Street near to Wapping and a plaque there records, "William Bligh RN FRS who transported bread fruit from Tahiti to the West Indies lived in a house on this site 1785-90." He was notorious for his involvement in the mutiny on the *Bounty* in that period and was also briefly Governor of N.S.W.

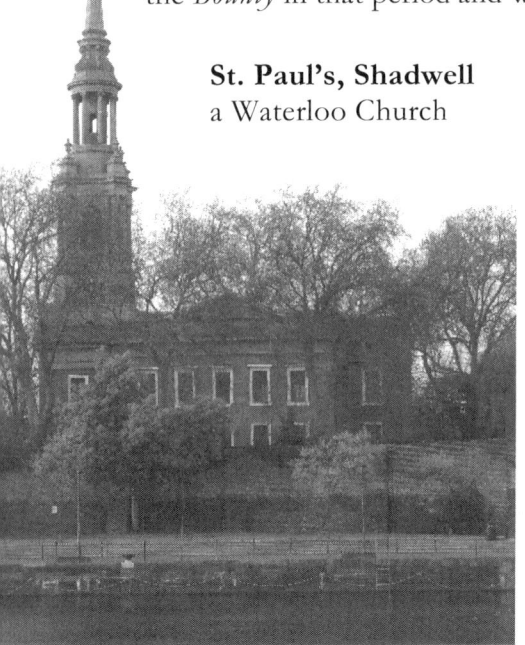

St. Paul's, Shadwell
a Waterloo Church

The "Church of Sea Captains"
was attended by **Captain Cook** and rebuilt in 1820.

Regarding the church, John Wesley came and preached there but it was demolished in 1817 and a new building designed by John Walters was erected in 1820. This was funded by the Commissioners for the *Waterloo Churches* and had a rectangular nave, shallow but broad transepts, two tiers of plain windows, and a west tower. As with St. Leonard's the spire harked back to the time of Wren and was very similar to St. Mary le Bow.

Shadwell Basin, an extension of London Docks, was built directly south of the church in 1828-32 (and is the only part surviving), thereby leaving the edifice on a distinct rise. Connections at this time included Walter Pater b.1835 a writer/critic (see Stepney) and William Henry Perkin b.1838 who attended the City of London School at Milk Street. He was attracted to chemistry, and at the age of just 18 discovered the first aniline dyes (or purple) in a crude laboratory in his home at Cable Street.

There was a great demand for such a colour for textiles in the Industrial Revolution, in particular due to its Royal associations, and after a faltering start Perkin earned himself a sizeable fortune. He continued to pursue his research and discoveries being knighted in 1906 and a plaque in Cable Street records his achievements there.

The church was combined with St. James's, Ratcliffe after the war, whilst the basin was redeveloped, including new housing and an original bascule bridge, in 1987. A team from Holy Trinity, Brompton have supported the work of the parish since 2005.

C. 25 February 1720/21 Jane the daughter of Isham Randolph in Shakespeare's Walk a mariner and Jane his wife [m. at St. Botolph's, Bishopsgate in 1717]
1 November 1763 James the son of James Cook a mariner and Elizabeth his wife of Upper Shadwell [or The Highway - five other children 1764-76]
1 July 1838 William Henry s. of George Fowler and Sarah Perkin of King David Lane carpenter baptized by W.W. Lutyens [founder of Holy Trinity, Bangalore]

Bow, Hackney

The last two areas of East London to consider are Bow bordered by the River Lea and Essex, and Hackney which on Stanford's Map was almost a separate suburb. The latter was separated from the city by London Fields, Hackney Common and Victoria Park.

St. John at Hackney

Continuing northwards along Cambridge Heath from St. John's, Bethnal Green a traveller arrived at the ancient township of Hackney. In this respect Stow recorded that, "On the other side of the River Ley [sic] is situate the pleasant and healthful town of Hackney; where divers nobles in former times had their country seats."

The church on Mare Street was dedicated as St. Augustine's in Stepney parish in 1275 and sat on land owned by the Knights Templar who held twelve acres and a mill. When they disbanded in 1307 this passed like other property to the Knights of St. John, who also had a mansion. There were memorials to Henry Earl of Northumberland d.1537, Sir Thomas Rowe d.1570 and John Nevill Lord Latimer d.1577. Edward de Vere, Earl of Oxford poet and playwright married Anne Cecil daughter of Burghley, but had to sell Earls Colne and lived at King's Place, Hackney being buried at the church in 1604.

Regarding the environs the Bishop of London held lands whilst there was a chalybeate well at Dalston and several manors: Shacklewell held by the Rowe family who had three mayors, Shoreditch Place held by St. Thomas's Hospital, Bryck Place home of Sir Ralph Sadleir, Tan House home of Sir Thomas Sutton of Charterhouse, and the Black & White House residence of Sir Thomas Vyner a mayor - later a school for gentlewomen.

In deference to the landowners the dedication was altered to St. John's in c.1660 and it then took on an augmented nature. With the arrival of numerous merchants and private schools the capacity was raised up to 1,000 seats through the addition of several galleries. However by 1788 it was concluded that another 3,000 spaces were needed!

After much consultation it was decided to buy Church Field to the north for £875 and some plans were drawn up by William Blackburn at £15,000, but after his decease James Spiller was employed and built a structure for 2,000 people in 1792-97. The old church was demolished a year later and the memorials transferred, but the bell tower was retained due to lack of funds and the private Rowe Chapel (of 1614) was also left standing.

A new rector Rev. John James Watson was appointed in 1799 and did much to establish the new church. His brother Joshua (a merchant) and his brother-in-law Henry Handley Norris (minister of the chapel at Well Street) were philanthropists and reformers.

A white classical tower was added to the plain brickwork of the square nave in 1814, and a trustee Harry Sedgwick planted many elms and horse chestnut around the church. The large parish was then divided into St. James's (W) by R. Smirke (1823), Well Street chapel (S) later St. John of Jerusalem by E. Hakewill (1847), and St. Thomas's, Stamford Hill (1827) an existing chapelry. St. James's, Clapton (E. Hakewill), St. Philip's, Dalston (H. Duesbury) and St. Barnabas (A. Ashpitel) were also added in the 1840s.

The Rowe Chapel itself collapsed in 1877 but one memorial survived, whilst after a fire in 1955 a Mandor organ was brought there from All Saints, Ennismore Gardens. Today, the tower of St. Augustine's remains beside the old Town Hall and there are (annotated) memorials to Beaufort, Watson, Hunter, Loddiges and Sedgwick nearby. Behind the new church are some memorial gardens and Sutton Place (built in 1809). [13]

Notable Parishioners - *Henry S.H. Wollaston* merchant and brother of William Hyde chemist resided at Clapton. His son Charles was vicar of Felpham, Sussex (1847-70) and Amport, Hants (1870-86), whilst grandson Charles H.R. was educated at Lancing College and played for the Wanderers in five Cup Finals and four times for England.

John Hunter was born at Leith in 1737 and was second in command to Arthur Phillip when the first fleet sailed to Sydney Cove in 1788 (see St. Mildred's, Bread Street Vol. I). He was then the second Governor of New South Wales from 1795-1800 and his name was reproduced regarding both a river and a valley in Australia.

Conrad Loddiges came from Hildesheim, Germany where his father was a gardener to George II, Elector of Hanover. He purchased an ancient house with small nursery on the east side of Mare Street from John Busch in 1771, and there he established a palm house and arboretum (the first so-named) containing many rare plants.

---

[13] Thomas Sutton (1532-1611) resided at Tan House which was later replaced by Sutton Place a Georgian terrace; whilst Sir Ralph Sadleir (1507-87) the Secretary of State to Henry VIII lived at Bryck Place nearby which was erroneously given the title Sutton House (now N.T.).

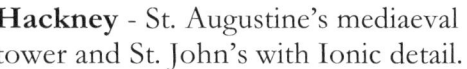

Hackney - St. Augustine's mediaeval tower and St. John's with Ionic detail.

He was the first to grow wisteria and introduced the rhododendron. His son George (1786-1846) expanded the business and Charles Darwin visited, but it closed down when the lease expired in 1854 (now St. Thomas Place). The building inspired Paxton's Crystal Palace and much of the stock passed to Sydenham when Kew declined to take it.

Francis Beaufort was born in Ireland in 1774 of Huguenot descent and served with the E.I.C. and Navy during the Napoleonic Wars. He spent his time mapping, surveying and produced a wind-scale during his first command on *H.M.S. Woolwich* in 1805, and was head of the Hydrographic Office from 1829. In addition he trained Capt. Fitzroy for the *H.M.S. Beagle* and was a founder of the Royal Geographical Society.

C. 5 June 1816 Charles Buchanan son of Henry Septimus Hyde and Frances Wollaston Clapton, Hackney merchant J. Paroissien (seven others 1803-05, 1814-25)

M. 1 March 1719/20 George Dance of St. Margaret Lothbury and Elizabeth Gould of this parish were marryed by ye lycens [architect] - see St. Luke's, Old Street [14]

B. 28 April 1818 Harry Sedgwick of Homerton, Hackney age 66 P. Paroissien
21 March 1821 John Hunter of St. Pancras age 83 G. Paroissien
20 March 1826 Conrad Loddiges of Church Street age 88 J.K. Roper
17 June 1839 John James Watson rector o.t.p. Rectory House age 71 H.H. Norris
22 December 1857 R. Admiral Sir Francis Beaufort K.C.B. of Gloucester Place,
Portman Square age 83 off min D.A. Beaufort & William Palmer

Captain John Hunter (1737-1821), second Governor of New South Wales. His family of Upper Clapton have a memorial just east of the church.

---

[14] James Gould, the father of Elizabeth, was a surveyor of Hackney and worked with George Dance his son-in-law on St. Botolph's, Bishopsgate from 1725-28.

St. Leonard's, Bromley (by Bow)

A Cistercian or Benedictine convent (of white monks) was founded by Henry II on the banks of the River Lea in about 1166, and the complex included a lady chapel. Stow noted that there were a number of significant burials including: John de Bohun, Earl of Hereford d.1336, and Elizabeth the sister of Queen Philippa d.1375. There was also a stone of ancient origins with the unusual inscription of "Wodehouse."

Geoffrey Chaucer who was customs official at Aldgate and did much travelling wrote *The Canterbury Tales* at the end of the 14th century. The convent featured in the prologue to *the prioress's tale*, explaining the prioress had learnt an Anglicised form of the language from the nuns rather than "proper" French as spoken on the Continent viz.

> *And Frensh she spake full faire and fetishly*
> *After the scole of Stratforde atte Bowe*
> *For Frensh of Paris was to hire unknowne*

At the Dissolution the convent was suppressed and the land passed to Sir Ralph Sadleir the courtier of Hackney, while the Lady Chapel became the parish church of St. Leonard's which separated from Stepney in 1536. A hunting lodge or palace was built nearby with stone from the convent for James I in 1606, but by the 18th century it was two houses for merchants and then a Board School (demolished in the late 19th century).

St. Leonard's was situated at the eastern end of Bromley High Street, and there was a memorial to Captain Sir Richard Munden who engaged in fourteen sea fights and took St. Helena d.1680. The whole church was rebuilt in the Victorian period and there was a gateway entrance in memory of Rev. George A.M. How rural dean of Stepney (1840-93), but most of it was destroyed in the war. In addition further land was lost to the Blackwall Tunnel Approaches leaving just an arch, wall, and garden remaining.

St. Mary's, Stratford le Bow

Confusion should be the middle name of this parish. The Romans had a crossing of the River Lea at Old Ford on the road to Colchester, and a paved way or *Street Ford* was built to join the two sides. In the early 12th century Matilda the wife of Henry I reputedly fell while traversing it and a bowed bridge was then constructed.

The outcome of this was that the settlement on the western bank was called Stratford of the Bow, and that to the east was termed Stratford (Langthorne) - the latter having a large Cistercian Abbey with some 1,500 acres from 1135-1538. Of course St. Mary Bow as it came to be known had nothing to do with St. Mary le Bow and its bells.

Regarding the former a licence was granted in 1311 to build a chapel for the inhabitants of Oldford and Stratford, since in winter it was impossible to reach Stepney for services. It was agreed they would pay 24s per annum to the mother church for repairs, go there for the feast of St. Dunstan's, and join the annual procession to St. Paul's.

The curate of Stratford le Bow was appointed by the vicar of Stepney; and the chapel of slint and stones had a nave/chancel with narrow aisles on octagonal columns, pointed arches, and a plain stone tower to the west. Helen Hilliard gave land and tenements for a chantry which were confiscated at the Dissolution, while with Westminster a bishopric the procession was reduced to "attendance" by the curate and wardens.

Rev. William Gouge long-term minister of St. Anne's, Blackfriars was born there as was his son Thomas vicar of St. Sepulchre (1638-62). The latter was ejected for refusing to use the *Book of Common Prayer*, but was well-known for charitable acts and travelled widely in Wales where he established many schools and printed 8,000 *Welsh Bibles*.

At the east end of the north aisle was a marble memorial to Alice daughter of Thomas Coburne gent and brewer who died of smallpox just before her marriage in 1689. Her intended, William Wollaston, then married Catharine Charlton later that year and lived at Charterhouse Square where he spent a life studying (see St. Botolph's Aldersgate). There was a memorial in the nave to her mother Prisca Coburne, a generous benefactor to the parish, and to Rev. Thomas White rector of Stepney and minister of Bow d.1709.

A separate parish was established on 26 March 1719 (despite nearby St. Leonard's) and money allotted for a rector, but the tithes remained with Brasenose, Oxford. Its location in the middle of the road was always a problem and the tower fell down in 1829, whilst it was only repaired in 1898. Sylvia Pankhurst took a shop opposite at 198 Bow Road for the Suffragettes in 1912 - writing *Votes for Women* instead of a trade name.

Outside there are memorials to Joseph Danson (1791-1854) "who devoted his time to the welfare and religious education of the humbler classes," and a statue to W.E. Gladstone given by Theodore H. Bryant of Bryant & Mays match factory. The latter was notorious for a campaign by Annie Besant and the *Match Girls Strike* of 1888. Earlier industry was calico printing, dyeing for the E.I.C. and the manufacture of china.

C. 6 November 1575 William Gowge son of Thomas was christened
19 August 1590 Henry [Earl of Holland] s. of R.H. Robert Lord Rich
29 September 1605 Thomas the sonne of William Gouge gent

M. 8 April 1591 William Whitaker Dr. Theologiae of Cambridge wid and Joan Fenner widower [a theological writer]
22 November 1714 William Penkethman bach. of St. Paul's, Cov Gdn and Elizabeth Hill maiden of St. Paul's, Shadwell [a comic actor]
1 Feby 1725/26 Rev. John Henley of St. Andrew, Holborn and Mary Clifford [a famous Orator and entertainer at Lincoln's Inn Fields]

B. 1 April 1591 A Portuguese, treasurer to the King of Portugal, died in the house of Rob. Ridgdaile innholder when the King laid in the parish [15]

St. Mary, Stratford of the Bow sits awkwardly among the busy traffic of Bow Road.

[15] Don Antonio Pérez (1539-1611) statesman to Phillip II of Spain, self-styled King of Portugal, was accused of treason. But he escaped to France disguised as a shepherd and came to England.

Hawksmoor's Baroque composition with Greek temple,
tower from Halicarnassus and lion and unicorn is crowned
by a statue of George I appearing in Roman dress.

London North

Moving on from the mother parish of Stepney and its fledglings we come to the *four elements* of Islington, Clerkenwell, Holborn and Bloomsbury. This area north of the City and the Strand consisted mainly of improving suburbs but also had earthy slums of Dickensian proportions.

It was the stomping ground of Whitefield and Wesley with their *hell fire and brimstone*, whilst entrepreneurs abounded who brought water to the city and longed for the refreshing air of the colonies - An area of grand classical churches challenged by numerous Nonconformist chapels.

From such basic elements there was a fine Renaissance in the locality and artisans and artistes produced exquisite works of great moment. Amongst its skilled craftsmen were Cruikshank the caricaturist, Niemann the artist, Talman the sculptor, Richardson the novelist and Trollope the chronicler. Then on another level again we have several architects of the highest calibre and a sculptor falling in the Roubiliac category.

But most of all this was a place where churchmen and designers challenged the existing ideas, creating chapels and edifices of lasting significance.

Bunhill Fields, City Road

Detail on a memorial to John Bunyan d.1688. *The Pilgrim's Progess*, a Christian allegory, was written by Bunyan whilst in prison for preaching outside of the Anglican fold. It became a best seller especially in Puritan America.

Islington

A person visiting the Angel today might be somewhat surprised at Stow's description, "Isledon, corruptly and commonly called Islington, placed pleasantly upon a hill; whence is a fine prospect of London, on the northwest side of it."

Despite the fact this was still a rural area the town was of some significance, since the Great North Road came there from Aldersgate. It then went along Upper Street past a toll house, up the Holloway Road and eventually reached Highgate Hill. To the rear was a back route (renamed Liverpool Road) where drovers rested their stock on the way to Smithfield, and here were extensive cattle and sheep pens for their constraint.

Both the Bishops of London and Dean and Chapter of St. Paul's owned estates, and there were moated manor-houses at Canonbury and Highbury. Originally the City was supplied with water from ancient springs below Finsbury hill, but Sir Hugh Myddelton constructed *New River* from the source of the River Lea in Hertford to New River Head at Clerkenwell in 1613. Today, his posed statue is located on Islington Green.

Likewise the Duke of Bedford, Sir Joseph Banks &c. formed a club to show livestock in 1798 and the Royal Agricultural Hall replaced its pens on Liverpool Road in 1862. It was a show venue and parcels depot in the war but is now a business design centre. This was also an area of leisure with Sadler's Wells *musick house* (1683) by a spa, music halls like the Eagle (Grecian Theatre) on City Road where Marie Lloyd began her career, others at Islington Green, and a Lyons Corner House on the site of the Angel Inn.

Initially Islington was developed with a number of Georgian squares and attracted the well-to-do, but with slum clearance in the centre (i.e. at Holborn) poorer people moved in. There was then multiple occupancy as the population of 10,000 in 1801 had reached 300,000 by 1891. One consequence was several new churches including Holloway Road Chapel built by W. Wickings in 1814 which was St. Mary Magdalene parish in 1894.

St. Mary's with its surviving Georgian tower and porch (built 1751-54) - now in an improving, chic area. Nearby is a statue to **Sir Hugh Myddelton** whose New River was most certainly visionary.

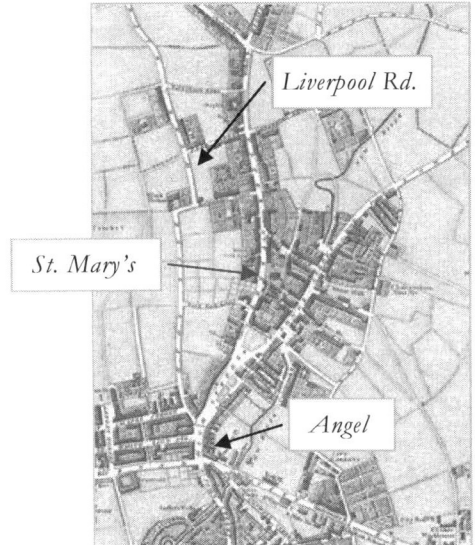

Islington (map 1805) showing its rural location with growth by St. Mary's, drovers route to the west and Angel on City Road.

Bishop Daniel Wilson (1778-1858) - Whitefield and Wesley once kicked up a religious storm here, and their evangelical work was carried on by Rev. Wilson.

St. Mary's, Islington

A church was located on the current site, just east of Upper Street, from Norman times and the mediaeval structure was rebuilt in 1483. Stow had little to say regarding Islington however several significant memorials were later recorded there:

John Markham d.1610 sergeant of arms to King James, Nicholas Kempe d.1624 of the High Court, Sir Thomas Fowler d.1624 husband of Jane Charlet and of Mary the widow of Sir John Spencer of Althorp (mother of Lord Spencer), Anne Chitting d.1632 wife of Henry Chitting the *Chester Herald*; and in the churchyard Richard Cloudesley Esq., "A benefactor of the parish," d.1517 (restored in 1690).

Islington was a centre for religious upheaval and at the Reformation statues were taken out from the church and smashed on the Green, whilst there were also several prominent ministers. William Cave was born at Pickwell, Leicester in 1637, and the son of a rector expelled for Royalist leanings. Despite this he was educated at St. John's, Cambridge and was vicar of Islington in 1662-91 during which time he wrote several learned pieces, the content of which apparently went over the heads of the parishioners.

His works included the *Apostolici* or *History of the Apostles in the First Three Centuries* (1677) and an *Ecclesiastical History* (1688) bringing him into conflict with Jean Leclerc. He held the livings of All Hallows the Great (1679-89) and Isleworth (from 1690), was a chaplain in ordinary to Charles II, and a canon at Windsor where he died.

In the second instance, Rev. George Stonehouse became the vicar in 1738 at the time of the *Great Awakening* and Charles Wesley joined him as curate. As a result he invited John Wesley and George Whitefield to come and preach there - the former came on ten occasions in the next year, but the latter was prevented from entering the pulpit by the churchwardens. Due to such disturbances Stonehouse was forced to resign in 1740, and there were said to be "no Methodists in the parish" over the next few years.

The edifice was rebuilt by Lancelot Dowbiggin in the Georgian style from 1751-54 and Rev. Daniel Wilson a leading evangelist came there as minister in 1824-32. Initially he was at St. John's, Bedford Row with links to the Clapham Sect, and started the *Islington Conference for Evangelical Clergy* in 1827. He was then appointed Bishop of Calcutta but his family retained the advowson which was given to an Evangelical trust, and his son Rev. Daniel Wilson junior was the long-term minister from 1832-86.

This tradition was continued into modern times however the building was destroyed in the blitz in 1940, and services took place in the memorial hall until it was rebuilt in 1956. Despite this the *church* grew at this time under another evangelical Rev. Maurice Wood who went on to become Bishop of Norwich, while David Sheppard (the cricketer) and George Carey (later Archbishop of Canterbury) acted as his curates.

St. Mary's Parish Records

C. 7 March 1813 Edmund John the son of John Diedrich and Mary Louisa Niemann of Astey's Row, merchant, by Mr. Rose born 8 February [1]

M. 27 March 1843 Henry Dorling wid. bookseller of Epsom s. of William bookseller and Elizabeth Mayson wid. of 14 Duncan Terrace d. of Isaac Jerrom a stable-keeper licence by J. Ray presence Jno. Thos. Stelms, Louisa Elliott [mother of Mrs. Beeton]

B. William Cave D.D. buried 7 August 1713 [d. 4th]

Royal Agricultural Hall, Islington - opened in 1862.

Charles William Alcock (1842-1907) was secretary of the F.A. from 1870-95 and of Surrey C.C.C. at the Oval from 1872. In this joint capacity he started the F.A. Cup competition and wrote sporting annuals. His restored memorial is at West Norwood Cemetery.

---

[1] John Niemann came from Minden near Hanover, Germany but worked for Lloyd's and his son Edmund was born at Astey's Row in 1813. The property was on a terrace beside the New River at the junction of Canonbury and Essex Roads. Edmund was initially a clerk at Lloyd's however then devoted himself to "art" at High Wycombe, and produced scenic views of the Thames and Yorkshire. He exhibited at the Royal Academy in 1844-72 and his distinctive paintings were in general characterised by romantic realism, while he died at Brixton Hill in 1876.

His son Edmund H. Niemann was an artist in similar but not as exacting style, and married Emma Harriet the sister of Edward Gibbon Blythe another artist of Clapham. These three were the aunt and uncles of Colin Blythe (1879-1917) the Kent and England cricketer.

Holy Trinity (front and rear) was on a leafy square by Liverpool Road. Sir Charles Barry designed this and orchestrated two others in the district viz. St. John's and St. Paul's.

Holy Trinity, Cloudesley Square

The area around Liverpool Road received a number of squares from the 1820s-30s, with Milner and Gibson Squares to the east and Lonsdale and Cloudesley Squares to the west. The church of Holy Trinity was built at the latter in 1826-29 - one of three edifices in the locality designed by Sir Charles Barry, architect of the Houses of Parliament. In addition he produced several designs in Sussex including St. Peter's, Brighton (1826) one of the earliest examples of Gothic Revival, and also the church at Hurstpierpoint.

Barry's model for these edifices was formulaic with a variation on a theme and Holy Trinity had a grand west window with corner turrets (which now need restoration). The lofty nave had pinnacles along its length reminiscent of King's College, Cambridge, and adjacent were lower but quite distinct aisles. It was then occupied by the Pentecostal or Celestial Church of Christ from 1980 (formed in Benin in 1947).

Apart from the gentry who inhabited its Georgian-style housing the most notable link was to George Cruikshank (b. 1792). He initially made his name with political and royal satire in the 1820s, but then turned to book illustrations in particular *Sketches by Boz* and *Oliver Twist* for Charles Dickens - later employing his wealth to support the temperance movement. He first married Mary Ann Walker but after his second marriage moved to 263 Hampstead Road, Camden, where he lived until his death in 1878. A brown plaque was erected at the latter address by the R.S.A. in 1885.

M. 7 March 1850 George Cruickshank wid. artist of Amwell Street, Clerkenwell son of Isaac artist and Eliza Widdison spin. of 24 Dolly Terrace, City Road d. John gentleman lic. by A. Stock, *C* [flamboyant signature] wit. John Sheringham, Isaac Armstrong

St. Phillip the Evangelist, Arlington Square - This was designed by A.D. Gough next to the Regent's Canal, just north of City Road, in 1855. A parish was created three years later although part was transferred to St. James's, Prebend Street in 1875. However the structure was demolished and the remaining parish joined to the latter in 1953.

M. 10 December 1864 Charles William Alcock shipbroker 33 Sherborne Street s. Charles shipbroker and Eliza Caroline Ovenden 45 Morton Road d. Francis Webb O. artist banns by James Sutherland B.A. incumbent wit. H. Sedgwick, J. Brooks, Lily and S. Beale

St. John's, Upper Holloway - Rev. Daniel Wilson vicar of Islington conceived a church at Archway and it was built to a Barry design on land of Rev. James Palmer, vicar of St. Bride's, in 1826-28. Again it had a Gothic remit with pinnacles on the tower, nave, and aisles - like the minarets of a mosque; whereas Wilson designated a three-tier pulpit and little separate chancel for his envisaged form of worship. Barry was not pleased with the outcome and destroyed all his drawings, whilst a prominent feature was the Puritan box pews. This is still an Anglican church and the vicar emanates from Nigeria.

St. Jude's, Mildmay Park - This was built by A.D. Gough with a distinctive ragstone spire, school, and vicarage in 1856 - he was also architect of St. Matthew's, Essex Road and St. Mark's, Tollington Park. Rev. William Pennefather, son of a Baron of the Irish Exchequer, arrived there from Barnet in 1864-73 then wrote hymns and founded the Mildmay Institution with its *Conferences* which aimed to help the poor. During his time there the church was also extended and outside is a tablet to that effect.

St. Paul's, Canonbury - Barry designed the church with a stone tower, distinct aisles and pinnacles east of New River in 1828. This was a very fine building but the parish combined with St. Jude's and it became a school and social centre from 1982.

St. Peter's, Islington - This was a plain church which some attribute to Barry, built east of the Green, in 1834-35. The partners Roumieu and Gough were architects of Milner Square to the north and later embellished the building with flying buttresses; however it was joined to St. James's, Prebend Street also in 1982 and converted to flats.

Kingsland Road Chapel - A leper or Lock Hospital was founded in the hamlet of that name on the eastern border of Islington in 1280, and came under St. Bartholomew's in 1549. Its ancient chapel then became a *chapel of ease* for the parish of Hackney, but the hospital closed in 1760 and its decayed church building was demolished in 1846.

Union Chapel, Compton Terrace - This independent or Congregational chapel with a red-brick tower and white stone entrance was "founded 1799, built 1806, rebuilt 1877." Rev. Henry Allon who trained at Cheshunt was minister from 1844-92 (bur. Abney Park) and was editor of the *Quarterly Review* from 1865. He employed James Cubitt, who used a broad central space, to rebuild it from 1874-90 and it is now a music venue.

St. Barnabas, King Square, with its Ionic portico and slim spire, had a façade similar to Soane's work at Euston and Walworth. It is now surrounded by flats and is called St. Clement's.

A sign located on **St. Luke's** gates.

The City Road

The Commissioners debated overcrowding in London parishes in 1711, and in particular noted that St. Giles Cripplegate parish covered a large area up to Islington and across to Shoreditch. Meanwhile nearby St. Stephen Coleman also included Finsbury Circus.

Parochial returns revealed that St. Giles had 4,600 houses with numerous alleyways and courtyards in the area between Moorfields and Redcross Street, leading up to Old Street with extensive fields beyond. As a result St. Luke's was created to serve this area, and other churches followed later. In addition an inaugural by-pass linked Paddington Green to the Angel Islington in 1756 and was initially called New Road, but was later renamed as Marylebone and Euston Roads with Pentonville Road just beyond.

This was also extended at the eastern end as City Road through to Old Street and down to Moorgate in 1761. The former became an important city artery - the location of many retail outlets and workplaces for artisans, whilst the Regent's Canal tunnel emerged near the Angel and to the east were the City Road and Wenlock Basins.

St. Barnabas, King Square

As housing filled the adjacent areas new churches were needed and Thomas Hardwick designed an imposing *chapel* between City Road and Lever Street at £12,853 in 1823-26. This was in the classical style on a new square with shallow Ionic portico, four columns, entablature and tall slender spire - its façade reminiscent of Soane's work. The rector of St. Luke's was appointed the patron and it became a separate parish in 1842.

However, the church was badly damaged during the war and the square was reduced to merely a cul-de-sac. Services were then held elsewhere and it was used to store furniture, but it was renovated and united with St. Clement's and St. Matthew's once on City Road in 1954. Since then it has been known as *St. Clement with St. Barnabas, King Square.*

St. Luke's, Old Street

Initially Mr. Willmers offered a plot to the south at Whitecross Street for £550 - but this scheme was then deferred in September 1712. A new site owned by the Ironmongers Company adjacent to Old Street was then considered in late 1714, but with the arrival of George I and a new Whig ministry this was all promptly mothballed. As a consequence St. Luke's was one of the last of the "Fifty Churches" to be sanctioned in June 1727 and with a new directive, namely, to be built in a much cheaper fashion.

John James was the architect of the nave with its plain walls and two rows of square and round-headed windows, plus top-stones. However it was the innovative Hawksmoor who added the staircase and distinctive west tower with its extremely unusual obelisk for a spire. The whole composition was finished in 1733 and the parish covered an area from just north of Chiswell Street reaching across to the City Road.

Dr. William Nicholls was the first rector of St. Luke's and vicar of St. Giles, hence his portrait can be found in the tower of the latter; whilst the two most notable parishioners were William Caslon (memorial in front) and George Dance architect (see over).

The Whitbread brewery was situated either side of Chiswell Street on the site of the former King's Head brewhouse from the mid-18th century, however by that time Caslon was already well established in the area. William Caslon was born at Cradley, Worcester in 1692 and came to London as an engraver, then opened a type foundry in 1720. The *Caslon Typeface*, based on the earlier Dutch Baroque, became an instant favourite.

He initially traded at the Minories and at Ironmonger Row just behind the church, but moved to the Caslon Foundry on Chiswell Street opposite to Moor Lane (or Type Street) from 1737-1909. The family retained an interest throughout that time and it then passed to Stephenson, Blake & Co., whilst today a plaque marks the site.

Just west of the church at the south end of Bath Street were a series of public buildings including Alleyn's Almshouses, a Lying in Hospital (1773) and St. Luke's Asylum (1789). Regarding the parish this was then sub-divided into St. Paul's, Bunhill Row (1839-1932), St Thomas Charterhouse (1842-1909) and St. Mary Charterhouse (1858-1940) or Golden Lane Church on Playhouse Yard - the site of the Fortune Theatre.

St. Luke's, Old Street

Elton John may have pumped up the decibels but the church's subsidence was strictly historical.

These three churches were combined and then re-united with St. Luke's in 1952. St. Bartholomew, Moor Lane (1848-1902) was designed by C.R. Cockerell like its namesake at Threadneedle Street, but was demolished for the railway and went back to St. Giles. One other link was John Wood an artificial florist at 3 Bath Place (Street) in 1881, whose daughter Matilda (Marie Lloyd) began her career at the Grecian Theatre nearby.

Regarding St. Luke's it was a prominent feature on Old Street with its small churchyard behind, but was closed due to subsidence in 1964 and the parish reunited with St. Giles. The font and organ case were removed to the latter, whilst after the roof was removed the edifice became a stark ruin with trees growing out of it for some forty years.

Being a Grade I listed building it was finally restored as a concert hall for the London Symphony Orchestra - with a new acoustic, concrete roof supported on steel columns. Performers there have included Bruce Springstein, Paul Simon and Elton John whilst it has hosted other significant musical events.

C. 22 Oct 1775 Ann Mary d. Edw. Underwood packthread spinner & Mary b. 2 Oct [2]

M. 3 January 1809 George Wilson Addison of Almondbury, Yorks bach. and Elizabeth Brook o.t.p. spin. lic. by John Busby curate wit. Wm Brook, Jn. A. Addison [3]

B. 4 February 1766 William Caslon a man apoplexy
17 February 1768 George Dance a man

William Caslon I (1692-1766) pioneer of a typeface worked in nearby Chiswell Street.

George Dance the elder (1694-1768) was born at St. Dunstan in the West son of Giles a mason and merchant taylor. He trained with his father then married Elizabeth daughter of James Gould a surveyor of Hackney, and lived by St. Luke's which he saw built. He was appointed City of London Surveyor in 1735 and designed St. Botolph's, Bishopsgate (1728), St. Leonard's, Shoreditch (1740), the Mansion House (1739-52), St. Botolph's, Aldgate (1744), and St. Matthew's, Bethnal Green (1746).

George Dance the younger (1741-1825) succeeded his father as City Surveyor and designed Newgate, the Guildhall, All Hallows, St. Bartholomew the Less and St. Luke's Hospital (1782-89).

St. Mary Moorfields

The first Roman Catholic chapel in the district was opened in 1686 but was suspended in 1689. It re-opened at Ropemaker Alley (St.) from 1736-80 however it was destroyed in the Gordon Riots. This was followed by a building in White Street and a large classical church St. Mary's designed by John Newman on the east side of Finsbury Circus in 1817-20; the latter also near to the London Institution, Finsbury and Unitarian Chapels.

Cardinal Wiseman was born in Seville but with the changes of the Oxford Movement the Pope made him first Archbishop of Westminster in 1850, and this was his pro-cathedral from 1850-69. The building was sold in 1899 and George Sherrin who designed the dome of the Oratory built a new St. Mary's at Eldon Street in 1903. It had an impressive interior which included Newman's altar columns, despite being in "a façade of shops."

---

[2] David Watson married Ann Mary Underwood of St. Luke's parish with her father's consent at Westminster in 1793. Their daughter Eleanor married Dr. Robert Willis of Dover Street and Barnes whilst their grandson Robert Watson Willis was second F.A. secretary.

[3] William Brook & Sons were wool staplers in Meltham, Yorkshire and Addison worked there after his marriage. He was a mill owner at Bowling, Bradford from 1828 and died at Manningham in 1861; whilst his son George continued the business and grandson George William was a major R.E., played in the first Cup Final, and was an assistant to Lord Iveagh (see Kensington).

Wesley's Chapel

Rev. Samuel Wesley (1662-1735) was initially educated at a grammar school in Dorchester but then trained as a dissenting minister at Stepney and Newington, at which time he met fellow student Daniel Defoe. He attended Oxford as a poor student and married Susanna youngest daughter of Samuel Annesley another dissenting minister on 11 November 1688. However, over a prolonged period he moved back towards *Conformity*.

Consequently, he was appointed to the parish of Epworth, Lincoln after his poetry put him in favour with Mary II in 1697, and on one occasion he was criticised for backing Rev. Sacheverell in an intolerant attack on Dissenting Academies! Meanwhile, the couple had ten surviving children including Samuel (1690) a master at Blundell's School, John (1703) the founder of Methodism and Charles (1707) the celebrated hymn writer.

The latter two brothers were educated at Charterhouse and Westminster then after a failed mission to Georgia in 1735-36 turned to the Moravian movement. As a result John experienced a conversion at their meeting house at 28 Aldersgate Street on 24 May 1738, after hearing a reading of Martin Luther's, *Preface to the Epistle to the Romans*. He was followed shortly afterwards in such convictions by his brother Charles.

John Wesley was a friend of Whitefield from his days at university and initially helped him, preaching at Bristol and Kingswood, but his Arminian Methodism was a distinct branch and doctrine from that of Whitefield's Calvinism. He taught personal salvation by faith through *God's Grace* and after he was banned from preaching in parish churches, he took to the open air and started his own chapels - the first of these at Bristol.

His creed was a direct affront to the existing institutions and therefore a social threat, but he believed they were failing to minister to the poor or bring salvation to the sinner. The construction of the New Room at Bristol was followed by the Foundry Chapel, in a disused cannon foundry on the eastern side of Windmill Hill (Tabernacle Street), on 11 November 1739. This was just above Moorfields (Finsbury Square) and Worship Street, being shown on Rocque's map as "Methodist Meeting House."

There was a growing rift with the Church - hence the first Methodist conference took place there on 25-30 June 1744, and aimed to establish rules for chapels, preachers and groups. Wesley initially balked on ordination due to a belief in Apostolic Succession and the Bishops, but had created ordained priests for home and the colonies by 1748. The conflict continued for several years, although Wesley never wanted to stray too far from the precepts of the Established Church and preached around the country.

A new chapel was built on City Road opposite Bunhill Fields in 1776-78, the architect George Dance the younger who was City of London Surveyor. This was a fine example of Georgian architecture with classical entrance around a courtyard, while John Wesley resided in the adjacent property and was buried behind the chapel in 1791. Its gallery was modernised in 1864 and the columns (masts donated by George III) were replaced by jasper, using subscriptions from overseas, in 1891.

Today the building houses a congregation, a *Museum of Methodism* and the *Foundry Chapel* which includes benches from the original chapel and Wesley's pipe organ. In the courtyard is a memorial to Susanna Wesley his mother and a plaque on the south house records that Wesley lived there (for his last eleven years).

Wesley's Chapel, City Road with memorials to John Wesley and mother Susanna Wesley d.1742 (erected 1870). Her father was ejected from St. Giles.

Bunhill Fields - This was part of the manor of Finsbury and an Artillery Ground was laid out for archers and military exercise in 1498 (later cricket), whilst the Hon. Artillery Co. came from Spitalfields in 1641. Nearby were some windmills and the City planned a burial ground in 1665 but Tindal took the lease and it was named after him. It was mainly for dissenters who were well established in the area, but was used by anyone who could afford the fees. The Quakers burying ground was adjacent and is now a park.

An inscription notes it was opened under the mayoralty of Sir John Lawrence and on the walls are names of significant people buried: Henry, Richard and William Cromwell, Daniel Defoe, Thomas Hardy (radical), John Bunyan, Isaac Watts (hymn writer, mayor), Susanna Wesley and William Blake. There are prominent memorials to Defoe, Blake and Bunyan but it was closed in 1854 and Abney Park at Stoke Newington took over.

The Tabernacle - George Whitefield (1714-70) also went to Georgia and encouraged the Wesleys to preach outside, then built chapels at Kingswood and in a rural location by Windmill Hill in 1741 (rebuilt 1753). He was a chaplain for the Countess of Huntingdon a Calvinist and spent much time in America preaching to large crowds.

Two more Tabernacles were opened at Penn Street, Bristol (birthplace of Penn senior) and Tottenham Court Road in the 1750s, whilst the registers at Moorfields began in 1768 and Whitefield carried out the first baptisms. Andrew Kinsman of Devonport preached there and Rev. John Morley who was baptized by him recorded in Wesleyan terms:

"The thunder rolled tremendously loud and the lightning flashed vividly, there was an earthquake in my conscience and I feared the earth would swallow me up. But my mind was set at happy liberty under a sermon preached in the Tabernacle by the Rev. Edward Parsons of Leeds (Acts 13 v. 38-39). The reading of the text melted me into tears, every sentence in the sermon bringing Holy unction to my spirit." Rev. Matthew Wilks was the minister in 1775-1829 and also attended Tottenham Court Road, but the chapel closed in 1907 and was replaced by the Central Foundation School on Leonard Street. [4]

---

[4] John Morley (1770-1863) trained at Spa Fields then was pastor of the independent chapel at Alford, Lincoln (allied to the Countess of Huntingdon) and spent 50 years at Hope Street, Hull. His son Rev. Ebenezer Morley (1801-62) was minister at Holborn Street in Hull and Brentford; whilst grandson Ebenezer Cobb Morley a solicitor of Barnes and Temple took up the ideas of "muscular Christianity" and was first secretary of the F.A. in 1863 - formulating the rules.

Clerkenwell

Regarding this locality there was a transparent clue in the name, since it referred to the location of the clerics or clerks' well. Indeed, this was an historic site just beyond West Smithfield by the drovers' road up to Islington (St. John's Street), and had no less than three major religious institutions in its bounds. There were also a number of significant chapels and churches in the area other than the parochial ones (see below).

Charterhouse Chapel

The Carthusians were an enclosed order who were formed in the Chartreuse Mountains in the Lower Alps in 1084 (hence the name). Despite having no abbeys they developed their own statutes, and each priory had a leader with lay brothers or hermits.

Baron Walter de Manny established a Carthusian order just north of Smithfield on the former site of a plague burial ground in 1371, but after a short existence it was dissolved like the other monasteries in 1537. The property was sold to Sir Edward North who promptly developed it into, "A very large and goodly mansion, beautified with spacious gardens, walks, orchards and other pleasures, enriched by divers dependencies of lands and tenements, and very aptly seated for the wholesome air."

Sir Thomas Sutton (1532-1611) was a Master of the Ordnance and married Elizabeth Dudley, thus securing connections to the Earls of Leicester and Warwick. Being very rich with large estates and a house in Hackney, he searched for a site to establish a hospital and school for the poor. Little Hallingbury was purchased from the Earl of Essex and he engaged in "fervent plans" to start a *Hospital of King James* there, but finding the site at Charterhouse more convenient entreated with the Earl of Suffolk its owner.

The good Earl warmed to such a Godly scheme and £13,000 was paid by Sutton for the site. However, before the plan was finished the latter died and his executors John Lawe and Richard Sutton carried it through - therefore the hospital opened on 3 October 1614. Within the precincts of the house were the old chapel (1500) and an ante-chapel with groined roof (1512). The institution was initially called "Sutton's Hospital" and in the northeast corner of the sanctuary was his memorial with coat of arms:

"Here lyeth Thomas Sutton late of Castle Campes co. Cambs at whose only costes and charges this hospital was founded and endowed with large possessions for ye relief of poor men and children; he was a gentleman borne at Knayth, Lincs of worthie and honest parentage d. 12 December 1611, aged 79."

Sutton's Hospital, Charterhouse in c.1770 and the chapel (little changed from that time).

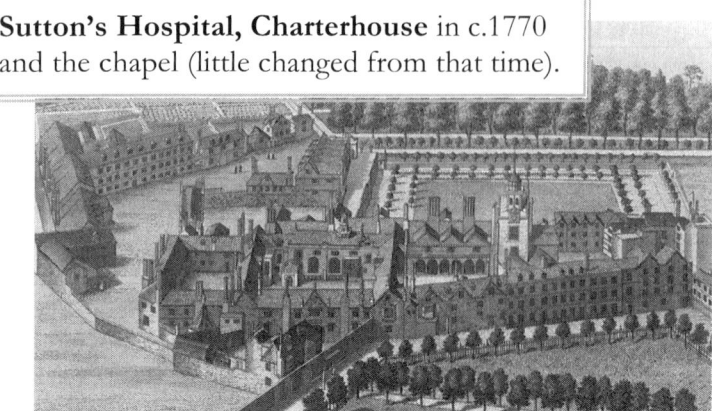

Charterhouse Square
The historic buildings and almshouses conceal the cloisters behind.

The foundation provided for 80 male pensioners - gentlemen in poverty, soldiers of sea and land, shipwrecked merchants and Royal servants and to educate 40 boys. It gained a fine reputation under Dr. Henry Levett who came from St. Bartholomew's in 1713. His widow married Andrew Tooke F.R.S. a professor of Gresham College who was briefly the headmaster from 1728 (both were pupils and have memorials there).

An adjacent site called Pardon Churchyard was turned down by the Commissioners for a parish in the early 1700s, whereas the chapel witnessed the marriages of John Talman art collector who had toured Italy and Samuel Richardson author of *Pamela, Clarissa* and *Sir Charles Grandison*. Meanwhile the school had some eminent pupils: Richard Lovelace, Nathaniel Lee, Joseph Addison, Sir Richard Steele, John Wesley, the Earl of Liverpool, A'bishop Charles Manners-Sutton, Francis and William H. Wollaston, William Heberden junior, Robert Baden-Powell, Sir George Barrow and W.M. Thackeray.

The chapel was enlarged in 1824 and repaired in 1842, but the school outgrew the site and under headmaster Rev. Dr. Haig Brown moved to Godalming in 1872. The adjacent St. Thomas Charterhouse was un-connected (see over), whilst the almshouses remain by the chapel and still hold the patronage of Little Hallingbury in Essex. [5]

M. 3 July 1718 John Talman bach. of St. Andrew, Holborn married Frances Cockayne spinster of Hinxworth, Hertford by Fa. Maddox, Mr. John King
23 November 1721 Samuel Richardson of ye parish of St. Bride's and Martha Wild of ye parish of St. Botolph Aldersgate by Ralph Welstead

B. 26 September 1811 Rev. Mathew Raine D.D. head school master of this hospital was buried in the chapel d.17 September, age 51 [memorial south wall by Flaxman]
22 December 1818 Right Hon Edward [Law], Lord Ellenborough of St. James's Square, age 68 [pupil and Lord Chief Justice, memorial south wall by Chantry]

Cloisters - Lt. Col. Wm Havelock [1793] fell at head of regiment 14th Light Dragoons charging the Sikhs at Ramnegger 22 Nov. 1848. He served in the Peninsula 1810-14 and Netherlands 1815 wounded at Quatre Bra, and was Sir H. Havelock's elder brother.

Outside - Guilielmo Makepeace Thackeray Carthusiani H.M.P.C. *Natus* MDCCCXI *Ob* MDCCCLXIII, *Alumni* XXIII - XXVIII (buried at Kensal Green)

---

[5] The school at Godalming was designed by Philip C. Hardwick (s. of Philip); whilst they had a significant role in soccer the Old Carthusians winning the F.A. Cup in 1881, and its memorial chapel was designed by Sir Giles Gilbert Scott in 1927. The Smithfield site was occupied by the Merchant Taylor's School until 1933, then passed to St. Bartholomew's now the London School of Medicine which is situated around the great cloister (with information plaque).

St. Thomas Charterhouse was built by Edward Blore in Romanesque style at a cost of £5,560 in 1842, being one of 29 new churches at this time. The land on Goswell Road was donated by Charterhouse and the parish separated from St. Botolph's and St. Luke's, whilst educational reformer Rev. William Rogers was minister of this crowded parish in 1845-63. After depopulation it was demolished in 1909 and united with St. Mary's then St. Luke's - the resultant funds going to St. Thomas, Acton Vale in 1915.

St. James's, Clerkenwell

Baron Jorden Briset founded a Benedictine nunnery dedicated to St. Mary on the site in 1140 and this became quite wealthy and influential. Local residents used the church and at the Dissolution in 1539 the surviving part became the parish of St. James's. The land then transferred to Thomas, Duke of Norfolk. The steeple fell down in 1623 and during rebuilding the south aisle and gallery were damaged, but it was all repaired at a cost of £1,600 by 1627 and the east part of the church was renovated in 1638.

 The living came into the hands of trustees in 1656 and remained so after the Restoration with the election of vicars and a Low Church tradition. The founder and his wife Muriel were buried in the priory while later memorials were to: Sir William Weston last prior of St. John's d.1540, John Bell the Bishop of Worcester d.1556, Lady Elizabeth Berkeley of the Queen's Chamber d.1585, Elizabeth the Countess Dowager of Exeter d.1653, and finally Gilbert Burnet the Bishop of Salisbury d.1714.

 Other residents included Thomas Briton who was born at Rushden in 1644 then a coal merchant at Aylesbury Street to the east, and as *the singing coalman* had many strings to his bow (a plaque marks the site). He built up a library and laboratory to study chemistry whilst as a patron of music invited many top musicians to come and play there.

 Meanwhile, the church with remains of the nunnery and later additions fell into decay and a new one was built by James Carr in 1788-92. Its exterior with Classical pediments and Gothic spire was like Wren but the interior with narthex, high oblong nave and oval ceiling was strictly for the pulpit. Rev. H. Foster a founder of the C.M.S. was vicar and Bishop B. Porteus dedicated the building - the upper galleries being added in 1822.

St. James's, Clerkenwell from the Green

Interior with England organ and Royal arms dated 1792.

The tower and spire were restored by W.P. Griffith in 1849 and Sir Arthur Blomfield rearranged the main nave in 1882. The church and adjacent area remain little changed, its winding lanes being a favourite location for filming. In the vestibule are memorials to Burnet, Crosse and Penton, benefactors from 1577-1879, and arms of Coade stone, and inside a brass to Bell and memorials to Exeter and Wood in the southeast corner.

Regarding radicalism in the locality there is a long memorial to those lost in the *Fenian Conspiracy* of 1867, an attempt to release prisoners from the nearby House of Detention (built in 1615, then a school, now flats). Lenin, founder of the Communist State, lived at Percy Circus to the north in 1902 and his writings were published at 37a Clerkenwell Green before moving to Geneva. This became the Marx Memorial Library in 1933.

C. 15 December 1730 Thomas Birch aged 25 was bapt [went to St. Mgt. Pattens]

B. 4 March 1653/54 Elizabeth Countess Dowager of Exeter chancel - with arms
10 September 1691 Sr. William Wood marshall to the archers from the hospital
1 July 1712 Thomas Crosse Esq. bur. in the church vault [memorial by Roubiliac]
1 October 1714 Thomas Briton was buried in the vault
11 February 1714/15 Henry Penton Esq. of Lincoln's Inn in the chancel
22 March 1714/15 Gilbert Burnett, Lord Bishop of Sarum chancel - with mitre

St. John's, Clerkenwell

The second Clerkenwell priory was also founded by Baron Briset and Lady Muriel, after they purchased ten acres of land from the nearby nuns, in 1144. In exchange they gave them a site of similar size at Welling, Kent. Here they established a Benedictine priory which became the principal seat of the Knights of St. John of Jerusalem.

Heraclius, Patriarch of Jerusalem, came to England due to a religious crisis in 1185 and during the visit dedicated the Temple Church of the Knights Templars and the Church of St. John's. At the latter place a council was held and Heraclius persuaded Henry II to send troops on a crusade, but could not secure the services of the King himself. [6]

The Knights of St. John inherited the lands of the Templars in 1325, but found it hard to support the expenses of the Grand Master and his retinue - who entertained Royal guests such as King John, Edward I and his wife Queen Eleanor. Two priors Theodoric and Grendon went to fight in the Holy Land, while the rebels of Kent and Essex burnt down the priory in 1381 and it was then gradually restored.

Thomas Docwra the penultimate prior of the Hospitallers completed the great church, palatial buildings and south-gate of the inner precincts in 1504. After the fall of Rhodes, Henry VIII initially confirmed their privileges, but at the Dissolution he granted William Weston and other knights small annuities whereby most of them retreated to Malta. In the first instance the site became a Royal storehouse for tents and the like; but under

---

[6] The Knights of St. John of Jerusalem were founded in the Holy Land in 1099 but were removed to Cyprus and Rhodes by 1310. After a siege by Suliemann of the Ottoman Empire they left in 1522 and eventually accepted a new base on Malta in 1530. They settled at Birgu with an auberge and eight langues but after a "great siege" the Grand Master built the fortified Valletta in 1565. Napoleon came in 1798 and the British established a colony by the Treaty of Amiens in 1802.

Edward VI in 1549, "The church for the most part, to wit the body and the side aisles with the great bell tower, was undermined and blown up." Its stone was used by the Lord Protector to build Somerset House and to restore All Hallows, Lombard Street.

Under Queen Mary the surviving quire and side chapels were sealed at the west end and Sir Thomas Trensham was made prior by Cardinal Pole, and mass was held there, but this was again suppressed by Elizabeth I in 1558. Many of the brethren were buried there including William Mallory but it is unclear if he was related his namesake Thomas.

With the Knights definitely back in Malta for the final time the buildings then received a number of uses, and in general the complex decayed from its former glory. Initially the old choir was repaired in 1623, and Robert Bruce, Earl of Aylesbury and Elgin, made it into the private Aylesbury Chapel. It was also a Presbyterian meeting house, but the pews were burnt by the Sacheverell rioters before Bishop Burnet's property in 1710.

The building then came under scrutiny and despite much opposition regarding tithes and maintenance the Commissioners purchased it for £3,000 as the parish church of St. John's in 1723. John Langhorne the poet who translated *Plutarch's Lives* was curate and lecturer there in 1764-66, while Dr. Johnson and others were ridiculed by Churchill after a visit to the crypt - "where they trembled on seeing the Cock Lane Ghost."

An old postern gate at the end of Jerusalem Passage (by Briton's house) was demolished in 1780. But the church remained on St. John's Square with the south/east walls, capitals, ribs, and painted east window of Docwra's priory - as restored by W.P. Griffith in 1845. The area with its narrow streets was transformed by a cutting of the Farringdon Railway in the 1860s, and Clerkenwell Road joined Old Street to Theobalds Road in 1878.

The latter went through the middle of St. John's Square and buildings on Albemarle Way became reminiscent of the flatirons in New York and Vancouver. Regarding the ancient gate to the south Richard Hogarth ran a coffee house in 1701-09, whilst Edward Cave began the *Gentleman's Magazine* in 1731 and Dr. Johnson worked for him in 1737. It was also a tavern and after restoration H.Q. of the Order of St. John's Ambulance from 1873, whereas a garden to the south demarks the outer precincts (cont. over).

M. 8 January 1847 George Frederick Cambridge gent of St. Paul's, Deptford s. of ditto and Sarah Fairbrother spin of Baker Street d. of John gent lic by Hugh Hughes rector wit George Cooper, Eliz. Brown [Queen Victoria did not recognize the Duke's marriage and his actress wife was known as Mrs. FitzGeorge] - see Christchurch, Mayfair

St. John's showing *The Round* of Docwra's priory and entrance.

Mediaeval nave and priory gatehouse

St. John's ceased to be a parish in 1931 and became the chapel for the order, but was badly damaged in the blitz and restored with assembly hall at £80,000 in 1958. The Duke of Gloucester, Grand Prior opened the memorial garden and the Docwra family donated some wrought iron gates at the entrance. Features are a 12th century crypt, mediaeval walls, a triptych given by Prior John Weston after the siege of Rhodes in 1480, and some 18th century carvings. The Docwra gatehouse itself is now a museum.

Pentonville Chapel (St. James's) - Henry Penton of the Admiralty and M.P. for Winton laid out a suburb in 1777, and asked for a chapel but the rector of St. James's would not pay a minister. Aaron Hurst then built one in Palladian style with houses on Pentonville Road in 1788 (and was buried), and Joel A. Knight of Spa Fields was incumbent. It had a brick façade, cupola and lay north to south, and the parish bought it the next year.

Of its connections R.C. Carpenter of Russell Square advocated ideals of the Cambridge Camden Society (Ecclesiological) and tutored B.W. Mountfort (NZ), his works including Lancing College and St. Mary Magdalene, Munster Square. Joseph Grimaldi was a clown in Covent Garden but died at Southampton Street and has a memorial of 1837.

The church became St. James's in 1854 but Rev. A.L. Courtenay the curate fell out with the parish over tithes and founded Christchurch (St. Silas) by S.S. Teulon in 1860. It was redundant by 1959 and replaced by offices with a replica-façade in Grimaldi Park in 1985, whilst nearby was the prison panopticon with entrance by Barry of 1840-42.

C. 25 November 1812 Richard Cromwell Carpenter s. of Richard & Sophia b. 21 Oct.

St. Mark's, Myddelton Square - Rev. Thos Handley, incumbent of St. James, reported a severe situation in 1822: "The parish contains about 36,000 inhabitants and there is not accommodation in the two parochial churches and chapel for more than one tenth that number." Hence the New River Co. donated some land and their surveyor W.C. Mylne designed a Gothic church for £16,000 and houses in 1825-28. To the south was Sadler's Wells theatre and the New River Head constructed by H. Myddelton in 1613, the latter replaced by the Metropolitan Water Board building in 1915-20 (see picture p. 311). [7]

Spa Fields Chapel - The Pantheon, Exmouth Market had Egyptian columns, pediment and rotunda and was a tearoom from 1770-74 then a proprietary chapel. Nearby were the Quakers' Workhouse, Bridewell, New Prison, Cold Bath and New Wells. The Countess of Huntingdon who joined Whitefield and the Methodists bought it in 1779, but due to conflicts with St. James's seceded under the *Toleration Act*. She resided next door and was buried at Bunhill Fields in 1791, her movement joining the Independents. There was a burying ground adjacent and nearby a riot with the Spenceans and Wedderburn.

St. Philip's, Granville Square was built to the north by Edward B. Lamb in 1830-33 but was repaired due to the railway in 1860. The Church of the Holy Redeemer was built as its mission in Romanesque style with campanile on the Spa Fields Chapel-site by Sedding in 1888. It was extended and took over St. Philip's when it was demolished in 1936, and has a park adjacent. Granville Square featured in Riceyman Steps by Arnold Bennett, and Lubetkin designed the modernist Finsbury Health Centre nearby in 1938.

---

[7] On the square are plaques: No. 30 Dr. Jabez Bunting (1779-1858) Wesleyan Methodist 1833-58; No. 60 Fenner Lord Brockway (b.1888) peace activist 1908-10 - his statue in Red Lion Square.

Holborn

St. Andrew's Holborn, a Wren church located in the City, is discussed in Volume I but its history is inextricably linked with the area. Generally it was of exalted stature and eight of its ministers were appointed bishops, while the most notorious Rev. Henry Sacheverell preached against the neglect of the Whigs from St. Saviour's, Southwark.

His printed sermons were burnt at the Royal Exchange in 1710 and he was suspended for three years leading to unrest and a new Tory Ministry. Once this period had expired the Tories installed him in the valuable rectory of St. Andrew's and he died at The Grove, Highgate in 1724 - but his presence was not universally accepted (see later).

Another significant parishioner was Thomas Coram (1668-1751) who established the Foundling Hospital in nearby Hatton Garden on 20 November 1739. It rapidly outgrew the premises and a new building was begun just to the north at Lamb's Conduit Fields in 1742. The project became a *cause célèbre* with notables such as Burney, Handel, Hogarth and Stanley involved, plus an Italianate-style music school attached.

The layout of the hospital, with three buildings around a courtyard and entrance with loggias, was reminiscent of the Hospital of the Innocents on the Piazza St. Annunziata in Florence - designed by Brunelleschi in 1419-27 (with adjacent facades in 1520 and 1601). However, its central fountain was absent in London. Thomas Coram was buried in the chapel with memorial bust by Roubiliac, but after the hospital left in 1926 it was moved to St. Andrew's and a museum was established on the site at Coram's Fields. In addition, a number of prominent churches were situated nearby:

Lincoln's Inn Chapel

In Plantagenet times law was generally taught by the clergy, but Henry III banned legal practices in the City in 1234 and a papal bull prevented them teaching common law. As a result the Earl of Lincoln d.1310 encouraged lawyers to Furnival's and Thavie's Inns at Holborn. Lincoln's Inn became one of the four *Inns of Court* soon afterwards and has documents dating back to 1422 whereas several buildings are 17th century.

The chapel was in poor repair and Inigo Jones put forward plans but took no further part, while the benchers erected an edifice on pillars with open crypt below in 1620-23. Of its preachers John Donne gave the first sermons and John Tillotson came there.

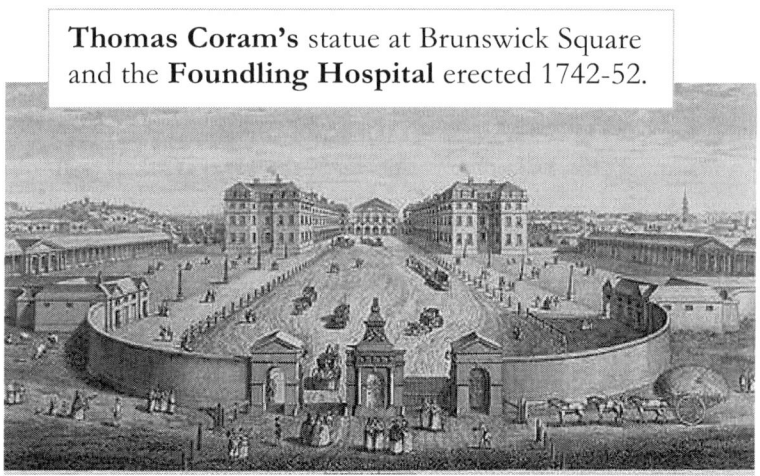

Thomas Coram's statue at Brunswick Square and the **Foundling Hospital** erected 1742-52.

Lincoln's Inn Chapel with its "mediaeval" undercroft below.
The fields attracted preachers, had a theatre on the south side and
appeared in Dickens' *Bleak House* - Sir John Soane lived at No. 12
now a museum **(right)** and William Marsden at No. 65.

Wren made repairs in 1685 and it was enlarged with western bays, vestibule and vestry
in 1883 - as delineated by the box pews. In more recent times the barrel-vaulted ceiling
was replaced by one in Gothic Revival style. The nearby *Manor* of Gray's Inn also had
an ancient chapel but this was rebuilt in the later 19th century and after the war.

M. 4 May 1733 Peter Vidal to Mary Studley - had links to the Eyre family, see Temple
15 March 1736/37 Thomas Augustine Arne [actor] and Cecilia Young [singer]

Holy Trinity, Lincoln's Inn was designed by Francis Bedford in the Gothic style with
spire, pinnacles and buttresses west of Little Queen Street in 1829-31. It was denoted as
New Church in Holborn but came within St. Giles parish, however was demolished when
Kingsway arrived in 1909. Belcher and Joass built a replacement above Kingsway Hall
based on Santa Maria della Pace but this closed in 1986 and is now offices.

Holy Trinity, Gray's Inn Road was built by James Pennethorne in 1837 with pilasters,
pediment and small tower like Christchurch, Albany Street. It lay within St. Pancras but
had a detached parish in Holborn and St. Bartholomew's was built to the south in 1860.
The church closed in 1928 and was replaced by St. Andrew's Gardens after the war.

M. 8 Nov 1853 Richard Doddridge Blackmore bach writer for the press Rochester Sq.,
Camden s. John a clergyman and Lucy Maguire of Guernsey spin d. Edward Paul govt
secretary lic. by J. Stevens wit Charles Foster, Cyrus Maguire [author of *Lorna Doone*]

St. Peter's, Saffron Hill - This was the first new church in the area and was designed by
Charles Barry in a narrow lane amongst tenements in 1830-32. With its octagonal towers
it was similar to Holy Trinity, Islington and had a William Hill organ, but was destroyed
in the war and joined with St. Alban's in 1952. Nearby was St. Peter's an Italian Catholic
basilica by Sir John Miller-Bryson based on San Crisogono in Rome (of 1863).

The City Temple - Thomas Goodwin started an Independent chapel at Lime Street in
1640 which moved to Poultry. However T. Binney laid a new foundation by St. Andrew's
and after £70,000 was spent the *Cathedral of Nonconformity* opened on 19 May 1874.
Joseph Parker was minister until 1902 and also chair of the Congregational Union.

Father Mackonochie and **St. Alban's** with its memorial porch.

St. Alban's, Holborn

Arthur Pember wrote a poignant article "Ritualism in England by an English Ritualist" for *Atlantic Monthly* in February 1869. He described how the movement, which placed the Sacrament at the centre of worship, had spread since the time of the Tractarians and then taken hold in the Anglican Church - while he added descriptively:

"In many parts of England, Ritualism has so thoroughly undermined the ordinary religious currents of society that it has well-nigh produced a convulsion. It has parted friends, it has disunited families; stormy meetings have been held advocating its suppression; bodies of rioters have sacked churches, attacked the houses of priests, and openly insulted and ill treated many inoffensive persons in the streets, simply because they were Ritualists. For many months during the year 1867 the church services were disturbed Sunday after Sunday, and the congregations were obliged to be protected by large bodies of police."

The problem was referred to a *Royal Commission on Ritual* which concluded that most practices were legal and within the Church laws. Many priests introduced ritual the next Sunday but the Low Church took proceedings in the Ecclesiastical Court to halt Father Mackonochie of St. Alban's, "one of the most advanced Ritualists of the day." [8]

Around High Holborn were the Bishop of Ely's palace, Thavie's, Barnard's, Staple's and Furnival's inns plus Gray's Inn itself. But to the north were a warren of alleyways and courts near Baldwin's Gardens and Brooke's Court. These covered an area 500 x 200 yards yet 8,000 people, the dross of humanity, were crammed into this small space - a situation reminiscent of Seven Dials and Five Points/Water Street in New York.

As a result a parish was created and Mackonochie held the first service above a fish bar in Baldwin's Gardens on 11 May 1862, and was made perpetual curate on 3 January next. Baron Leigh a merchant donated a site and William Butterfield designed a Gothic edifice with clergy house and yard in 1863. The Brooke Street courts had cowsheds, destitute hovels, poor lodging-houses, children's brothels, workshops, and a thieves' kitchen thus Dickens used them as a template for Fagin's Den in *Oliver Twist*.

---

[8] Alexander Heriot Mackonochie (1825-87) attended Wadham, Oxford and came under Pusey's influence then ministered at Westbury and Wantage with a daily mass. He went to the Mission Chapel, Wellclose Square under Rev. Bryan King of St. George in the East in 1858.

Indeed, Mackonochie exclaimed, "What are Christian people doing who are content to allow them to live in apartments which in the country would hardly be thought fit for a pig to live in?" He advocated ritual on a daily basis with a spiritual presence then fared forth amongst the slums to seek the people and help alleviate the social-ills. His courage was *contagious* to rich and poor thus many held him in high esteem, but he was often in trouble with the Court of Arches, Parliament, Press and the general public.

From the start of his ministry he added High Mass, vestments, ceremonial, music, and candles and none were surprised when he appeared in a green chasuble in 1865, or, when he introduced Gregorian psalms, canticles and incense in 1866. Over twenty years he was at odds with the authorities being suspended and forced to resign in 1882, then C.H.M. Mileham designed his memorial chapel with windows by C.E. Kempe in 1891.

One of his assistants Father Stanton preached for fifty years, whereas Robert Suckling the second vicar has a brass in the sanctuary. The church was literally destroyed in 1941 and Ninian Comper gave a statue of St. Alban in memory of Fa. Eves vicar at the time, then Adrian Gilbert Scott carried out the restorations completed in 1961.

The saddleback tower and clergy house survived with some moving inscriptions, whilst there is a dominant mural by Hans Feibusch and an organ by John Compton & Co. In fact the font itself stands symbolically on the site of a thieves' kitchen.

St. Etheldreda's (R.C.)

This was the city chapel of the Bishops of Ely from 1250-1570 and is the oldest Catholic building in London, being one of only two from Edward I's reign. Etheldreda was born in 630 A.D. and set free all her bondsmen leading to a shrine at Ely, while the bishops were most influential and there was a large palace with extensive grounds.

The church itself was built by Bishop Longchamp treasurer to the King in 1290 and a palace, orchards, vineyards, gardens and ploughlands were added to a site covering 58 acres from 1316. John of Gaunt, Duke of Lancaster, lived at Ely Place after the Savoy Palace was burnt by Wat Tyler and his rebels, letting it from Thomas Arundel the then Archbishop (the Duke makes an oration there in *Richard II* by Shakespeare).

In fact Henry VIII was a guest in 1531 but the estate passed to Sir Christopher Hatton who built Hatton House in the grounds and part of the undercroft became a tavern. The Spanish Ambassador came there in 1620 and mass was said but it was requisitioned in 1642, whilst Matthew Wren (uncle of the architect) was the Bishop of Ely. Hatton House was demolished in 1689 and Ely Place declined, passing to the Crown in 1772, then to Charles Cole an architect who laid out roads - leaving only the chapel remaining.

The chapel with its Gothic entrance, east window, box pews, pulpit and plaster ceiling provided Anglican worship for residents of his Georgian houses. It passed to the *Society for Education of the Poor* and galleries were added in 1820, but the saffron fields became Dickensian slums and the arrival of Holborn Viaduct meant it faced St. Andrew's.

Cardinal Henry Manning wanted Fa. Lockhart and the Rosminians from Italy to serve there and bought it at auction for £5,400 in 1873, out-bidding the Welsh Episcopalians who departed. It was restored with a 13th century ceiling but the box pews, galleries and crest of Charles I were removed (as a challenge to Rome). The first mass was on 23 June 1878 and there are now arms to Abp. Simon Langham abbot of Westminster.

St John's Chapel, Bedford Row

After Rev. Sacheverell arrived at St. Andrew's in 1713 many parishioners seceded and started a new chapel on fields at Great James Street above Bedford Row - named after Sir W. Harper a mayor born in Bedford. A plain square edifice was built on land owned by Rugby School but it was noble inside and was for fifty years the H.Q. of Evangelism. In fact it was never consecrated and the minister was licensed by the bishop.

When Rev. Richard Cecil arrived in 1780 it was already the largest Episcopal chapel in London, but was much neglected and a large sum was required for its repair. He then joined with John Newton, John Venn, Thomas Scott and Henry Foster to establish the Eclectic Society which met fortnightly in the vestry from 1783. In addition, Rev. Josiah Pratt was his assistant from 1795 and married Elizabeth the sister of Rev. William Jowett two years later, then was instrumental in starting the *Christian Observer*.

There were already a Baptist and a London Missionary Society thus the group with John Jowett and members of the Clapham Sect formed the Church Missionary Society on 12 April 1799. Their aim was to carry out mission work with indigenous peoples and Rev. Scott was the first secretary but was replaced by Rev. Pratt from 1802-23.

Rev. Cecil provided the sermon for John Newton's funeral at St. Mary Woolnoth and lectured at Long Acre, Orange Street, and Christchurch, Spitalfields but died in 1810. His curate Rev. Daniel Wilson (see Shoreditch) was minister in 1812-24 and the C.M.S. sent William Jowett as their first missionary to the Mediterranean (later secretary). At this time there were carriages the length of the street and the galleries were extended and a fine H.C. Lincoln organ was installed in 1821. The organist was Miss Cecil. [9]

The next two incumbents were Rev. Charles Jerram of Chobham in 1824-26 and Rev. Baptist W. Noel in 1827-48. The latter left to be a Baptist at their chapel at John Street, Gray's Inn and was president of the Baptist Union, however St. John's declined and the roof collapsed in 1856 thus it was demolished in 1863. [10]

St. Etheldreda's - in 1772 and today: The chapel of the Bishops of Ely was located in the Saffron Hill Liberty and became Catholic again in 1878. But despite many local changes its façade is little altered.

---

[9] The organ was sold to Thaxted, Essex for £230 in 1858 and it was there that Gustav Holst worked on the Planets Suite in 1914-16.

[10] Baptist Wriothesley Noel (1798-1873) was son of Gerard Noel and Baroness Barham and his brother was the Earl of Gainsborough. His sister Louisa married William H. Hoare banker and their daughter Mary Jane spent her early years with Rev. Noel at Hornsey starting a school for domestic servants. She married Lord A.F. Kinnaird in 1843 and they supported the C.M.S., Lock Hospital, Barnardo's, London City Mission and others (see Mayfair and St. James's).

Bloomsbury

The land on which this affluent area was established belonged to William de Blemond and later devolved to Edward III and the monks of Charterhouse. At the Dissolution it fell to Thomas Wriothesley, 1st Earl of Southampton and Bloomsbury Square was the first development in the 1660s. Under his descendant Lady Russell two parish churches were built and it passed to the Dukes of Bedford while a market arrived in 1730.

Bedford House and Montagu House (British Museum) backed onto fields by Bedford Square, but the land to the north was developed after 1800 notably Russell Square by H. Repton and Gordon/Tavistock Square by T. Cubitt. There is a plaque to Sir Hans Sloane physician and benefactor at 4 Bloomsbury Place (1695-1742), a statue to C.J. Fox Whig associate of the Russells on the Square, and tablet to Isaac Disraeli of No. 6 in 1817-29. Meanwhile, three chapels were constructed on Bloomsbury (Charlotte) Street:

Bedford Chapel - This began as a proprietary chapel in 1771 under Rev. John Trusler author of the first English thesaurus. The façade was redesigned with arches, belfry, arched windows and galleries when New Oxford Street arrived in 1846. Rev. John C.M. Bellew was minister in 1862-68 then a Catholic; and Rev. Stopford Brooke chaplain to Victoria and writer was a Unitarian there from 1880 but it was demolished in 1896.

French Protestant - The congregation of the Savoy was started by Charles II and they moved to Bloomsbury when Ambrose Poynter designed a chapel in 1845. There was a school attached (dating to 1747) and both survived the building of Shaftesbury Avenue by George Vulliamy and Joseph Bazalgette in 1877. However, as most Huguenots went over to the Anglicans it was no longer needed and all was demolished in 1924.

Bloomsbury Chapel - The first Baptists had met at Spitalfields in 1612, but they only developed after Carey founded the B.M.S. in 1792 and the Union was formed in 1832. Sir Samuel M. Peto wanted a new witness in Bloomsbury near the slums of St. Giles, but the Commissioners were reluctant to take a lease as such chapels were often dull without spires - so Peto exclaimed, "A spire, my Lord? We shall have two!"

Their new chapel opened on 5 December 1848 putting the Nonconformist faith in full public view, and Rev. William Brock from Norwich was minister in 1849-72 while by the mid-1860s there were some 900 members. Generally they had an open door policy to all-comers but did not allow Americans who supported slavery at the time of the Great Exhibition, which was backed by Peto with a guarantee of £50,000.

As the slums were cleared the area altered and people left thus it became the Central Baptist Church in 1905, the spires were removed as unsafe in 1951, and the organ and gallery during major renovations in 1962.

Bloomsbury Chapel, built by Peto in 1848, was originally the middle one of three chapels and had two spires.

Isaac Disraeli writer and father of the P.M. lived at 6 Bloomsbury Square.

St. George's, Bloomsbury

This was another of the Commissioners churches and was involved in the general debate regarding sites. A chapel of ease for Holborn was built at Queen Square in 1707 but the adjacent St. Giles in the Fields parish, which reached all the way to Bloomsbury, was still inadequately supplied. A site offered by Lady Russell was surveyed despite the fact it was limited in extent and the church would have to be located north to south.

A sum of £1,000 was then paid for the plot on Hart Street west of Bloomsbury Square and near to Lady Russell's home. Gibbs and Vanbrugh were initially considered for the design, but the job was given to Hawksmoor whose estimate was £10,000, although the project eventually lifted £23,000 from the coffers. Construction took place in 1716-31 and Edmund Gibson the Bishop of London consecrated it on 28 January 1730.

The design included a classical portico reminiscent of the Temple of Jupiter at Baalbek, Lebanon; however its "tower like a temple" which had for a blueprint the Mausoleum at Halicarnassus marked it out as an exceptional piece of architecture. William Hucks M.P. for Abingdon funded a statue of George I in Roman dress at the top and Horace Walpole commented on such theatricals, stating, "It is a masterpiece of absurdity."

Regarding the interior the nave was a perfect cube a piece of symbolism linked to the Masons, however this also solved the problem of a north-south orientation. There were three galleries on rows of Corinthian columns facing an apse to the east, whilst the pews were turned inwards as in a college chapel. This created a large degree of light with altar and pulpit clearly visible - well suited to the liturgy of the *Book of Common Prayer*.

On each side was an arch and entablature with a flame at the centre representing the Holy Spirit; while the ceiling was by Isaac Mansfield and symbols such as crosiers, mitres and pelicans reinforced its Episcopalian aims. The reredos was of Cuban mahogany and exhibited Moravian influences being without commandment, creed, or prayer. In fact the church appeared in Hogarth's propaganda engraving of gin lane in 1751.

However there were soon significant changes and it was re-organised north to south in 1781, with a gallery on the east side and the apse a baptismal area - the latter featuring in a christening in *Sketches by Boz*. Likewise G.E. Street removed the east/west galleries and inserted a chancel and choir stalls to suit Victorian High Church needs.

A memorial service was held for Emily Davison in 1913 and Haile Selassie attended a requiem in 1937, while it was the University Church from 1956 up until the mid-1970s. However it suffered from the ravages of time and closed for a major restoration project in 2006 funded by the estate of Paul Mellon, World Monuments Fund, the Lottery and other smaller donors. This saw the building restored to its east-west alignment with the reredos in the apse, a new north gallery and an organ in the south gallery. Finally the lion and unicorn on the exterior removed in the 19th century were re-created.

Bloomsbury Parishioners - *George Cruikshank* born 1792 was apprenticed to his father also a caricaturist, and after making his name with political satire moved into illustrations with the likes of Dickens. He died in 1878 and has a memorial at St. Paul's.

Anthony Trollope was born at 16 Keppel Street off Russell Square the son of a barrister and was educated at Harrow and Winchester. After financial problems his mother took the children to America and as a writer published *Domestic Manners of the Americans* (1831),

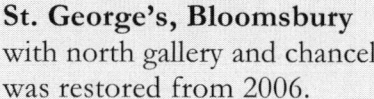

St. George's, Bloomsbury
with north gallery and chancel
was restored from 2006.

but later they moved to Bruges and London. Anthony entered the Post Office and rose to fame with his own work including the *Barchester Chronicles* and *Pallisers* d.1882.

Richard Meux Benson was born at Bolton House, Russell Square his father High Sheriff of Surrey, while his mother had links to the Clapham Sect and he grew up in countryside estates. After attending Christchurch, Oxford he was vicar of Cowley in 1850 and ran a retreat to Cuddesdon in 1858, then Wilberforce let him establish the first Anglican order of monks: St. John the Evangelist or the "Cowley Fathers." Initially he remained a vicar but devoted all his time to the mission from 1886 and died in 1915. [11]

C. 6 November 1792 George son of Isaac and Mary Cruikshanks b. 27 September
18 May 1815 Anthony son of Thomas Anthony and Frances Trollope of Keppel Street barrister at law by N. Forth born 24 April
6 August 1824 Richard Meux son of Thomas Starling and Elizabeth Benson of Russell Square merchant by J.W. Wallington born 6 July

M. 25 August 1812 John Venn rector of Clapham wid & Frances Turton lic J. Sharpe
11 March 1820 Thomas Earnshaw wid and Rachel Walton spin b.o.t.p. lic by David Felix curate witness John Harrison, Jane Colborn - see St. James's, Piccadilly

B. 6 December 1821 Sir James Mansfield of Russell Square, 87 by J. Wynne [12]
8 November 1823 Charles Grant of Russell Square, 77 by Rev. Daniel Wilson [13]
9 July 1827 Edward Parry of Gower Street, St. Giles, 77 [director E.I.C., south wall]
16 Nov 1827 Rev. Thomas Willis L.L.D. rector o.t.p. Rectory House, 72
2 April 1844 Robert Bell of Russell Square, 86 [general E.I.C., west wall]

---

[11] Bolton House (S.E.) was built for 6th Lord Baltimore in 1759 prior to the Square and went to the Duke of Bolton. Sir Charles Flower mayor of St. Botolph's, Aldgate died there in 1834.

[12] James Mansfield the son of an attorney was born at Ringwood in 1734 and attended Eton and Cambridge. He entered the Temple and presided over prominent cases and advocated human rights - being Solicitor General, an M.P., and counsel to John Wilkes in 1768 (south wall).

[13] Charles Grant was a civil servant in India for fifty years, chairman of the E.I.C and friend of Wilberforce. His large memorial under the tower was sculpted by Samuel Manning senior.

St. George the Martyr, Holborn

Holborn was an expanding district during the 18th century and Arthur Tooley designed a chapel of ease above Gloucester Street in 1703-07. Its elegant layout was meant for the residents of Queen Square which was built in fields just above from 1716-25.

The Commissioners for Fifty Churches considered it as an option from the start and on 17 October 1711, stated, "St. George's chapel, Ormond Street fit for a parish church for 2,000 people." For a time an alternative at Red Lion Square was considered, but a letter was sent to Sir Nathaniel Curzon and John Kent Esq. regarding terms of purchase for the building - and in reply they stated "£1,000 to inherit the site."

There were further deliberations in 1712-13 including a minister's house and the selling of the old pews, whereas £600 was to be paid to Dr. Proctor for 3 acres in St. Pancras as a churchyard for the parish - its plan from Hawksmoor. In 1714 they discussed grazing beside the church and a wall and road for the churchyard at a cost of £470.

St. George the Martyr on Queen Square was originally a chapel of ease for Holborn built in 1703-07 - with tablet in Gloucester Street and boys' school by the church.

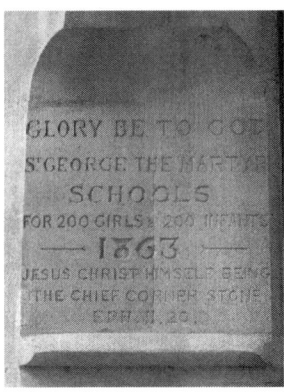

The latter was of particular interest and was located in Lamb's Conduit Fields beyond the housing, and had an access road in the east leading to the Hampstead and Highgate Road (Gray's Inn Road). It was consecrated by the Bishop of London in 1715 but there was some reticence regarding its rural location, and relatives' minds were only put at rest when Rev. Nelson a Commissioner was buried there. The plot had a section on the north side for St. George's, Bloomsbury, separated by a long wall (now by markers).

Meanwhile, the chapel was purchased and duly turned into a parish church by 1723 with 30 vestrymen including two churchwardens, one of them Sir Edward Gould of Queen Square. Twenty years later the Foundling Hospital with its hall, wings and chapel was built just south of the churchyard and accessed across the fields from Red Lyon Street, whilst a pump with arms of two patron saints was erected by the church in 1840.

Of the parishioners, William Rogers son of a barrister was baptized there and attended Eton and Oxford. He was made perpetual curate of St. Thomas Charterhouse by Bishop Blomfield in 1845 and spent 18 years on social problems in a parish of 10,000 starting a network of schools. Rogers was chaplain in ordinary to the Queen, prebend of St. Paul's, a member of the London School Board and at St. Botolph's, Bishopsgate from 1863. In addition he helped to create Alleyn's School in 1882 and died in 1896.

Today, St. George's is a community church beside an old school and some elegant buildings, whilst there are a number of significant hospitals nearby. A statue in the square was thought to be of Queen Anne and for a time the location was known by her name, but it is now attributed to Queen Charlotte the consort of George III.

C. 30 December 1819 William son of William Lorance and Georgiana Louisa Rogers of Guildford Street an Esquire by J.L. Martyn rector

B. 28 January 1714/15 Robert Nelson Esq. of Gloucester Street *in Latin* (south wall)
15 December 1727 Anne Gibson of Bidford Row widow (in front)
21 December 1729 R.H. Richard [2nd] Lord Coningsby from Brunswick Court [14]
9 October 1730 The Rev. John Marshall L.L.D. rector of the parish

---

St. George's Gardens above Coram's Fields has markers to delineate the *parish boundary wall* which separated it from that of Bloomsbury. Among the memorials are those to Rev. Robert Nelson and Anne wife of Thomas Gibson, favourite daughter of Richard Cromwell the 2nd Lord Protector from 1658-59 (who fled to France). Nearby is a mysterious obelisk attributed to Thomas Falconer dated 1729 which has no corresponding entry in the parish records.

An obelisk to **Thomas Falconer** and memorial to **Anne Gibson** granddaughter of Cromwell.

---

[14] He was the grandson of Thomas Coningsby, 1st Lord of Clanbrassil. The latter fought with William III at the Battle of the Boyne and held some senior posts under him and George I.

St. Giles in the Fields

The first church on the site was a chapel for a monastery and leper hospital founded by Matilda wife of Henry I in 1101, on a bend of the road leading to Tyburn and Oxford. A village developed nearby and it was administered by the order of Lazars from 1299, but was briefly with St. Mary de Graces in 1391-1402 then returned to the former, while John Oldcastle based his Lollard rebellion in the adjacent area in 1414.

During this time it was a chapel to Westminster but when the monastery was dissolved it became the parish church of St. Giles in 1547 and the land went to Lord Lisle. It had a round mediaeval tower and dome then a spire in 1617, but was replaced by a Gothic building in 1623-30 paid for by Alice wife of Robert Dudley and consecrated by Bishop Laud. The first victims of the plague were buried and twelve Catholic martyrs in 1678-81 whilst the importance of the church was confirmed by its prominent rectors.

St Giles (once in the fields) is at the centre of London on an ancient routeway and has a stunning neo-Palladian interior.

Memorial at the rear to Lord Baltimore erected 1996.

However, by 1711 there was extreme damp in the old church and the Commissioners agreed to pay £8,000 for its rebuilding. As a result Henry Flitcroft designed a Palladian style church with barrel vault, galleries and vestry house in 1730-34 (the model is on the north side), and the building appeared in a Hogarth satire published in 1738. [15]

St. Giles was near Seven Dials and the Rookery a notorious slum described by Dickens, but the more fashionable Bloomsbury was also in the parish hence it had some eminent connections (see below). Alterations were made by Sir A. Blomfield and W. Butterfield during 1875 and 1896, and there was a successful restoration in 1952-53.

---

[15] Henry Flitcroft (1697-1769) started his career under Lord Burlington and became a leading neo-Palladian architect working on Stowe, Wimpole Hall, Stourhead and Woburn Abbey.

St. Giles - the Wesley pulpit from West St. Chapel and one donated by Rev. Sharp the minister.

Today, the interior has a pulpit and lectern given by John Sharp rector in 1676; whilst there is part of a *three-decker* pulpit in the north aisle used by John and Charles Wesley at West Street Chapel. Above the altar are *Ten Commandments*, a pelican, and on either side paintings of Moses and Aaron. On the reverse is an inscription, stating they are by Francisco Vieira the younger who was court painter to the King of Portugal. To the rear is an impressive Schmidt organ dated 1699/1734 (but restored at a latter date).

After the building of New Oxford Street the church was more isolated away from the main road and is now delineated by Centre Point and Central St. Giles (by Renzo Piano). It is known as the Poets Church due to links with Milton's daughter, George Chapman translator of *Homer* d.1634 and Andrew Marvell poet d.1678. There are memorials to the latter two and also to other notaries Flaxman, Hansard and Earnshaw inside.

Selected Rectors (from the first appointment in 1547)

1547 Sir William Rowlandson
1616 Roger Manwayring chaplain James I, Dean of Worcester, Bishop of St. David's
1635 Brian Walton the Bishop of Chester
1636 William Heywood (later restored) chaplain to A'bishop Laud and Charles I
1675 John Sharp chaplain to Charles II, Dean of Canterbury, Archbishop of York
1691 John Scott the Canon of Windsor
1695 William Hayley Dean of Chichester, chaplain to William III
1715 William Baker Bishop of Bangor and of Norwich
1732 Henry Gally chaplain to George II
1788 John Buckner Bishop of Chichester
1824 Christopher Benson a Master of the Temple
1851 Robert Bickersteth the Bishop of Ripon
1857 Antony W. Thorold Bishop of Rochester and Winchester

Notable Residents - Regarding marriages, Caius G. Cibber was a sculptor and his son Colley (b.1671) was an actor, playwright and poet laureate; whilst Everard Fawkener was Ambassador to the Ottoman Empire and entertained Voltaire in Wandsworth, his wife of 'natural birth' being a relative of the Duke of Marlborough.

The burials initially took place at St. Giles (registers start 1636) and then at St. Pancras old church from the mid-18th century. Of these Edward Rooker an engraver did works depicting the Foundling Hospital, St. Paul's, the ruins of Spalatro and *London Views* with Paul Sandby but was also an actor and he died at Great Russell Street. His son Michael 'Angelo' Rooker a watercolour painter trained under Sandby (who gave him the name) however fell into debt and died at 23 Dean Street, Soho.

Others of note were Balmain a surgeon under J. White on the first voyage to N.S.W. in 1788 returned in 1802, Flaxman a premier sculptor who spent time in Rome, Hansard who printed the House of Commons journals from 1774, Earnshaw watch chronometer maker and Sir John Soane architect and curator (with memorial at St. Pancras).

St. Giles in the Fields parish registers

C. 7 November 1647 (or 8) Mary daughter of John Milton Esq. and Mary uxor

M. 24 November 1670 Caius Gabriel Cibber widr and Jane Colley spin by licence
19 February 1746/47 Sir Everard Fawkener kt of St. James Westminster and Harriott Churchill of St. George's Hanover Square by Wm. Gibbon

B. 10 March 1653/54 Margaret wife of Winceslaus Hollar [engraver]
7 December 1675 Sisell Ld. Baltemore - Cecilius Calvert, founder of Maryland in 1632
18 August 1678 Andrew Marvill Esq. [poet and Parliamentarian]

St. Pancras (old church)
28 November 1774 Edward Rooker of Bloo [sic]
7 March 1801 bur Michael Rooker of St. Anne's
25 November 1803 Willm. Balmain of St. George's Bloomsbury
15 Dec 1826 John Flaxman Esq., Buckingham St., Marylebone, 71
6 November 1828 Luke Hansard Esq. of Great Turnstile, 77
8 March 1829 Thomas Earnshaw of Chenies Street, 80
30 January 1837 Sir John Soane of Lincoln's Inn Fields, 84

Park Crescent, Portland Place, Marylebone
dates from the 1820s ....

.... but is strictly a Nash façade, the interiors being
rebuilt as offices in the 1960s.

London North West

Marylebone and St. Pancras like Bloomsbury were quite plutocratic having elite addresses for the gentry, although not quite in the class of Belgravia and St. James's. The area north of Oxford Street up to "New Road" was laid out in broad grid-like thoroughfares with names such as Cavendish, Harley and Portland designated in tribute to their benefactors.

This was a locality with glimpses of the past in the winding High Street and village of Marylebone, but looking to the future with the Eyre Estates and imprint of those opulent designers Hardwick, Inwood and Nash.

Within the grandiose stucco crescents and terraces were doors calling to any aspiring Copperfield or Twist - a place for writers, philosophers, artists and musicians to hone their skills. Thus we have those great amanuenses Byron, Dickens, Browning and Sheridan plus Mrs. Beeton cooking up a stew.

British ingenuity and talent abounded with Bach, Gibbs, Nollekens, Pugin and Stubbs, whereas William Godwin analysed the makeup of society and his nemesis Wesley looked more to *the music of spheres*. Then, reaching up into the Elysian Hills beyond one finds Constable painting a noble scene, Keats in romantic rapture and Coleridge at his stately pleasure dome.

St. Pancras (area)

The site was north of Saxon Lundenwic and its church was one of the oldest places of Christian worship in Britain. However, the settlement was abandoned in the mediaeval period due to water-logging of the Fleet and the residents moved to Kentish Town. The area then developed from the 1790s with the expansion of Bloomsbury, and Camden and Somers Towns beside the Regent's Canal and Park Terraces. St. Pancras was something of anathema, just "a church and station" in most people's minds, whereas above Holborn there were 33 ecclesiastical parishes by 1890 - including some earlier chapels:

Kentish Town Chapel - This was erected on land given by Robert Warner in 1449 but was rebuilt several times, the site being just above Prince of Wales Road. It was pulled down in 1784 and the oak panelling and stone used by Richard Morgan for his house. A new chapel with portico/cupola was designed by James Wyatt on Highgate Road, but was replaced by a Gothic edifice with spires in 1845 and became St. John the Baptist in 1863 - with St. John's College opposite. It passed to Christ Apostolic in 1993.

The Percy Chapel - This was built by William Franks on the west of Charlotte Street in 1766, and the first minister was Rev. A.S. Matthew until 1804 - lecturer at St. Martin's. He lived at 27 Rathbone Place and entertained Blake, Stothard, Flaxman &c. the latter decorating his rooms. James Stewart of Boston a former lawyer was minister in 1812-28 supporting the C.M.S., Jewish converts, and prayer, but the chapel was demolished in 1867 and the site covered by 15-17 Rathbone Street next to Percy Street.

Fitzroy Chapel (St. Saviour's) - A site was leased for an Episcopal chapel on the north side of Maple Street where it met with Whitfield Street, near to Fitzroy Square, in 1777 and opened in 1788. It became a separate parish in 1863 but eventually declined and was attached to St. John the Evangelist, Charlotte Street, in 1913. The latter was founded in 1846 and constructed in the Romanesque style but was destroyed in 1945.

Regent Square Chapel (St. Peter's) - William Inwood designed this with a portico and round tower above St. George's Gardens in 1822-25. It became a parish in 1868 but was lost in the war. A Presbyterian church with Gothic towers was built to the west in 1827 with Edward Irving as minister, and after war damage was demolished in 1959.

Somers Town Chapel (St. Mary's) - W. and H. Inwood constructed this with Gothic tower, pinnacles and ogee façade in 1824-27, while Rev. T.J. Judkin was a minister and Dickens worshipped there as a student. Ewan Christian added a chancel in 1878 and the galleries were removed in 1890. It remains on Eversholt Street near Euston (see p. 311).

Tabernacle, Tottenham Court Road - The vicar of St. Martin's opposed Whitefield at Long Acre so he built this with octagonal façade above St. Giles in 1756. It attracted the Prince of Wales, Garrick and Walpole and Wesley preached there when he died, and had memorials to wife Elizabeth (1768), Rev. Toplady (1778) and John Bacon (1799). It was refaced with stucco/pilasters in 1827 then was Congregational after a fire in 1856, and was rebuilt due to poor foundations and opened by Rev. Parker of City Temple in 1898. It was rebuilt again after the war and was the American Church from 1976.

Christchurch, Albany Street

This was designed by Sir James Pennethorne, an employee in John Nash's office, under Bishop Blomfield's *Church Extension Scheme* of 1837, and aimed to serve the working class Cumberland Hay Market beside an offshoot of the Regent's Canal. It was built in the classical style with rectangular nave, yellow brick, and a small steeple, whilst inside were galleries and an inlaid marble floor added by W. Butterfield in 1867.

The first minister William Dodsworth came from Margaret Street chapel near Cavendish Square and advocated the Oxford Movement but resigned to join the Catholics in 1851. His successor (as perpetual curate) was Rev. Henry W. Burrows a graduate of St. John's, Cambridge who published several sermons. These included one to Christina Rossetti a parishioner of Albany Street with her views on Lewis Carroll and a second advocating an end to pew renting. His memorial of 1878 was in the sanctuary, whilst her brother Dante Gabriel provided a stained glass window for the church, *Sermon on the Mount*. [1]

Ebenezer Cobb Morley, "The Father of Football" and president of the F.A. in 1867-74 was married there, and the funeral of Eric Arthur Blair (George Orwell) author of *Animal Farm* and *1984* was in 1950. One of the assistant clergy established St. Mary Magdalene, Munster Square (built by R.C. Carpenter and based on Austin Friars), but the two joined in 1989 and the church became St. George's Greek Orthodox Cathedral (see p. 312).

M. 14 October 1869 Ebenezer Cobb Morley attorney at law of Barnes s. Ebenezer cong min to Frances Bidgood of 304 Camden Road d. of Alexander Masters Bidgood woollen merchant licence by H.W. Burrows witness W.E.A. Bidgood, E.L. Morley

Ebenezer Cobb Morley (1831-1924) was first secretary of the F.A.

Fitzroy Square (south) by Robert Adam

---

[1] Gabriele Rossetti (1783-1854) was a native of Sicily but a change of policy forced him into exile and he lived on Malta in 1821-24 then came to London. He was a professor of Italian at King's College and its school and married Frances Mary Lavinia Polidori daughter of another exile in c.1826 - whose brother was John Polidori (see St. Pancras old church). The couple had two sons who were Pre-Raphaelites and their daughter Christina was a poet.

Christ the King, Gordon Square

In the 19th century, in tandem with the Oxford Movement, there were preachers who witnessed to the *Power* of prayer and prophecy. In particular, Rev. James Haldane Stewart sent out 500,000 pamphlets calling for a revival of the Holy Spirit, and Rev. Edward "Orator" Irving preached to large crowds at Regent Square and outdoors in Scotland. He also led 800 away from the London church when the doors were closed against him.

After Irving's death in December 1834 his followers termed Irvingites formed a sect the Catholic Apostolic Church, with six apostles leading and a number of coadjutors. Like the Mormons and other such groups it was centred in prophecies from the Bible. They then built the Church of Christ the King at Gordon Square designed by Raphael Brandon in 1851-54. It was a Gothic masterpiece, but only had five bays in the nave and the west end was unfinished, while like Westminster Abbey there was no crossing tower.

However the east end, transepts, and rose window, in perpendicular style, are clearly mediaeval in design like the High Gothic of Amiens, Beauvais and Rheims, France but *en miniature*. It also compares to Arundel Catholic Cathedral built by Hansom twenty years later. The sect declined in the later 19th century, and it served the university in 1963-94 then went to Forward in Faith. Nearby is Dr. Williams Library once at Cripplegate.

Local Residents - Bloomsbury and St. Pancras had many prominent residents living in its wide avenues and opulent squares, and Charlotte Street (built in 1765) had at No. 30 Charles Dibdin dramatist and songwriter in 1808, No. 36 John Nash architect in 1824, and No. 76 John Constable R.A. artist from 1822 until his death there in 1837. Constable owned another property at Well Walk in Hampstead, but rented out part of the London house whilst retaining a studio, gallery, and parlour there for his own use.

Meanwhile to the north was one of its crowning glories! Fitzroy Square, named after Charles Fitzroy Duke of Grafton, was designed by Robert Adam in 1794-98 although the north and west sides were completed in the 1820s-30s. It attracted many notable residents including the following who are recorded there with plaques:

E. No. 7 - Sir Charles Eastlake (1793-1865) painter and first director of Nat. Gallery
No. 9 - A.W. Hofmann (1818-92) prof. of chemistry of Geissen who influenced Perkin
W. No. 21 - Robert G. Cecil, Marquess of Salisbury (1830-1903) P.M. after 1885
No. 29 - George Bernard Shaw from 1887-98 and Virginia Woolf during 1907-11
S. Nos. 36-37 (now displays a modern tablet) - "R. Adam 1728-92 architect"
SE. (bust) - Gen. Francisco de Miranda re Latin America independence 1802-10

Just to the east was University College and Charles Darwin lived with his wife Emma Wedgwood nearby at 110 Gower Street (formerly 12 Upper) from 1840-42. J.E. Millais had a studio at No. 7 (formerly 87) by Bedford Square, and it was there that he formed the Pre-Raphaelite brotherhood with Holman Hunt and D. Rossetti in 1848-49.

In addition several architects were drawn to this profitable area and George Dance y. lived at 91 Gower Street in 1790-1825, John Shaw senior and junior lived in that same street, and relatives Philip Hardwick and son resided at 60 Russell Square for ten years. Further, William Inwood died at Upper Seymour Street (later Eversholt Street), Somers Town in 1843, and William Butterfield resided at 42 Bedford Square.

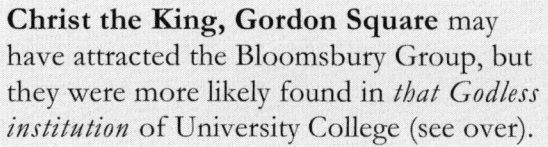

Christ the King, Gordon Square may have attracted the Bloomsbury Group, but they were more likely found in *that Godless institution* of University College (see over).

Sir Leslie Stephen (1832-1904) was connected to an eminent circle, being well-suited as editor of the *Dictionary of National Biography*.

Other local residents were Charles Dickens who lived at 48 Doughty Street when first married, and then at the palatial Tavistock House on the northeast of Tavistock Square in 1851-60 (a plaque marks the site). In addition, railway engineer Edward Ladd Betts lived at No. 29 on that square, while the poet and publisher T.S. Eliot worked for *Faber & Faber* at 23-24 Russell Square in the years 1925-65 (also has a plaque).

Vanessa Bell the painter and Virginia Woolf the writer were daughters of Sir Leslie Stephen and moved to 46 Gordon Square after their father's death in 1904. It was here that the Bloomsbury Group met - an intellectual, literary and philosophical association comprising John Maynard Keynes, E.M. Forster and Lytton Strachey (see inset). [2]

At the start of this period New Road (later Euston and Marylebone Roads) was built to connect Islington with Paddington in 1756, and the district was soon occupied by opulent stucco housing and grand churches. However, as stated, St. Pancras and the adjacent area became dominated by three station termini in the mid-19th century, all of which were built on the (then) outskirts of London viz.

Euston (1837) with railway by William Cubitt and station, grand hall and Doric arch by Philip Hardwick (demolished 1961-62); King's Cross (1851-52) by Lewis Cubitt who was younger brother of William and Thomas Cubitt; and St. Pancras (1866-73) with Midland Hotel façade by architect George Gilbert Scott. In fact when the latter was built St. Luke's, Euston Road was demolished and replaced by Christchurch, Chalton Street.

---

[2] Sir Leslie Stephen (1832-1904) was born at Kensington and his g.father James was a member of the Clapham Sect. He worked on both the *Cornhill Magazine* and *Pall Mall Gazette* and was a pioneer Alpine mountaineer, whilst he married Harriet daughter of W.M. Thackeray (d.1875) and Julia Prinsep Jackson with whom he had children Vanessa Bell and Adeline Virginia Woolf. Stephen was then editor of the *Dictionary of National Biography* in 1885-91.

Henry Thoby and Sarah Prinsep were hosts to the Pre-Raphaelites at their home Little Holland House whereas the latter had sisters, Julia Margaret Cameron the photographer of "Dimbola," Freshwater, Isle of Wight and Maria wife of Dr. Jackson. Their circle included G.F. Watts the painter and sculptor and Rev. Dodgson (Lewis Carroll) author of *Alice in Wonderland*.

Euston Arch (built 1837) - A massive controversy surrounded its demolition in the 1960s, but much of the stone went in the Prescott Channel of the River Lea and it may be rebuilt between the surviving hotel lodge gates (top right).

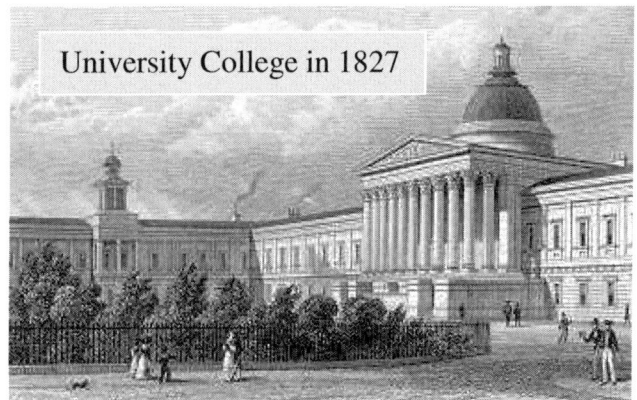

University College in 1827

Academia, Bloomsbury

Just west of Gordon Square was *University College, Gower Street* founded by James Mill and Henry Brougham with radical inspiration from Jeremy Bentham in 1826. Its classical façade was designed by William Wilkins architect of the National Gallery. But due to its secular nature it did not receive a Royal charter for some ten years thus Northampton, Durham and Nottingham challenge its claim to be "the third university." The surrounding area attracted academics and the long façade of Gower Street was home to many prominent people (as noted).

Meanwhile, it was involved in controversy from the start and Rev. George D'Oyly rector of Lambeth and the Duke of Wellington established King's College in the Strand as an answer to "that Godless institution" in 1829. The Duke was a supporter of the Catholic Relief Act while Lord Winchilsea chair at Exeter Hall sent a letter to the secretary of the college, stating, "Under the cloak of some show of Protestant zeal, the Duke has carried on an insidious design for the infringement of our liberties and the introduction of Popery into every Department of State." This led to a duel between the two men at Battersea Fields on 21 March 1829 and the Duke apparently missed while Winchilsea fired into the air and apologised!

A second movement designated as the *Bloomsbury Group* then followed at Gordon Square, a highbrow leafy suburb, just east of the university and close to St. Pancras new-church. It was built as a pair with Tavistock Square by Thomas Cubitt on land leased from the Bedford Estate in the 1820s. After the death of Leslie Stephen, his children including Vanessa and Virginia moved to 46 Gordon Square on the east side and attracted a group of academics who met at Cambridge. J.M. Keynes the economist also lived in the house while Vanessa married Clive Bell and later resided at No. 50 a home to the group, and Virginia moved to Fitzroy Square and married Leonard Woolf. The writer and critic Lytton Strachey was a resident at No. 51 but there were several extra-marital relations and *who lived where* was not always clear (three plaques and an information board are present).

All Saints, Camden

A long ascent took puffing trains up the hill from Euston Station to the Chalk Farm depot with its roundhouse turntable for engines (built to designs of Robert Stephenson in 1847). Just to the east was the growing suburb of Camden Town which was centred on the Regent's Canal, and here were long-boats in attractive, glistening basins.

The settlement was originally in the manor of Kentish Town and named after Charles Pratt, 1st Earl of Camden who also owned Camden Place, Chislehurst. He sold the first plots for housing in the 1790s and the area soon became highly populated. The edifices of Christchurch and St. Pancras to the south were built solely for their local areas, thus a new church was scheduled for Camden under the Church Building Act (1818).

This was erected by the parishioners at a cost of £20,000 from 1822 and consecrated as Camden Town Chapel on 15 July 1824. The design was carried out by William Inwood and his son Henry, one of four in the locality erected by the two architects. It comprised a large rectangle with continuous gallery and apse however the main feature was the west façade with tower in Portland stone. Its Greek design was a result of research by Henry W. Inwood during a sojourn to Greece. In fact, the Ionic columns of the portico were based on fragments he brought back which are now in the British Museum.

The first incumbent was Rev. Alexandre C.L. d'Arblay from 1824-36 who was son of an exiled French officer and Fanny Burney the novelist. A survey then revealed there were large congregations at *three services* in the mid-19th century, and it was a district chapelry from 1863 with a vicar soon after - being unofficially known as St. Stephen's.

An official dedication to All Saints was applied in 1920, but with falling attendances it was leased in 1948 and was thereafter a cathedral of the Greek Orthodox Church. The exterior is little changed, although was later embellished by the National Trust, and it is a listed building with round cupola-style tower encased in mini Ionic columns.

All Saints, Camden was built in the Greek style by the Inwoods and "prophetically" it became Orthodox.

St. Michael's, Camden Rd. whose foundation was laid by Marquess Camden was built in 1880-81. Its nave cost £10,000 with £6,000 coming from St. Michael's, Queenhithe (1877), the chancel added in 1893-94. The main feature was flying buttresses above straight aisles, although a Gothic tower was never built. It took over the parish of All Saints after the war.

Just opposite the church was farmland called Upper Brook Meadow which was sold to St. Martin in the Fields for a churchyard and consecrated by Bishop B. Porteus in 1805. There was a chapel and clergy house whilst almshouses, from Crown Street in the City, were built on the western side in 1818. It was closed in 1855 and Hannah Rothschild, Countess Rosebery heiress of £2 million opened St. Martin's Gardens for the St. Pancras District in 1889. A Celtic cross was erected by public donations (see St. Martin's).

A number of churches followed including Holy Trinity, Clarence Road by T.H. Wyatt in 1849-50, and St. Mark's, Albert Road by Thomas Little from 1851-53 both in Gothic style. Later additions included St. Michael's (see over) and all three are still in use.

St. Katharine's (Danish)

The history of this church was inextricably linked to the foundation of St. Katharine by the Tower and its demise. An Act was passed to build St. Katharine's Dock on 10 June 1825 and the last service in the old church was on 30 October that year, while ships first entered the new dock designed by Telford in the winter of 1828.

At this juncture the Royal Foundation for a *Hospital and College of St. Katharine*, which was established in 1148 and the only monastery to survive the Dissolution, was removed to Regent's Park between the eastern Nash Terraces. A church reminiscent of a college chapel was built of stone and brick in Tudor Gothic style by Ambrose Poynter in 1827, and attached to it were a lodge, school and almshouses. [3]

St. Katharine's - the Classical façade of Gloucester Gate contrasts with the Gothic lines of Poynter's church.

[3] Ambrose Poynter (1796-1886), a pupil of John Nash in 1814-18, went to Italy in 1819-21 and attended Keats' funeral in Rome. He initially had an office at Westminster, but went to Paris in 1830 and married Emma Forster grand-daughter of Thomas Banks the sculptor at the Embassy Chapel in 1832. Two years later he was a founder of R.I.B.A., whilst his other significant works Christchurch, Westminster (1841) and French Prot., Bloomsbury (1845) were demolished.

His son Sir Edward John Poynter (1836-1919) painter/designer was born in Paris and trained there with Whistler. He married Agnes MacDonald daughter of a minister and by that marriage was brother-in-law to Burne-Jones and uncle of Rudyard Kipling and Stanley Baldwin. He was director of the National Gallery from 1894 and president of the R.A. after Millais in 1896.

The building, elegant and functional, was strangely out of place in its location and might have sat better beside the Cam or Isis - but instead was inserted among the ultra classical Gloucester Gate by Nash and Mott to the north, and Cumberland and Chester Terraces with their Wedgwood-ware relief by James Burton and W.M. Nurse to the south. It was an unusual idea of Poynter's to juxtapose such radically different architectural genres, but today the chapel is a pleasant surprise to any sojourner in the Outer Circle.

To the rear of the church was a large cavalry barracks and Christchurch with its school was to the south. Just beyond was a cutting of the Regent's Canal, leading to a basin of that name on Cumberland Hay Market. Inside the park were St. Katharine's Lodge and the Zoological Society Gardens laid out by Decimus Burton in 1827-28. [4]

During the First War *the foundation* was moved back to Bromley Hall, Poplar and after the next it removed to the vicarage of St. James's, Ratcliffe whose church was destroyed. In the meantime Queen Alexandra of Denmark wife of Edward VII granted the chapel site to the Danish Church, and a replica of a rune stone erected at Jelling, Denmark by Harold Bluetooth (first Christian King in 980) is located in the gardens.

St. Pancras (Old)

Tucked away behind the ultra-modern Eurostar terminus, with its refurbished halls and tribute to John Betjeman juxtaposed with Barlow's Derby steel span and Scott's Gothic hotel, slumbers the rather innocuous St. Pancras church.

Despite a lack of documentation it is thought to be one of the first Christian sites in London, dating to A.D. 314 and the time of St. Pancras after which it is named. A more permanent structure was erected in Saxon times and there is a restored 6th century altar, but it was in ruinous condition by the 13th century and was completely rebuilt.

This was a somewhat swampy location due to the seasonal flooding of the River Fleet and soon after many of the inhabitants removed north to Kentish Town. The church was positioned on the east side of the road leading from Bloomsbury up to Highgate - just above the bucolic byways and open pastures of Lamb's Conduit Fields.

Due to its "backwater location" it remained generally obscure being largely abandoned by the 16th century, although Cromwell used it for a barracks and stabling at the time of the Civil War. After the Restoration it was again restored then continued as a country church by a stream among the hedgerows, but lost its parish status and extensive parish after a Greek Revival edifice was built just to the south in 1822.

However, being located close to the expanding districts of Bloomsbury, Camden and Somers Town it had some important connections. Indeed the new church was strictly neo-Classical but the mediaeval structure harboured far more Gothic associations.

William Inwood was born at Caen or Kenwood, Highgate in 1771 his father Daniel a bailiff for Lord Mansfield thus he received architectural training under Lord Colchester. He married at the church in 1793 and at the same time produced *Tables for the Purchasing of Estates* which was to enjoy many reprints. Of his sons Henry William (1794), Charles Frederick (1799), and Edward (1802) were also architects and he collaborated with the former, whereas the other two were baptized at St. Marylebone.

---

[4] Today, the Gloucester Gate Bridge (1878) is just north of the church but covers no water.

Other developments saw John Wood the elder design the Bath Circus in the Palladian style in 1754-68, but St. Pancras soon had its own version. Indeed an inverted form was built at Somers Town on a site once occupied by the barracks of the Life Guards.

Sir Charles Cock, Baron Somers, leased the rural land lying between Euston Road and Hampstead to Mr. Jacob Leroux who laid out a rectangle of streets, the main feature being *The Polygon* an architectural experiment at the centre of Clarendon Square. The former was the first building on the development in 1793, and consisted of 32 houses in an outward facing circle part of a sixteen-sided figure (or polygon).

As was common in such developments (see Clapham Park) Leroux built himself a large property on the north side of Clarendon Square (No. 31), while William Godwin writer and philosopher initially resided at Chalton Street just to the west. [5]

"Gothic Architects" - Godwin, whose father was a Nonconformist minister, trained at Hoxton Academy with the intention of entering the church. He was then influenced by Samuel Newton a disciple of Robert Sandemann who preached against Calvin. After some ministerial posts north of London, he came to the capital to spread social welfare through the pen and wrote *Enquiry Concerning Political Justice* in 1793.

At this time the French Revolution was in full swing and Somers Town looked destined to be a prosperous suburb. However its houses were sold below cost price and the area soon deteriorated - being inhabited by impoverished exiles from France.

Meanwhile, Mary Wollstonecraft who was baptized at Bishopsgate in 1759 was a young woman of social conscience and initially worked as a schoolmistress and governess. Being of enlightened disposition she came to London and with the help of publisher Joseph Johnson established herself, writing *A Vindication of the Rights of Women* (1792). She had an initial affair with artist Henry Fuseli then met industrialist Gilbert Imlay on a trip to turbulent France, and they had a daughter thus she used the cognomen Mrs. Imlay.

After a period of despair she returned to London and writing in 1795, re-entering the circle of Johnson and meeting William Godwin. The couple seemed a perfect match and were married at St. Pancras in 1797 then lived at 29 The Polygon. A daughter Mary was born on 30 August that year - but the mother died soon after the birth.

However, this was not the end of the story and Godwin produced a true biography of his wife which damaged her reputation until the 20th century. His next door neighbour at the Polygon was Mary Jane Clairmont who already had a daughter, and he married her at Shoreditch in 1801. In later years he confronted Thomas Malthus over his *Essay on the Principle of Population*, stating that an intellectual solution was possible.

The next generation were destined for further greatness and Shelley who learnt to hate tyranny at Eton was sent down from Oxford after his piece, *The Necessity of Atheism*. He eloped with and then re-married Harriet Westbrook, but after becoming an advocate of William Godwin became infatuated with his daughter Mary at their home and bookshop. The two undertook illicit meetings at the churchyard of St. Pancras and in 1814 ran away to France with her step-sister Claire Clairmont.

---

[5] Other residents of Clarendon Square were Edward Scriven (1775-1841) engraver and Samuel de Wilde (1748-1832) a portrait painter of actors, whilst Charles Dickens lodged at 17 The Polygon in the 1820s. The Polygon became slum housing and was demolished in the 1890s and after the war was occupied by modern flats between Phoenix and Polygon Roads.

All of this became part of a notorious tangled web and Lord Byron who had finished a number of dangerous liaisons, including with Lady Caroline Lamb and Claire Clairmont (resulting in a child), headed for the Continent. He took with him his young physician John Polidori and settled at the Villa Diodati by Lake Geneva in 1816, while Shelley came to an adjacent house the next summer with his new wife and sister-in-law.

Being a somewhat temperate rainy climate in the days before global warming, the five turned to writing fantastical stories, and Mary Shelley produced *Frankenstein* and Polidori devised a version of *The Vampyre* although this was initially attributed to Byron. However tragedy was not very far away and Polidori was dismissed by his employer; then returned to London where depression led to his premature death in 1821.

During this period Shelley produced some of his greatest works whilst staying at various Italian cities including *Ozymandias, Odes, Prometheus Unbound* and *The Masque of Anarchy*, the latter a call to freedom in response to "Peterloo." However he died the year after Polidori and was cremated on a beach north of Livorno in the presence of Byron; while his wife Mary died at Chester Square in 1851 and was buried at St. Peter's, Bournemouth.

The Polygon was home to the Godwins, whilst **St. Pancras** stood by the banks of the River Fleet for many centuries.

The Church Today - By the mid-19th century the mediaeval building was derelict and the ancient tower was pulled down, but the nave was extended and rebuilt by Roumieu (trained by B. Wyatt) and Gough in 1847-48. Thus the small mediaeval-style church seen today is basically Victorian with a few traces of Norman stonework.

Dickens, a long term resident of the area, mentioned St. Pancras church in *A Tale of Two Cities* in 1859, whereas Arthur Blomfield &c. were controversially employed to clear the east part of the churchyard for the Midland Railway in 1862-67. At this time writer Thomas Hardy was a trainee architect under Blomfield and received the harrowing task, thus a tree artistically surrounded by relocated gravestones enjoys his eponym.

At the entrance to the churchyard a large memorial sundial was unveiled by Baroness A.G. Burdett-Coutts the philanthropist in 1879. It records famous names there, while its composite of sandstone, limestone, marble and granite would please any geologist.

In fact St. Giles in the Fields churchyard was located immediately to the north from the mid-18th century, thus Flaxman and Soane of St. Giles have memorials there. The two were combined as a garden on 15 July 1891 and there is also a memorial to William and Mary Godwin, although their remains were removed to Bournemouth. [6]

St. Pancras Old Church - parish records

C. 25 June 1794 Henry William s. of William and Mary Inwood born 22 May
18 July 1802 Decimus s. of James and Elizabeth Burton born 30 Sept 1800 [architect]
21 April 1819 Eliza Denne d. Alex and Hannah M. Orme Fitzroy Sq. gent b. 20 Dec

M. 8 July 1793 William Inwood o.t.p. and Mary Townsend o.t.s by banns by
Edward Sawyer minister witness Patrick Henderson and C. Fothergill
29 March 1797 William Godwin o.t.p. bach and Mary Wolstonecraft o.t.s.
spin by licence by J. Michall curate presence of Jan Marcher, W. Monrose
24 December 1801 Joseph Grimaldi wid. and Maryann Cath. Bristow

B. 6 January 1782 John Christian Bach [7]
10 September 1797 Mary Wollstonecroft Godwin, 38
25 November 1813 William Franklin of Marylebone, 82 [8]
29 August 1821 John Polidori [38] Gt. Pulteney Street, 26
14 April 1836 William Godwin of Whitehall, 81

The Hardy Tree at St. Pancras old church and **London Bach** who influenced Mozart.

---

[6] Sir Giles G. Scott, a trustee of the John Soane Museum, utilized the latter's design for his mausoleum at St. Pancras (and Dulwich Gallery) to create the Red Telephone Box in 1924.

[7] J.C. Bach (1735-82) was born in Leipzig the youngest son of Johann Sebastian and established himself in London from 1762. He composed operas, chamber music and symphonies.

[8] William Franklin (1731-1813) was born in Philadelphia the illegitimate son of Benjamin and was a soldier there, but trained for the bar in England and thus became Governor of New Jersey. He was a Loyalist opposing his father and imprisoned in 1776-78, then left New York for England without his money in 1782 and died at 28 Norton St. (Bolsover St.), Marylebone.

St. Pancras (New)

The sole development was the creation of St. James's chapel in Hampstead Road as a parish in 1793. Consequently the original parish had 46,000 residents but only places for 150 people in the church, and a like number at Kentish Town, in 1811.

Rev. James Moore arrived there in May 1814 and it was during his incumbency that this situation was completely altered. The original church was erected on the site of a Roman encampment, but despite such classical associations, it was deemed quite unworthy of the properties built on the Duke of Bedford's estate to the south.

There was considerable local opposition to the projected costs when many were still starving in the parish; however an Act was passed in 1816 to build a new church and a competition to find a blueprint was promptly instigated.

Indeed, this was to be a watershed for one particular family. Henry Inwood, who visited Rome and Greece in 1818, produced an ambitious design which was victorious, fighting off thirty other tenders including competitors like Francis Bedford. A foundation stone for the new church was then laid by H.R.H. Frederick the Duke of York, at the corner of Euston Road just above Tavistock Square, on 1 July 1819.

In general, the exterior proudly exemplified the Greek Revival genre. Inwood, who had studied the Acropolis as both archaeologist and architect, introduced three components which were then executed by Isaac Thomas Seabrook the main contractor:

(1) An Ionic propylon and portico drawing on Gibbs' St. Martin in the Fields, which was seen with better clarity than today since Euston Square then extended to the south.

(2) An octagonal drum tower in two sections based on "the tower of the winds" situated in the Roman agora in Athens, all of this faced with Portland stone.

(3) A reproduction of the caryatids from the temple of the Erectheum on the Acropolis of 406 B.C. built on each side of the church. These were sculpted by John Charles Felix Rossi who also did the terracotta ornaments, but are out of proportion to the originals and provided entrances to the burial vaults below.

St. Pancras New Church (opposite) and detail from the Inwoods' innovative design - the caryatids, ornate font and theatrical chancel with its rotunda apse.

The church was consecrated by William Howley Bishop of London on 7 May 1822, and in addition to its opulent façade had a lavish and expansive interior with galleries on every side. However at a cost of £89,296 it was the most expensive ecclesiastical building constructed since St. Paul's Cathedral. Among its detractors there were many regarding the high costs, whilst in terms of architectural merit opinion remained divided.

James Ferguson decried its arrival stating, "More than any other it hastened a reaction towards the Gothic," although at a latter date Sir John Summerson curator of the Soane Museum evinced that, "It is the Queen of the early 19th century churches." William and Henry Inwood were then employed on three other local churches, although the design for St. Mary's at Somers Town also came in for some serious criticisms. [9]

The next vicar was Rev. Thomas Dale from St. Bride's in 1846-61, while the lack of pews was further corrected as new churches were added: Christchurch and St. Katharine (see above), All Saints Gordon Square (1842), St. John's Charlotte Street (1846) and St. Bartholomew's Gray's Inn Road (1846). Indeed, no longer were parishioners distracted from the vitality of sermons by cramped discomfort and miserable draughts!

William Inwood went forward from such success despite any polemics and employed both William Railton and (briefly) William Butterfield as pupils, whilst his son designed an Ionic temple for Lord Onslow at Clandon in Surrey. However, in later life the father was assisted by *The Soane Fund for Distressed Architects*, and died at his home in Upper Seymour Street (Eversholt Street) in 1843 being buried at the new church.

Other residents of note included Charles Dickens who was at 48 Doughty Street south of Coram's Fields in 1837-39 (now a museum), but then went to Marylebone. He moved to Tavistock House on the square of that name in 1851-60, although separated from his wife at this time. Indeed, several of his children were baptized at the church.

During both world wars the crypt was used as an air-raid shelter but it was damaged in the latter and suffered from dry rot being closed for restoration in 1951-53. However the close proximity of Euston Road meant that pollution had infiltrated the Portland stone and it defied attempts to clean it properly. A new north chapel was added in 1970 and there was further restoration during the 1980s.

Church Memorials - Entering the portico one does not discover a columned temple with golden statue to Athena or Zeus, but instead one sees an octagonal domed narthex and a record of the church's foundation. There is also a tablet to Henry Baker FRIBA who was district surveyor to the parish for 53 years and died in 1878.

Arriving in the nave there are six Ionic columns to the west supporting a large organ, whilst low fluted Corinthian pillars support the side balconies and there is a high pulpit with thin iron rails. A white apse with columns of dark marble and gold scrolls inscribes the raised sanctuary, this being an inverse form of the porch at All Saints, Camden. On each side of this there are two Lady Chapels, and above is a flat roof with bosses, whilst the pristine white interior is generally dark and theatrical in its aspect.

To the rear there are a number of memorials and on the north side is one to William Page (1765-1826) late of Fitzroy Square for many years in the HEIC Civil Service on the

---

[9] St. Mary's was very expensive at £10 per pew, and A.W. Pugin satirised its imperfections contrasting it with Bishop Skirlaw's mediaeval chapel at Skirlaugh, Yorkshire.

Bombay establishment, buried St. James's chapel in Hampstead Road. Nearby is another to Mary Frances wife of William Westoby and also her father Edward Holmes Baldock of Hyde Park Place and Buxted, Kent d.1845 and their families.

In addition there is a perplexing memorial to Rev. Henry Hughes M.A., "The founder and first minister of this church d.1852 aged 46, a faithful pastor, a discreet counsellor, a sympathizing friend. Members of his congregation erected this frail perishable memorial believing his most enduring record is in the book of God's remembrance." However, the tablet was actually moved there from All Saints, Gordon Square by the university "upon the union of that benefice with St. Pancras" in 1909.

On the south side of the church is a memorial to the real founder, "Rev. James Moore L.L.D., for 32 years vicar of this extensive parish died 10 June 1846, 78. His ability as a preacher was attested to by a large and grateful congregation and he used much zeal in building both churches and schools. The church which was erected through his exertions is his best and noblest monument." Adjacent to this is a plaque to Henry Smart (1813-79) Hon. F.R.C.O. who was organist of the church from 1865.

Rev. Henry Hughes (memorial) originally came from All Saints at Gordon Square…. which was joined with St. Pancras in 1909.

Charles Dickens (1812-70) resided at Tavistock Square but was photographed by J. Gurney in New York….

"Do you mean to say child that any human being has gone into a Christian church and got herself named Peggotty?" Betsey Trotwood in *David Copperfield* (1850)

However, the most interesting engraved epithet was erected there by a son, and William Kitchiner M.D. was described as, "The epitome of the Christian spirit deeply conversant with medical science but fortune rendered it unnecessary to pursue such a field, thus he was a musical theorist, composer, improver of the telescope and a writer."

William Kitchiner was baptized at St. Clement Danes in 1778 the son of a prosperous coal merchant and stated he was educated at Eton with a medical degree from Glasgow. Neither of these facts were proven - however he was financially independent and married in 1799, although parted for another liaison. He resided near an observatory in Camden Town and at 43 Warren Street, penning *The Cooks Oracle* in 1817 which inspired Mrs. Beeton, wrote on optics, owned 89 telescopes, composed operettas and sea shanties and was F.R.S. in 1819. He died in February 1827 and was buried at St. Clement's.

At the rear of the church are memorials to Rev. Edward Balm AM RSS ASS d.1822 of Russell Place fellow of Magdalene "science and literature;" Pierre Fournie clerc tonsure (1738-1825) of Charlotte Street, Bloomsbury born Bordeaux a member of the order of Elus Cohen; and Daniel Beale Esq. d.1842 of Fitzroy Square and Edmonton formerly of Canton and Macao, "a most zealous promoter of the building of the church and one of the original trustees." All three are buried in the new church. [10]

Marital Vows - Despite some poverty in the area it was mainly opulent and the church witnessed significant marriages. John Edward Pember a stockbroker from South London married Fanny one of fourteen children of John and Deborah Robson in 1831.

The Robson family resided at Hamilton Place by New Road (near to King's Cross), and the father was also a member of the Stock Exchange. The young couple then moved to Clapham Park and had eight children including Edward, Arthur, Frederick and Ellen (all discussed under Brixton) - with important links to the Darwin family.

Joseph Bonsor was baptized at St. Bride's in October 1807 his father Joseph owning a stationery business at 132 Salisbury Square. This was most pecuniary and he purchased Polesden Lacey from Charles Sheridan in 1818 converting it into a villa with extensive grounds. Major Alexander Orme of the H.E.I.C. lived at 39 Fitzroy Square from 1805-40 (home of Sir Charles Wilkins company librarian), whereas Bonsor junior sold the estate and moved to Belgravia becoming an owner of the Combe & Co. brewery.

C. 9 December 1837 Charles Culliford Boz son of Charles John Huffam and Catherine Thomson Dickens of Doughty Street a gent born 6 January (also Mary 1839)
6 May 1852 Edward Bulwer Lytton son of Charles J.H. and Catherine T. Dickens of Tavistock House esquire born 13 March by James White of Bonchurch [11]

M. 9 August 1831 John Edward Pember esq. wid of St. Mary Lambeth and Fanny Robson a minor o.t.p. by licence consent of father John Robson esq. by E.D. Bannam curate presence of M. Robson, Katherine Robson, John George Barrow
14 June 1836 Joseph Bonsor of St. Bridget esq. bach and Eliza Denne Orme o.t.p. spin a minor by licence consent of father Alexander Orme by Alfred Williams off. minister presence of A. Orme, Mary Jane Denne and W.J. Denne

B. 23 March 1843 William Inwood of Up. Seymour Street, 73 at St. Pancras pr. vault
27 June 1846 Rev. Dr. James Moore vicar of St. Pancras of Upper Gower Street, 78 at St. Pancras church by F.J. Stainforth

---

[10] The Elus Cohen (elite priests) was a Masonic organisation founded by Martines de Pasqually the theosophist in 1764, but despite its rituals was really a religious movement of Gnostic ideals stressing levels of spiritual attainment. Fournie was a leading member but it dispersed in 1781 and he came to England at the Revolution and published a book of his experiences in 1801.

[11] Rev. James White (1803-62) a writer for *Punch* was husband of Rosa Hill owner of the manor of Bonchurch, Isle of Wight who donated the new church there. Dickens was friends with him and visited them at "Woodlynch" then rented nearby "Winterbourne" in 1852, whereas Carlyle, Macaulay, Swinburne and Stacpoole were all residents of Bonchurch.

Marylebone (parishes)

The locality was originally the manor of Tybourne or Tyburn and at the time of the Domesday Book it was held by Barking Abbey, whereas the more familiar cognomen of Marylebone arose from the church of St. Mary at or by the bourne.

A deer park was created in the area of Regent's Park by Henry VIII and the locality was used for dairy produce and market gardens to supply London. However with other local environs such as St. James's and Soho already well developed there was ever-increasing pressure on available land, thus John Holles 1st Duke of Newcastle and his wife Margaret Cavendish purchased the manor for £17,500 in 1710.

Their daughter and heir Lady Henrietta married Edward Harley 2nd Earl of Oxford in 1713, and the couple realised the need for fashionable housing above the Oxford road. Thus they employed John Prince a builder to design a grid plan with Cavendish Square at the centre. This took place at the same time as the Grosvenor Estate was inaugurated to the west and radically altered the Georgian landscape of West London.

Matters moved on further when the heiress Lady Margaret Cavendish Harley married William Bentinck the 2nd Duke of Portland in 1734. At this time there were still fields west of Marylebone Lane and little beyond Cavendish Square other than a basin, but the area was then developed northwards using family names for the streets. Meanwhile fields to the west were owned by Henry William Portman who leased two farms to William Baker - and began his own developments there from 1755.

All Souls, Langham Place

Harley and Portland Streets were major thoroughfares leading away from Oxford Street and Cavendish Square. But in 1746 the area in between was occupied by Mortimer and Margaret Streets, the Grenadiers Mewse [sic] and little else. The region up to Euston Road was then built up, although the extra-wide Portland Place by the Adam Brothers only reached down to Duchess Street. The reason, Foley House sat across its route and Lord Foley did not want his view of the countryside interrupted!

However, Royal designs then interfered with such aims and John Nash extended the "Place" across to his new Regent Street and onwards to Carlton House. At the same time he was the architect of All Souls which was meant to be a feature at the kink in the road created by the existing street topography. The church was completed in December 1823 at a cost of £18,323, two-thirds of which came from the Church Commissioners, and it was consecrated by the Bishop of London on 25 November 1824.

This was an unusual design built in Bath stone with a plain nave barely connected to the entrance-round harking back to the days of the Knights Templar. The lower portico had an inner cylinder surrounded by free-standing Ionic columns and capitals of Coade stone, although cherubs atypically linked the scrolls. Above was a steeple of similar form, the drum having seventeen sides with Corinthian columns and a slender spire above.

Generally, the church was criticised for lack of proportion or ornamentation, and does appear too small in perspective past the bustling crowds of Oxford Circus. But despite this Nash's circular design provided a necessary foil to its awkward location.

Nash also supplied the organ in its mahogany case, whilst the rector was by Crown appointment from No. 10 Downing Street since they owned the land around the church. Regarding this Dr. G. Chandler a supporter of the High Church movement arrived there from Southam as the first minister, and introduced some plans to redevelop the nearby Margaret Chapel as a separate parish church (see later).

In addition, the itinerant Rev. W.J.E. Bennett was a curate there having previously been at the Oxford Chapel and Holy Trinity, Marylebone. He went on to be minister at the Portman Chapel; however his greatest work was at St. Paul's, Knightsbridge where he was an evangelist to the poor of Pimlico. A number of significant parishioners were connected to All Souls and these are discussed in detail below.

The church was severely damaged in December 1940 and the congregation then met at St. Peter's, Vere Street until it was finally repaired ten years later. At this time the main name connected with the church was Rev. John R.W. Stott who came to All Souls as a boy and was curate and minister from 1945-75. He wrote over forty books being a leader of the evangelical movement and was appointed *rector emeritus* at the latter date.

Meanwhile, a new project was instigated during May 1975 after it was discovered the foundations were 13 feet deep! The new Waldegrave Hall was inserted beneath and the nave remodelled for modern worship, whilst it re-opened in November 1976 retaining a musical tradition. There are few memorials but there is a tablet to Maj. William R. Moore who died during the Indian Mutiny, son of Major J.A. Moore director E.I.C.

Just near to the church were three significant buildings. The opulent Langham Hotel on Portland Place was built facing north at £300,000 from 1863-65 and was opened by the Prince of Wales. It attracted many celebrity guests including Mark Twain, Napoleon III and Oscar Wilde, whereas Conan Doyle used it as a location in his mysteries.

During the Depression the owners nearly sold the site to the B.B.C., but instead the new Broadcasting House was built across the road in Art Deco style in 1932. Its curving modernist façade patently designed in sympathy with the adjacent church.

A short distance to the south the Queen's Hall replaced Portland Bazaar in 1893, and its owner Robert Newman asked (Sir) Henry Wood to conduct promenade concerts there from 1895. The mainly classical venue had seating for 3,000 people in a large auditorium, but was destroyed in May 1941 and the "Proms" and bust of Wood were transferred to the Royal Albert Hall. A plaque denotes the site of the Hall, and another at 63 Portland Place records that Frances Hodgson Burnett (1849-1924) lived there during the 1890s. Perhaps with a secret garden concealed just behind!

"John Nash 1752-1835 architect" bust by Cecil Thomas in 1956…. and re-furbished **interior of All Souls** with painting by Richard Westall.

All Souls, Langham Place by John Nash with Auntie peeping out from behind.

Sir Henry J. Wood (1869-1944) learnt his music at St. Sepulchre and was organist at St. Mary Aldermanbury. He entered the Royal Academy of Music, but became famous near to All Souls church.

Local Promenaders - There were four generations of Henry Revell Reynolds the first a doctor at Middlesex and St. Thomas's in 1773-83, and physician in ordinary to George III. In fact the latter job was most tiring and he was questioned in the House of Lord's! His son and grandson were barristers the first Commissioner of Bankrupts & Debtors in 1806-53 living at 5 Upper Wimpole Street, and the second the father of Eleanor (1824) and Henry (1827) a minister. The daughter was married to Rev. Wollaston whose family came from Charterhouse Square and uncles were chemists of renown. [12]

Meanwhile, Gabriele Rossetti professor of Italian at King's College married Frances Mary Lavinia Polidori (sister of John) in c.1826 and then had four children, two of whom were baptized at All Souls. The most famous was Dante Gabriel who with his brother William Michael, an editor, helped start the Pre-Raphaelite movement in 1848. Of their sisters Maria joined All Saints an Anglican order and Christina a poet wrote *Goblin Market* and *In the Bleak Midwinter* from which Gustav Holst created the popular carol.

Regarding the Creswell family they emanated from Funtington and Kingston in Sussex but operated the postal service in Gibraltar, over three generations, in 1822-1910. Of the children William Rooke (1852) was a rear admiral and "Father of the Australian Navy," John Edwards (1864) was a physician at University College and Egypt, and Frederic Hugh Page (1866) was engaged in mining in Venezuela, Asia Minor and the Transvaal.

Their brother Edmund William Creswell was born at Hargraves Parade, Gibraltar on 7 November 1849 and was educated at Bruce Castle School, Tottenham and Brackenbury's army school at Wimbledon then entered the Royal Engineers in 1870. [13]

---

[12] Other residents were J.L. Pearson and Edwin Lutyens both at 13 Mansfield Street (plaque).

[13] Bruce Castle School was established by Rowland Hill and his brothers, educational and postal reformers, at Tottenham in 1827 and implemented the "Hazelwood System" with sport, science, self-government and liberal punishment. John Brackenbury established his military school at Wimbledon in 1852 and Samuel Teulon built a Gothic school-house south of the town at Edge Hill in 1859. This prepared students to enter the Royal Military Academies but closed in 1887 and became Wimbledon College. Both the Carvers and Creswells resided near the school.

Creswell played in the first Cup Final as a forward despite a broken collar bone and was married to Emma Mary Carver at Christchurch, Byculla, Bombay, in 1875 - her family were long term residents of Gibraltar and Alexandria merchants. He was then involved in major irrigation works in the sub-continent and for the Ordnance Survey in England but his wife Emma died at Mussoorie, India, a famous mountain retreat, in 1899.

Retiring as a colonel the next year he went to live at Cobham in Surrey, and did some work for the Land Registry, then he made a new association with the Vulliamy family. The latter were French Huguenots and Benjamin Vulliamy was clockmaker to George III, whilst sons Benjamin (1780) and Justin T. (1787) were also appointed to the Royal family and put forward a design for Big Ben. The latter had sons Justin and Theodore and the first settled at "Hawksview," Cobham, thus Edmund Creswell was remarried and went to live at "Copse Hill," Ewhurst near the home of G.F. Watts. [14]

C. 3 July 1827 Henry Revell s. of Henry Revell and Mary A. Reynolds, 25 Berners Street gentleman born 4 June - also three other children from 1825-33
8 June 1828 Gabriele Charles Dante s. of Gabriele and Frances Mary L. Rossetti of 38 Charlotte Street, teacher b. 12 May [Charles Lyell geologist was his godfather]

M. 30 July 1846 Rev. Charles Buchanan Wollaston o.t.p. and Eleanor Reynolds of Holy Trinity by licence by G. Chandler rector witness H.R. Reynolds jun., A.S.C. Reynolds, H.R. Reynolds, H. Revell Reynolds and B. Reynolds
19 October 1907 Col. Edmund William Creswell late R.E. of 31 Cavendish Square and Isabel Agnes Vulliamy of Hawksview, Cobham (d. of Justin) by W. L. Crane wit. Justin Vulliamy, Edmond A. Creswell, Mary D. Creswell, Theodore Vulliamy

Holy Trinity, Marylebone Road

Cleveland Street de-marked the parish boundary of Marylebone and St. Pancras and the road orientation on each side reveals there were different developers. In fact, at the same time as the Inwoods were working to the east, Sir John Soane was employed to build a new edifice at the edge of Marylebone to supplement the main parish church.

This was funded as a *Waterloo Church* and Soane, who trained under George Dance the younger and Henry Holland (architect of the nobility and Hans Town), designed this as one of his better creations in 1828. The building with its shallow portico of four Ionic columns surmounted by square tower and round cupola above, compared favourably to his other ecclesiastical projects at Bethnal Green and Walworth.

Built shortly after St. Pancras a short distance away on Euston Road, the two came in for comparison. However this was an erroneous exercise since Holy Trinity relied on a delicacy of classical touch, proportionate scale, and three contrasting stones rather than the Acropolean grandeur of the other. It was like saying the Louvre was similar in style to Giza simply because they both had pyramids (or in this case classical churches).

---

[14] Lewis Vulliamy (1791-1871) son of Benjamin was born at 68 Pall Mall and articled to Robert Smirke an architect. His designs included Gordon and Tavistock Squares, Christchurch Woburn Square, St. Michael's Highgate and St. James the Less and St. Peter's, Bethnal Green, using both Classical and Gothic influences. George John son of Benjamin jun. was also an architect.

This was another Crown living and the rectors included Rev. George Saxby Penfold in 1828-46, Rev. Gilbert Elliot in 1846-50 chaplain to the Archbishop and dean of Bristol, Rev. Thomas Garnier in 1850-59 dean of Ripon and Lincoln, and Rev. William Cadman M.A. in 1859-91 who was a canon of Canterbury and prebend of St. Paul's viz.

A record in the *London Gazette* in January 1860 noted "The Queen was pleased to present Rev. Cadman to the district rectory due to the resignation of Thomas Garnier," whilst an external pulpit with tablet records, "For fifty years in the exercise of his ministry here and elsewhere he was sympathetic and zealous in preaching the gospel."

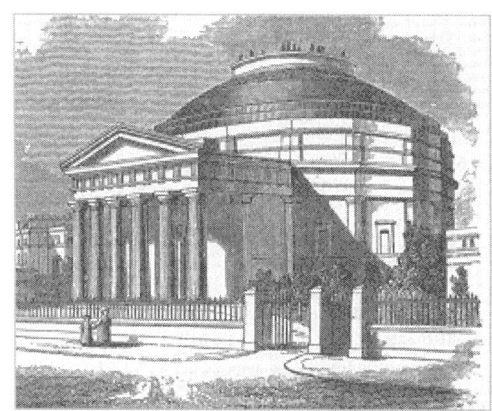

Holy Trinity built by Soane in 1828 and the nearby **Colosseum** which only lasted from 1824-75, "but Rome still stands."

Despite such successes the church attendance declined and the newly-formed *Penguin Books* used part of the building as a bookstore from 1936, whilst the church closed and became the H.Q. of the *Society for Promoting Christian Knowledge* from 1956-2006. Grade II listed it now stands on a traffic island in a prominent location with apse to the rear, opposite the façade of Great Portland Street underground (opened 1863). Meanwhile the future of the building is likely to be a mixed retail and café complex. [15]

The land just north of the church was the domain of Sir Samuel Morton Peto and that Regency sensation - The Diorama. On the east side of Park Square, which was an open field with rustic gates before Nash arrived, architects J. Morgan and A. Pugin sen. erected a strange building with circular heart and two straight wings, in four months, in 1823. It was called The Diorama and was designed to exhibit two dioramic views shown in Paris by the originators Bouton and Daguerre (inventor of the Daguerreotype).

[15] Thomas Bray (1658-1730) formed the S.P.C.K. aimed at establishing parish libraries in 1699 and the *Society for Propagation of the Gospel* in 1701. The latter was linked to his missionary work in Maryland and he was rector of St. Botolph's, Aldgate in 1706-30. The S.P.C.K. produced tracts and pamphlets from the start and now prints eighty Christian or spiritual titles a year, whilst it is the third oldest publishing house after Oxford and Cambridge Universities.

The large pictures 80' x 40' were exhibited in the two rooms and depicted the interior of Canterbury Cathedral and the Valley of Sarnen in the Alps. These utilized the varying natural light from the roof to illuminate the calico transparencies, whilst 200 spectators sat in the central area which turned automatically to give alternating views of the prints. Despite some valuable receipts in Easter 1824, it was not a commercial success, and the machinery and sixteen pictures on cylinders were sold off in 1848.

Peto, who had already built Bloomsbury Chapel that year, purchased the building and converted it into Regent's Park Chapel in 1852. Its first minister was Rev. Dr. William Landels later chairman of the Baptist Union whereas the structure, no longer a church, remains in Peto Place (formerly Albany Mews) just beside Holy Trinity.

A short distance to the north by Regent's Park was the erroneously named Colosseum, which was similar to the Pantheon in Rome but with fluted Doric columns at the portico. Designed by Decimus Burton and built by the firm of (Henry) Peto in 1824 it housed dioramic panoramas illuminated by its dome. One of the most popular, "London" was sketched by the owner Mr. Horner from St. Paul's and painted by Mr. E.T. Parris.

A rising platform exposed the pictures to view and other attractions included grottoes, conservatories, an aviary, Temple of Theseus and a Swiss cottage. The building was put up for auction in 1855 but did not reach the reserve of £20,000 (a tenth of the money invested), and after several schemes it was demolished for housing in 1875.

St. Mary's, Bryanston Square

At the extreme antipodes of Marylebone the Commissioners employed Robert Smirke to build *The District Rectory of St. Mary's* from 1823-24. The church cost nearly £20,000 of which three-quarters was directly funded and the main emphasis was towards the square in the south - a fact confirmed by the bare brick walls on the north side. [16]

Indeed, when considering comparisons, this was almost identical to its mirror image of Holy Trinity, the only differences being the curved Ionic portico and round tower with cupola above. This fact was clearly not surprising given Smirke's mentor. The portico in rotunda style was also reminiscent of All Souls but sat awkwardly on the plain nave, and just beyond was Wyndham Place leading to the residences of the gentry.

However, all was not well in the neighbourhood and after the advent of the Spa Fields Riot and Peterloo the followers of Thomas Spence the radical philanthropist gathered at Cato Street. Arthur Thistlewood who was involved in previous unrest plotted against the Liverpool Government and the conspirators were apprehended there in 1820, whilst it was renamed Horace Street for a time and today has a blue plaque.

The church was built to the east four years later and soon witnessed some significant baptisms and marriages. Rev. Thomas Frognall Dibdin was born in Calcutta in 1776 and was the nephew of Charles Dibdin the musician (see St. Martin in the Fields). He was ordained in 1804 with a curacy at Kensington, but was belatedly given the living of Exning, Sussex and the rectory of St. Mary's by Lord Liverpool in 1823.

---

[16] Robert Smirke (1781-1867) studied under Sir John Soane and worked on many public buildings including the Royal Mint (1809), St. Anne's Wandsworth (1822), British Museum (1823-31) and General Post Office at St. Martin le Grand (1825-29 - but demolished in 1910).

St. Mary's, Bryanston Square and the bibliographer **Rev. Thomas F. Dibdin** who was first rector from 1823-47.

Dibdin wrote several bibliographical works and his *Introduction to Editions of the Classics* brought him to the attention of Earl Spencer, who became his patron - giving access to the Althorp library. After publishing the *Bibliotheca Spenceriana* in 1814-15 he went to the Continent to buy books, wrote about his travels and started the Roxburghe Book Club with the Earl. He held the living of St. Mary's until his death in 1847.

As the area developed two further significant churches were built nearby. St. Luke's, Nutford Place was designed by Ewan Christian with a Gothic hall in 1854 but was lost in the war, and St. Mark's, Old Marylebone Road a red brick edifice with tower was erected by A.W. Blomfield in 1871-72. It then took over the former parish in 1952.

Some Matrimonial Matters - John Mayson was curate of Thursby, Cumberland and married Isabella Trimble there in 1793, whereas a son Benjamin was born in 1801. The latter came to London in his late twenties, and was a Manchester warehouseman with a house at Upper Baker Street and premises at Milk Street in the City.

Meanwhile, Isaac and Mary Jerrom had stables and a taxi service at 1 Wyndham Mews on the Portman Estate and through business links became acquainted with horse racing at Epsom. In addition, Henry Dorling clerk to the racecourse married in 1834 and his first child was baptized "Henry Mayson" with Benjamin as godfather; whilst the latter married the daughter of Isaac Jerrom at St. Mary's the following year.

The most significant event was the birth of a daughter Isabella on 14 March 1836 who initially grew up at her father's premises in Milk Street. However Benjamin died in 1840 and her mother remarried Henry Dorling at Gretna on 24 March 1843, and confirmed this at St. Mary's, Islington on the 27 inst. As a consequence Isabella grew up beside the Epsom grandstand and its kitchens helping to look after several children from the two families. She then married Samuel O. Beeton a publisher whom she knew from her days at Milk Street and became famous with her book on household management.

Other residents had grander designs and Walpole Eyre (1773-1856) the main landowner east of Edgware Road, employed James Burton to develop St. John's Wood in the 1820s. His son-in-law Edward Urch Sealy of Bridgwater, Somerset was a barrister, but inherited a fortune from Robert Studley Vidal of Abbotsham, Devon. The will stated he was to occupy Cornborough House and take the name Vidal, thus when his benefactor died he altered his name by *Royal Licence* on 12 February 1842 - just prior to his marriage.

The couple resided at Cornborough and raised a large family including Robert Walpole Sealy Vidal (1853-1914) who like his father went to Westminster. He excelled at soccer on Vincent Square under the sobriquet the *Prince of Dribblers*, and played for the Wanderers in the 1872 Cup Final when his "middling" led to the winning goal. Vidal also played for England whilst at university, sat on the F.A. committee and won the Cup with Oxford. After attending Cuddesdon College he was ordained in 1877 and was vicar of Abbotsham in 1881, but changed his name back to Sealy by deed poll in May 1892.

The third marriage of note had links to Jamaica and William James Stevenson married Mary Lawrence James at Trelawny parish in 1795. Their son William was a judge on the island and married Caroline O. Biscoe at Barnwood, Gloucester in 1852 then became the Governor of Mauritius in 1857. Lt. Francis Arthur Marindin R.E. his A.D.C. married his daughter Kathleen in 1860, however Sir William Stevenson died at Moka in 1863 and his widow then remarried Rev. Zincke a second cousin from Jamaica.

Regarding other links, Samuel A. Barnett was curate under Rev. Fremantle in 1867-73 and married Henrietta Octavia Rowland then went to St. Jude's, Whitechapel that year. They worked with Arnold Toynbee and Octavia Hill regarding social reform, and Barnett founded and became the warden of Toynbee Hall in Commercial Street from 1884-1906. This implemented the theories of Ruskin and aimed to place those from university where they could help the deprived, being a centre for social improvement.

C. 20 April 1836 Isabella Mary d. of Benjamin and Elizabeth Mayson of 40 Upper Baker Street gentleman [sic] by W.H. Charlton curate born 14 March

M. (Marylebone) 16 February 1818 R.H. Charles John Gardiner the Earl of Blesington o.t.p. wid. and Margueritte Fermor [Farmer] a widow sp. licence at 43 Bryanston Square in Marylebone parish by Luke Heslop D.D. minister of Blesington presence Ellen Hume Purves, John T. Power, J. Purves Hume Campbell, and L.S. Cole [17]

M. 2 May 1835 Benjamin Mayson of St. Marylebone and Elizabeth Jerrom of St. Mary's a minor by licence consent of Isaac Jerrom father by W.H. Charlton curate
19 March 1842 Edward Urch Vidal gent of Cornborough and Emma Harriet Eyre a minor of 22 Bryanston Square by licence by Henry S. Eyre off min witness E.C. Sealy, Alethea S.H. Eyre, F. Eyre, Walpole Eyre, and Septimus Burton [18]
30 May 1865 Foster Barham Zincke clergy of 15 Montagu Place gent and Caroline Octavia Stevenson widow of Milton Brean, Beds. lic by C. Merivale rector of Lawford witness Wm. Lawrence, Mary C. Ryett, and F.A. Marindin
28 January 1873 Samuel Augustus Barnett 28 bach clerk holy orders 34 Up. Montagu St. and Henrietta Octavia Weston Rowland 21 spin 7 Serle Court d. of Alexander by banns by W.H. Fremantle witness Henry E. Rowland, Francis A. Barnett (father)

---

[17] Charles John Gardiner, 1st Earl of Blessington (1782-1829), was an Irish peer and married Margaret Farmer (née Power) who left her first husband and had a lover Capt. Thomas Jenkins. The latter was paid off £10,000 for jewels and clothing prior to the marriage, and they then leased 10 St. James's Square - a home to three P.M.s and Lord Kinnaird. After travelling to Italy in 1822 they met Lord Byron whilst daughter Harriet Gardiner married Count D'Orsay.

[18] Walpole Eyre Esq. died at 22 Bryanston Square on 23 February 1856, aged 82.

St. Marylebone

If St. Pancras was monopolised by the Inwood family in terms of church design, then Marylebone was surely cornered architecturally by the Hardwicks who built a number of prominent religious buildings in the locality.

In addition, St George's Hanover Square on the Grosvenor Estate to the south was often touted as "the church of the rich and famous." But this was something of a fallacy, since in terms of numbers it was Marylebone which reigned supreme, with carriage after carriage of gentry and nobility arriving for baptisms and marriages. This was one of those strange quirks of history as not long before it was just a country village.

The geography of the area included *Oxford road* which started at the City and Holborn then went past St. Giles in the Fields, and *Marybone Lane* which turned north opposite to the site of Bond Street - whilst Edgware Road branched off at Tyburn corner.

In fact, the first church in the locality was St. John's built between Marble Arch and Marylebone Lane in 1200, but this was some distance from the main settlement which sat to the north on the road leading up towards Hampstead. Consequently, a second church renamed St. Mary's was built "by the bourne" opposite the manor house in 1400.

Marylebone Church (1400-1741)

The mediaeval building witnessed the marriages of Sir Francis Bacon in 1606 and Rev. Samuel Wesley in 1688.

Here the interior is depicted by William Hogarth - regarding the marriage scene from *The Rake's Progress*.

As the area was developed Edward Harley, Earl of Oxford donated an irregular piece of ground amongst fields to the southwest for a burying ground in 1730. Whereas the large mediaeval structure fell into decay and a third church was built on the site, on the west side of the High Street, in 1741. This was a smaller building located opposite the ornate Marylebone Gardens and amongst some ribbon housing along the lane.

The Duke of Portland and his wife then continued development past Cavendish Square and the village was swallowed up in a grid of avenues and piazzas, although not all were solely for the gentry. Paddington Street was constructed at the top of the burial ground in the 1760s, and Henry Portman who was developing to the west gave a second burial plot north of the road in 1771. One condition of the first grant was that a work-house should be built nearby and there was also an infirmary in the locality.

The church itself was then subjected to new schemes and became "an architect's work in progress." The population of Marylebone was only 5,000 in 1740 but by the end of the century reached 64,000 and the small edifice proved grossly inadequate. A majestic new structure was proposed as early as 1770 and plans were submitted by Sir William Chambers who was tutor and architect (with Robert Adam) to George III. However, the scheme was eventually abandoned until the next century.

A site was finally purchased north of the old church in 1811 and Thomas Hardwick a pupil of Chambers and local resident was employed to construct *a chapel* there. At the time the main intention was to build *a parish church* at the centre of "Portland Circus," a proposed development to the north of Portland Place. However this also fell through and a crescent was built instead whereas Holy Trinity followed soon after.

Consequently, Hardwick received a revised remit to turn his chapel into "a church" and was asked, "to heighten the architecture of the building accordingly." Despite the fact the construction was under way the plans were altered with two extra columns in the portico, Corinthian pillars in place of the Ionic superstructure, greatly extended wings, and grand tower with cupola on caryatids as oppose to a simple bell turret.

Hardwick's opulent edifice was completed in 1817, and with the arrival of Nash's York Gate entrance to Regent's Park soon afterwards, became assured of a beneficial view. The interior was no less impressive with double galleries, a flat ceiling reminiscent of a stately home and behind the altar a Holy family painting by Benjamin West.

Regarding the church's layout there was only really one flaw, as the site was orientated north-south and the sanctuary faced away from Jerusalem. This then provided the scene in *Shakespearean terms* for a series of society weddings under the guise, "All the world's a stage; all the men and women are merely players." Samuel Wesley (son of Charles) was organist in 1817-34, and Rev. W. Barker with the aid of Thomas Harris remodelled the interior taking down the upper galleries to let in more light during 1884-85.

There was also a new sanctuary with carved choir stalls, mediaeval style apse, mosaic floor and marble pulpit, and the resulting opulence reminds one of those Mediterranean colossuses seen in Valletta and Malta. Rev. H.J. Matthews, rector, produced a history of the church and its people in 1941, while the Browning Chapel was created to the rear after the war and a bronze relief of Wesley was presented by N. Dimbleby.

St. Marylebone was originally intended to be a chapel but it was upgraded by Thomas Hardwick from 1811-17. The interior was then remodelled during 1884-85.

Hardwick was invited to *heighten the architecture* as seen in the new plans. The nave and steeple are viewed from the east.

The burial ground at Paddington Street closed in favour of St. John's Wood in 1814 and was gardens in 1885, while most memorials were removed except a fine monument to the wife of Richard Fitzpatrick (1759). The old church to the south was retained as a parish chapel until 1926 but after war damage was demolished in 1949, and the site beside Beaumont Street was converted to a garden by the *Marylebone Society* two years later. A number of old memorials were retained there including de Crespigny and Oliver, whilst there is an information tablet and obelisk to Charles Wesley.

Gentry and Nobility at Marylebone (parish records)

C. 21 February 1758 Frederick Ponsonby son of the Right Honourable William Lord Viscount Duncannon and Caroline his lady b. 24 January
15 February 1765 George Martin of William and Arabella b. 17th ultimo
12 December 1785 Carolina Ponsonby [daug.] of Frederick Lord Viscount Duncannon and Henrietta Frances b. 12th ultimo
27 May 1787 William Crake son of John and Mary b. 16 April [married there in 1809]
1 March 1788 George Gordon son of John Byron Esq. and Catherine b. 22nd inst
19 July 1792 Philip Hardwick of Thomas and Elizabeth [Esq.] b. 15 June
27 June 1793 Augustus Earl[e] son of James and Caroline b. 1 June [travel artist]
13 May 1803 Horatia Nelson Thompson born 29 October 1801
28 Nov. 1810 Fanny d. of John Robson & Deborah his wife b. 25 Nov - see St. Pancras
4 June 1815 Elizabeth d. of Isaac & Mary Jurrum [sic] servant b. 24 May - see St. Mary's

18 May 1824 Eleanor d. of Henry R. and Mary A. Reynolds b. 30 Mch - see All Souls
7 July 1824 William Hamilton son of William and Mary Ann Crake "trade" b. 22 May
25 August 1840 Catherine Elizabeth Macready d. of Charles and Catherine Dickens Esq. of 1 Devonshire Terrace b. 29 October 1839 by B. Burgess (also five others)

A number of the baptisms are well known and combine with the marriages to produce stories of intrigue and desire. Frederick Ponsonby married Henrietta Frances daughter of Earl Spencer, whilst her sister Georgiana married the Duke of Devonshire and as stated their house in Piccadilly became a centre for Whig politics, gambling and liaisons.

Caroline Ponsonby whose brother was the Governor of Malta was raised by her aunt at Devonshire House, and married William Lamb who later became Lord Melbourne and P.M. (with Lord Althorp as his Chancellor). Lord Byron, who was born at Holles Street, made his first speech about the Luddites in 1812 and then had a four month affair with Lady Caroline Lamb who described him as - "mad, bad, and dangerous to know."

Meanwhile, regarding slightly more perfunctory matters Sir George Martin was the son of Capt. William Martin and Arabella Rowley daughter of the Admiral of the Fleet. He also entered the Royal Navy and served in the American and Napoleonic Wars, receiving the surrender of Valletta after the blockade of Malta in 1800. Martin was also married on two occasions: firstly to Harriet Bentinck sister of a vice admiral and then to Mary Lock whose brother was the minister of St. Margaret's, Lee.

William Crake was a plumber, painter &c. at 18 Old Quebec Street in 1820-35 and his son John was an architect, thus they developed the terraces of Hyde Park Gardens - part of a speculative development (see Paddington). A younger son William Hamilton Crake was born at Notting Hill and became an East India merchant in Madras. Due to such pecuniary success the family resided at 10 Stanhope Street (or Southwick Place), and the son at 34 Gloucester Square - living in the houses they had built.

In terms of design, Thomas Hardwick (1752-1829) was born at Brentford the son of a master mason and travelled in France and Italy to produce his portfolio, then associated with John Soane. He gained a reputation as a church architect after building St. Mary's, Wanstead in 1790 and restored St. Paul's, Covent Garden and St. James's, Piccadilly. At a latter date he worked on St. Bartholomew the Less as well as his projects in Marylebone and died at 55 Berners Street adjacent to Middlesex Hospital.

His son Philip Hardwick was born at 9 Rathbone Place, Marylebone near Soho Square where he was educated, and went to the R.A. Schools, then married Julia daughter of John Shaw another architect. He worked on the Bethlem, Bridewell, St. Bartholomew's, Goldsmiths Hall, St. Katharine's Dock, Euston Arch, and other projects in Marylebone then lived at Cavendish and Russell Squares and died in 1879.

Returning to the naval theme - Admiral Horatio Nelson was born in 1758, the child of Edmund Nelson a minister in Norfolk and Catherine Suckling grand-niece of Sir Robert Walpole. His career including the Battles of the Nile and Trafalgar is well documented; however he married Frances Nesbit a young widow on the Island of Nevis, West Indies in 1787 and they settled at his family home in Burnham Thorpe.

After France had declared war he was posted to Naples and met Sir William Hamilton the ambassador (1764-1800), who was also an antiquarian and archaeologist. Meanwhile Amy Lyons (Emma Hart), a beautiful young actress, had a liaison with Charles Greville nephew of the ambassador. She fell pregnant by a baronet who passed her over, thus Sir William married her and in exchange settled his nephew's gambling debts.

In fact there was an age difference of 35 years and despite a certain fondness, she liaised with Nelson during negotiations in 1793, and conceived a child before they all returned to England in 1801. The child was born at 23 Piccadilly by Clarges Street the Hamiltons residence, but she was only baptized after Sir William died on 6 April 1803 and prior to Nelson joining the *H.M.S. Victory* in the May. Initially she took the name of Vice-Admiral Charles Thompson with Horatio and Emma as godparents, but was later "adopted" by them, eventually marrying a curate near to her father's home in Norfolk.

The last point of interest regarding births is the writer Charles Dickens who lived with his family at 1 Devonshire Terrace, just east of the church, under a lease from 1839-51. A number of children were born there including Kate a painter who married Charles Alston Collins (brother of Wilkie) and Charles Perugini, and was painted by Millais in *The Black Brunswicker* (1860). A son Alfred D'Orsay Tennyson Dickens was baptized in 1845.

R.B. Sheridan created real life drama when he eloped and a modern collage to **Dickens** on Marylebone Road.

M. (Mediaeval) 10 May 1606 Francis Bacon and Alice Barnham [19]
17 November 1688 Samuel Westley [Wesley] and Susannah Angly [Annesley]

M. (Georgian) 13 April 1773 Richard Brinsley Sheridan Esq. of St. Paul Covent Garden and Elizabeth Ann Linley a minor by licence with consent of Thomas Linley her father by Daniel Boote D.A. witness Thomas Linley, James Swale [20]
5 February 1774 Joseph Nollekens Esq. o.t.p. and Mary Welch of the same by licence by S. Russell curate witness Samuel and Anne Welch ["the younger" a sculptor]
6 September 1791 R.H. Sir William Hamilton wid. and Amy Lyons spin b.o.t.p. by licence by Edward Barry M.D. clerk pres "Abercorn," L. Dutens rector of Elsdon, Northumb.
2 February 1802 Augustus Charles Pugin o.t.p. bach and Catherine Welby of St. Mary's Islington spin by lic. by Benj. Lawrence wit. Thos Hind, Selina Welby (see Southwark)
3 April 1804 George Martin Esq. and Harriet Bentinck b.o.t.p. by lic by George Saxby Penfold witness "Portland," J.H. Hardon, W. Fairchild, W. Bentinck and E. Gibbs
3 June 1805 Hon. William Lamb of Lincoln's Inn and the R.H. Lady Caroline Ponsonby o.t.p. a minor consent of parents by special licence at *2 Cavendish Square* house of the Earl of Bessborough by James Preedy wit. "Bessborough," "Spencer"
8 May 1806 R.H. Charles Lord Kinnaird of Lr. Grosvenor Street and R.H. Lady Olivia Letitia Cath. Fitzgerald o.t.p. consent guardian sp. lic at *7 Stratford Place* house of R.H. Lord Kerry by Edward Legge, Dean of Windsor wit. Henry Fitzgerald, "Lecale" [21]
25 June 1806 Rev. George Augustus Lamb clerk of Rye and Julia Louisa Bancroft o.t.p. lic by Wm. Dodson wit. Edw. Bancroft, Eliz. D. Lamb (see St. Stephen's, Hampstead)

M. (Present) 12 September 1846 Robert Browning gent of St. Paul's Deptford s. Robert gent and Elizabeth Barrett Moulton Barrett o.t.p. d. Edward gent lic. by Thomas Woods Goldhawk curate witness James Silvahorn and Elizabeth Wilson

---

[19] The marriage of F. Bacon (1561-1626) was described in a letter from Dudley Carleton to John Chamberlain, which gave the details since the records did not start until 1668 (see Vol. I).

[20] R.B. Sheridan (1751-1816) dramatist attended Harrow School while Thomas Linley a musician lived at the Royal Crescent, Bath and a plaque records - "His daughter Elizabeth eloped with Sheridan on the evening, 18 March 1772." The latter owned Polesden Lacey from 1796.

[21] The Kinnairds came from Perth and were bankers and Whigs with links to the Spencers.

Regarding the old church - there is a tablet to notable people buried and a memorial to Claude Champion de Crespigny a refugee from France after the revocation, received at the Savoy in 1687. His restored epitaph states he died 10 April 1697 but the parish record is unreadable, while his wife is down as Mary Champion buried 23 June 1708.

Others recorded are James Gibbs (1682) of Aberdeen who worked on churches in the Strand and Oxford Chapel, but lost St. Giles to Flitcroft died 11 Henrietta Street; John Michael Rysbrack sculptor of Antwerp who produced major works died at Vere Street; James Ferguson a former Scottish shepherd who invented clocks in the Strand and did a book on the orrery for Stephen Poyntz died Bolt Court, Fleet Street; and artist George Stubbs from Liverpool who painted horses and died at 24 Somerset Street.

The parents of Rev. Charles Wesley (1707-88) hymn writer were married there and he himself married Sarah Gwynne in 1749, then went on evangelising trips until 1765 but settled at Great Chesterfield Street (now Wheatley Street). Hon. Andrew Oliver (1706-74) was a merchant and Lt. Governor of Massachusetts in 1771, and his son Brinsley Sylvester a physician and graduate of Harvard has a memorial to that effect.

B. 9 August 1754 James Gibbs Esq.
11 Jan. 1770 John Michael Ryssbrack
23 November 1776 James Ferguson
5 April 1788 Revd. Charles Wesley
18 July 1806 George Stubbs Esq.

> There is a restored memorial to Rev. Charles Wesley outside, which records his sons Charles J. and Samuel who were both composers and organists.

9 Nov 1809 Most Noble William H.C. Bentinck, [3rd] Duke of Portland
1 May 1828 Brinsley Silvester Oliver of Grafton Street, 73
17 October 1837 Samuel Wesley Esq. of Kings Row, Pentonville, 71

Marylebone (Chapels)

Bentinck Chapel was erected at the junction of Chapel and Lisson Streets in 1772, the minister appointed by trustees but was demolished in the 1830s (now a flyover). It was replaced by St. Paul's chapel and school on Rossmore Road east of Lisson Grove, built by James W. Higgins in 1839, but the district was overcrowded and Octavia Hill began her reforms there. Most old housing was demolished after the war and the church closed in 1976, but was rebuilt and re-opened for community use ten years later.

Brunswick Chapel was on the north of Upper Berkeley Street below Brunswick Mews and was erected by an unidentified builder in 1795. An initial lease went to George Saxby Penfold for 14 years, and the Church Army H.Q. had some connection from 1905 but was generally listed at 55 Bryanston Street (see St. Mary at Hill Vol. 1). The building was still present after the war but the site is now occupied by Rutland Court.

Oxford Chapel or St Peter's, Vere Street was built in 1722 (see the main text).

Portman Chapel on (R) Adam Street was a proprietary chapel for the Portman Estate from 1779, but became St. Paul's, Portman Square in 1899 and was rebuilt in 1970. A chapel of ease for All Souls from 1988 it was a base for Billy Graham's mission the next year, but is now used for meetings/training. A tablet outside records its history.

Hinde Street Methodist with façade like St. Paul's and **Rev. Charles Wesley (1707-88)** the hymn-writer with his memorial behind Marylebone church.

Portland Chapel on Great Portland Street was built in 1766 and as an Episcopal chapel had a Crown income of £350. It was located behind All Souls and was likewise dedicated to St. Paul - thus it should not be confused with the Portman Chapel. Charles Dickens attended the nearby Unitarian chapel at Little Portland Street in 1843 and at that time wrote *A Christmas Carol*. The former despite its dedication remained as a chapel, whilst a red brick office building with pilasters replaced it after the war.

Quebec Chapel was built on Bryanston and Quebec Streets in 1787 the name from the battle in Canada, and like Portman Chapel was a gift of the proprietor. It was made into a parish and dedicated as the Church of the Annunciation in 1894, then rebuilt by Walter Tapper in High Church style under Rev. Bernard Day Douglas Shaw (unrelated) in 1914. It was one of his finest works, with organ by Sir Frederick Rothwell, and the minister has a brass memorial dated 1922 in the chancel (see picture p. 312).

Nearby Seymour Street had famous residents at: **30** Edward Lear (1812-88) a writer of Limericks born at Bowmans Place, Holloway and baptised at the Haberdashers Chapel; **32** Major Herbert Hugh Muirhead (1850-1904) R.E. a son of James Patrick Muirhead (biographer of relative James Watt) and Katherine E. Boulton - he played in the first Cup Final and was buried at Great Haseley, Oxford with Greek memorial.

Welbeck Chapel was located on Westmorland Street just above Welbeck Street and was constructed in 1774. Like the Portland Chapel it had an income of £350 and received a dedication to St. James - under which name it was denoted on Stanford's map. However it was replaced by the National Heart Hospital in 1874.

Hinde Street Methodist was built above Wigmore Street by James Weir with façade like St. Paul's Cathedral in 1887. It operated as part of the West London Mission founded by Hugh Price Hughes which included the Kingsway Circuit; however after the retirement of Lord Soper in 1978 this was based entirely at the Hinde Street location.

St. Peter's (Oxford Chapel)

This is one of the few surviving chapels - located at the south end of Marylebone Lane where it met with Oxford Street. Edward Harley, 2nd Earl of Oxford, descended from the Noel family and married Henrietta Cavendish Holles at her family property Wimpole Hall on 31 August 1713, and also came into Welbeck Hall by the marriage.

The speculative development of Cavendish Square was laid out in 1717 although work was held up by the South Sea Bubble, and the Earl built a church "to accommodate the inhabitants of his manor" in 1722. The Marybone or Oxford Chapel designed by James Gibbs was considered to be one of the most beautiful of its kind in London, while it was located in a street named after the de Vere family who once held the Earldom.

Regarding significant events Lady Margaret, their only child, grew up at Wimpole and was married at the church in 1734. However the union was recorded in the Marylebone register since no records were kept until 1736, the location detailed thus, "The register for use of the Oxford Chapel by order of R.H. Edward Harley, Earl of Oxford is at his lordships house in Dover Street - dated 5 October 1737" (until 1754).

William Boyce had his first position as organist in 1734-36 and was master of the King's music (see Garlickhythe), while the interior was in Hogarth's set of moral satires *Industry and Idleness*. The Earl died in 1741 and the title passed to his cousin Edward, while Rev. John Harley son of the latter was rector of Marylebone and a friend of Charles Wesley. In fact, the 2nd Duke of Portland was a governor of the Foundling Hospital and his son William 3rd Duke was a figurehead P.M. in 1783 (Whigs) and 1807-09 (Tories).

In addition John Michael Rysbrack (1693-1770) sculptor lived in Vere Street for many years and collaborated with James Gibbs, his most famous work to Sir Isaac Newton in Westminster Abbey. Also, the Rev. F.D. Maurice was the minister from 1860-69 and had much controversy with the Dean of St. Paul's over his socialist philosophies.

At this time the chapel was dedicated to St. Peter's but pollution made the exterior look like "a nondescript edifice of George I." As a Government church the incumbent was paid £450 while the pew rents were appropriated, there being no district attached.

The church was re-licensed for marriages again in 1930 and became a chapel of ease for All Souls in 1952; however it closed down in 1983 and from that time was used by the *London Institute for Contemporary Christianity*. This was founded by Rev. John Stott and aimed to equip Christian missions around the world.

M. 11 July 1734 The most noble William [2nd] Duke of Portland and ye Right Hon. the Lady Margaret Cavendish Harley by licence

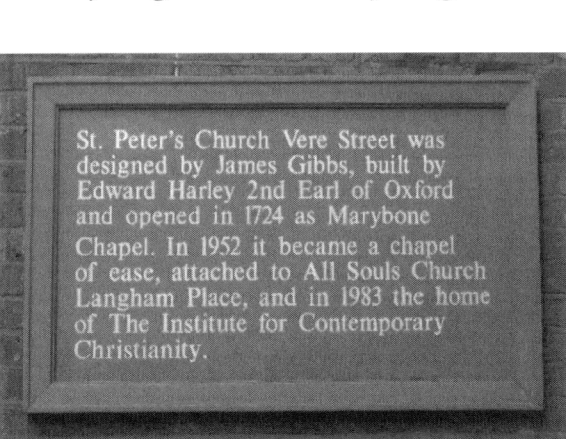

St. Peter's Church Vere Street was designed by James Gibbs, built by Edward Harley 2nd Earl of Oxford and opened in 1724 as Marybone Chapel. In 1952 it became a chapel of ease, attached to All Souls Church Langham Place, and in 1983 the home of The Institute for Contemporary Christianity.

St. James's, Spanish Place was linked to the Spanish Embassy and built in 1890.

West London Synagogue designed by N.S. Joseph in 1870, as part of the British Jewish reform movement.

St. James's (R.C.), Spanish Place

This had a long history and the Spanish Embassy was originally at Ely Place, however after the Restoration was re-established at Ormond Street and then at Hertford House, Manchester Square (which now houses the Wallace Collection).

A site was leased on the south side of George Street next to Spanish Place, and a chapel was built there by the architect Joseph Bonomi in 1791. Dr. Thomas Hussey, embassy chaplain, was responsible for its growth and was also Bishop of Waterford and Lismore. The connection to Spain ended in 1827 and it transferred to the London Vicariate, whilst it was famous enough to appear in *Vanity Fair* by W.M. Thackeray. A freehold site was purchased opposite and Edward Goldie, great grandson of Bonomi, built a new edifice with impressive flying buttresses - which was completed in 1890 and remains today.

West London Synagogue

A group of prominent families which were led by Mocatta, Montefiore, Henriques and Goldsmid made a resolution on 15 April 1840, and thus broke away from Bevis Marks to create the first Reform Synagogue in Britain. A new congregation was established the next year and initially they took premises at Burton Street, St. Pancras, but then moved to Margaret Street just west of Cavendish Square from 1849-70.

Their main aims were a shorter service, new prayer book (denounced as heretical) and a sermon in English rather than Hebrew. The first minister was Rev. David Woolf Marks who was also the professor of Hebrew at University College and combined the Ashkenazi and Sephardic traditions - as a single religion of modern British Jews.

Sir Moses Montefiore the banker and philanthropist, a relative of the Rothschilds, was a great critic of the new synagogue which moved to its current site at 34 Upper Berkeley Street on 22 September 1870. The design was by architect Nathan S. Joseph who worked on the striking New West End Synagogue at Bayswater some seven years later, whilst the movement gathered pace and the building was extended in 1934/64. [22]

---

[22] David Mocatta (1806-82), architect, studied under Sir John Soane and travelled in Italy. His works included a synagogue for Sir Moses Montefiore (his cousin) at Ramsgate, and Brighton Railway Station with other stations on that line.

St. John's Wood

The Knights of St. John of Jerusalem (Hospitallers) owned woods above Marylebone in the mediaeval period, the parish reaching to Hampstead. The area had clear development potential, which was brought forward with New Road in 1757 and Regent's Canal and the Park by John Nash in 1816. Regency houses in London were generally terraces with little or no garden thus the Eyre family, who owned St. John's Wood, planned *A Garden Suburb* with detached villas in 1796. This was put on hold during the Napoleonic Wars, but was revived in 1813 and they employed the builder James Burton (1761-1837).

He enjoyed some distinctive credentials and his father John Haliburton of Roxburgh was married to Janet Scott, thus he was a first cousin of Sir Walter Scott. A family dispute meant he changed his name to Burton and had sons James (1788), Septimus (1794) and Decimus (1800); whilst Nash employed him to work on Regent Street and the Terraces and he also worked with Decimus who was architect of London Zoo. [23]

In particular he designed many villas for St. John's Wood and the first phase was Park Road, North and South Bank, and Grove Road in 1820. The area, centred on Wellington Road, was known as the Eyre Estate and the Eyre Arms (now Eyre Court) at the north end of Grove End Road had assembly rooms, balloon ascents and jousting. In fact the last development was at Alma Square as late as the 1860s.

St. John's Wood Chapel

Despite a number of chapels there was limited provision in Marylebone in the early 19th century, and the vestry purchased six acres from Walpole Eyre and the Duke of Portland for a burial ground in 1807. The plot known as Great Garden and Willow Tree Fields was at the north end of Park Road just above the bridge of the Regent's Canal.

Thomas Lord the pioneer cricketer established his first cricket ground and the M.C.C. at Dorset Square east of Marylebone Station in 1787 (a plaque marks the site) - this being done at the request of members of the White Conduit Club of Islington. When the lease expired a second location was obtained on two fields at North Bank from 1809-13, and another plaque marks the position of "The 2nd Lord's."

However, the Regent's Canal Co. required the land which was close to the labourers housing in Lisson Grove, thus the turf and other fittings went to St. John's Wood Road in 1814. At this time Thomas Hardwick designed a chapel quite different to his church at Marylebone and it was consecrated by Bishop William Howley on 24 May. After the opening ceremony the guests were entertained on fields at Lord's just opposite.

This was an elegant church in the Regency style with a portico of four Ionic columns, a small cupola, and austere nave. The interior of white and gold with galleries and quaint box pews (which still survive) all produced the aura of a New England chapel.

---

[23] James Hali-Burton (1788-1862) lived in Italy and Egypt from 1815-35 until his father stopped his allowance, and worked on the *Excerpta Hieroglyphica* with Joseph Bonomi (an Egyptologist and curator of the Soane Museum). His brother Septimus designed country villas and Decimus worked on The Holme, Clarence and Cornwall Terraces, and the Palm House at Kew.

Other changes saw St. John's Wood Farm converted to a barracks with gymnasium and parade ground in the Napoleonic era (by All Saints and the Eyre Arms), and a cemetery opened at Finchley in 1855. The chancel was extended with a window to St. John (lost in the war), and when the burial ground closed the parish went to Christchurch in 1889. It was restored in 1938 and the galleries closed-in for meeting rooms, while it was a parish again replacing the damaged St. Stephen's, Avenue Road (by Daukes) in 1952.

The organ was transferred from the west gallery to the side in the early 20th century and was rebuilt in 1957, a statue of St. John was erected by Hans Feibusch regarding the new hall in 1977, and an attractive limestone pavement was laid in the chancel with the altar moved to the centre in 1991. The result was an impressive and peaceful sanctuary.

"Local Players" - There is some confusion with baptisms in the registers as the chapel came under Marylebone parish, whilst burials were generally at St. John's from 1814-55 and a number of prominent people had memorials both inside and out.

Regarding the residents Hugh Mitchell (1787-1851) was a colonel in the Royal Marines and Madras N.I. then married Jessie (1813-87) daughter of Sir John McCaskill. The latter took part in the 1st Sikh War or Sutlej campaign and was killed at the battle of "Midnight Mudki" near to Ferozepore (see Kensington). They had a child at Cuttack but returned to 29 Cavendish Road West, an impressive villa just behind Lord's Cricket Ground. An entry for their daughter Mary under St. Marylebone was probably at the chapel. [24]

Other locals were Edwin Landseer painter of *Monarch of the Glen* and *Scene in Braemar* (for E.L. Betts) at 1 St. John's Wood Road from 1827, Madame Tussaud at Wellington Road in 1838-39, and George Eliot at The Priory, 21 North Bank from 1863-76.

Inside the chapel are several fine memorials. On each side of the chancel are those to the daughters of Robert and Agnes Gillespie (1832-33) and John Capel (1846), the first being attributed to Chantry of woodcock fame although both are similar. To the rear are ones to John Josiah Holford (1836) and John Farquhar (1826) of Fonthill Abbey and this parish (see over). To the west is that of Richard James Lawrence (d.1830, 85) and his son James of Fairfield, Jamaica who were relatives of the Stevensons - see St. Mary's.

---

[24] Their son Hugh Mitchell (born 1849) went to Harrow and entered the Royal Engineers on the same day as Edmund William Creswell. They played together in the first Cup Final and during a posting to Gibraltar he met Mary. C.E. Creswell (sister) whom he married at White Notley, Essex in 1878. After leaving the army he was a solicitor at 6 Douro Place (see later) and Gibraltar, but died on the goldfields at Brakpan, Transvaal in 1937.

The churchyard itself was closed in 1886 and now has a garden with pretty borders and forest paths, whilst an information plaque records its memorials: Johanna Southcott local prophet who had visions and printed her beliefs leading to a sect d. 38 Manchester Street; Samuel Godley born 1781 a private in the lifeguards who carried out heroic acts and a charge at Waterloo (memorial by comrades); and John Sell Cotman painter, etcher and teacher at King's College whose pupils included Dante and William Rossetti. [25]

C. 22 April 1846 Mary d. of Lt. Col. Hugh & Jessie Mitchell of 29 Cavendish Rd. W.

B. 2 January 1815 Johanna Southcott of St. Marylebone, 65
22 January 1832 Samuel Godley of Boston Place, 53 Peter Moody
6 August 1836 John Josiah Holford Esq. of York Place, 72 W.H. Charlton
21 Sept 1840 Chevalier James Lawrence of Quadrant, St. James, 67 Wm. Dent MA
30 July 1842 John Sell Cotman of Hunter Street, 60 Thom. Warton MA

St. John's (interior) has a memorial to **John Farquhar** the owner of Fonthill Abbey at the rear, "a record to man's folly."

Central London Mosque - There were several attempts to establish a mosque, the first by Rowland Allanson-Wynn, 5th Baron Headley, who converted to Islam in 1913. He wrote various books and being much travelled was a rival to T.E. Lawrence. Negotiations were made by Lord Dolobran secretary of state to the colonies in 1939, and Churchill donated a site west of Regent's Park for those who fought in the Empire in 1940.

A sum of £100,000 was allocated and the offer was accepted in 1944 thus a cultural centre opened three years later. Various designs were submitted and Frederick Gibberd who was influenced by Le Corbusier completed a large new mosque in 1969-77, with much of the £6.5 million coming from overseas principalities. This included a library, reading room and offices, the building in stark contrast with St. John's nearby.

---

[25] William Thomas Beckford novelist, art collector, and M.P. employed James Wyatt to build Fonthill Abbey, Wiltshire, in 1795-1807, on land inherited from his father William a plantation owner. He was forced to sell to John Farquhar an ammunition dealer for £330,000 in 1822 and the main tower collapsed for the final time in 1825. The building reminiscent of Ely is mostly gone, while Farquhar left no will and his fortune went to his nieces and nephews.

Christchurch, Cosway Street by T. Hardwick (left).

St. Mark's, Hamilton Terrace went towards the High Church with Rev. Bellew, until it was underpinned.

Christchurch, Cosway Street - Thomas Hardwick used another classical design for his third local church on Gt. James (Bell) and Stafford Streets, finished by his son Philip in 1822-25. It had a portico of Ionic columns with open tower and cupola, and served the working class Lisson Grove near Portland Market. Early rectors were George S. Penfold in 1825 and Robert Walpole in 1828-56; but it joined St. Paul's, Rossmore Road in 1971 and became a recording studio then offices for the Braemar Shipping Agency. [26]

All Saints, Finchley Road

This was built by Thomas Little in Gothic style with spire in 1845, and Henry William Maddock of St. John's, Bethnal Green and Hereford was vicar from 1850-70. He married Elizabeth Grey daughter of Edward Bishop of Hereford and niece of Charles Grey P.M. (sons of 1st Earl), and was followed by Henry S. Eyre son of Walpole from St. Mary's, Newington in 1870-87. The church itself closed and united with St. John's in 1974.

Of the parishioners Thomas Henry Huxley (1825-95) was born at Ealing then went to Charing Cross Hospital and Haslar, Gosport. As with Darwin and the *Beagle* he voyaged on the *Rattlesnake* in 1846-50 visiting the Barrier Reef and met his wife Nettie in Sydney. Through research he knew Kingsley, Lubbock, Lyell, Spencer and Wallace and promoted Darwin's theories. He was at the School of Mines and Royal Institution and did coastal studies during his honeymoon then confronted Wilberforce at Oxford in 1860.

Huxley also promoted science, worked for F.D. Maurice, and was the R.S. president in 1883-85. He resided at 14 Waverley, 26 Abbey and 4 Marlborough Places but moved to Eastbourne in 1890 and has a memorial at Marylebone Cemetery. His son Leonard had Darwin and Hooker as godparents and married Julia Arnold daughter of Tom, niece of Matthew - children of the head. He was a master at Charterhouse, editor of the *Cornhill* and biographer of Darwin, Hooker and Huxley his sons being Julian and Aldous.

C. 11 Oct. 1861 Leonard s. Thos. and Henrietta Huxley 26 Abbey Place, H.W. Maddock

M. 21 July 1855 Thos. H. Huxley prof. School of Mines 14 Waverley Pl s. George master and Henrietta Anne Heathorn 41 North Bank d. Henry gent lic by H.W. Maddock

---

[26] Rev. Walpole was grandson of Horatio Baron Walpole brother of Robert, 1st Earl of Orford P.M. of Houghton Hall. He also held Itteringham, Norfolk in 1809-56 the earl being a patron.

St. Mark's, Hamilton Terrace

This was started in a small temporary building as an outpost of Christchurch in the early 1840s, and the freehold was purchased from the Harrow trustees for £600 in 1846. St. Mark's was built by Thomas Cundy and his son Thomas for £9,300; but one critic called it "a large broad Gothic riding school" for unknown reason, and the *Ecclesiologist Magazine* stated "another vast hall with galleries around three sides."

However, many appreciated its space and light with 1,000 rented seats and 450 free, and it was consecrated by C.J. Blomfield the Bishop of London on 24 June 1847. It aimed to cater for the new villa-dwellers in the rural fringes and Ashley Haselwood the curate of Christchurch who organised the project was the first vicar. He promoted a school next door "for the sons of poor clergy" and his curate Dr. Thomson was headmaster, but some thought it was there simply to provide choristers and to pay the priest's wages.

Haselwood who lived in Bond Street was often absent and there were criticisms of his handling of pew-rents - with suggestions of speculation in railway shares! Lady Burdett-Coutts of the banking family put up £600 for the school which was moved to Greville Mount, Kilburn and later became St. John's School at Leatherhead (in 1872). There was also a parish school which was constructed in 1864 and rebuilt in 1873.

Meanwhile the incumbents were presented to the living by the P.M. thus it had some notable ministers. John C.M. Bellew (1823-74) arrived from India in 1857-62 and was an author and later a Catholic, whilst Canon Robinson Duckworth who was previously tutor to Prince Leopold youngest child of Victoria came there in 1870. He announced that his mission was: "To provide a service identified with no party in the best spirit of the Church of England and void of offence in the eyes of all loyal to the prayer book."

Duckworth, who was chaplain in ordinary in 1870-1901, went with the Prince of Wales to India in 1875-76, and was present on a boating expedition when Alice daughter of his friend Henry Liddell was introduced to Rev. Charles Dodgson. As a result he appeared as a duck in an early edition of *Alice* while *The Looking Glass* was written in his vicarage. He then oversaw the addition of a chancel in 1877-90 and continued as vicar until 1906 whilst he was buried in the choir of Westminster Abbey in 1911.

Rev. John Magee, son of the Archbishop of York, followed and attracted prominent preachers, but was criticised for taking the church too high - and maybe due to this it was underpinned in 1908 and electricity installed in 1925. There is a baptistry in memory of Duckworth and the *St. John's Wood Preservation Society* started there in 1965.

Of the residents, Arthur Pember was born at Brixton Hill on 15 January 1835 and had a private education unlike his brothers, then entered the Stock Exchange with his father. He married the daughter of a broker and moved to Carlton Road, Kilburn in 1860 but his wife Elizabeth died and he married Alice Mary Grieve of nearby Waterloo Place at Willesden. After starting the *No Names Club of Kilburn* he was first president of the F.A. in 1863 establishing the rules and was an advocate of Ritualism. He immigrated to New York in 1868 and as a reporter wrote on political, religious and social issues.

M. 13 March 1860 Arthur Pember stockbroker of Clapham Park s. John Edward stockbroker to Elizabeth Hoghton of 7 Abbey Road d. Aubrey Alexander stockbroker licence by J.M. Bellew witness A.A. Hoghton, Emma Hoghton, John E. Pember

Hampstead & Highgate

Although these suburbs were beyond the city boundaries of Stanford's Map they were too important to exclude. In general the wealthy lived on the "twin hills" by the Heath, and in the 18th century Hampstead had a chalybeate spa with many notable occupants. The railway caused certain changes but it still remained a desirable location.

One consequence was a proliferation of plaques and tablets around the winding streets of the town today. John Keats visited Leigh Hunt in the Vale of Health in 1816 and took lodgings at Well Walk, then moved with his friend Charles Brown to a semi-detached property called Wentworth Place at John Street in 1818. They occupied the smaller side and next door was Charles Wentworth Dilke (1789-1864) the literary critic, although about a year later Dilke departed and Fanny Brawne and her family moved in.

Keats did not remain long but wrote some of his most famous poetry there, whilst the house was saved in 1925 and has a library dated 1931. A plaque at 40 Well Walk records that John Constable lived there near to Wellside, site of the old pump room.

Leaving the leafy eastern suburbs we then arrive at the parish church and precincts of Holly Hill. Robert L. Stevenson (1850-94) was castaway for a time at 7 Mount Vernon and George Romney (1734-1802) lived at the weather-boarded 5 Holly Bush Hill, while *Fenton House* dating from the 17th century was home to a merchant. Further on we find 28 Hampstead Grove, abode of George du Maurier in 1874-95, and then the twinned properties "The Admiral's House" and "Grove Lodge." Sir George G. Scott architect resided at the former and John Galsworthy playwright at the latter from 1918.

Walking across the heath one passes Robert Adam's opulent Kenwood House which was remodelled in 1764-79, and just beyond is the triangle of Highgate. The cemetery has memorials to Dickens' parents, G. Eliot, Michael Faraday, Karl Marx, the Rossettis and Sir Leslie Stephen, whilst Waterlow Park was bequeathed by the Mayor in 1889 and nearby was located *Lauderdale, Elms Court, Fairseat House* and *Hertford House*.

A plaque by the park on Highgate Hill records, "4 feet below is the step entrance to the cottage of Andrew Marvell (1621-78) poet, wit, and satirist, colleague with John Milton in the foreign secretary-ship during the Commonwealth and for 20 years M.P. for Hull." On and on down the hill towards Archway is a statue to Sir Richard Whittington and his cat "thrice Lord Mayor" which was erected in 1821 and restored in 1933.

The Admiral's House (The Grove) was actually home to a captain and Constable painted it as *Romantic House at Hampstead*.

Kenwood House on Hampstead Heath was the epitome of a Robert Adam design.

Keats House was built in c.1815. The poet composed *Ode to a Nightingale* whilst sitting under a plum tree in the garden:

"I cannot see what flowers are at my feet, nor what soft incense hangs upon the boughs..."

St. John's - a shade of New England comes to Hampstead.

Turning again, the Great North Road had a steep gradient up to Highgate Hill and was thus diverted by Thomas Telford onto a toll road to the east in 1810. A planned tunnel collapsed leaving a cutting therefore John Nash built a bridge or archway over the top to carry the road leading to Hornsey in 1813 (replaced 1897-1900). Another oddity was the *Highgate Hill Cable Car Tramway* which operated on the hill from 1884-1909.

St. John's, Downshire Hill - This was a proprietary chapel in the London Diocese and was independent being owned by the congregation. Rev. James Curry, Edward Carlisle a lawyer and William Woods developed Downshire Hill and the church was opened on 26 October 1823. It had a Regency stucco façade, Doric porch, clock by John Moore & Son of Clerkenwell, and a double staircase vestibule. There was a school attached and mission work, whilst the organ by Bevington & Sons was installed in 1880, and the east window with the eagle of St. John two years later. Some Bible texts were discovered on the gallery and reredos in 1923 and the box pews remain as a rare survivor. John Street was renamed as Keats Grove, and the church was restored and underpinned with aid in 2004.

Christchurch, Hampstead Sq. - This was built in Early English style of ragstone by S.W. Daukes in 1850-52. The first ministers were John T. Pelham son of the 2nd Earl of Chichester, and Edward Bickersteth in 1855-85 later the Bishop of Exeter. A gallery was added by George Gilbert Scott and porch and aisle by Ewan Christian (see p. 313).

Flinders Petrie, son of William and Anne (née Flinders), was born at Charlton in 1853 and was the *father* of archaeology in Egypt and Palestine. He used a modern approach with pottery and was the first professor at U.C.L. Residing at 5 Cannon Place (plaque) he married a student Hilda M.A. Urlin at St Mary Abbots on 29 November 1897, with banns at Christchurch. He controversially sold artefacts to fund his digs (d.1942). [27]

M. 10 January 1922 Clement Richard Attlee lecturer [L.S.E.] 638 Commercial Road s. of Henry solicitor and Violet Helen Millar of Heathdown, Hampstead d. of Henry Edward merchant by banns by B.E. Millar curate of St. Saviour's [first Labour PM 1945-51]

---

[27] Matthew Flinders (1774-1814) hydrographer was born at Donington, Lincs. and his father a doctor married Elizabeth Weekes. He served under Captain Bligh and on the *Investigator* with his step-cousin John Franklin son of Willingham and Hannah Weekes of Spilsby. Emily Sarah Sellwood wife of Tennyson was daughter of Sarah Franklin a sister. He married Anne Chapelle at Partney, Lincs. in 1801 just before the voyage and daughter Anne married W. Petrie.

St. John's, Hampstead

The living was originally held by the Benedictine monks of Westminster Abbey with the first reference in 1312, and at the Dissolution it passed to the Bishop of Westminster under the rector Thomas Thirlby. When the see was abolished by Edward VI the manor and benefice went to Sir Thomas Wrothe and in the vestibule is a list of rectors.

However, the mediaeval church became inadequate to the needs of the spa clientele and was declared as unusable in 1744. A new building was erected three years later by Henry Flitcroft and John Sanderson but this too became deficient and architect Lewis Vulliamy was approached in 1827. However his ambitious design was too expensive thus Robert Hesketh added some transepts thereby extending the west end in 1843.

Ten years later Henry Willis fitted and played the organ there, whilst plans were made for further enlargement in 1871. But these involved knocking down the tower, and there were objections from many including Morris, Burne-Jones, Holman Hunt, Trollope and du Maurier. Instead, F.P. Cockerell a relative of Pepys came in and extended to the west again in 1877-78, although this moved the altar to that end of the church.

The dedication was adjusted from St. John to St. John the Evangelist in 1917, and the final change came in the 1950s when the original whitewashed interior was re-instated. A number of memorials are recorded in the churchyard with information plaques and the most significant are to a romantic painter and a chronometer maker:

John Constable from Suffolk was married at St. Martin in the Fields in 1816 then had his greatest success with *The Hay Wain* and *Salisbury Cathedral*. He had property at 40 Well Walk from 1827 and at 76 Charlotte Street, St. Pancras, where he died in 1837.

John Harrison was born in Yorkshire in 1693 and made his first long-case clock in 1713 but came to fame when he solved the problem of longitude. A very accurate timepiece was needed to correctly identify location east-west and more random methods had led to shipwrecks, in particular the naval disaster under Sir Cloudesley Shovell at Scilly in 1707. An award was offered by Parliament (but never presented) and Harrison produced his first timepiece for the Navy in 1736. He then spent a lifetime on the work with his son, while a peeved George III tested one at his palace over ten weeks in 1772.

St. John the Evangelist, Hampstead received its appendage in 1917 while…

…. **John Harrison** was always punctual for appointments.

Eventually Harrison received all of the accolades and then resided at Red Lion Square (where there is a plaque). A copy of his chronometer was utilised by Captain Cook on his later voyages, having used the lunar distance method on the first.

His memorial and lengthy tribute south of the church were restored by the Worshipful Company of Clockmakers in 1879, even though he was not a member, and he is also commemorated at Westminster Abbey. Other burials included George du Maurier author and cartoonist and Walter Besant the social novelist and historian.

M. 5 April 1831 Rev. Thomas Henry Causton of St. Botolph's and Hon. Frances Hester Powys o.t.p. by licence by Horace Powys pres. Thomas Causton, "Lilford"

B. 2 April 1776 Thomas Harrison [sic]
8 April 1837 John Constable of St. Pancras age 61 by T.J. Judkin off min [28]
13 October 1896 George Louis Palmella Busson du Maurier of 17 Oxford Sq. 62
19 June 1901 Walter Besant of Frognal End age 64 by Brook Deedes vicar

St. Michael's, Highgate

A chantry of eight acres with a priest and hunting ground was established in 1100; and Sir Roger Cholmeley chief justice of the Queen's Bench founded a free school for boys there after the Dissolution in 1565, with six governors under the bishop. A schoolhouse was erected in 1578 and "a chapel of ease" for school and village was donated by Bishop Grindal in 1583 - it being a long distance from Hornsey and St. Pancras (in whose parish it fell). The chapel was enlarged in 1616-23 and the registers dated from 1633.

Thomas Carter the schoolmaster was imprisoned in 1641-42 for continuing to use the *Book of Common Prayer* and for speaking against Parliament, saying, "None but fools would take the Protestation." Despite, or because of this, he was restored in 1660.

However, the governors began to see themselves as administering a charity and placed the chapel first thus it was rebuilt in 1719-20. They also paid for almshouses and a school for poor girls - with only some money from pew rents and donations. As a result the schoolmaster, who imparted a classical education, protested over the misuse of funds in 1771. But it was to no avail since the Foundation repaired the chapel the next year!

A new structure was built for 120 boys in 1819 and the *Madras System* introduced like a National School, since before this there was little education taking place. The governors also launched an appeal for a new church and introduced a bill for a parish in 1821, but a village group contested this, saying the foundation was just for a grammar school. Lord Eldon then judged that the trust was only for teaching, thus the school and chapel were separated in 1824-26. The old chapel was pulled down in 1832 and materials sold, whilst the resulting funds went towards a new church on a different site. [29]

---

[28] The memorial to Constable is in a glade south of the church and his wife Maria Elizabeth who d.1828 was the daughter of Charles Bicknell, solicitor to George IV and his Administration. Rev. Thomas James Judkin (1788-1871) the minister of Somers Town Chapel was a frequent visitor at Charlotte Street and being a great admirer tried to emulate the artist.

[29] John Bradley Dyne a fellow of Wadham, Oxford became head in 1838 and introduced a new curriculum, library, and cricket field, also a schoolhouse and chapel in 1866-67 (at the west end of the High Street with memorials). Dyne who was "the second founder" retired in 1874.

Samuel Taylor Coleridge (1772-1834)

St. Michael's built in 1832 and **3 The Grove** - home to Coleridge in 1823-34, author of *Rime of the Ancient Mariner* and "*In Xanadu did Kubla Khan a stately pleasure dome decree,*" and J.B. Priestley in 1931.

To the west was the mansion of Sir William Cornwallis on South Grove which passed to Thomas Howard the Earl of Arundel and became "Arundel House," while Sir Francis Bacon, Lord Verulam, died there after catching a chill in 1626. It was then replaced by Ashurst House (1675), Old Hall (1691), Voel House and South Grove Mansion.

A neo-Gothic design for a new church was exhibited by Lewis Vulliamy at the R.A. in 1831, and the site of the semi-derelict Ashurst House was then chosen. St. Michael's was dedicated on 8 November 1832, it being higher than any other church in London, and took land from three other parishes viz. Hornsey, Islington and St. Pancras.

The total cost was £8,171 and the Church Commissioners paid £4,811 while the school whose pupils had seats contributed £2,000. In fact at £5.25 per seat it compared well to Kensington at £8.30 and there was accommodation for 1,500 people with 1,000 renting. Its main features were a spire of Bath stone, corbels by the west door to Cholmeley and Grindal, and a bell given by George Crayshaw. The parish was divided into St. Anne's, West Hill (1853) and All Saints, Church Road (1874); then the emphasis moved away from the pulpit when it was extended with a chancel and choir stalls in 1881.

After the new school chapel was built, the churchyard in the High Street was overhung and neglected. However it had significant memorials: John Browne M.A. chaplain 1728, Thomas Causton Esq. 1763, 71 (listed), and Rev. Edward Yardley preacher in 1731-69. A memorial to Samuel T. Coleridge the poet who lived at 3 The Grove was originally in that location, but was removed to the middle aisle of the new church.

Other residents of note were Rev. Thomas Causton created a prebend of Westminster in 1779, Charles Causton esquire who died in 1811, and the Rev. Thomas Henry Causton who was rector of St. Botolph's, Aldersgate in 1824-38 and St. Michael's in 1838-54. In addition he was a governor of the grammar school residing at Old Hall near the church and married on two occasions within the locality (see entries).

Another link was James Hooman who arrived in 1858 after the demise of Hooman & Pardoe carpet manufacturers at Kidderminster, and lived at 6 Holly Terrace, West Hill and Fitzroy Villas, 7 Hampstead Lane. His son Thomas attended Charterhouse and played in the Cup Final then was a shipbroker and manufacturer of Portland cement.

M. 7 April 1842 Thomas Henry Causton wid. clerk s. Thom. Causton D.D. and Frances Louisa Tatham spin. b.o.t.p. d. Thomas T. Tatham (wit) solicitor lic by Ralph Tatham

B. 2 August 1834 Samuel Taylor Coleridge of Highgate, age 61 by S. Mence

St. Jude's, Hampstead Garden Suburb - Henrietta Barnett established the suburb to the north on land owned by Eton College in 1907. This had a school named after her, model housing and two churches designed by Lutyens who provided the *Master-plan*. St. Jude's itself was built in the hybrid Queen Anne style from 1909-11.

St. Saviour's, South Hampstead - King Henry VI bestowed the Chalcot Estate on Eton College and houses were erected at Eton Villas and Provost Road by 1848. A temporary church was built that year and Edward M. Barry designed a permanent one of ragstone in 1856 with a spire erected in 1864. The parish was then separated from St. John's.

As the area grew several churches were added including: St. Paul's, Avenue Road by Samuel Teulon (1812-73) of Greenwich in 1859, and St. Mary the Virgin, King Henry's Road, Primrose Hill also on land of Eton College in 1872. Percy Dearmer was vicar of St. Mary's in 1901-15 and wrote *The Parson's Handbook* a liturgical guide to Ritualism, while the parish was combined with St. Paul's which was demolished in 1956.

St. Stephen's, Rosslyn Hill - Rev. Joshua of St. John's chapel and Charles L. Wood promoted the church which was built by Teulon in the French Gothic style in 1865-71. Lord Ebury laid the foundation and it was consecrated with Rev. Joshua as vicar but the porch, aisles, transepts, organ, vestry and tower took several years. Teulon had worked on many churches, country estates and a memorial at Westminster, but this was his most expensive at £27,000 and had a coarse flamboyance - being a climax to his career.

The exterior was of Kentish ragstone and granite with plum-brick banding and inside were sandstone columns. There was a three-quarters nave at 120 feet, a west gallery above the narthex, a font donated by Ewan Christian and mosaics by Salviati. Despite its attention to historical detail the concrete foundations were on the River Fleet and moved in 1969, thus it closed down in 1977 and was restored by English Heritage.

Regarding its connections, John Forster Alcock (1841-1910) helped to start Forest F.C. (the Wanderers) with his brother Charles secretary of the F.A. and Surrey C.C.C. in 1859. He then had a tumultuous marriage with Catherine R. Rowse (see Victoria), but was married again and moved to "Exhims," Northchurch. He was then a shipbroker and ice merchant at Great St. Helen's, with an ice farm and property near to Kragerø in Norway, whilst he was a respected local councillor and grew orchids in his conservatory.

M. 21 April 1886 John Forster Alcock 45 bach a merchant of Kensington and Augusta Lackland White 18 of Hampstead lic. wit. James A. Davies, Maggie A. McGilchrist [30]

(See pictures of St. Saviour's and St. Stephen's on p. 313)

---

[30] Augusta Lackland White was born at Pelham Street, Brompton in 1867 the daughter of Sarah White and Edward Lackland *name erased*. However her reputed father was Edward Augustus Lamb a barrister the son of Rev. G.A. Lamb of Rye and Julia Louisa Bancroft. The latter was born at Chaillôt, Paris in 1779 the daughter of Edward Bancroft a double-agent who worked for Benjamin Franklin and William, 1st Lord Auckland in France.

London Central East

And so we come to the area of Old Lundenwic and the stomping ground of Dr. Johnson, who never tired of London with its fine streets and alleyways! Not forgetting those compatriots Francis Bacon and Horace Walpole.

Here were the grand churches of St. Clement's, St. Mary's and St. Martin's delineating the ancient routeway from the City to the old Royal Mews and Westminster. Whilst in the elegant Stuart squares behind were St. Anne's and St. Paul's with a few chapels and temples besides.

Tenements crowded in on the main thoroughfare and its mansions but this did not stop the blossoming of creative ability, and the Royal Opera House and Theatre Royal represented only the pinnacle of theatre-land. From here came those artistes Arne, Cibber, Gilbert and D'Oyly Carte, followed by an encore from "Nellie" that any King might have approved of.

Artistic flair abounded in the environs with Roubiliac, Perigal, Chippendale and Gibbons, whereas Dryden and Hazlitt penned the story and Turner and Constable painted the scene. Noble palaces nestled in with blacking factories and the parents of Dickens hoped something might turn up, and it did in the form of the King of Corsica, Old Awdley and Boyle's Law.

"An Old Curiosity"

The 16th century building in St. Clement's parish was possibly the inspiration for Dickens' story, and inside we might find Little Nell helping her grandfather and Master Humphrey's clock to boot.

Aldwych (area)

For an initial understanding of the locality we can do no better than by turning to Stow, whilst other ecclesiastical buildings of note are discussed later:

"The street called the Strand has many buildings memorable for their greatness situated on the River Thames including the Bishop of Excester's House, Leicester [Essex] House built by Robert Dudley, St. Sprite's chapel, Milford Lane down to the river, the Bishop of Bath's Inn lately new built by Lord Thomas Seymour admiral which passed to the Earl of Arundel thereof called Arundel House. Then the monastery of St. Ursula at the Strand [otherwise St. Mary's parish church], Chester's Inn of chancery, the Bishop of Llandaff's house, the Bishop of Worcester's Inn and the Strand Bridge...."

Such appellations are reflected in road names of today with Essex and Arundel Streets on either side of the still extant Milford Lane. Edward Seymour, Duke of Somerset and Lord Protector, pulled down Chester and Worcester inns and other houses in 1549 then built a property on the site of Strand Bridge which passed to the Crown in 1552.

Somerset House was developed by Inigo Jones with a chapel for Henrietta Maria to the west in 1630-35, and it was the Queen's residence in the Stuart reign except in the war. It received a new river frontage and Wren did repairs, while Catherine of Braganza was the last occupant. Sir W. Chambers and Thomas Hardwick (then James Wyatt) rebuilt it from 1775 and it housed Government offices, the Navy Board and learned societies.

Immediately to the east was King's College located on Surrey Street. This was proposed by Rev. George D'Oyly rector of Lambeth with support from Wellington in response to the creation of U.C.L. It was established on 14 August 1829 and a building by R. Smirke opened in 1831, but it could not confer degrees and had eleven *feeder schools* - including its own King's College School situated in the basement and the Forest School.

The two colleges combined as London University in 1836 and its lecturers included Gabriele Rossetti (whose son was a pupil) and John Sell Cotman. The school itself was separated and moved to Wimbledon in 1897. Today, the college today still operates from its Strand Campus and uses the Maughan Library in the old P.R.O. building.

To the north was Lincoln's Inn, one of four Inns of Court dating back to the 15th century; and across in Chancery Lane were offices of the Master of the Rolls (or records), a position created in 1286. Within its precincts was a chapel initially for Jewish converts to Christianity. An archive was built for the P.R.O. by Sir James Pennethorne in 1851-58, but the ancient chapel was replaced when new wings were added in 1895.

Exeter Hall was a large religious venue beside the Strand built in 1831.

St. Anselm's, Kingsway was preceded by the more historic Sardinian Chapel.

Exeter Hall - The site was occupied by Burghley or Exeter House and was replaced by the Exeter Exchange just beside the Strand in 1676. The Bible Society and C.M.S. had problems at the Freemasons Hall, where the capacity was only 1,600 and women were excluded. Thus J.P. Gandy designed a new building in 1829-31 with Corinthian columns in a recess, main auditorium for 4,000, a smaller hall for 1,000, and shops in front.

This was a centre for religious and philanthropic gatherings hence Lord Kinnaird and Lord Shaftesbury (Ashley-Cooper) were at the *May Meetings*, it was synonymous with the Anti-Slavery Society and George Williams started the Y.M.C.A. there in 1881-1907. St. Michael's, Burleigh Street was built adjacent by James Savage in 1833, but the site was replaced by the Strand Palace Hotel in 1907 next to the Lyceum Theatre of Peto and Grissell. A rectory (No.14) added by Butterfield went to St. Paul's, Covent Garden.

New Court Independent - There was a somewhat complex history behind this small meeting house in an alley off of Carey Street. Initially, Dr. Thomas Manton was ejected from St. Paul's, Covent Garden under the Act of Uniformity in 1662, and his new chapel at Russell Court near to Brydges Street was closed down by the Five Mile Act.

However, after the *renewed* Declaration of Indulgence was implemented, Rev. Daniel Burgess started a Presbyterian congregation there in 1687, and soon removed to Crown Court near to Drury Lane Theatre. Once the lease expired, he built a chapel with three galleries in a secret location at New Court and was the first pastor in 1705.

Despite such efforts many left to join up with Dr. Earle at Hanover Street, whilst Rev. Sacheverell's mob broke all the windows, and burnt the pulpit and pews in Lincoln's Inn Fields in 1709. As a result the remaining members had a debt of about £700 and the situation only improved with the arrival of Rev. Thomas Bradbury from Fetter Lane in 1727. He brought many people with him and had some rich acquaintances. It became an Independent church from that time, with ministers of Calvinistic leanings.

Bradbury remained in the position until 1759 and was later followed by Rev. Robert Ainslie (1802-76), a Unitarian and secretary of London City Mission. The most famous member was William Butterfield High Church architect, whose parents were strict non-conformists and had a chemist shop in the Strand. It was demolished for the Law Courts in 1873 and the church moved to Tollington Park, Crouch Hill (until 1976).

C. 3 October 1814 William Butterfield s. of William and Ann b. 7 Sept. (seven 1813-24)

Great Queen Street Chapel - In the early 18th century the area west of Lincoln's Inn was very different to today, and a significant Wesleyan chapel was located south of the street with Stable Yard behind. There were three main thoroughfares going east to west namely High Holborn, The Strand, and a third along Long Acre and Great Queen Street linking St. Martin's Lane to Lincoln's Inn Fields. Drury Lane itself went south towards Wych Street then turned east past St. Mary's and across to St. Clement's.

The properties 66-68 Great Queen Street were built in about 1640 with a stream on the south side, and a *dissenting chapel* was added by Mr. Baguley in the rear garden in 1706. It soon came into conflict with the rector of St. Giles who tried to stop any title agreement, but prospered and Rev. Thomas Francklyn purchased it for the Wesleyans in 1758. The latter remained there until his death in 1784 and his executors sold it to the Society for £3,507 in 1798 - at which time they left West Street Chapel and moved there.

St. Clement Danes and Gladstone with nave detail, Dr. Samuel Johnson in literary pose and R.A.F. motif.

An alleyway entrance led to the building whose structure was mainly below the street, but it was rebuilt and extended with galleries in 1817 and a portico of four Ionic columns was added in 1840. It then formed the centre of a circuit up to Barnet and Finchley. However after Kingsway was built next door it was given to the West London Mission in 1906, but the building was condemned and they briefly went to the Lyceum Theatre. A new structure *Kingsway Hall* was erected in 1912 and under Donald Soper pacifist and socialist it was a recording venue, but the Mission had departed by 1978 and the edifice was demolished with the adjacent Wesley Hall in 1996.

Regarding the three houses in front of the chapel there were some significant residents. Elizabeth Paulet wife of Robert Devereux, 3rd Earl of Essex was first to live at No. 66, and Sidney Montagu husband of Anne Wortley was an occupant in 1703-15. In fact their son Edward Wortley Montagu was married to Lady Mary Pierrepont, the latter being a descriptive letter-writer of some prominence (see St. Paul's C.G. and Mayfair).

Another resident in 1748 was celebrated composer Thomas Augustine Arne under the name "Augusti Arne." His works included a setting of Addison's *Rosamund* at Lincoln's Inn Fields theatre and later on *Rule Britannia* (see St. Paul's). In addition Rev. Thomas Francklyn resided at No. 67 from 1761-84 and his widow until 1795.

Great Queen Street was home to the Grand Lodge of the Masons from 1717 and the Freemasons Hall and Tavern were built by Thomas Sandby (brother of Paul) at No. 61 in 1775. The building was later extended and two organisations were inaugurated there: the first Geological Society in 1807 (a plaque records this) and the F.A. on 26 October 1863 its founders including A. Pember, J.F. Alcock, E. Morley, F.W. Campbell and H. Steward. Meanwhile a grand Art Deco Lodge with tablet was completed there in 1933.

The Sardinian Chapel - This significant building in Duke Street west of Lincoln's Inn was the oldest Roman Catholic chapel in London, being attached to the residence of the Sardinian Ambassador. It was there from 1648 and took the name in 1720, whilst it was a sanctuary for ceremonies and worship when Catholicism was banned. The practice was gradually tolerated, but it was damaged in the Gordon Riots and then enlarged taking in some former stables. However, it was superseded by St. Mary Moorfields and others in the 1820s and was then used mainly for local residents, often foreigners.

The organists included George Paxton in 1766-76, Samuel Webbe from 1776-95 who also composed glees, and Vincent Novello a former chorister who was there and at the Portuguese chapel in 1796-1822 and then at St. Mary Moorfields. Webbe and Novello did the first performances of masses by Haydn and Mozart, whilst the latter was father of Clara Novello a famous soprano (and perchance, unrelated to David Ivor Davies).

To the north where the square met with Great Queen Street (now Remnant Street) was a house built by the Marquis of Powys in 1686, which was notable for its arches above the pathway. Powys and his family were Roman Catholics and it was constructed there to be near the chapel. It was also home to the Duke of Newcastle P.M. under George II and to the *Society for Promoting Christian Knowledge* in the 19th century.

The old chapel had a fine choir and was renamed St. Anselm's (1853) then St. Anselm and St. Cæcilia (1861), but with the arrival of Kingsway was demolished with many other historic houses. The last mass was on 6 July 1909 and Sardinia Street is south of the site. A new church was built east of Kingsway with Sardinian coat of arms, the old high altar in the Lady Chapel, and *Descent from the Cross* reputedly by Marcus Rigaud or Benjamin West. This was painted to replace the altar piece destroyed in the Gordon Riots.

C. Die 10 Augusti 1823 natus et die 21 Septembris 1823 baptizatus fuit Joannes filius Eduardi et Isabella Cotter olim Wilkie conjugum suscepere Joannes Heney et Maria Reed a me Fred. Edgeworth Misso Apeo [1]

M. 3 May 1733 Joseph Francis Nollekens and Mary Ann Lesack ["the elder" a painter]

St. Clement Danes

The ancient church was built just beyond the precincts of the City (and Temple Bar), but the origins of the name are open to conjecture with three alternative theories in vogue: Harold Harefoot a Danish King and his compatriots were buried there; The Danes met there under Ethelred after sacking Chertsey Abbey; A group of Danes settled there when others were driven out, married English women and erected a church. The latter concept emanated from Lord Burghley a resident who quoted Fleetwood the antiquarian.

A church probably stood there from the 9th century and it was rebuilt by the Normans whilst Stow noted that John Fabian a great historian resided in the parish. He produced *Books of Mediation* and *Chronicle*s then left land at Ovington, Essex (died 1541).

So-called "unthrifts" from the Inns of Chancery were unruly at night, thus the Recorder and six inhabitants kept watch by the church in 1582 and met Mr. Robert Cecil who gave a civil salute. They were most impressed at the nobleman's son, noting, "How he putteth off his cap to poor men," and wrote to his father complimenting such virtues.

---

[1] Edward Cotter was a poor tailor from Youghal, Ireland and lived with his wife at White's Alley in the Liberty of the Rolls. His son John Cotter entered the 3rd Foot (Buffs) and as adjutant was raised to lieutenant in the Crimea. The latter's children then included: Edmond William R.E. a lieutenant colonel who played in the first Cup Final, Francis Gibson a commandant in the Navy, and half-sister Isabella Kate the wife of Sir William W. Pryn surgeon rear admiral.

St. Thomas, Liberty of the Rolls was between Bream Buildings and White's Alley, the scene of 1,000 evictions of poor people by the Ecclesiastical Commissioners in 1886. Questions were then asked, "Was this a precursor to demolishing the church, there being no population?"

The edifice was located in a small ground at the end of the Strand, which was very narrow at this point, due to housing and tenements occupying the space up to Holywell Street. To the south were the Bishop of Bath's Inn and to the north Clement's, Lyons, Danes and New Inns then a warren of alleyways and Carey Street. A large churchyard for the parish was situated at the latter's junction with Portugal Street.

Inside there were a number of memorials - including in the chancel to: "Hippocrates de Otthen descended from the noble family of Otthen of Holsatia, doctor in Montpellier University and incorporated in Oxford University… died 13 November 1611." However the mediaeval edifice was mainly in poor repair. An area 20 feet square was added to the east end in 1608, a new chancel was built for £1,000 and the steeple improved at £496 in 1616, and the exterior was roughcast and interior beautified at £90 in 1631-32. Clearly it was a large expenditure for the period but apparently it was all in vain.

St. Clement's by Wren with its organ, pews and chancel.

The old church was taken down in 1680 and a new one built slightly to the south by Edward Pearce under the direction of Wren, whereas the ornate steeple was added to the composite tower by James Gibbs in 1719-20. St. Clement was patron saint of feltworkers and sailors thus local buildings had anchor motifs and the church featured white stone, Corinthian columns, a circular Ionic portico (gone) and Tuscan altar and pulpit.

Strype then recorded, "The church and steeple have lately been new built, there is a fine pulpit wrought with carved work, the ceiling is arched with fret work, and there is a good organ." A number of the parishioners were gentry and rich tradesmen; although the houses of the nobility viz. Arundel and Essex were replaced by fair courts and squares. Likewise a survey in 1732 recorded that the church was some 730 years old. [2]

---

[2] Essex Street itself was built by Nicolas Barton in the grounds of Essex House in 1675 and was home to some famous people: Sir Orlando Bridgeman, Henry Fielding, Brian Crosby (lawyers), James Savage architect, the Unitarian chapel of Thomas Lindsay, and the *Evening Club* of Dr. Samuel Johnson at the "Essex Head" in 1783 (a tablet records these facts).

Rev. William Webb Ellis came from St. George's, Albemarle Street as rector in 1843-55, and after his death a myth was created that he was first to run with the ball at Rugby. In the north gallery a brass plaque was erected in 1851 stating that for many years Johnson sat there for services. Indeed the seat was revered like *The Squire's Pew* of old. The parish owned land in Holborn from the 16th century, and the funds allowed them to open a school in nearby Houghton Street in 1862 (moved to Chorleywood in 1975).

Princess Alexandra of Denmark stopped there on 10 March 1863 and the parishioners provided an address, noting the absence of any "olde feuds" from 800 years earlier. The warren of alleyways lying below Carey Street was then swept away, and George E. Street designed the Royal Courts of Justice in the Gothic style during 1873-82.

Just to the west was the narrow passage of St. Clement's Lane which linked the church to a churchyard beside Clare Market, Carey Street and Portugal Street. A workhouse for the parish was built on the site, and King's College Hospital was started in the building in 1840 but became a separate entity moving to Denmark Hill in 1909. It was then taken by the *Fabian Department* of the London School of Economics from 1920.

Across the road on Sheffield Street, near to the Old Curiosity Shop, was located the *St. Clement Danes & Clare Market Parish House*. A tablet records the site was given by Hon. W.F.D. Smith M.P. and it was built by donations in 1887. Rev. J.J.H. Septimus Pennington (formerly Sparrow) was rector in 1889-1910 and his name appears on the building, while his brother Rev. Montagu P. Sparrow was chaplain to the Earl of Mornington. [3]

The church was destroyed in the bombing on 10 May 1941 and after an R.A.F. appeal it was restored and re-consecrated on 19 October 1958. It became their church in London with motifs of 800 commands on the slate floor, and to the rear is an organ donated by the U.S. Air Force. Outside are statues to Sir Arthur Harris and Lord Dowding wartime leaders erected in 1992 - although their role made these controversial at the time.

Famous Parishioners: *Robert Cecil* was the son of 1st Baron Burghley, Master of the Court of Wards. He became Secretary of State after the death of Francis Walsingham in 1590 and senior minister after his father died in 1598. He was created 1st Earl of Salisbury and as a protégé of Walsingham became a spymaster to James I (d.1612).

The marriage of *Ananias Dare* and *Eleanor White* took place at the church in 1583, although St. Bride's claimed it was sanctified there. In fact her father Thomas White was the first Governor of Roanoke Island - a colony in North Carolina established by Sir Walter Raleigh. The couple had a daughter Virginia on 15 August 1587 who was the first white child born in America. With the demise of that colony in unknown circumstances she passed into myth and folklore (the island is now located in Dare County).

Hippocrates de Otthen the son of a physician to the Emperor of Germany was sent for by Queen Elizabeth in 1579. He attended the Earl of Leicester at home and in the Low Countries, also the Earl of Essex with whom he travelled to Cadiz. **(cont. p. 120)**

---

[3] William Pole Tylney Long-Wellesley (1788-1857) was the 4th Earl of Mornington from 1845 and led a dissipated life using money from his wife and uncle the Duke of Wellington. He was commemorated in a famous line of verse, "Bless every man possess'd of aught to give, long may Long Tylney Wellesley Long Pole live!" His son William R. the 5th Earl of Wanstead House sold land at Snaresbrook to the Merchant Seamen's Orphan Asylum from St. George in the East (1817-59), and G.S. Clarke a pupil of Barry built a Gothic Venetian structure in 1861-62.

The "Great Audley" and the Grosvenor Estate

The Manor of Eye (or Ebury) was held by Westminster Abbey until 1538 and part was enclosed as Hyde Park by the King, while the remainder was located in Belgravia, Pimlico and by Park Lane. The Crown let it in two leases and trustees of Sir Lionel Cranfield, 1st Earl of Middlesex purchased one in 1618 and the other came to him in 1623.

Hugh Audley was baptized at St. Michael's, Wood Street in 1577 - the tenth child of a Cheapside mercer. After entering the Temple in 1603, he became clerk of the Court of Wards & Liveries amassing a great fortune as a lawyer, moneylender and philosopher. He then purchased the Ebury Estate from Cranfield for £9,400 in 1626 whilst a number of players shortly entered into this rather avaricious narrative.

Richard Dukeson became rector of St. Clement Danes in 1634 and lived in the rectory in Milford Lane, a fashionable quarter, but was locked up by Parliament twice in 1642-43 for taking an adverse position (d.1678). Several of his children were baptized at the church including Mary who married Alexander Davies, and Rebeckah wife of William Docwra who was an adviser to the Grosvenor family (see Vol. I).

The sisters of Hugh Audley played a part and Alice married John Clarke and Sebastian Bonfoy; while Elizabeth married John Jennings and Stephen Peacock - and had a daughter the wife of John Davies (parents of the above). Audley survived financially despite the suppression of the Court in 1646 and its abolition in 1660, being a skilful and cunning lawyer who took out lawsuits and the like to secure his pecuniary position.

He was a good friend to his neighbour and relative Rev. Dukeson, a staunch Royalist, and employed John Rea who was in a position of trust, and his great-nephews Nicholas Bonfoy and Alexander Davies as scriveners. There were serious machinations around his will and he amended a settlement in favour of Nicholas Bonfoy in 1656, then created a trust to John Rea and two others in 1660, then left all his estate to Bonfoy and Davies in 1661, and finally bequeathed it to Thomas and Alexander Davies in 1662.

The will of "Hugh Awdeley of the Inner Temple" was dated 4 November that year and he died eleven days later then was buried at Temple Church, whilst the document was proved on the 24th inst. His legacy included money to Barts, Christ's and St. Thomas's Hospitals, a repayment to his half brother William Harvie, and 500 acres to his nephews which later became Belgravia, Pimlico and Mayfair. A pamphlet was also published, "The way to be rich according to the practice of the Great Audley!"

Thomas Davies sold his portion to his brother Alexander for £2,000 and the latter built property along the river at Market Meadows in Millbank, including the site for a mansion called Peterborough (Grosvenor) House. However he died during the plague in 1665 and his heir was an infant daughter Mary Davies who was just 6 months of age.

His widow married John Tregonwell a Dorset squire but much had to be spent repaying his brother and the uncompleted mansion cost £4,000. The money was then recovered in three ways - some from the squire, by selling Goring House (Buckingham Palace), and the sale of land in Knightsbridge (later repurchased). In 1672 an agreement was reached that Mary Davies would marry Hon. Charles Berkeley when she attained the age of twelve and £5,000 was paid to Tregonwell regarding this. **(continued)**

However the agreement broke down since he had just built Berkeley House, Piccadilly and was short on the agreed funds and land. Instead, her uncle William Docwra secured a new contract, and she married the 21 year-old baronet Sir Thomas Grosvenor who came from an ancient Cheshire family - with a seat at Eaton Hall and two lead mines.

The bride was just twelve at the time thus she spent two years in the care of her aunt, and Lord Berkeley and Tregonwell had to be repaid with interest. In addition some rents came in and land was sold at Buckingham Palace, Green Park and Hyde Park Corner. Sir Thomas died in 1700 and Dame Mary who was unstable was lulled into a marriage (later annulled) and the money was put in Chancery, whilst she died in 1730.

As a postscript their three sons started Grosvenor Square in 1723 and the eponymous Audley Street was one of the thoroughfares, whilst their descendant Robert Grosvenor, Marquess of Westminster (1767-1845) eventually laid out Belgravia and Pimlico.

St. Clement Danes - parish registers

C. 6 June 1563 Master Robert Cicill sonn of ye Lord Highe Treasorer of England [4]
17 December 1640 Marie Dukesonne the daughter of Richard parson of this parish and Anne uxor - also four others baptized 1634-46
17 May 1778 William Kitchener s. of William Esq. and Mary Cecil b. ye 11th ultimo
28 Dec. 1778 Joseph Grimaldi s. of Joseph and Rebecca b. 18 Dec. [at Clare Market]
24 June 1810 Ralph Wedgwood s. of Ralph and Mary born Burslem, Staffs 19 June 1793
1 July 1866 John Edward Pember the son of Frederick and Eliza Georgina of 91 St. Andrew's Road, Southampton clergyman born 23 April

M. 24 June 1583 Annainas Dare and Elinor Whyte [sic]
16 May 1661 William Docwray and Mrs. Rebekah Dukeson married
10 October 1677 Sr George Grosvenowre [sic] of Eaton in the co. palatine of Chester baronet and Mrs. Mary Davis of St. Margaretts, Westminster
10 April 1768 Robert Studley Vidal o.t.p. bach married Elizabeth Blinch o.s. spin licence by John Lewis curate witness Wm. Betney, Ann Worthington [5]
3 August 1799 William Kitchiner o.t.p. esq and Elizabeth Oram of St. Martin in the Fields by licence by George Laurance curate witness Thos. Gotobed and Ann Oram
14 October 1865 Frederick Pember 28 gentleman of Coleshill, Amersham s. John Edward gent and Eliza Georgina Gibbard 23 of 16 Serles Place d. John Henry artists' colourman by R. Henry Villiate rector licence witness J.W. Gibbard [only one]

B. 14 November 1611 Docktor Otten a doctor of physyke
6 May 1692 Nathaniell Lee a man was buried
6 March 1827 William Kitchiner M.D. Warren Street, 51 by Jas. Knight

---

[4] He was the son of William Cecil, 1st Baron Burghley and his second wife Mildred Cooke. Her sister Ann married Sir Nicolas Bacon and they were parents of Sir Francis Bacon (1561).

[5] Their son also R.S. Vidal b. 1770 was an antiquarian of the Temple and Abbotsham, Devon.

Regarding the later parishioners *Nathaniel Lee* (b.1653) was the son of a Presbyterian minister of Hatfield and attended Charterhouse. He failed as an actor due to stage-fright then made his name with blank verse poetry; however was committed to the Bethlem as a result of excessive living in 1684. After stating that *they were mad* he was outvoted by them (or so it is said) and died shortly after his release in 1692.

William Kitchiner was connected with the parish throughout his life and was the son of a coal merchant, but his reputed education at Eton and Glasgow was probably a fallacy. He parted from his wife soon after marriage and had a liaison with Elizabeth Gifford, then wrote on gastronomy and optics while composing operettas and sea songs. He lived at 43 Warren Street and as a fellow of the Royal Society improved the telescope, whilst his son erected a memorial to him at St. Pancras new church.

Thomas Wedgwood was a cousin and partner with Josiah at "Etruria" near Burslem, and had a son Ralph born in 1766 who had his own pottery company. The latter married on three occasions and had a son Ralph in Burslem, Samuel at Knottingley, Yorks (1800), and Triane at 328 Oxford Street (1810) all baptized together at St. Clement's.

His company produced cameos, medallions and ornamental pieces, whilst Ralph junior was married at Covent Garden in 1818 and established a stationery business. He was the inventor of carbon paper at Cornhill and settled at Barnes; thus his son John Raphael resided at "Etruria House," 49 Lonsdale Road until he died in 1902. [6]

Frederick Pember, the last connection of note, was the brother of Edward and Arthur (the F.A. founder). After attending Christchurch, Oxford he was imbued with the ideals of the Oxford Movement and was ordained by Bishop S. Wilberforce in 1861. In fact he married someone from a different social class and 16 Serles Place (Sheer La.), his bride's residence, was in "that warren of alleyways" below Carey Street.

John Henry Gibbard artists' colourman of Cumberland Hay Market married Elizabeth Johns daughter of a doctor at Trinity, Marylebone in 1841. A child Eliza Georgina was born that year and her mother was "a laundress at chambers," thus the link may have been Edward a barrister at Lincoln's Inn. Rev. Pember took up mission work and was in Christchurch, N.Z. from 1868-75 and Canada, Maine and Boston in 1877-1914.

Nathaniel Lee (1653-92), on the left, was a poet/dramatist of acclaimed aptitude.

Rev. Frederick Pember (1837-1914) was a missionary in Christchurch and brother-in-law William Reeves was a leading politician there.

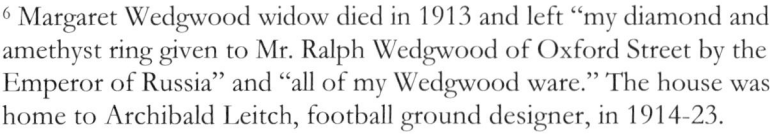

[6] Margaret Wedgwood widow died in 1913 and left "my diamond and amethyst ring given to Mr. Ralph Wedgwood of Oxford Street by the Emperor of Russia" and "all of my Wedgwood ware." The house was home to Archibald Leitch, football ground designer, in 1914-23.

St. Mary le Strand

Of all the churches in London this was the only one that was created, removed for 150 years, and returned again in even greater glory! Stow rather glossed over such issues and in general was more concerned with deliberating grand houses and legalistic inns.

However, the first mention of the church south of the Strand came in 1222 and it was dedicated to St. Mary and the Innocents, although others knew it as St. Ursula's due to a brotherhood that was established there. No doubt to great protestations, it was pulled down by Edward Seymour, 1st Duke of Somerset, to facilitate the building of Somerset House in 1549. But more significantly - the church was not replaced.

The parishioners then used St. Clement's and the Savoy Chapel whilst a large Maypole was erected in the middle of the road on the site of the present church. Not surprisingly the parish petitioned the Church Commissioners in November 1711 and the Queen gave leave for a new edifice on the Maypole site in June 1713. [7]

A design from the courtier Thomas Archer was accepted in 1714 and any gravel that was excavated was moved to St. John's, Westminster and Somerset House. There were several problems, and *a memorial* was received from the residents stating the work had stopped-up the water-courses. The Commissioners also altered their plans and resolved to use a design by Gibbs in December that year - then the work continued.

James Gibbs had trained under the famous Baroque architect Carlo Fontana in Rome from 1704-09, and on his return was a surveyor for the Commission in November 1713. Due to his Tory convictions he only retained this post for a brief time, although this was long enough to secure his first commission to build the church.

Only the lower storey was ready by 1716 and Gibbs had to provide more estimates, as under the new regime the purse strings were tightened. Eventually the masterpiece was completed at £16,000 in 1714-23 but all was not well in the State of Denmark, and the architect was unhappy with changes made by the Commission. The original design was purely Italianate with a campanile at the west end and square nave, while after the death of the Queen plans for a statue in front were abandoned. As a result the stone was used to build a steeple instead - and the nave was eventually oblong in shape.

The church was situated at the west end of Holywell Street with tenements behind and the Strand on the south side, but there were serious problems due to adjoining traffic noise right from the start. The parish was created out of St. Clement's to the east and included an area below the church across to the Savoy Chapel and Somerset House. St. Clement's itself covered a far larger area reaching from the rear of St. Mary's to Temple Bar and then up to Drury Lane and across to Portugal Street.

Externally, there was a distinct Baroque appearance with influences from Rome. The two-tier façade with apses and recesses was reminiscent of Fontana's San Marcello al Corso near to the Piazza Venezia, and the porch was inspired by Cortona's Santa Maria della Pace (see St. Paul's, Deptford). However, the vagaries of the site meant there was a three-tier tower and the lower levels had blanked-out walls facing the roads.

---

[7] The Maypole was incommodious to the building of the church and was purchased by Sir Isaac Newton then moved to Wanstead House. Rev. Pound had obtained leave of Sir Richard Child, Lord Castlemaine (later Tylney) to place it there and a fine telescope was erected on top.

However, the chief glory was inside. The plain pilasters of the walls provided a stark contrast to the exuberance of the decorated ceiling and columned apse beyond - the roof being inspired by Fontana's Santi Apostoli and Cortona's Santi Luca Martina near the Capitol in Rome. A shade of antiquarianism transposed to London.

The building was consecrated on 1 January 1723 and Rev. John Heylyn D.D. (1685-1759) was the first rector. There was little room nearby thus the main churchyard was situated behind Thomas Manton's chapel at Russell Court (now Kemble Street).

Rev. Heylyn was educated at Westminster School and in addition to being rector was a lecturer at All Hallows, Lombard Street, a prebend of St. Paul's and chaplain to George II. He had a major influence on religious thought and John Wesley was inspired by his preaching after assisting at a service on 19 May 1738, while Bonnie Prince Charlie is alleged to have renounced his Roman Catholic faith at the church in 1750.

Meanwhile, the most notable connection was with John Dickens (1785-1851) a clerk in the Navy Pay Office at Somerset House who worked with Thomas Culliford Barrow. The latter introduced him to his sister and they were married at St. Mary's then moved to Landport, Portsmouth and their son Charles was born there in 1812.

The Strand and its church already had traffic problems in the 19th century.

John Dickens suffered a pecuniary setback and was the original Mr. Micawber.

The father's next position was in Chatham followed by another job at Somerset House hence the family moved to Camden Town in 1822. Shortly afterwards he spent time in the Marshalsea due to some debts and in later life wrote to friends of his son asking for money. As a result the author found his parents a cottage in Devon, but they returned to London and provided the model for Mr. and Mrs. Micawber (see Highgate).

The church was nearly demolished on the building of Aldwych and Kingsway in 1906 but was saved by a campaign, although its site was severely restricted with vehicles racing by on either side (as at Monte Carlo!). There is a model in the V & A and its painting of "The Annunciation" by Mather Brown dates to the 1780s, whilst Percy Dearmer of St. Mary's, Primrose Hill author of *The Parson's Handbook* preached from the pulpit.

Indeed, John Betjeman expostulated in rhyme: "Great Gibbs of Amsterdam who gave Cambridge its Senate House and sons of Oxford the Radcliffe Dome, but nothing is quite so grand as the Baroque of the chapel of St. Mary in the Strand."

M. 13 June 1809 John Dickins o.t.p. married Elizabeth Barrow o.t.p. a minor by licence consent of Charles Barrow father by T.J. Ellis curate wit. Mary and Sarah Barrow

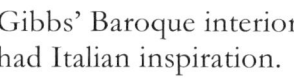

Gibbs' Baroque interior had Italian inspiration.

St. Mary le Strand, one of the "island churches," with St. Clement's just behind in the distance.

Temple Church

Although strictly speaking situated within the City, the legal precincts of the Temple are included here for their numerous links beyond. The location may be familiar to many passers-by, but perhaps the ancient church within its grounds is more of a mystery.

In fact, on visiting the Embankment today, it is hard to imagine how it once appeared. First came the houses of Somerset, Arundel and Essex with terraces leading down to the river, followed by ecclesiastical and royal palaces such as Temple, Whitefriars, Bridewell, Blackfriars and Baynard's Castle - all sequestered amongst trading wharves.

The Knights Templar were formed in 1118 and dwelt in the palace of the patriarch of Jerusalem by the *temple* where they protected pilgrims visiting the Holy Sepulchre. They took part in the Crusades in the 12th century, but were often at odds with other orders such as the Teutonic Knights and Knights Hospitaller. In London they were originally based in Oldbourn (or Holborn) but moved to the New Temple at the time of Henry II in 1185, whereas Jerusalem fell to Saladin two years later.

From that time they amassed considerable wealth, and treasure was often associated with their precincts. For instance, Hubert Earl of Kent was a prisoner in the Tower in 1232 and kept his valuables there under ecclesiastical protection, but the King confiscated all his gold, silver and precious stones "which were of unimaginable worth."

A new temple was re-edified in 1240 and Pope Innocent Nuncio arrived in 1245 and demanded 6,000 marks of the Bishops, but Henry III forbade this, while ambassadors and princes were grandly entertained there. Edward I, whose mother's jewels were kept in the treasure house, arrived on a pretence to see them - but broke into the coffers of sundry other "investors" and took away £1,000 in valuables.

Such wealth created problems and Phillip IV, King of France was in debt to the Order through a war with England and manipulated Pope Clement V who lived in his country. Initially there was an attempt to amalgamate them with the Hospitallers, but when this failed a policy of persecution ensued with the main leaders being imprisoned.

All the Templars in England were arrested for heresy in 1310 and were condemned to perpetual penance in several monasteries, "where they behaved themselves modestly." Soon afterwards, the King of France procured their overthrow throughout the world and took all their property in 1313. Thus Edward II gave the New Temple to Aimer de la Valence, the 2nd Earl of Pembroke (great grandson of William Marshal).

The precincts were then usurped by Hugh Spencer and passed to Edward III, but a council at Vienna gave all their lands to the Knights Hospitaller of St. John in 1325. This was a reward for removing the Turks from Rhodes, the latter being famous for their occupation and embattlement of Valletta, Malta in the early 16th century.

Meanwhile, the Hospitallers already possessed an estate at Clerkenwell thus they rented the Temple "to students of the common law," dividing the area into two Inns of Court but with one central church dedicated to *St. Mary*. The latter was late 12th century and of impressive design with a circular western tower and oblong nave to the east. Just to the north was Serjeant's Inn granted by Henry III to the Bishops of Chichester, and divers judges and sergeants lodged there during term times.

The rebels of Kent and Essex destroyed the Temple houses in 1381 and burnt records taken from the church, but the precincts were restored and at the Dissolution the Crown seized them. Their future was secured when they were given to a group of lawyers and a hall was built at Middle Temple in 1572. Initially there was a master and four stipendary priests, but from this time there was a master, reader and lectures by preachers.

Most buildings survived the Great Fire although King's Bench Walk, Tanfield Court and the Crown Office were lost; while Strype noted, "Eight images of knights are found in the *Round Walk* with five of legs crossed, as men vowed to the Holy Land against the infidels and unbelieving Jews." This was in fact one of its most notable features.

However, a serious fire started in Pump Court in 1678 which destroyed many of the chambers and an inscription above the portico recorded this. Only the church, refectory and halls survived and everything else had to be rebuilt - including the entrance on Fleet Street with its brick façade, four Ionic pilasters and circled lettering dated 1684. The fire damaged much of the church and several ancient records were lost, but Wren provided plans to repair the chancel and the round with its arched doorway.

Temple Church

The western door and the "Round"

The Round: Ackermann's *Microcosm of London* 1808-11, by A.C. Pugin with figures by Thomas Rowlandson.

Dorset Garden or **Duke's Theatre** was home to one of the two patent theatre companies in 1671-1709. Its main feature was moveable scenery.

A *Saxon* inscription in a half-circle above the old cloister door was broken by workmen in 1695, but G. Holmes recorded it, "Dedicated by Heraclius patriarch of the Church of the Holy Resurrection to the Blessed Virgin in 1185." The Inner Temple then wanted an organ by Harris and the Middle Temple preferred one by Smith. In the *battle of the organs* Baptiste Draghi organist to Queen Catherine tried out the former, and Blow and Purcell the latter which was selected by Chancellor Jeffreys in 1687. John Stanley represented Inner Temple from 1734-86 and each inn presented an organist until 1814.

There was a Victorian restoration of the church but it was severely burnt in the blitz on 10 May 1941, and much was lost including all the wood and the organ. The dark Purbeck marble columns of the chancel were also damaged by the heat and had to be replaced, although retained their *mediaeval lean*. The work was carried out by Walter Godfrey who also renovated Chelsea Old Church, and the result was comparable to some of the City churches detailed in Volume I viz. St. Mary le Bow, Walbrook and Woolnoth.

Whitefriars - This was founded by Sir Richard Gray in 1241 and Edward I gave a plot in Fleet Street, but was rebuilt by the Earl of Devonshire in 1350 and later repaired by Sir Robert Knowles 1407 and Robert Marshal Bishop of Hereford 1420. The memorials included those to many knights and Countess Margaret wife of Richard Grey, Earl of Kent. The friary was surrendered in 1539 and pulled down by Edward VI then replaced by lodgings for noblemen, while the refectory was briefly Whitefriars Theatre. The area remained a liberty for many years - known as Alsatia or a place outside the law.

Adjacent was Salisbury (Dorset) Court home to the Bishops which went to Sir Richard Sackville in 1564 and son Thomas, Lord Treasurer the Earl of Dorset (1604). A theatre was built there in 1629, but all the property was lost in the fire and replaced by Dorset Street. Wren or Hooke added Dorset Garden a *patent theatre* by the stairs in 1671-1709 which went to Lincoln's Inn and the area became wharves. On the site were the City Gas Works 1814, Sion College by A. Blomfield 1884 (now offices) and two City schools.

Templar Connections - The church is located on Inner Temple Lane just opposite to Dr. Johnson's Buildings, and its circular west end with porch, buttresses and embattled cupola comes straight from the era of the heraldic knights. Regarding the interior it is no less impressive but much is the result of a modern restoration.

Entering into the ambient light of the round with its interlocking detail at the triforium one is soon drawn to the black-based pillars and simple rib-vaults of the nave. But the chief glory is surely the effigies of eight knights recumbent at the west end, which evoke the period of the Crusades and all they embodied in film and folklore.

The most significant is on the south side to William Marshal the 1st Earl of Pembroke d.1219 said to be "the greatest knight of his age" or perhaps of all time. Marshal rose up through the ranks by courting the Royal favour of the early Plantagenets, coupled with success in battle, and it was he who dealt with the barons at Runnymede when King John signed the *Magna Carta* in 1215. The other effigies to the south are to his son Gilbert Marshal d.1241 plus two family members, and opposite is Geoffrey de Mandeville, 1st Earl of Essex d.1144 prominent at the time of King Stephen.

Quite naturally this discussion brings us to a clue. Dan Brown in the *Da Vinci Code* provided a tantalising riddle by stating, "In London lies a knight a Pope interred," hence Langdon and company arrived at Temple church, only to find there were no burials lying beneath the eight effigies. In reality this was discovered during renovations after the war while in alternative literature the church had a more significant role. [8]

Regarding other memorials and burials Henry II was most likely present at the dedication in 1185; and his grandson Henry III had the nave rebuilt in 1240 with the intention of being buried there, although this was altered in his last will to Westminster Abbey.

Quite naturally there are several memorials to great lawyers including to Richard Martin reader by the south door, to Edmund Plowden opposite, and to John Selden a scholar of law at Whitefriars on the south side. Other notables connected to the precincts are:

Richard Levett - His father Sir Richard Levett (d.1711) resided at Cripplegate and with brother Francis built a business empire. This included the tobacco trade with the Virginia Co. and in the East Indies, whilst he was an early director of the Bank of England. As a result he socialised with Pepys, became Mayor in 1699 and owned Kew Palace which was later leased to Frederick Prince of Wales and rebuilt by George III. But his son Richard a sheriff and alderman mismanaged affairs and filed for bankruptcy by 1730.

The Temple Nave with memorials to William Marshall and Richard Martin.

---

[8] In the author's own book *The Wizards of Wight* the last clue in the Diachronic Rubicon was "seek the answer to the final question in the round church within the square temple." This led Cornwall, Rebecca and Layabout the cat to the denouement beneath the building.

Oliver Goldsmith - He was born in 1730 the son of a rector of Lissoy, Co. Westmeath and was part of the circle of Samuel Johnson, residing at 6 Wine Office Court where he composed *The Vicar of Wakefield* (1766). He also penned *The Deserted Village* in 1770. In fact "Sweet Auburn" was based on Lissoy but discussed the clearance of land by wealthy landowners and immigration of poor farmers to the New World.

   There is a quote in Wine Office Court (connected with the Excise Office) by Johnson and a record of the famous writers who visited, "Sir, if you wish to have a just notion of the magnitude of the great city, you must not be satisfied with seeing its great streets and squares, but must survey the innumerable lanes and courts."

Ebenezer Cobb Morley (& Co.) - The Temple provided an unlikely precinct for the emergence of the sport of soccer, but perhaps like the knights of old this was a new form of conflict, coupled with its own brand of religion.

   Morley (1831-1924) came from a family instrumental in the Congregational faith with links to Whitefield (see Spa Fields) and was born in Hull in 1831; but moved to Barnes by 1858 where he was involved with rowing and the formation of Barnes F.C.

   He played in inaugural games against Richmond and was the first secretary of the F.A. when it was formed at the Freemasons Tavern in 1863. Regarding work he was a solicitor and partner at 3 King's Bench Walk, Inner Temple from that time and the club captains met at his chambers to debate the first game against Sheffield in 1866. The latter formed part of the deliberations regarding the rules and as stated he was "The Father of Football," whilst other members of the chambers also promoted the game (cont. over).

M. 7 December 1669 Christopher Wrene married Faith Cogg [hill] by the Reader
27 October 1692 [Capt.] Robert Studley married Anne King by the Reader [9]

B. 1557 Nicholas Hare of Bruisyard Abbey master of the rolls, speaker re. Hare Court
1584/85 Edmund Plowden lawyer, produced a treatise on succession for Mary I
1618 Richard Martin a recorder of London and reader of the Temple

14 December 1654 John Selden a learned antiquary and bencher near steeps of saints bell - marble with Latin inscrip [m. Elizabeth wid. Henry Grey, Earl of Kent]
21 November 1662 Hugh Audley of the Inner Temple Esq. bur upper end of the south isle [chancel] where the vestry now standeth [10]
9 October 1707 William Petyt Esq. bencher of Inner Temple at Temple bur Thur [11]
15 November 1740 Richard Levett Esq. in the rounds on the Inner Temple side
9 April 1774 Oliver Goldsmith B.M. of Brick Court, Middle Temple in the ch'yard

---

[9] Robert Studley attained his sea skills with the aid of Christian V of Denmark and was made captain of the *Experiment* by Prince George in 1707. He took the *Weymouth* to the Baltic in 1715 and received a memento from Frederick IV of Denmark and one from the people of Naples for repelling the Algerine corsairs. His daughter Mary married Peter Vidal and their grandson Robert S. Vidal resided at Abbotsham, Devon with links to the Eyres (see Bryanston Square).

[10] Hugh Audley (1577-1662) entered the Temple in 1603 and as previously discussed left the land that formed the Grosvenor Estate in his will. He was friends with Rev. Richard Dukeson of St. Clement Danes and died at the Old Rectory, Milford Lane on 15 November.

[11] William Petyt (c.1641-1707) was a learned antiquarian and keeper of the Tower records.

Arthur Pember the first F.A. president had lodgings at Temple probably through his brother Edward a parliamentary counsel; while John Welch a special pleader in 1829-82 was at Hare Court but moved to 3 King's Bench Walk. His son Reginald de Courtenay played in goal for the Wanderers in the first Cup Final, and Albert C. Meysey-Thompson a defender with Lubbock in that game had chambers at 9 King's Bench Walk. These were rebuilt after the serious fire in 1678, whilst at the western entrance is the mock-Tudor *Astor Estate Office* on Temple Place built by J.L. Pearson in 1895.

Temple Bar a successor to the 13th century *post and chain* demarked the liberties of the City and Westminster. A timber structure survived the fire, but Charles II ordered a new gate in 1672 and it is the only one still extant. It was designed by Wren, built by Thomas Knight and Joshua Marshall, and had statues by sculptor John Bushnell.

After the Royal Courts were built in 1877, it was acquired by Sir Henry Meux for Theobalds Park, Herts, whereas a griffin statue was designed by Sir Horace Jones to mark the site. A trust was formed to reinstate the Temple Bar in 1976 and it became part of Paternoster Square in 2001-04.

Strand (west)

A number of significant properties lined the famous route The Strand which emanated from the Olde English term for the riverbank - like Deptford Strond.

To the west of the Savoy were Salisbury House built by Robert Cecil below his father's later Cecil Street (Hotel) and Shell Mex; Durham House site of the Adelphi of R. Adam; York House home to the Archbishops whose Watergate remains by the Embankment; and Northumberland House (demolished in 1874) whose gate was moved to Bow.

St. Martin in the Fields sat away from the main thoroughfare on its own lane with its churchyard opposite; whilst Cockspur Street and Whitehall intersected with the Strand at Charing Cross, a small triangle of land with the Eleanor Cross at the centre.

However there were soon major changes and Trafalgar Square by John Nash replaced the Royal Mews in 1820. The National Gallery had its first building in Pall Mall in 1824 but this was described by Trollope as "most dingy," thus William Wilkins designed a new one on Trafalgar Square in 1832-38 - partly on the site of St. Martin's churchyard.

Hungerford Market was designed by C. Fowler and built by Peto & Grissell in Italian style on Craven and Villiers Streets in 1831-33, and Barry developed the Square in 1845 with Nelson's Column (designed by Railton and built by the partners) at the centre. The market was replaced with Charing Cross Station by Sir John Hawkshaw in 1864-65, and the attached hotel was by E.M. Barry with a *cross replica* in front. Apart from this there were many theatres and three churches of major architectural importance.

St. John the Baptist, Savoy

This is an ancient location and harks back to the days when grand palaces and mansions lined the riverbank. Henry III granted the land to Peter Count of Savoy, who was uncle of his wife Eleanor, and there he built "a noble palace of the Savoy" in 1245.

Upon his death in 1268 it passed to Edmund, Duke of Lancaster and was later home to the powerful John of Gaunt, while Chaucer worked there as a clerk. It was a liberty with its own rights and customs, but was burnt down during the Peasants Revolt in 1381. The first chapel was constructed on the west side during the 14th century, but was rebuilt in the perpendicular style with impressive ceiling and windows from 1490-1512.

Meanwhile, the palace was no longer needed, and Henry VII rebuilt it as a hospital and charitable foundation under his will (but carried out in 1512). Above the door it stated: "King Henry the Seventh to his merit and honour, this Hospital founded poor people to succour." He also provided 200 beds in a long nave, land to support the foundation, a master and four chaplains - plus the innovation of hospital attendants.

Despite this, Edward VI directed Sir Roger Cholmeley Baron of the Exchequer to look into "staff expenses" in 1552, and he found they exceeded revenue by £205 leaving the hospital in a ruinous state. His disposition was to dissolve the foundation but instead it was briefly removed to the Bridewell with all its beds. Queen Mary re-established it and under Elizabeth the chapel became a parish church for those in the precincts.

Over the years its charitable nature was generally misused and idle beggars and rogues took shelter there. At the time of the Commonwealth it was a place for *Divines* to debate with Foreign Churches, then under Charles II it was a garrison, but the last master Henry Killigrew retired and the buildings were converted to private tenements in 1702.

Within the precincts was a French Protestant Church on Dutchy Lane for refugees and residents with twin organs for singing psalms, a Dutch one beside the main square, and a German Lutheran on Savoy Stairs. However it was all demolished for Waterloo Bridge in 1820 and the only part to survive was the chapel of St. John the Baptist.

Adjacent developments were carried out by Richard D'Oyly Carte (1844-1901), who was born at Greek Street, Soho son of a flautist and instrument maker. He entered the industry composing comic operas and was manager of a theatre, thus he was acquainted with W.S. Gilbert and Arthur Sullivan bringing them together in 1875.

The Savoy Chapel is accessed to the south and sits below a raised garden.

Earning great profits from a series of light operas by the duo, he purchased property along the Strand and built the *state of the art* Savoy Theatre in 1881 and the Savoy Hotel in 1889. However, Gilbert and Sullivan parted company the next year; and he also built the Royal English Opera House or Palace Theatre on Shaftesbury Avenue.

During these years Helen Lenoir an actress (born as Susan Helen Couper-Black) was his business manager and helped produce the operas at the Savoy, thus they were married at the chapel in 1888 with Sullivan as best man. There is a memorial planter by the hotel noting his achievements and a plaque to the Fountain Club opponents of Walpole P.M., however the building itself overshadows the ancient chapel below.

Today, the Savoy precincts are operated by the Duchy of Lancaster who appoints the chaplain. There are some seat-markers for the Royal family and many plaques to those of note who worshipped there. To the east there is a memorial window to D'Oyly Carte and his family, and there is a font presented by Helen de Wint for her husband erected after a fire in 1864. Just south of the church is a tablet to the *Electrical Engineers* laid by Queen Victoria and a replica statue of Michael Faraday the scientist.

Marriages solemnized in the Chapel Royal in the precinct of the Savoy

M. 12 April 1888 Richard D'Oyly Carte 42 widower gent of St. Michael's, Burleigh Street son Richard Carte a gent and Helen Couper-Black 29 spinster of The Savoy daughter of George a gent by licence by Henry White chaplain witness James Caird, Arthur Sullivan, E.J. Caird, Henry W. Carte, Eliza Carte

The Savoy interior (and font) had ample light for **D'Oyly Carte** the producer of light operas.

The Adelphi - Durham House was built with a hall and large chapel in c.1345 and was occupied by the Bishops of Durham except in the Tudor period. It was in decay by the 1640s and initially the ruins were replaced by Durham Yard, then by Adelphi Terrace 24 neo-classical houses with wharves beneath by the Adam brothers in 1768-74.

A tablet records its residents such as Topham & Lady Diana Beauclerk, David Garrick, D'Oyly Carte, Thomas Hardy and George B. Shaw. The elegant houses were replaced by the *New Adelphi* an Art Deco building in 1936 but nearby are: 1-3 Robert St. home of Robert Adam, Hood, Galsworthy and Barrie; 1-5 Adam St. "Ivybridge House" offices of the N.Z. Co. 1839; 8 Adam St. Sir Richard Arkwright industrialist; 16 John Adam St. Thomas Rowlandson artist and nearby the Royal Society of Arts built 1772-74.

St. Martin in the Fields

Recent excavations have suggested this may have been a Christian site from the earliest of times, namely during the Roman occupation but the first record dates to c.1222. The church was on St. Martin's Lane in fields by the Royal Mews and was rebuilt by Henry VIII in 1542, whilst the area developed out towards Soho in the next century. According to Stow, "it was low and ordinary, in a triangular ground, much in need of new building and enlarging." Therefore it was extended to the east with a fine chancel at the expense of King James I, his son Prince Henry, and the parishioners in 1608.

Within its precincts was Whitehall Palace and a standard was hoisted on the steeple on days of importance. In fact the incumbents were presented by the King and included: Nathaniel Hardy *Dean of Rochester* in 1661-70, Rev. Thomas Lamplugh in 1670-76 later Bishop of Exeter and Archbishop of York (1688), and Dr. Thomas Tenison in 1680-92 who was then Bishop of Lincoln and Archbishop of Canterbury (1695).

A workhouse was erected between Castle Street and St. Martin's Lane, and Tenison asked Evelyn and Wren to help build a library there in 1685. This had gilt-edged books, while there were two masters (one a librarian) each receiving an annual salary of £30. He then endowed a charity school on the site with help from the S.P.C.K. in 1699. [12]

The church's prominence was confirmed by its memorials: John Worsley of Whitchurch Salop messenger to the Queen of twenty years benefactor 1595, Sir Carew Keynell usher to the Privy Chamber 1624, Susan wife of William Price a P.C. from Winchester 1632, Nathaniel Hardi Dean of Rochester and vicar 1670, Henry Coventrie ambassador son of Baron Coventry 1686, Benjamin Colinge secretary to the Lord Chamberlain 1700, and (outside) John Lloid controller of the tents, pavilions and revels 1703 age 92.

Originally the parish environs encompassed an area over to Oxford Street but Strype recorded, "Although such large portions of the parish of St. Martin's have been, by Acts of Parliament, taken away from it, and proportioned out into three distinct parishes as St. Paul Covent Garden long since, St. James and St. Anne more lately; yet it remaineth a very great parish and too populous for one church to receive the inhabitants."

Due to this fact there were two chapels: one at Oxendon Street near the Hay Market built in 1676 (see below) and Trinity Chapel, Conduit Street built in 1691 (see Mayfair). In addition St. George's Hanover Square followed under the Commissioners.

The remaining parish covered an anomalous area from St. James's Park to Drury Lane, and Whitehall up to Leicester Square and Long Acre (with St. Paul's as an island parish in the middle). It also encompassed parts of Buckingham Palace and Green Park.

Meanwhile, James Gibbs completely rebuilt the church in 1721-26 with a grand portico of Corinthian columns, pediment, tower, and dimpled steeple in ascending layers. This was despite the fact the façade only faced housing at the time. It was as if he predicted the advent of Trafalgar Square, which set-off the edifice so nicely at a latter date, thereby giving much fuller credentials to his sumptuous Baroque creation.

---

[12] According to Gilbert Burnet - Archbishop Tenison (1636-1715) endowed schools at Lambeth Oval in 1685 and at Croydon in 1714, whilst he was a poet of distinction, crowned Queen Anne and George I, and preached at the funeral of Nell Gwynne. A Girls School was built in 1797 and moved to Charing Cross Road ref. the gallery in 1868 and then to Tulse Hill in 1928.

Its spacious and illuminated interior had rows of Corinthian columns, double capitals, aisles with low domed roofs and galleries above. The main ceiling had moulded plaster bays that might have graced a stately home, leading to a chancel recess framed by golden-headed pilasters, and in the resulting quadrants were the parish rooms.

All of this, clearly from the pages of *Italian Renaissance Monthly*, emulated designs of Christopher Wren at St. James's and studies Gibbs carried out in Rome. Finally to the northwest was the churchyard and wrapped around it the school and workhouse.

At the time, the design was heavily criticised, but it quickly became a model for New England churches and St. Andrew's, Chennai (Madras) built in 1821 was largely a replica. Its organists included John Weldon (1676-1736) the composer from 1714 and Benjamin Cooke (1734-93) who was also at Westminster Abbey from 1781.

However, the churchyard became inadequate by the late 18th century and Upper Brook Meadow was purchased in Camden Town in 1802. Bishop Beilby Porteus consecrated it three years later, whilst almshouses (of 1683) were moved there with a clergy house and chapel in 1818, and All Saints was erected opposite in 1822-24. The site at St. Martin's Lane was then occupied by the workhouse and later by the National Gallery.

The new churchyard which was by St. Martin's Place was closed in 1855, and Countess Rosebery opened a garden there by public subscription in 1889 - with large Celtic cross at one end. It has a mound of uncertain origins, memorials to Sir John Barrow rear and Dr. George Swiney north (in Latin), and information about a restoration in 2006.

St. Martin's church itself rose to fame under Rev. Dick Sheppard preacher and pacifist who helped the homeless and dubbed it, "The Church of the Ever Open Door." Twelve bells including some from Whitechapel were donated to the Swan Memorial, Perth in 1988, and it was refurbished with a social centre in the crypt for £36 million in 2006-08. This included a novel spiral entrance and east window "Cross in Water."

The crypt is of some interest since it contains the *London Brass Rubbing Centre* and at the west end a number of memorials rescued from the mediaeval church. These include one to Nathaniel Hardy the Dean of Rochester on the west wall, and a plaque (of 1952) to John Hunter (1728-93) surgeon. This records his removal to Westminster Abbey after diligent research by Frank Buckland, surgeon and natural historian, in 1859.

In the north aisle is an exquisite font and ancient chest. At the east end there is a plain memorial to *Louisa Louis*, servant of H.R.H. Princess Charlotte of Wales, born Erbach, Germany 1771 died Buckingham Palace 1838. She was attached to Queen Victoria from her infancy and it was the latter who erected the commemorative tablet. [13]

Oxendon Street Chapel - This was built by Margaret Baxter on the west side of the street near Haymarket in 1676, and had two houses in front to screen it. Her husband Rev. Richard Baxter, a Presbyterian divine and hymn-writer, then *attempted* to preach there. However, Henry Coventry the Secretary of State lived just behind at Coventry House from 1673-86, and took exception to such rebellious teachings. Consequently, he regularly disturbed the services "by beating the *King's Drums* under the window."

---

[13] Princess Charlotte Augusta only child of George IV by Caroline of Brunswick married Leopold of Saxe-Coburg at Carlton House on 2 May 1816. She briefly resided at "Claremont," Esher in Surrey with Louisa Lewis acting as her personal servant.

St. Martin in the Fields, the parish church of the Royal Family, is a centre for the homeless and also many musical concerts.

Coventry, who was the uncle of Sir John, also took legal action under the Justices to seek redress. Hence, Rev. Baxter was induced to approach the vestry and lease it to the parish at £40 per annum - then the pew-holders fitted it out for Anglican worship.

Coventry House was pulled down and converted into smaller properties in 1690 whereas Oxendon Street was described as, "A good, open well-built and inhabited street with the tabernacle on the west side." After the arrival of St. James's nearby the chapel appeared to be superfluous, but continued in use as such until the new St. Martin's opened in 1726 and maybe beyond. A Scotch Presbyterian congregation (begun in 1737) came there under Rev. George Jerment in 1808 then removed to Haverstock Hill in 1878, and the chapel was then pulled down and replaced by the Civil Service Stores.

Residents of note at St. Martin's - York House in the Strand was appropriated from the Bishop of Norwich in 1556, and was home to the Lord Keepers of the Great Seal in 1558-1620. Their main duty was to approve and store documents of State.

Sir Nicholas Bacon (1510-79) was first *Keeper of the Great Seal* at York House and with his wife Ann Cooke had a (youngest) son Francis there on 22 January 1560/61, the latter spending his early years at the property when his family resided in town. From 1620 the Duke of Buckingham was owner and after a break during the Commonwealth era, it was returned to George Villiers, the 2nd Duke, who sold it for redevelopment in 1672.

Meanwhile, there were many significant baptisms in the 17th century including Erasmus Dryden son of the poet, Maria Musard wife of Christopher Wren junior (with memorial St. Paul's), Admiral Edward Vernon famous for his victory at Porto Bello, John son of Delariviere Manley female writer (see St. Benet's), Roger Morris architect with Colen Campbell, and William Elliott of Wells, Roxburgh an army officer and M.P.

Later baptisms at the old church were of Theophilus Cibber actor, son of a playwright and manager, who married into the Arne family (see St. Paul's); and Horace Walpole son of the Prime Minister - a famous historian and antiquarian of Strawberry Hill.

Gibbs mighty creation then witnessed further significant baptisms and Charles Spencer was married to Anne Churchill then became Duke of Marlborough. His son Robert was an M.P. and a friend to the Prince of Wales, Charles James Fox and R.B. Sheridan; but lost and won a fortune through his gambling habits. Other noteworthy people are listed below, whereas several important marriages were linked to the baptisms:

Louis François Roubiliac (1695-1762) was born at Lyons but made his name in England with statues and busts. Amongst his works are Sir Isaac Newton for Trinity Cambridge, Shakespeare for Garrick at Hampton and five memorials in Westminster Abbey.

Benjamin Duterrau was born at Soho in March 1768, and his aunt Mary married Francis Perigal of 57 New Bond Street watchmaker to George III, whereas Perigal & Duterrau formed in 1794. He was an engraver and married the daughter of a jeweller of Coventry Street, but then immigrated to Tasmania as a teacher of art. His work *The Conciliation* (or National Picture) depicted G.A. Robinson as Protector of the Aborigines in 1835 but was an inaccurate portrayal of events. His daughter Sarah, who went with him, married John Bogle a Glasgow merchant and their two sons became Royal Engineers.

Sir Richard Birnie was born at Banff in 1760 and worked as an apprentice saddler to the MacIntoshs at Haymarket who supplied the Royal family, thus he came into favour with the Prince of Wales. He married the daughter of a wealthy baker who lived in Oxendon Street, and as churchwarden at St. Martin's helped establish almshouses at Bayham Street, Camden Town. After serving as a captain in the volunteers, he was a commissioner and chief magistrate at Bow Street - thereby overseeing the Cato Street affair.

William Cuffay emanated from St. Kitts and became a Westminster tailor active in the Chartist movement. He married twice at St. Martin's including to Ann Broomhead on 12 February 1825 and later at St. James's, Piccadilly. After planning an uprising he was sent to Hobart and his third wife followed, whilst he continued his union activities there.

C. (Old) 25 January 1560/61 baptizatus fuit Franciscus Bacon filius dm: Nicho: Bacon magni Anglie sigilli custodies [Francis Bacon polymath]
20 Maii 1669 Erasmus Henricus Dryden filius Joannis et Elizabethre nat. 20
12 September 1677 Maria Mussard pa [daughter of] Phil. et Constantiae id
3 December 1684 Edward Vernon s. of James [sec of state] and Mary b. 12 Nov
13 July 1691 John Manley son to John and Dela. born 24 June
28 Apr 1695 Roger Maurice [sic] son of Owen and Rebecca borne 19 April
17 January 1696/97 William Ellot [sic] of William and Eleanor b. 17 January
19 December 1703 Theophilus Cibber of Colley and Catharine born 25 November
22 October 1717 Horatio Walpole of Robert Esq. and Catherine 24 Sept

C. (New) 31 May 1747 Right Hon. Lord Robert Spencer son of his grace Charles Duke of Marlborough and her grace Elizabeth his duchess 8 May
9 January 1813 Jane Sarah Duterrau d. of Benjamin and Elizabeth of 9 Buckingham Street "insurance broker" by J. Tillotson curate
11 October 1813 James Birrell son Richard Birnie Esq. and Louisa of [14] Oxendon Street justice of the peace [mag.] by J. Tillotson curate (also William 1815)
23 October 1856 Edward s. of Edward and Mary Nesbitt Stanford of 6 Charing Cross a map-seller born 27 May by G.J. Gowring curate (**see Introduction**)

York Gate and **The Adelphi** (c.1850)
Both were prominent landmarks on the Thames … The former, the last vestige of "the Grand Houses of the Strand," is now left high and dry; whereas the latter was demolished for profit in 1936.

M. (Old) 20 April 1626 Johis Underhill de nupit preconowidele domina Viscountess gri Alborn ye civra [Alice Barnham the widow of Francis Bacon]

M. (18th C.) 12 April 1735 Lewis Francis Roubiliac mar Caroline Magdalene Helot [sic]
15 August 1765 Francis Perigal of St. Giles in the Fields and Mary Duterrau o.t.p. mar by licence Bishop of London by L. Dixon cur pres. James Duterrau, Rosa Perigal
19 March 1796 Joseph Bonsor of St. Ann Blackfriars bach and Jane Hartshorne otp spin by lic. by Plaxton Dickinson cur wit Geo Hartshorne, Sarah Smith (see St. Pancras)
7 February 1798 Richard Birnie bach and Louisa Birrell spin b.o.t.p. by Archbishop's lic by P. Dickinson curate pres. James Birrell, Grace Martin, Catherine Birrell

M. (19th C.) 7 May 1811 Benjamin Duterrau bach and Elizabeth Perigal spin b.o.t.p. lic. by Jno. H. Howlett curate in pres of J. and Mary Perigal, Sarah Moon
24 July 1814 Isaac Jerrom and Mary Standage b.o.t.p. by banns by John Tillotson cur witness Nehemiah Sager, Elizabeth Standage (see Bryanston Square)
2 October 1816 John Constable of St. Pancras bach and Maria Elizabeth Bicknell o.t.p. spin by lic by John Fisher prebend of Sarum pres of Willm. and Sarah Manning [14]
24 May 1819 William Cuffay and Ann Marshall b.o.t.p. banns by John Tillotson curate (both signed) witness Jon Roberts and Mary Moss Sharp
9 September 1821 Edward Cotter and Isabella Wilkie b.o.t.p. by lic by John Miles min (both signed) pres Maurice Hearn, Thomas C. Olten (see Sardinian Chapel)

Regarding burials at St. Martin's there was a lengthy list of notaries including Nicholas Hilliard the Royal portrait painter; and Lady Anne Calvert wife of Baron Baltimore who was the *de facto* founder of Maryland. She was the daughter of George Mynne who came from Hertingfordbury and was moved to St. Martin's on her death on 6 August, although the details are unclear. Baltimore, who lived at Lincoln's Inn, was left with ten children but James I rewarded him with a 2,300 acre estate at Longford the next year.

A second mystery is Nathaniel Hardy the minister and Dean of Rochester who has a memorial at the church, but despite claims he was buried there has no entry in the main register. Regarding Sir Christopher Wren he married Faith daughter of Sir John Coghill a neighbour at the Temple, and secondly Jane who was daughter of Lord Fitzwilliam. In fact Robert Hooke, his esteemed friend, had never met her prior to the marriage.

---

[14] John Fisher (1748-1825) was a canon of St. George's, Windsor, chaplain to George III and the R.A., and Bishop of Salisbury in 1807-25 thus he commissioned a painting of the cathedral. His nephew John Fisher (1788-1832) became best friends with the artist and was a chaplain at Sarum, while the couple honeymooned at his rectory at Osmington, Dorset.

The actress Nell Gwynne first appeared in a play by John Dryden and came under the wing of the 2nd Duke of Buckingham. She was then long term mistress of Charles II and had two sons: including Charles Beauclerk, Duke of St. Alban's. After leaving the stage she resided at 79 Pall Mall a Crown property, whilst Tenison preached a sermon from Luke 15:7, "There will be more joy in Heaven over one sinner who repents...."

Other famous names were: Robert Boyle the chemist who resided with his sister Lady Ranelagh in Pall Mall, Jack Sheppard a highwayman born Stepney notorious for escaping from Newgate Prison, and Thomas Chippendale cabinet maker whose family business was operated at 60-62 St. Martin's Lane from 1754-1813.

B. 7 Januarii 1618/19 sepultra fuit Nicholaus Hilyard
10 August 1622 Lady Anna Calvert uxor hon siri Georgii Calvert equities garter, moriens en Thursday ultimo - brought here from Hertford re-buried
9 June 1670 *Dr. Nathaniel Hardy, Dean of Rochester* (**see right**)
4 September 1675 Dame Faith Wren mulier in cancella
6 October 1680 Lady Jane Wren w
17 November 1687 Elinor Gwin (**margin note:** Nell Gwynne, she died at her house in Pall Mall age 38 and buried in vicars vault in old church)
7 January 1691/92 Robert Boyle Esq.

16 November 1724 John Sheppard
15 January 1762 Lewis Francis Roubiliac
13 November 1779 Thomas Chippendale
15 October 1789 Cecilia Arne w (see Covent Garden)
22 October 1793 John Hunter Esq. m

St. Martin's Gardens, Camden (from 1805)

Charles Dibdin (1745-1814) was born at Holy Rood, Southampton son of a parish clerk and his brother Thomas was a sailor in India (see Bryanston Square). Initially he was a chorister at Winchester and in Covent Garden, but began to compose and then acted in Bickerstaffe's *Maid of the Mill* in 1765. He produced music for Garrick at Drury Lane and had links to Richmond, Ranelagh, Sadler's Wells and Marylebone then erected the *Sans Souci* theatre at Leicester Square. Most famous for his patriotic shanties he retired to Cranford and resided briefly at Arlington Street, Camden.

Regarding the other entries - George Swiney M.D. was educated at Edinburgh and was considered an eccentric on his retirement to London. He left £5,000 to both the Society of Arts and British Museum and large numbers attended his funeral. Sir John Barrow had government posts in the Cape and the Admiralty and was a founder of the R.G.S. in 1830; while Robert Batty was a physician and his son Robert, an army officer and artist, married Johanna Maria daughter of Sir John Barrow in 1821.

B. 29 July 1814 Charles Dibdin of Camden Town, 69 W.B. Champneys
6 May 1832 Sir Richard Birnie kn of St. Paul Covent Garden, 73 D. Morgan curate
29 January 1844 George Swiney M.D. Grove Street, Camden Town, 50 E. Chaplin
25 Nov 1848 Lt. Col. Robert Batty Ridgmount Place, Ampthill Sq., Pancras, 59
29 Nov 1848 Sir John Barrow of 7 New Street, Spring Gardens, 84 E. Chaplin

St. Paul's, Covent Garden

It may be pure conjecture but St. Paul's is probably the only "parish within a parish" in the whole of England. The large living of St. Martin's covered an area by the Strand then reached out into the fields of Westminster, also up to Marylebone and the Oxford road. At the eastern end was an area of forty acres belonging to the Abbey of St. Peter's, which was previously a *Convent Garden* under King John.

At the start of the 17th century there were just some fields, thatched houses and stables in this locality, but the Earl of Bedford had designs on the portion beside Drury Lane and secured leases and the like to form a new precinct. He removed all the old buildings, laid out a large piazza (400' x 500') and created a grid of streets. To the south were the walls of Bedford House, and in the north and east stately buildings upon arches, with a walkway below like the Royal Exchange or St. Mark's Square in Venice.

This then became an exclusive area for the nobility, gentry and wealthy tradesmen but had an absence of poor people, courts and alleys. Stow also noted that the parish of St. Martin's out of which it was taken "begirteth the new parish on all parts."

Bedford House was one of the few major properties on the north side of the Strand, and Francis Russell, 4th Earl set aside some land for a church. He then employed Inigo Jones who had just returned from a tour of Italy. The work which cost £4,000 took place in 1631-33, and the result was an unusual temple-style building. At the east end was a portico of four Tuscan columns and recessed pediment (but no entrance).

The church was then accessed by a garden and tunnels at the west end and comprised a brick façade, large tomb-like doorway, and sparse window space. Meanwhile, part of its purpose was to attract wealthy residents to these more affluent properties.

This was the first new church in London since the mid-16th century and caused a good deal of debate. In fact, one anecdote suggested Bedford did not want too much expense and asked for little more than a barn, so Jones retorted, "It will be a grand one!" Comedy sketches apart, the work began on 5 July 1631 but the licence to build was retrospective on 30 June 1635. The Earl disposed of his pew in St. Martin's and argued with the rector while it was consecrated by the Bishop of London on 27 September 1638.

St. Paul's, Covent Garden, "The house that Jones built"

It once gave shelter to a poor flower girl and is now popular with street entertainers.

Inigo Jones the Court architect then built the piazza and surrounding houses over the next few years, and also designed Catholic chapels for Somerset House and St. James's. However at Covent Garden he produced a structure that echoed the innocence of the early church, and it was this centrepiece that received the most attention.

The design was almost certainly influenced by liturgical controversies of the day, and the grand portico with false door behind the communion table was a change of design, added during building. This may have been insisted on by Archbishop Laud and aided by William Bray the vicar of St. Martin's one of his chaplains, whilst it was initially a chapel of ease until the matter of its parish status was sorted out.

Further developments took place under William Russell, 5th Earl and his two brothers John and Edward in 1641 - then an Act of Parliament was passed to make it parochial on 7 January 1645/46. At this time the curate was replaced by a rector, being appointed by the Earls of Bedford who retained the patronage.

With its portico-style façades and pavement leading in from Bedford Street it certainly commanded attention, and the incumbents included Rev. Thomas Manton in 1656-62 and Simon Patrick in 1662-89. The former was a famous Puritan preacher and although he supported the King was ejected under the Act of Uniformity for retaining reformed principals. Patrick himself went on to become Bishop of Chichester and Ely.

There were a number of internal changes and galleries were added on all three sides in 1643-70, while the chancel (cause of so much controversy) was moved to the north wall. Inigo Jones rejected any plans for a steeple or vestry since they would despoil his temple, but there was a belfry on the southwest side and this became a schoolroom in 1701. The span itself had no supports and the timbers were repaired at a cost of £600 in 1714-15, whilst the first organ by Abraham Jordan was installed in 1726.

The adjacent thoroughfares of Bedford Street, King Street and Henrietta Street all had fine houses with eminent tradesmen, while Bedford House had a yard to the front for coaches and an extensive garden to the rear with stables and terracing.

Many fair monuments adorned the church due to its rich associations including a white marble statue to Petrus Lelius d.1680 by Gibbons (who also did the pulpit), the family of George Villiers of Brooksby, Leicester 1683/84, and Dame Margerie the widow of Sir Edmond Fortescue of Valiput, Devon d.1687. In the churchyard was that to Marmaduke Conway a Royalist and servant of the Royal family who d.1717 aged 108 years.

Amongst its admirers were Lord Burlington's circle and much attention was lavished on the venerated building. Thomas Hardwick the *parish surveyor* estimated repairs would cost £10,300 in 1788 and the vestry asked Pitt the P.M. for more funds. This included a cupola and new reredos for the east end sculpted by Thomas Banks friend of Hardwick, but there was a serious fire in 1795 when much of the interior was destroyed.

Regarding the piazza a fruit and vegetable market was present from the 1500s, but the 6th Duke cleared away the old sheds and stalls, then Charles Fowler designed a neo-Classical building in 1828-30 (with new roof in 1872). Its large open space with shops and galleries might be compared for significance to the Piece Hall at Halifax (1779).

In the 19th century all the original houses disappeared then William Butterfield made major changes to the church in 1871-72. He removed the box pews, side galleries, and most wall monuments then installed decorated pilasters and ephemera, while the seating fell from 832 to 528 places. However this work did not receive universal approval.

Henry Clutton produced a new plan to return to Palladian ideals in 1875-76, the work carried out over the next ten years. This included removal of the bell turret and rejection of a scheme by the 8th Earl to dispense with the portico. Clutton explained that it was this which integrated the church with the piazza - and was the genius of Jones!

St. Michael's, Burleigh Street was demolished in 1905 and the vicarage was taken; while Shaw wrote *Pygmalion* in 1913 with the opening scene in the portico, a lime-wood wreath by Gibbons was given by the Dean and Chapter for the screen in 1965, and the organ was restored by N.P. Mandor in 1967. It was dubbed as the *Actors Church* and has many plaques to famous stars such as Chaplin, Coward, Fields, Leigh and Novello.

"Arne Family" - The Puritans suppressed public entertainment but Charles II licensed two patent theatres for serious drama. One was at Lincoln's Inn (Lisle's Tennis Court) in 1661/95 and the second at the Theatre Royal, Drury Lane in 1663. After the former had success with Gay's *The Beggar's Opera* the profits built Covent Garden (Royal Opera Ho.) in 1732, and these were the main centres for acting until the Theatre Act (1843).

Thomas Arne a box numberer of Covent Garden married Mary Thursfield at St. Mary Woolnoth in 1681 then lived at Islington and St. George's, Southwark, but ended up in the Marshalsea. His son Thomas (1682-1736) a theatre servant and upholsterer married Mary Sharpe prior to 1703 and Anne Wheeler at the Mercers Chapel in 1707.

The latter had a number of theatrical children and Thomas *Augustine* Arne (1710-78) who was born at King Street took the middle name due to his Catholic faith. He went to Eton and was intended for the law, but was drawn into English opera and Drury Lane through his sister Susannah who was a distinguished contralto. In addition their siblings Esther and Isabella also sang on a professional basis.

Theophilus Cibber actor and playwright, son of Colley theatre manager and laureate, married Jane Johnson at St. Benet's in 1725 then Susannah Arne by a Catholic priest at an *Embassy Chapel* on 21 April 1734. To complete the duet Thomas Arne married Cecilia Young, a singer and pupil of Geminiani, at Lincoln's Inn on 15 March 1737 - although her father Charles a famous organist objected to his faith.

Arne resided at Lincoln's Inn Fields writing operas and masques and did masses for the Sardinian Chapel, whereas *Masque of Alfred* with "Rule Britannia" written after Vernon's victory was performed at Cliveden home to patron Frederick, Prince of Wales in 1740. He collaborated with David Garrick, his apprentice C. Burney was a musical historian, and his only son Michael was also a composer. He died at Bow Street in 1778.

C. 30 December 1682 Thomas s. of Thomas Arne by Mary his wife
22 or 26 February 1702/03 Mary d. of Thomas Arne by Mary his wife
28 May 1710 Thomas s. of Thomas Arne by Ann his wife
28 Feby 1713/14 Susannah Maria d. of Thos Arne by Anne his wife

B. 4 April 1693 Mary wife of Thomas Arn in ye church
24 December 1713 Thomas Arne from ye Marshalsea
28 January 1732/33 Jane wife of Theophilus Cibber
17 June 1736 Thomas Arne from St. Giles in the Fields
22 June 1757 Anne Arne wido from St. Martin in the Fields
15 March 1778 Thomas Arne bur

Arne Tablet on the north wall.

St. Paul's, Covent Garden (main register)

Apart from such theatricals there were a number of residents of note. Robert Harley was born in Bow Street and a prominent Whig and Tory politician, being the Chancellor and Lord Treasurer. He also promoted literature and was a patron of the Scriblerus Club thus he met with Arbuthnot, Defoe, Gay, Manley, Pope, Swift and Henry St. John, and was created 1st Earl of Oxford. His only son Edward by his wife Elizabeth Foley developed Marylebone, while his granddaughter was married to the Duke of Portland.

Mary Pierrepont the daughter of the 5th Earl of Kingston upon Hull a privy councillor was a prolific letter writer, and through her friendship with Anne Montagu married her brother Edward Wortley Montagu. Initially she was in the country but this changed when her husband became M.P. for Westminster and Ambassador to Istanbul in 1716-18. Her letters recording Eastern life and travel were both acclaimed and descriptive.

Thomas Chippendale married at St. George's, Mayfair in 1748 and designed high quality furniture at St. Martin's Lane, although he also resided at Kensington and Hoxton. His son Thomas continued to run the business after he died in 1779, however had to leave the premises due to bankruptcy in 1813 - but left an important legacy.

St. Paul's (interior) with masterpiece by Turner a favourite son, and **W.S. Gilbert** who was "the very model of a modern major general."

In addition to these J.M.W. Turner the son of a wig-maker was born in Maiden Lane, south of Covent Garden, in 1775 - a plaque on a modern building demarks the site. He entered the Royal Academy Schools in 1789 and had an interest in architecture but soon concentrated on painting, travelling to the Continent and residing in Chelsea. Likewise the dramatist W.S. Gilbert son of a naval surgeon was born in the parish in 1837.

Regarding marriages consecrated at the church these included John Wall Callcott a most eminent composer of glees (see Kensington), and Ralph Wedgwood a stationer who had links to St. Clement Danes and moved to 11 Castelnau Villas, Barnes (d.1866).

Other residents in the registers included Margaret Ponteus the first victim of the plague, Samuel Butler poet who sold works to Pepys, Sir Peter Lely a portrait painter who came from Holland, Grinling Gibbons the famous sculptor and Elizabeth his wife, and Charles Christian Reisen son of a silversmith who was a noted engraver of intaglios under his patron Robert Harley and had a collection of prints, medals and curios.

The writer Jane Austen stayed with her brother at 10 Henrietta Street in 1813-14 when visiting publishers John Murray, and another plaque by Bedford Street states, "Charles Dickens as a boy worked here 1824-25." A tablet at William IV Street and Chandos Place records: "The first stone of Charing Cross Hospital laid by Charles, Duke of Richmond knight of the garter, postmaster general and vice president on 27 June 1831."

C. 6 December 1661 Robert Harley e. sonn of Sr Edward Harley kt of the Hon Order of the Bath and Lady Abigail his wife borne the 5th of the same monthe
26 May 1689 Mary d. of Evelyn Pierpoint Esq. by the Lady Mary his wife
23 April 1749 Thomas son of Thomas Chippendale by Catherine his wife
14 May 1775 Joseph Mallad [sic] William son of William Turner by Mary his wife
11 January 1837 William Schwenck the son of William and Ann Mary Bye Gilbert of Southampton Street gent born 18 November

M. 14 July 1791 John Wall Callcott o.t.p. bach and Elizabeth Mary Hutchins o.t.s. spin by banns by Edward Embry curate pres J. Callcott, William Smith, John Gold
23 March 1818 Ralphe Wedgwood the younger o.t.p. bach married Hannah Englishe of St. Clement Danes spin minor by lic consent of Isaac Englishe her lawful father by Francis Wm. Johnson Vickery cur. wit. Susanna English, R. Wedgwood sen [sic]

B. 12 April 1665 Margaret daughter of Dr. John Ponteus in church
27 September 1680 Samuell Butler Esq. 25 September
7 December 1680 Sir Peter Lely knight in the church
30 December 1719 Elizabeth wife of Grinlin Gibbons
10 August 1721 Grinlin Gibbons (also five children baptized 1678-83)
19 December 1725 Charles Christian Reisen

Spring Garden Chapel

Simon Osbaldeston was "keeper of the Springe Garden and the bowling greene there" in 1631, but it was closed due to disorder by 1646 - although Evelyn said he went there ten years later. The section east of Arlington House was then divided into building plots, and the bowling-green became a garden for the Admiralty Office in 1694. There was a serious fire at Whitehall Palace four years later thus the houses became official residences.

Indeed, Edward Southwell then re-planned the area from 1730-55 and built properties on three floors with a stone cornice, whilst he also built a chapel at the corner of New Street for the local inhabitants in 1731. His heirs held the rights until it was transferred to St. Martin's in 1828, at which time it was dedicated as St. Matthew's.

Sir Robert Taylor lived nearby and may have been involved in the chapel design. This comprised a brick exterior with stone quoins, moulded cornice, a northeast porch with pediment, and a domed-cupola with Doric columns and a bell. The shape was irregular and the altar/chancel was in an alcove with elliptical arch to the southeast. There were also galleries to the north and west, and a flat roofed covering above.

The chapel held 300 but the site was acquired by the Admiralty in 1882 and it became a store for records. An annex was added to the naval building and an opening created from The Mall out into Charing Cross in 1891. The church itself was demolished in 1903, and Sir Aston Webb R.A. designed the notable Admiralty Arch in 1910.

Soho (area)

The fields between St. Giles and St. Martin's were mainly used for grazing, but Henry VIII set them aside for a Royal hunting ground in 1536 at which time cries of "Tally-Ho" and "So-Ho" rent the air. Robert Sydney, 2nd Earl of Leicester obtained a section to the south and built a mansion on Leicester Fields enclosing the site by 1635. The remainder then passed to Henry Jermyn, 1st Earl of St. Alban's for building purposes in the 1660s and it devolved to William, 1st Earl of Portland later that century.

The Earls of Leicester and Portland hoped to develop the district in a similar fashion to Bloomsbury and St. James's, thus King (Soho) Square was built to the north in the 1670s. A statue of Charles II by C.G. Cibber was placed at the centre and Robert Frith built a large property No. 31-32 at the southwest corner in 1677-80. This was home to the Earl of Bolingbroke, Sir Cloudesley Shovell, Sir Joseph Banks in 1776-1820 and the Linnaean Society from 1821-57 (demolished in 1936 - a tablet marks the site). [15]

However this was the only fashionable square erected, and after the gentry had departed the area became home to immigrants especially Huguenots. It was a poor enclave among richer districts with courts, tenements and music halls, and James and Samuel Wyatt built The Pantheon assembly rooms and theatre on Oxford Street (1772-1937).

Its boundaries were quite clearly delineated by Swallow Street to the west, Seven Dials to the east - an intersection (like Five Points, New York) whose notoriety was highlighted by Dickens, Oxford Street to the north and Leicester Fields to the south. Indeed, it was to become even more isolated after the arrival of Regent Street (1814-25), and Charing Cross Road and Shaftesbury Avenue (1877-86).

Regarding the area to the south, the premier building Leicester House was the residence of George II in 1717-27 and his son Frederick, Prince of Wales (1707-51) from 1742. It became a court for *alternative politics*, whilst the latter was a great promoter of the Arts supporting an opera company which opposed Handel at Drury Lane. Likewise he was a patron of James Thomson and Thomas Arne who gave us "Rule Britannia."

Leicester Square - the Royal palace in 1750 and pleasure gardens in 1880.

---

[15] The statue was removed during landscaping of the square in 1875 and went to an island in the garden of Grim's Dyke, Harrow home of Frederick Goodall an artist. The house was bought by W.S. Gilbert in 1890 and his widow Lady Gilbert returned the statue in 1938. Later associations included the F.A. who were present in 2000-09 - between Lancaster Gate and Wembley.

Leicester Fields declined and the house was demolished in 1792 but the area remained a centre for entertainments. The Sans Souci Theatre was to the north in 1796-1830, and the Royal Panopticon for Science opened to the east in 1854 but became the Alhambra Music Hall in 1857, later being managed by C. Morton. The *Great Globe* of James Wyld was at the centre from 1851-62 and was replaced by gardens with a fountain.

Just to the east at Wood Yard, Castle Street between Long Acre and Seven Dials was a brewery started in the 1650s which traded as Gyfford & Co. until 1787. Joseph Delafield arrived there from Whitbread's at the latter date and introduced steam power, whereas Harvey Christian Combe joined the company bringing further innovative ideas.

Combe, Delafield & Co. was very successful and the buildings soon occupied a large plot between the modern Neal, Langley and Sheldon Streets. Sir Charles Flower and his son James became partners in 1818, whereas Joseph Bonsor joined in 1852 injecting a sum of £80,000 - part of the capital of £400,000. At his decease in 1873 his sons Henry Cosmo and Alexander George Bonsor took over and a merger created Watney, Combe and Reid in 1898, whereas the premises (still present) closed seven years later.

However, local problems were highlighted by Dr. John Snow a sceptic of the miasma theory regarding cholera epidemics. He discussed this with Rev. Henry Whitehead curate of St. Luke's, Berwick Street, and identified the source as a water pump on Broad Street (now Broadwick) in 1854 - a replica pump near the site commemorates this.

All Saints, Margaret Street

This significant building is more correctly located in Marylebone, however being close to the bustle of Oxford Market and not far from Carnaby and Broadwick Streets it seems to have a suitable *church-niche* in this over-crowded part of Soho. Indeed its architecture was designed for such a restricted, urbanised location.

The Margaret Chapel was established in the southeast of Marylebone by the 1770s, and was on the north side of the street opposite to the historic Marylebone Passage. It then came to prominence under Rev. Frederick Oakeley who advocated the Oxford Movement and its liturgical and social practices from the 1830s. A large congregation often attended and amongst the crowd were William Butterfield and W.E. Gladstone.

As a result a new Gothic-style church was designed by the architect Butterfield utilising a "model plan." Its aim being to reflect the ideals of design and furnishings advocated by the Ecclesiological Society and worship and pastoral care of the Oxford Movement. In fact he had a difficult conundrum - since he was asked to fit a church, vicarage, clergy college and choir school around a courtyard in an area just 100 feet square!

The foundation was laid by Dr. Edward Pusey and the church was built in 1850-59, while the architect succeeded with flying colours and fulfilled all the requirements. It had many accolades being re-created at St. Alban's, Holborn and John Ruskin noted, "It is the first piece of architecture, built in modern days, which is free from all signs of timidity or incapacity… it challenges fearless comparison with the noblest works of anytime."

Little expense was spared in glorifying the Faith and it had ornate pillars of Aberdeen granite on marble plinths - with alabaster capitals and clerestory windows above. John Betjeman a future admirer pronounced, "It was here in the 1850s that the revolution in architecture began." Indeed many features survive from the original work.

All Saints, Margaret Street remains one of Butterfield's finest High Church creations.

Entering the door examples of Butterfield's paintwork can be seen in the baptistry and also in the ceiling with a pelican. Yet the layout of nave at 63 feet and chancel at 38 feet completely conceals the limitations of site - always giving an appearance of space.

All of the emphasis was placed on the Eucharist thus the focus is towards the choir and altar from every angle, while the pulpit of marble cost £400 and although secondary still stressed the importance of preaching. A low wall separated the sanctuary from the nave and the altar-piece was painted by William Dyce but replaced by Ninian Comper in 1909, who also added further decorative panels on each side and a new organ.

The Lady Chapel left of the pulpit was added by Comper in 1911 and the tile picture on the north wall commemorates William Upton Richards, minister from 1845-73 during the rebuilding. The great west window was replaced under Butterfield's direction in 1877 and below it are panels to Rev. Berdmore Compton the vicar from 1873-86.

There is just one exposed façade on the south side and the ornate banding of the court-yard with its Gothic lines and clergy building are towered over by the 227 feet spire. This is higher than the western towers of Westminster Abbey and exemplifies in its skilful design the aims of the Ritualists as in Matthew 28.19, "Make disciples of all Nations."

Wells Street Scotch Church - There was a Presbyterian church located just to the east on Marybone Place (Wells Street) in 1753-1875, and nearby was St. Andrew's built by S. Daukes in 1846 but re-erected at Kingsbury in 1934. Rev. Alexander Waugh (1754-1827) son of a Berwickshire farmer arrived at the former in 1782 and had some success, sitting on the committee that began the L.M.S and touring the country. He died at Salisbury Place and had a marble tablet in the church and memorial at Bunhill Fields.

His son George married Mary Walker and was a chemist at 177 Regent Street then was appointed pharmacist to Queen Victoria. Their children who included Fanny, Alexander, Marion Edith and Alice Gertrude were baptized there and at Marylebone, being related to Woolner and Holman Hunt. The parents then moved to Paddington and Hampstead and have a memorial at Kensal Green (d.1873). Evelyn Waugh, grandson of Alexander j., was a prolific writer his works including the Pre-Raphaelites and *Brideshead Revisited*.

C. 20 March 1801 George Waugh s. Alexander and Mary Neill of Marylebone b. 11 Feb

St. Anne's, Soho

With the development of housing in the former hunting field a parish was needed, which covered an area from Oxford Street to Leicester Square, and Wardour Street across to Charing Cross Road. This was bounded to the west by the new St. James's parish which had a burying ground above Broad Street (later a workhouse), and to the east by St. Giles in the Fields - in particular the converging junction of Seven Dials.

A church was begun to the west at Kemp's Field by Wren or his apprentice William Talman in 1677. This was of a basic basilica-design and Bishop Henry Compton once a tutor to Princess "Anne" consecrated it on 21 March 1686. It also had a 70-foot high tower and wooden spire, but the building was not finished until 1718. By then it was surrounded by dense housing in a block between Prince (Wardour), Dean, Compton and King Streets - with narrow alleyways leading through to its western yard.

A school was started in 1699 and two organs arrived at this time from the chapel at St. James's Palace (who had too many!). In fact William Croft was the first organist and later went to the Chapel Royal and Westminster Abbey. During his sojourn there he composed the hymn "St. Anne," later set to a poem *O God Our Help in Ages Past* by Isaac Watts. Strype noted the cost of building remained below £5,000, while there was a chapel in the parish like at St. James's, as well as others for the French nation (see below).

Regarding the church memorials these included ones to: Thomas Agar Esq. surveyor general to Charles II and James II 1687, Grace the wife of Hender Mouldsworth Esq. Governor of Jamaica 1687, Sir John Lanier lieutenant general died Flanders 1692, James Hays apothecary to William III 1701, and Lady Grace Pierrepont daughter of Henry the Marquess of Dorchester (and a relative of Mary Pierrepont) 1703.

The tower was found to be unstable and was rebuilt by Samuel P. Cockerell designer of Admiralty House in 1801-03. This had a lower level of brick with vestry/robbing room, whilst above was a Portland stone bell-chamber and moulded brass cupola. The church became less isolated due to Shaftesbury Avenue and had a lengthy musical tradition, but burnt-out in September 1940 and worship continued nearby and at St. Thomas's, Regent Street (with which it combined). There were plans to keep the ruins as a memorial, but the east wall was demolished in 1953 and the tower partially restored in 1979.

Eventually the complex was rebuilt in 1991 including a social centre, houses, garden, and chapel (at the east end) - which contains the original foundation stone laid by Henry Compton (1677) and St. Anne watch-house (1801). Much of the work was encouraged by the *St. Anne Society* and there were literary links, while Centrepoint Charity was started there. Just south of the church is the modern China Town on Gerrard Street.

"The Soho Society" - A number of notables had links including Benjamin Duterrau sen a clockmaker (see St. Martin's), William Duke of Gloucester and Edinburgh a favourite brother of George III (born 1738), and Edward Harley cousin of the 2nd Earl.

Regarding burials the poet John Dryden lived at the refined 43 Gerrard Street (plaque) and was removed to Westminster Abbey, whereas Sir Edmund Andros was governor of New York province from 1674-81 and of the wider New England in 1686-89. The latter was generally in conflict with the Puritans who abolished Christmas and other festivities, and was thus removed but was later a governor in Maryland and Virginia.

On a more mysterious note Theodore Baron Neuhoff a German adventurer, soldier, spy and alchemist arrived in Corsica to help fight for freedom against Genoa in 1736. He was crowned "King of Corsica" but left for London at the end of the year, then went in the King's Bench Prison due to insolvency and died penniless. Despite this he became a folk hero and friend John Wright an oilman of Compton Street erected a memorial and Horace Walpole gave the inscription. A modern version is on the south tower.

Rev. David Williams was born in Caerphilly and initially went to a dissenting meeting house in Frome, but became acquainted with Garrick and began a school in Chelsea. He lectured at the Margaret Chapel from 1776-77, but often used quotes from authors and talked in a coffee house at Charing Cross. After establishing the (Royal) Literary Fund for distressed talents in 1790, he ran the charity at 36 Gerrard Street from 1811.

However, the most poetic link was William Hazlitt son of a Unitarian minister who was born in Maidstone in 1778 and went to Boston, U.S.A. with his father. He then attended the short-lived Hackney Unitarian College where he developed interests in philosophy and met with William Godwin. But after he heard Coleridge preach at Shrewsbury near to his father's home he was inspired in both painting and poetry.

Hazlitt married Sarah Stoddart a friend of the Lambs at Holborn in 1808 and took a retreat at Winterslow, while he worked as a journalist and knew leading figures of the day. However he was divorced and re-married in Scotland, went to France and Italy, and fell into sombre moods. He had rooms in Chancery Lane, Bouverie Street and Frith Street but died penniless and has memorials on the tower and to the north. In addition Thomas Hearne (1744-1817) a watercolour artist lived nearby at 6 Meard Street (plaque).

C. 18 February 1741/42 Benjamin Duterau son of James and Mary b. 3 February
25 November 1743 His R.H. William Henry son of their R.H. the Prince and Princess of Wales was born [at Leicester House] on 14th and baptized 25th of the same

M. 16 March 1724/25 Edward Harley Esq. of Lincoln's Inn and Martha Morgan of St. James Westminster by licence [3rd Earl of Oxford]
8 April 1766 Benjamin Duterrau married Sarah Culverwell a minor b.o.t.p. by lic. by M.M. Merrick curate pres. E. Culverwell, Sarah Pine

B. 2 May 1700 John Dryden
27 February 1713/14 Sr. Edmund Andros m
15 December 1756 Baron des Newhoff of Chapel St. m
6 July 1816 David Williams Esq. of Gerrard Street, 74
23 September 1830 William Hazlitt of Frith Street, 52

St. Anne's - W. Hazlitt, south entrance and tower by Cockerell.

Other Soho Churches - The area briefly had a Venetian chapel in Dean Street and four French churches - the one on Crown Street becoming St. Mary's in 1854-1934. There was also a chapel on Oxford Street beside John Trotter's *Soho Bazaar* (present from 1816-89) and a Welsh Presbyterian chapel by James Cubitt on Charing Cross Road.

Orange Street Chapel - Just above the Royal Mews were the Duke of Monmouth's stables and here Col. Thomas Panton built some properties in the 1670s, while Leicester Fields Huguenot Temple was situated on Orange Street from 1693. [16]

Isaac Newton lived next door and went with his niece Catherine Barton to hear Jacques Saurin, "whose genius was equalled only by the ancient prophets." While Rev. Jean Pierre Stehelin minister in 1736-53 spoke 17 languages, and Rev. Charles de la Guiffardiere was a favourite at court - reading French to Queen Charlotte and her daughters. [17]

Friends of Rev. Augustus Montague Toplady secured part possession during the revival and he preached in 1776-78, publishing *Rock of Ages* which was first sung there. It was then sold to Thomas Hawkes as a Congregational chapel in 1787, the first minister being Rev. John Townshend. An adjacent property was obtained on St. Martin's Street in 1790 to extend the church and the pulpit and organ were removed to the east end.

There was a stucco façade and central porch with fluted Doric columns, whereas the nave had three bays, two tiers of arched windows, Corinthian pilasters and entablature. Inside there was a flat ceiling with octagonal lantern, a gallery on cast iron columns, and a higher gallery above the organ - the chapel providing seating for 700 people.

Jemima Luke the wife of Rev. Samuel Luke wrote *I think when I read that sweet story of old* at the church in 1841, and it revived under Rev. Isaac Harthill a member of the historical and philosophical society. The old building was demolished in 1913 but the fittings were kept and a new chapel was established next to the library in 1929. This was then run by the deacons however did not join the U.R.C. in 1973 (see picture p. 313).

St. Luke's, Berwick Street - James II incorporated ten French ministers for refugees in September 1688 and two churches of La Patente were set up, one at Berwick Street just west of the Soho parish boundary and the other at Spitalfields. Strype noted the liturgy was in French but the ministers were Episcopal and appeared in canonical habits of the English clergy - the communicants being foreign tradesmen and gentry.

Berwick Street opened in 1689 in a leased building but was over-assessed for rates and some moved to Little Chapel (Sheraton) Street in October 1694 - prefixed L'Ancienne and Petite. The former renewed its lease but had dispersed by about 1707.

---

[16] Orange Street was famous for a tennis court built by Simon Osbaldeston in c.1634. It fell into disuse after 1735 and was used as a theatre, but when tennis revived became H.Q. of the game from 1800-66 (a tablet on the wall of the court once stated "James Street 1673").

[17] 35 St. Martin's Street owned by the church was built in 1695 and Isaac Newton lived there with an observatory in 1710-27. Dr. Charles Burney was resident in 1774 and his *History of Music* was written there, whilst daughter Fanny (Madame d'Arblay) wrote of Newton and *Evelina* in 1778. It was pulled down in 1913 despite Lord Macaulay's assertion, "It will be well-known as long as our island retains any trace of civilisation!" The panelling and fixtures from the fore-parlour now grace the Isaac Newton Room at Babson College, Massachusetts, whilst the site is occupied by Westminster Reference Library and there is a tablet to the scientist's memory.

In addition Le Quarré Chapel was first recorded at Soho Square in 1690 and moved to a site in Berwick Street, just above La Patente, in 1694. This was to be more long-lasting and the Swallow Street congregation joined them in 1709 followed by Castle Street, St. Martin's Lane in 1762. However they departed for Bourchier Street in 1769 and the site was converted to an auction room and later on a theatre.

Meanwhile, La Patente was purchased by the rector of St. James's in 1707 as a chapel of ease, but costs of £1,100 nearly stopped the plan. Indeed there was much rebuilding over the years and the organ was purchased from Archbishop Tenison's Chapel in 1766, whilst Thomas Hardwick attended to the structure in 1794. The freehold was purchased in 1801 and many poor people came to the area displaced by street improvements.

A new church was begun in 1835 and Earl Grey laid the foundation, then Edward Blore designed a building at £14,000 and it was consecrated as St. Luke's on 23 July 1839. Two years later it had an ecclesiastical district, but was the most densely populated in London and pew rents were eventually abandoned. A large west gallery was later reduced in size. This was a rectangular Gothic building with seven bays and typical of a Commissioners Church but was demolished and joined to St. Anne's in 1935.

St. Patrick's, Soho Square - "Carlisle House," just east of the square, was built by the Earl of Carlisle in the 1690s but came into the possession of Mrs. Cornelys in 1760. She was a Venetian lady with a child by Casanova and an opera singer of large social circle. However, despite such attributes she fell into debt and was sent to prison.

Father Arthur O'Leary was an assistant in the embassy chapel at Spanish Place and with some others purchased a 62-year lease on the vacant house after the Relief Act in 1792. The ceiling was removed and two galleries inserted, but there was little seating. It then catered for the inhabitants of the Rookery a notorious area between St. Giles and Seven Dials, whilst 9/10th's of the parish register entries were of poor Irish Catholics.

A major requiem was held there for Pope Pius VI and a number of local schools were attached which joined together at Great Chapel Street. The present church with its tunnel vault, Romanesque arches, apse-like sanctuary and tower was designed by John Kelly of Kelly & Birchall in 1893 - an unsuccessful applicant for Brompton Oratory.

West Street Chapel - To the east near Seven Dials was a Huguenot church called La Pyramide with round-headed windows, three galleries and a lantern built in c.1700. John and Charles Wesley leased it as their first chapel in the West End with the adjacent house in 1743, but took some new premises at Great Queen Street in 1798. It was then used as a free chapel and school, while St. Giles purchased it for £5,000 as All Saints in 1888 but it closed due to war damage. The top of Wesley's three-decker pulpit a reading desk went to St. Giles, and the building remains as business premises (with plaque).

London
Central West

Of religion and politics this was the centre of power at Westminster with both Abbeys and Cathedrals of note. Nearby were some Royal connections and related births of historical moment, whilst those of the highest calibre such as Churchill and Roosevelt ingratiated the church doors.

Many architects made their mark in terms of property and prestige thus we witness those all time greats Inigo Jones, Sir Christopher Wren, Thomas Hardwick and the mediaeval mason of the cloister. Here were the rich and famous William Pitt, the Duke of Wellington, Benjamin Disraeli as well as some foreign nom de plumes "Maldonado" and "Sancho."

On a more sublime lyrical note one might find Blake's green and pleasant pastures, Pepys' diary, Cibber's theatricals, and Shelley's elopement. Such captivating images are depicted in the coloured tones of Sandby, while our rights and freedoms are eloquently pronounced by John Wilkes.

It was a place of grand houses, grandiose vistas and even grander weddings with some subterfuge at St. George's Mayfair to boot. Not forgetting a few Shakespearean diversions, an intrepid explorer dressed up in a grey coat and timekeepers extraordinaire to maintain the balance of power.

The Christie memorial in **St. James's Gardens**, and a duet of **parish markers** located on the old palace near to the Queen's Chapel.

Mayfair (churches)

In earlier times St. Martin in the Fields, itself once part of Westminster, administered an extremely large parish up to Oxford Street and across to Hyde Park and Sloane Street. However, St. Margaret's, formed a smaller enclave south of St. James's Park.

As the population developed beyond the precincts of Westminster new parishes were created, in particular: St. Anne's which was situated to the east and St. James's serving its own elite district. There was a strict correlation between the arrival of 'modern' housing and church building, thus the development of the Grosvenor Estate and its Square in the 1720s coincided with the erection of St. George's Hanover Square nearby.

The latter originally came under St. Martin's, and its new parish reached right down to the river - covering the fields that were later developed as Belgravia and Pimlico. All of this was the land of the Grosvenor Estate, totalling some 500 acres - with a fifth being above Piccadilly and the remainder on five fields below Knightsbridge.

A May Fair was established in the locality of Shepherd Market in 1686 but was removed to Bow, due to its demeaning nature, in 1764. However, the name stuck and many large houses were built in the district as well as speculative developments, whilst the two main parish churches were supplemented by a large number of chapels as revealed.

Queen's Chapel (St. James's)

There was a Royal presence in the neighbourhood for many centuries and the Palace of Westminster with its hall and chapel was home to the monarch from before the Conquest. Henry VIII then requisitioned York Place residence of Wolsey, Archbishop of York and built Whitehall Palace on the site in 1530. He transferred governmental functions there whereas it boasted wine cellars, bowling greens, tilt-yards and tennis courts.

The King also took over the leper hospital of St. James the Less in 1532, and there he built another palace in the Tudor-style with a gatehouse and red-brick buildings around several courtyards. A number of early Royal weddings took place in these palaces at or near Westminster, but are sometimes wrongly attributed to the Abbey.

With regard to this, the *Chapel Royal* had two designations: one a department of the Royal Household with its choir made famous under William Byrd and Thomas Tallis; the second referring to the actual buildings located within various properties. These included the Chapel Royals at Somerset House, Whitehall and St. James's Palace.

Inigo Jones also designed the Queen's Chapel for Charles I and his wife Henrietta on the east side of the St. James's complex in 1625-28. This was a refined Palladian edifice with the first Venetian window, and reminiscent of the Queen's House built for Anne of Denmark in 1614-17. The architect also re-developed Whitehall, and in particular added the Banqueting House (still survives) with ceiling by Rubens from 1622-34.

Later developments saw Mary and Anne born at St. James's in the 1660s, then Wren designed a chapel for Whitehall but it all burnt down in 1698. William III also purchased Kensington (Nottingham) House and St. James's was the main palace in the Hanoverian era. A fire destroyed the east side in 1809 and Clarence House was added in 1827, while Marlborough Road was built in 1856 - leaving the chapel by Marlborough House.

Buckingham Palace and **Marble Arch** dated 1837.

The Queen's Chapel was designed by Inigo Jones in 1625-28 but has a "non-Palladian" chimney!

Apart from this there were two other main buildings. Frederick Prince of Wales came into possession of Carlton House in 1732 and William Kent laid out the gardens, whilst his grandson George refurbished it at a cost of £60,000 from 1783-96 under the architect Henry Holland. The result was generally palatial and it was the residence of the Prince Regent until 1820, followed by the addition of Regent Street in 1825.

Meanwhile, the Manor of Ebury was a rural wasteland, while the hamlet of Eye Cross had fallen into decay. It was mostly sold in the reign of James I and fell to Hugh Audley except for a small mulberry garden retained to produce silk. Sir William Blake built the first house in 1624 then Lord Goring improved this with a garden in 1633, but after a fire it passed to Henry Bennet the 1st Earl of Arlington in 1674. He built Arlington House (now the south wing) and it was extended by the Duke of Buckingham from 1703.

His descendant sold Buckingham House to George III for £21,000 in 1761, a piece of legal manoeuvring aided by Royal ownership of the freehold on the mulberry garden. It was to be a residence for Queen Charlotte, like Somerset House, but when George IV came to the throne he transformed the building. John Nash carried out the initial work in 1826-29 but due to spiralling costs was replaced by Edward Blore.

The property comprised a western suite of rooms with two wings on a courtyard and at the centre was a grand *marble arch* entrance, thus it became the principal palace under Victoria in 1837. However after her marriage to Albert it was found inadequate and Blore designed a new eastern façade which was built by Thomas Cubitt in 1847. In addition a large ballroom and range of state rooms were added by Sir James Pennethorne.

The Marble Arch built by Nash, based on the Arch of Constantine at the Colosseum in Rome, was then moved to the corner of Hyde Park where it stands today. To complete matters, St. James's Park passed to Henry VIII as part of York Place and was drained and landscaped for exotic animals. John Nash later developed this with a less formal design, and The Mall became a tree-lined walkway similar to the Tuileries in Paris.

Queen's Chapel - C. 27 June 1630 Charles Stuart s. of Charles I and Henrietta Maria (d. of Henry VI of France) b. 29 May at St. James's by Wm. Laud, Bishop of London
24 November 1633 James Stuart s. of Charles I and Henrietta Maria b. 14 October

Whitehall Palace - M. 24 Feb. 1676/77 Christopher Wren and Lady Jane Fitzwilliam

St. James's Palace - 1677 William of Orange and Mary II by Bp. Henry Compton
1761 George III to Charlotte of Mecklenburg, 1795 George IV to Caroline of Brunswick
1840 Albert of Saxe-Coburg to Queen Victoria, 1893 George V to Mary of Teck

St. George's, Hanover Square

This fashionable district was situated east of Grosvenor Square and was developed in tandem with the church. Sir Richard Grosvenor and his brother Thomas were the sons of Mary Davies the heiress, and began the development with grid-like avenues in 1720. At the same time the Commissioners agreed to build St. George's which was constructed as a local initiative on land provided by General Steuart. In fact a design by James Gibbs was passed over in favour of one by John James their own surveyor.

The church was erected on a site below Hanover Square in 1720-25, but an attempt to include a vista from Hyde Park failed because the lines of Grosvenor and Maddox Streets were already laid out. Thus its grandeur was diminished and its regal façade was never set off in terms of location like St. Marylebone or St. Pancras.

Externally there was a grand portico with pediment, six fluted Corinthian columns and steps leading up to the main door. To the north was an exposed wall and to the east an irregular space on Maddox and Mill Streets - with a shallow chancel, Venetian window, twin supports, broken pediments and cornice. Inside was an opulent interior consisting of columns up to the galleries, low moulded barrel vault, and fine organ at the rear. The rich woodwork displayed churchwardens' names many of them viscounts &c.

George Friedrich Handel resided at 25 Brook Street from 1723-59 and was a regular worshipper, thus the *Handel Festival* is held there each year. It was also later used in the fiction of Conan Doyle and Bernard Shaw. The church survived in its original form and the parish was divided with the emergence of Belgravia and Pimlico, whilst there were some senior rectors and important proprietary chapels nearby (see p.164).

1725 Andrew Trebeck of Christchurch, Oxford also the vicar of Croydon 1720-27
1759 Charles Moss also Bishop of St. David's but left to be Bishop of Bath & Wells
1774 Henry R. Courtenay rector of Lee, Bishop of Bristol/Exeter bur. Grosvenor Chapel
1803 Robert Hodgson also Hillingdon, Dean of Chester/Carlisle ancestor of Elizabeth II
1845 Henry Howarth chaplain to the Queen introduced Ritual and helped the poor
1876 Edward Capel Cure canon of Windsor chaplain to the Queen who continued social work and opened the St. George's Institute in 1884, died in Cairo in 1890

St. George's, Hanover Square within the Grosvenor Estate had Viscounts as churchwardens.

Many society weddings took place here - "Please, get me to the church on time."

Local Environs - Hanover Square was home to several Tory aristocrats and has a statue to William Pitt the younger. Nearby in Savile Row there are plaques to Richard Brinsley Sheridan dramatist (14) and George Basevi architect (17) cousin of Disraeli.

With regard to Grosvenor Square, a grand façade was planned for the eastern side by Colen Campbell, but this was never built and most of the aristocratic residences were the result of individual designs. Campbell and Roger Morris both lived nearby and built No. 12 (also Wanstead/Waverley) for Chancellor John Aislabie in Palladian style in 1729; while Robert Adam rebuilt No. 26 for Edward Stanley, 11th Earl of Derby in 1773.

In addition John Adams established a house at Brook and Duke Streets from 1785-88 and from here sent an ambassador to the Court of St. James, thus Grosvenor Square was home to the American Embassy. Most of the original houses are departed and No. 12, a later residence of Lord Lytton, was demolished as "not important" in 1961.

Citizens of Note - With such American associations in mind Thomas Howard, 3rd Earl of Effingham was an army officer who resigned his commission in protest over the war and was also Governor of Jamaica. Later baptisms included de Crespigny a descendant of the Huguenots of Marylebone, Victoria and Alice daughters of the Queen whose brother Albert "Edward" was christened at St. George's, Windsor on 25 January 1842, and Robert Watson Willis member of Barnes F.C. and second secretary of the F.A.

C. 25 January 1745/46 Right Hon. Thomas Howard, Lord Howard s. of the Right Hon. Thomas Earl and Elizabeth Cs. [sic] of Effingham born 13th
4 July 1818 Claude William s. Augustus James Champion and Caroline de Crespigny of U. Grosvenor Street b. 25 June Esq. by E. Smyth vicar of Camberwell (see that parish)
10 February 1841 Victoria Adelaide Mary Louisa d. of H.M. Queen Victoria and H.R.H. Prince Albert of Buckingham Palace b. 21 Nov (also Alice Mary Maud 2 June 1843)
4 September 1843 Robert Watson s. of Robert and Eleanor Willis of Dover Street b. 26 January physician (also Frances de la Touche 1839 and Mary Watson 1841)

M. (18th C.) 20 May 1760 William Martin Esq. of St. Paul C.G. bach to Arabella Rowley o.t.p. spin special lic of Archbishop by John Oxford pres. Thos. Rowley, J. Rowley

20 February 1762 John Mayhew of St. James Westminster bach and Isabella Stephenson o.t.p. spin lic. AB of Canterbury by Thos. Vincent cur pres John Mayhew, Wm. Ince (On same day) William Ince of St. James Westminster bach and Ann Stephenson o.t.p. spin lic. AB of Canterbury by Thos. Vincent cur pres John Mayhew, Jno. Mayhew ⎤ Partners and sisters

5 December 1793 Augustus Frederick [Duke of Sussex] and Augusta Murray [d. of 4th Earl of Dunmore] b.o.t.p. banns by J. Downes curate pres Jno. Jones, Mary Jones
4 March 1797 John Allcock and Elizabeth Preston b.o.t.p. by banns by Thos. Ash cur. in the presence of John Cragg, Frances Sarah Woolley
22 April 1799 The Most Noble John Henry, Duke of Rutland of Belvoir Castle and R.H. Lady Elizabeth Howard of Castle Howard minor consent R.H. Frederick, Earl of Carlisle [5th Earl related to Byron] pres. "Carlisle," "Cawdor" and "Morpeth"
11 June 1799 John Shaw of St. Andrew's, Holborn and Elizabeth Hester Whitfield by licence by J. Greville A.M. curate pres of John Lender, Mary Halstead

Regarding such *society weddings* those in the early years included Capt. William Martin who married Arabella Rowley daughter of Sir William Rowley, Admiral of the Fleet; the partners Ince and Mayhew furniture and cabinet makers who were at Broad Street, Soho in 1763-83 and Marshall Street in 1783-1809; John Alcock a ship-owner and upholsterer of Sunderland the grandfather of John F. and Charles W. Alcock; and John Shaw senior the architect who trained under Gwilt and was a relative of Hardwick.

However, there were also marriages at the highest level but not without controversy. It was clear that being a Royal sibling might leave "time on one's hands" and Prince Henry, Duke of Cumberland a son of Frederick was born at Leicester House in 1745. He had a reputed marriage to Olive Wilmot in 1767, then a very costly affair with Lady Grosvenor in 1769, and an actual marriage to Anne Horton on 2 October 1771.

This was followed by the Royal Marriages Act (1772) which demanded consent of the *Sovereign* and was generally contravened including when Prince Augustus Frederick (sixth son of George III) married Lady Augusta Murray in Rome on 4 April 1793 and again at St. George's in London. This was done without the knowledge of the King and annulled under the Act the next year - although they remained together until 1801.

Marriages in the next century included the re-marriage of poet Shelley after elopement, Sir George Martin (s. of William) to the sister of Rev. George Lock minister of Lee, Rev. Joseph Wolff a Jewish missionary to a descendant of Robert Walpole, a young Disraeli, Samuel Parkes V.C. after "The Charge of the Light Brigade," Teddy Roosevelt a politician and rancher of North Dakota, and the daughter of Sir George Ferguson Bowen governor in the Ionian Islands, Australia, New Zealand, Mauritius and Hong Kong.

M. (19th C.) 24 March 1814 Percy Byshhe Shelley to Harriet Shelley (form Westbrook) spin a minor b.o.t.p. remarried by licence (the parties having been married by the rites of the Ch. of Scotland) in order to obviate all doubts that have arisen, or shall, or may arise touching, or concerning, the validity of the aforesaid marriage, by and with consent of John Westbrook father by Edwd. Williams cur pres John Westbrook, John Sternley

29 May 1815 Sir George Martin knight commander of the bath widr and Mary Augusta Lock spin b.o.t.p. licence by George Lock rector of Lee, Kent [signed with encircled G] witness William Lock, John Augustine, Elizabeth Lock

6 February 1827 Rev. Joseph Wolff clerk bach of St Mary le Bow and R.H. Georgiana Mary Walpole spin o.t.p. lic by Chas Simeon vicar Trinity, Cambs - nine witnesses

28 August 1839 Benjamin Disraeli full bach esq. M.P. of Park Street s. of Isaac Disraeli esq. and Mary Anne Lewis full widow of Grosvenor Gate d. of John Evans Capt. R.N. licence by W.H. Dickinson B.C.L. curate pres "Lyndhurst," William Scrope

13 February 1858 Samuel Parkes bach. soldier of Oxford Street son of Thomas labourer married to Ann Jeffrey spin of the same d. of Jonathan farmer banns by A.P. Whitmore presence of John White, Caroline Barnett

2 December 1886 Theodore Roosevelt 28 wid ranchman of Brown's Hotel, Dover St. to Edith Kermit Carow 25 spin of Buckland's Hotel, Brook St. lic by Charles E. Camidge, Canon of York witness Cecil A. Spring-Rice [best man], Emily Tyler Carow

18 October 1899 Robert Lydston Newman 34 bach gent 9 Great Cumberland Place to Alfreda Ernestine Alberta Bowen 30 spin of 41 Park Street by David Anderson witness J.M. Bowen, Robert M. Herbert, Lionel A. Newman, James Crichton-Stuart

Mount Street - St. George's was on a restricted site with no room for burials therefore Sir Richard Grosvenor provided an irregular plot at Mount Street in 1723. A workhouse was erected on the north side and plans were made for an attached chapel to the south, although this was eventually built to the west (see Grosvenor Chapel). In fact, there were still open fields beyond leading down to Piccadilly during the 1740s.

The churchyard, however, proved inadequate for the size of the parish and a five acre plot was rented by the churchwardens on Bayswater Road in 1763. This was situated in the area of Paddington just west of Connaught Square but never became part of that parish, and a chapel of St. George's was built adjacent to the site in 1765.

There were some further burials at Mount Street in particular those of important people in the Grosvenor Chapel until the 1830s, but both were closed like others in 1854. St. George's Chapel which had a cupola, round-headed windows and many monuments was disused until 1880, when it was renovated for domestic servants. It was replaced by the Ascension Chapel at the expense of Mrs. Emilia Russell Gurney from 1911-52.

The site itself remained closed whereas St. George's Fields was laid out for private use in c.1914 with allotments, tennis and archery - as witnessed by a nearby road. However, it was generally derelict and there was a bill in 1964 to change the use over to housing, and this was carried out with a gated development during the 1970s.

Colley Cibber (left), actor and poet laureate, was criticised by both Hogarth and Pope.

Paul Sandby (right) was acclaimed as "the father of the water-colour movement."

Of the parishioners, Colley Cibber who was born at Southampton Street, Bloomsbury in 1671 was an actor, manager and playwright connected with Drury Lane and appointed *Poet Laureate* by George II from 1730-57, whilst in later life he lived at Berkeley Square. Other burials at Mount Street included Lady Mary Wortley Montagu the letter writer and Garrett and Anne Wesley parents of the Duke of Wellington and William Wellesley-Pole. The father was a prominent Irish politician and the name was altered in c.1790.

John Wilkes was born at St. John's Square, Clerkenwell, in 1725 and through a dowry became an M.P. then published *The North Briton* against the King in 1762. Due to such libellous writings he fled to Paris but was then Lord Mayor in 1774, championed freedom of the press, became popular with the public, and supported American independence. He was considered a poor orator and fell out of favour, thus he took an eccentric property which he named "Villakin" at Sandown, Isle of Wight in 1788 (marked by a plaque).

At that time the settlement had just a few houses and in the garden was a Doric column with moving inscription to Charles Churchill, "divine poet and pleasant friend." Wilkes spent much of his time there entertaining, writing memoirs and bird watching but died at 30 Grosvenor Square and has "a statue to freedom" in Fetter Lane.

Regarding other burials, Rev. Laurence Sterne was born in Tipperary but spent time as a vicar in Yorkshire and travelled on the Continent, writing his most famous novel *The Life and Opinions of Tristram Shandy, Gentleman* in 1759. He died in his lodgings at 41 Old Bond Street in 1768 and was buried at St. George's Fields, Bayswater Road.

Likewise, Paul Sandby began life as a map-maker but became the leading advocate of watercolour painting and was a founder member of the Royal Academy. In fact he lived at 4 St. George's Row beside the chapel on Bayswater Road from 1772.

Grosvenor Chapel, Mount Street	**B.** 18 December 1757 Colley Cibber Esq. m 22 August 1762 Lady Mary Wortley Montagu w 29 May 1781 Garrett Westley, Earl of Mornington m 4 January 1798 John Wilkes man 17 Sept. 1831 Anne C. of Mornington St. Marylebone, 89
St. George's Fields	**B.** 22 March 1768 Lawrence Sterne m, G.S. Davids rector 15 November 1809 Paul Sandby m

St James's, Piccadilly

Henry Jermyn, 1st Earl of St. Alban's, was granted land for building near the palace in 1662, and developed a grid of streets on a square leading across to Haymarket. A parish church was built there by Wren in 1682-84 with carvings by Grinling Gibbons, and was reminiscent of his other City churches with red-brick façade and white quoins.

The tower was capped off by a spire, while the interior had low galleries on diminutive gold Corinthian columns with wood surrounds, leading to its chief glory a monumental barrel-vaulted ceiling. In some ways it was reminiscent of St. George's since the primary architectural activity was above, leaving the preaching and sacrament below.

Henry Compton, Bishop of London, consecrated the church on 13 July 1684 and Strype recorded that, "It is well adorned, has an excellent pair of organs, a curious font, and the galleries are well set off with tapestries and Persian carpets." The patronage alternated between the Bishop of London and Lord Jermyn (in a ratio of two to one), whereas Dr. Tenison the vicar of St. Martin's was appointed the first rector in 1686-92.

St. James's Square was home to the rich and famous but there were also tenements up to Oxford Street. This area was served by St. Luke's chapel from 1707 (see Soho), and a burial ground later a workhouse was above Broad Street. Likewise, the Oxendon Street chapel served the parish although it fell within the bounds of St. Martin's.

The total cost of the work was £7,000 including the steeple which was finished at the turn of the century. Indeed a large number of benefactors contributed to its munificence. The altar and woodwork was of cedar and portrayed flowers, doves, and pelicans; whilst the organ by Renatus Harris was donated by Queen Mary in 1691. It came from James's *Popish Chapel* at Whitehall which was begun in 1686 but was never required.

St. James's, Piccadilly (on Jermyn Street)

This "Wren Church" for the gentry of St. James's was built outside the City but had many similar features. Unlike St. Anne's, Soho it survives much in its original form.

There was a great clock presented by Henry Massey, a gilded vane and dials given by Mr. Highmore the Royal painter, and an altar costing £3,000 paid for by Sir Robert Geer. In addition Grinling Gibbons made some major contributions. These included a "new" font in 1686 the old one going to St. Anne's, woodwork for the altar and reredos in lime-wood (paid for by Geer), and the casing for the Royal organ from Whitehall.

A large number of monuments adorned the church including: Elizabeth wife of Col. Ben Fletcher the Governor of New York Province 1698 (chancel), and Mary le Coq who was gentlewoman to a French duchess of high standing living in St. James's 1702.

Of the ministers Rev. Samuel Clarke was born in Norwich in 1675 and was chaplain to the Bishop thus he became the Boyle Lecturer. He wrote religious items and translated Newton's *Opticks* then was appointed to St. Benet, Paul's Wharf in 1706 and St. James's in 1709. Other works were *Caesar's Commentaries* dedicated to the Duke of Marlborough and *The Scripture Doctrine of the Trinity* in 1712, while he died at the rectory in 1729.

Several repairs were carried out in the 18th century, but Thomas Hardwick did further renovations at £1,000 in 1788 and replaced the north door with a window in 1803-04, it being the first major change. He also advised on the tower with John Shaw due to a lean and cracking, whereas vestibules were created in 1856 and a new pulpit arrived in 1862. An outside pulpit was added to the north courtyard in 1902, then after some war damage the church was restored and the tower reduced in height during 1947-54.

Beside the door on Jermyn Street there is a plaque recording some of the worshippers in particular Defoe, Evelyn and Vanbrugh. Under the tower is a tablet to William Van de Velde and his son, Dutch marine artists in England from 1673 (erected by the Society for Nautical Research 1929). Opposite is a memorial to Charles Cotton of Beresford Dale a friend of Izaak Walton who wrote the second part of *The Compleat Angler*.

Inside the church at the northwest corner is a plaque to "William Blake artist, poet and visionary baptized in this church," and Memorial 1914-19 with Hon. Douglas A. Master of Kinnaird and Hon. Arthur M. Kinnaird M.C. of the Scots Guards. On the north wall is an original to William Yarrell, "Treasurer and Vice-President of the Linnaean Society, distinguished naturalist, author of illustrated works and a *Natural History of the British Isles*," and a modern one to Mary Beale artist of Pall Mall and protégé of Lely.

"Social Connections" - As with St. George's there were a large number of prominent residents and baptisms included Lord Stanhope, 4th Earl Chesterfield a Whig statesman and William Pitt, Earl of Chatham born Golden Square a Whig P.M. in 1766-68.

Later baptisms included: Charles Churchill who was born at Vine Street the poet and satirist so admired by John Wilkes, and Edgar Lubbock of the banking family from High Elms, Downe, Kent who appeared for the Wanderers and Old Etonians in the Cup Final. The latter was managing director of Whitbread's Brewery and deputy governor of the Bank of England, whilst from his large estate at Caythorpe, Lincolnshire he entertained various dignitaries of the age such as Waldorf Astor and Bache Cunard.

When considering grand houses in the locality there was no address of more prominence and prestige than 10 St. James's Square, at the corner of York Street. A blue plaque on the building records that, "Here lived three Prime Ministers: William Pitt Earl of Chatham, Edward Geoffrey Stanley Earl of Derby and William Ewart Gladstone."

The occupant after Gladstone was Arthur Fitzgerald Kinnaird son of Lord Kinnaird the great philanthropist and banker of 1-2 Pall Mall (East). The son was educated at Eton with the likes of Bonsor, Lubbock and Thompson and was a top soccer player being president of the F.A. from 1890-1923. He once stood on his head at the Oval to celebrate a famous victory over the professionals of Blackburn Rovers, and followed his father as Lord High Commissioner of the Church of Scotland and president of the Y.M.C.A. [1]

C. 9 October 1694 Phillip Dormer Stanhope of R.H. Lord Philip & Lady Eliz: 22 Sep

13 December 1708 William son of Robert Pitt esq. and Henrietta b. 15th

1 March 1731/32 Charles Churchill of Charles and Ann nat. 4th

11 December 1757 William Blake son of James and Catherine b. 28 Nov

27 June 1784 William Yarell son of Francis and Sarah b. 3rd

21 March 1847 Edgar son of John William and Harriet Lubbock of 23 St. James's Place bart born 22 February (also Alfred November 1845)

St. James's with font and organ case by Gibbons.

With a significant location by premier housing the church was the scene of many top weddings. A young Thomas Earnshaw was in business as a watchmaker at High Holborn near Red Lion Square (a plaque marks the site) then improved on Harrison's escarpment for marine chronometers and was married there. A year later came the wedding of John Hakewill a landscape/portrait painter who decorated the state rooms at Blenheim, and was the father of Henry (1771-1830) architect of St. Peter's, Eaton Square.

Other 18th century weddings included that of John Hunter surgeon who worked with his brother William in Great Windmill Street, then set up a practice in Golden Square and was appointed to St. George's Hospital. After making the acquaintance of Robert Boyne Home an army surgeon in Portugal during the Seven Years War (1756-63), he married his daughter then resided at Jermyn Street and Leicester Square (with statue).

In addition the registers record the marriages of: the parents of Lady Caroline Lamb "at home" who had links to Devonshire House, Philip Hardwick and Julia T. Shaw with two prominent architects in attendance, and Friedrich Wilhelm heir to the electorate of Hesse-Kassel which was lost to Prussia during the Austro-Prussian War.

M. (18th C.) 27 March 1769 Thomas Earnshaw and Lydia Theakston b.o.t.p. by licence of the Archbishop of Canterbury by Tho: Skinner a clerk in orders presence of Robert Johnstone, James Theakston, Mary Gardinere, Matthew Athis
9 September 1770 John Hakewill and Anna Maria Cook b.o.t.p. by licence Archbishop married by Tho: Skinner witness Minny Cook, Betsy Martin, Edward Hart
22 July 1771 John Hunter o.t.p. and Ann Home of St. Martin in the Fields licence from the Bishop of London by W. Parker rector presence of Robt. and Mary Home
10 May 1780 John Perigal married Jane Grellier b.o.t.p. banns by John Waring clerk in orders presence of Peter Grellier, Jo. Faivey [a jeweller of Coventry Street]

27 November 1780 Hon. Frederick Ponsonby commonly Lord Viscount Duncannon and the R.H. Lady Henrietta Frances Spencer a minor married with consent of the R.H. John Earl Spencer, father, *at his house* in St. James's Place by special lic. Archbishop of Canterbury by Charles Poyntz D.D., signed "Duncannon" and H.F. Spencer, in presence of "Devonshire," "Bessborough," "Althorp" [parents of Lady Caroline Lamb]

M. (19th C.) 2 January 1816 James Flower of St Luke Old Street esq. bach to Mary Jane Stirling o.t.p. spin minor consent of Sir Walter Stirling father by Samuel Carlisle pres of Walter Stirling, C. Flower, Georgina M. Stirling &c. [partner in Combe & Co.]
18 October 1819 Philip Hardwick o.t.p. and Julia Tufnell Shaw of St. Giles in the Fields a minor by licence with consent John Shaw esq. the father by Edward Repson off. minister witnessed by John Shaw [senior], Thomas Hardwick
4 January 1826 Sir Robert Arbuthnot KCB o.t.p. wid and Harriet Smith of St. Marylebone licence by Geo Brett pres B.W. and Esther Burdett [general - Peninsular War]
31 May 1827 William Cuffay and Mary Ann Marwell b.o.t.p. by banns by Thom Murray Perowne curate both signed witness H. Thos Newby, Ann Aniele (see St. Martin's)

23 September 1856 Friedrich Wilhelm Prince of Hanen, Ct. Schaumburg bach Lt. Life Guards of St. James's son of "F.W." 1st Duke of Hesse Castle to Auguste Aloise Susanna Georgina Birnbaum minor consent o.s. d. Carl Birnbaum Esq. lic by Philip Birney curate signed "F.W. 1st von Hanen & Grasson" pres. Charles Thomas, Fredk. Green

Regarding burials these included Dr. John Arbuthnot a writer of Dover Street who inspired Pope and Swift, William Poyntz consul general of Lisbon and uncle of the 1st Earl Spencer, Pedro Maldonado an explorer and scientist from Spain, William Elliot the army officer, and Benjamin Stillingfleet botanist of renown who lived in Piccadilly.

B. 16 February 1686/87 Charles Cotton
16 December 1693 William Vande Vilde
8 October 1699 Mrs. Mary Beale
11 April 1707 Willm. Vander Velde
22 May 1729 Rev. Dr. Samuel Clarke
4 March 1734/35 John Arbuthnot M.D.

22 October 1748 William Poyntz Esq.
7 November 1748 Don Pedro Maldonado
14 June 1764 The Honble William Elliot
19 December 1771 Benj. Stillingfleet Esq
12 May 1772 R.H. Lady Frances Elliot
5 April 1783 Dr. William Hunter m

7 June 1815 James Gillray of St. James's Street, 58 (caricaturist and printmaker)
1 August 1823 Sir Charles Asgill bart of Pall Mall, 58 (equerry Duke of York)

St James's Chapel, Hampstead Road - A burial ground was established above Euston Road near to Cumberland Hay Market, and a chapel was designed by Thomas Hardwick with pediment, galleries and Venetian east window. It was a parish from 1793 and Samuel Sebastian Wesley son of Samuel and grandson of Charles was organist in 1826.

Its many memorials included George F. Fitzroy Lord Southampton by Nollekens 1810; General James Stuart commander in chief at Madras 1815; Rev. John Armstrong minister from 1793-1836; and Rev. Henry Stebbing historian, chaplain to U.C.L., perpetual curate in 1836-58 and rector of St. Nicholas Cole Abbey d.1882 (bur. Kensal Green).

The east side was taken by the London & N. Western Railway in 1883 and the London Temperance Hospital opened a new building on land beside the chapel two years later. A public garden was then inaugurated by Olive wife of Harry Lawson M.P. in 1887 (tablet at entrance). The Insull Wing was added in 1932 after an American donation, but the chapel was demolished in 1954 and today there are memorials to Christie and Stebbing.

B. 29 October 1811 Henry Revell Reynolds Esq. (of Bedford Sq. - King's physician)
23 July 1814 Capt. Matthew Flinders of [14] London Street, 40 (hydrographer Australia)

St. Philip's, Lower Regent Street - This was built by George Stanley Repton son of the landscaper to a design of William Chambers with portico, dome and cupola in 1819-21. Henry Smart was organist in 1838-39 before going to St. Luke's (Old St.) and St. Pancras (in 1865) but it was always a chapel and was demolished in 1904. It was supplemented by St. Peter's, Gt. Windmill Street built by Raphael Brandon and George Myers (1861-1954). Nearby in Pall Mall were the United Services, Athenaeum, Travellers, Reform, Carlton, War Office, Oxf and Camb and Guards clubs - also Marlborough House, the Queen's Chapel and the Shakespeare Gallery.

Thomas Earnshaw made a timely sum from his chronometers, while

James Gillray (right) produced political and Royal satires which did not amuse the King.

John Boydell published a series of engravings on the bard and opened his gallery on the north side of Pall Mall designed by George Dance y in 1788. He exhibited some 160 paintings but interest gradually waned and the British Institution took the lease in 1805. It was then used for general exhibitions of paintings, and was demolished in 1869. A sculpture by Thomas Banks was moved from there to New Place, Stratford on Avon.

Craven Chapel, Marshall Street - The Earl of Craven hired the site for a pesthouse in 1665 and land was bought from William Pulteney and William Lowndes in 1735. Marshall Street was then laid out and named for the family seat in Berkshire with Carnaby Market to the north, but the latter closed in 1820 and the street was extended. Thomas Wilson, a retired merchant, established Congregational chapels from 1799 and with Lord Craven built one on the site for 2,000 people at £11,000 in December 1822. The architect was probably Robert Abraham and the builder was Thomas Finden, estate surveyor.

At first there were visiting preachers however Rev. John Leifchild (1831-54) attracted a large congregation "scattered over half London," and a lecture hall and school were added in 1874. Nearby were a workhouse, baths and wash-houses whilst the lease passed to the Methodist, West London Mission, in 1894. When this expired in 1898 it was a stable for the Lion Brewery, Broadwick Street and a warehouse &c. for Liberty's from 1907.

C. 14 October 1832 John Raphael Wedgwood s. of Ralph Wedgwood and Hannah [née] English was baptized - also Ebenezer in 1836 (see St. Paul's, Covent Garden)

Our Lady of the Assumption, Warwick Street - Two embassies in Golden Square established a chapel to the rear in 1724, but the Portuguese moved to Mayfair in 1747. Compensation was claimed during the Gordon Riots and after the Bavarians left it was rebuilt by Bishop Talbot to the designs of Joseph Bonomi in 1789-90. Alterations were made by J.E. Carew in 1853 and J.F. Bentley in 1875 then the new name was adopted. It remains today with its original brick façade as the only surviving embassy chapel.

Tenison's Chapel, Kingly Street - Dr. Tenison minister of St. Martin's in 1680-92 and of St. James's from 1686 established a wooden tabernacle, and under Isaac Newton who was one of the trustees a new chapel of ease was built in 1702. The endowment included two preachers, a schoolmaster, and a reader or chaplain to say prayers twice daily.

C.R. Cockerell designed a new Regent Street façade and Thomas Hardwick new rooms in 1824. It then became St. Thomas's under Rev. J.E. Kempe in 1854, with an entrance on Chapel Court and a west end converted into shops. With the loss of St. Anne's and St. Luke's it was the only Anglican church in the area but closed in 1954.

York Street Episcopal Chapel - A foreign ambassador lived at 8 St. James's Square and to the rear was the French chapel from 1676, although in the next century it was unused. Dr. Thomas Hussey ran it in unison with the Spanish Embassy in 1786-91 until moving to Spanish Place, while the Wedgwoods had showrooms in the house and it was held by Swedenborgians, Baptists and Unitarians until 1832. It was then an Anglican proprietary chapel but closed after Rev. Stopford Brooke left for Bedford Chapel in 1875.

Christchurch, Mayfair (Down Street)

This rather nondescript Decorated hall was built by F. and H. Francis for a new parish on the corner of Down Street in 1865. Little took place in these back streets behind the more avant-garde Piccadilly, and it may have disappeared into obscurity but for a number of weddings there - like its *neighbour of notoriety* St. George's Chapel just behind.

Regarding these Sir William Stirling-Maxwell was an historical writer, art historian and the M.P. for Perthshire, while his bride was the daughter of Thomas Sheridan paymaster Cape of Good Hope (1813-17) and granddaughter of R.B. Sheridan. She was previously married to G.C. Norton at St. George's Hanover Square back in 1827.

Secondly, the Earl of Rosebery had inherited his title in 1868 and married Hannah de Rothschild the richest heiress of the day. It is suggested this took place at the *Board of Guardians*, 104 Mount Street used by the vestry, union and registrar by the workhouse, but they probably went there for a licence due to her Jewish faith. She was given away by Disraeli and the witnesses included Edward Prince of Wales. Rosebery was Liberal P.M. in 1894-95, but Gladstone restricted his ambitions and he left the Party.

Another witness Prince George, Duke of Cambridge (1819-1904) the cousin of Victoria infamously married actress Sarah (Louisa) Fairbrother at St. John's, Clerkenwell, in 1847. He was son of Adolphus 1st Duke and Augusta daughter of Frederick of Hesse Cassel, but despite a number of children the union was not recognized by the Royal Marriages Act and he had a further liaison with a mistress Mrs. Louisa Beauclerk.

The third marriage was of Angela G. Burdett (1814-1906), who inherited the fortune of her grandfather Thomas Coutts and Holly Lodge, Highgate from his wife Harriet Mellon in 1837. She added the name Coutts, and as a philanthropist was friend to Dickens and Wellington, but married her American secretary later M.P. for Westminster.

Regarding the church there was a fire in 1906, and Mary daughter of George V and wife of Henry Lascelles Earl of Harewood attended when at Chesterfield House, but it closed in the 1990s then re-opened with help from St. Helen's, Bishopsgate in 2001. Nearby is Down Street underground part of the Piccadilly Line until 1932 - used by Churchill and the War Cabinet as an air-raid shelter. There are other similar facades at Brompton Road and Hyde Park Corner (later a Lyons Corner House) closed at the same time.

M. (3 Chesterfield St.) 1 March 1877 William Stirling-Maxwell wid M.P. of 10 Upper Grosvenor Street s. Archibald Stirling of Keir gent and Caroline Elizabeth Sarah Norton wid of No. 3 d. Thomas Sheridan paymaster at the Cape in the drawing room sp. licence by Henry Malcolm & M.R. Graham before John Halsard registrar wit Morice Sheridan, Carlotta Norton, M. Feversham, R.B. Sheridan, "Feversham" and others

M. 20 March 1878 Archibald Philip Primrose full bach Earl of Rosebery of 2 Berkeley Square s. Archibald, Lord Dalmeny and Hannah de Rothschild full spin of 107 Piccadilly d. Mayer a baron lic. by William Rogers off min signed "Rosebery" pres. "Beaconsfield" (*twice*), "Cleveland," "Albert Edward," "George," Edward Primrose

12 February 1881 William Lehman Ashmead B-C Bartlett Esq. [29] of 80 Piccadilly s. of Ellis gentleman and Angela Georgina Burdett-Coutts a peeress [67] of 1 Stratton Street d. of Sir Francis M.P. by W. Cardall vicar witness Francis & Mary Dorothy Burdett, Mary & Jane Keppel, G.J. Gordon, Jane E. Lindsay, C.C. Lacaita, Ellis Ashmead Bartlett

Christchurch, Down Street and **Cambridge House**

Piccadilly: The road, originally Portugal Street, received its current cognomen from a wealthy tailor who sold piccadills (stiff collars with scallop and lace) in the 17th century. It reached from Hyde Park over to Haymarket with its theatre which had a Royal patent of 1766 and later façade by Nash, whilst Lower Regent Street was built over St. James's Market in the 1820s. Whatever the reason for its terminology this was a desirable location and a series of mansions were erected to the north, three of which still survive:

Apsley House - designed by Robert Adam in 1771-78 was home to the Wellesleys including the Duke of Wellington from 1807-1947, and is now a Museum called "No. 1 London" but is isolated through road improvements into Hyde Park.
Gloucester House - Prince William, Duke of Gloucester (d.1805) brother of George III.
Hertford House - Richard Seymour-Conway, Marquis of Hertford built this in c.1850.
Cambridge House - built 1756-61 for Charles Wyndham, Earl of Egremont home to Adolphus, Duke of Cambridge tenth child of George III (1829-50) and Lord Palmerston (1855-65), then the Naval and Military Club until 1996 and still present today.
Bath House - William Pulteney, 1st Earl of Bath a rival of Walpole lived here and it was later Pulteney's Hotel; then a new house for Bingham Baring, Lord Ashburton.
Devonshire House (formerly *Berkeley*) - built by William Kent in Palladian style in 1720 and home to the Dukes of Devonshire prominent Whigs but demolished in 1924.
Clarendon House - built in 1664-67 and replaced by Albemarle Street in 1683.
Burlington House - was begun by Sir J. Denham in 1665 and remodelled by Campbell for the 3rd Earl of Burlington, then for the Royal Academy in 1867. Other organisations came including the Royal Society in 1873 (now at Carlton House); while today there are five societies and external statues to scientists &c. Liebnitz, Cuvier, Davy, Blake etc. Just opposite was the notable Egyptian Hall used for exhibitions from 1812-1905.
Melbourne House - by Sir William Chambers 1770-74 home to Frederick, Duke of York and Albany son of George III, became "The Albany" high class apartments in 1802; the residents including Lord Byron, W.E. Gladstone and the Kinnaird family. [2]

---

[2] 5 The Albany was home to George Kinnaird 9th Lord who married Frances A.G. Ponsonby niece of Lady Caroline Lamb. Also to his brother Arthur F. Kinnaird the 10th Lord who married Mary Jane Hoare a philanthropist and niece of Rev. Baptist Wriothesley Noel.

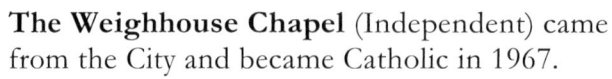

The Weighhouse Chapel (Independent) came from the City and became Catholic in 1967.

St. George's Hospital (left) occupied a country house in 1733 and William Wilkins designed a new facade in 1826-44. It became the Lanesborough Hotel when the hospital went to Tooting in 1980.

Apsley House (right) was built by Robert Adam in red brick in 1771-78 but was enlarged and refaced in Bath stone by Benjamin Wyatt in 1818-19. The similarity of the two is quite striking and both stand opposite the Wellington or Hyde Park Arch of Decimus Burton (1842).

Mayfair (chapels)

The parish of St. George's had a proliferation of Episcopal or proprietary chapels from its inception, many of which were speculative ventures aimed towards the local gentry. A number of these were built when the Church was slow to respond, however only one remains in use as a church today and the rest are consigned to history.

At the centre of all this religious construction was Berkeley Square above Devonshire House, which had a number of famous residents including No. 45 Clive of India soldier and administrator (1725-77) and No. 50 George Canning statesman (1770-1827). Other occupants were Joseph Bonsor partner in Combe & Co. at 6 Hill Street during 1853-68 while the celebrated Thomas's Hotel was at No. 25 in the northeast corner.

The Duke of Wellington once called on Mrs. Porter at Berkeley Square hoping she might arrange a meeting with the famous courtesan Harriette Wilson, stating: "If you have good news to communicate address a line to Thomas's Hotel." [3]

Berkeley Episcopal Chapel was at the corner of Charles and John Streets (Chesterfield Hill) behind Chesterfield House, and situated in the last area to be developed between Berkeley Square and South Audley Street in the 1750s. Sydney Smith (1741-1845) a writer was morning preacher from 1802 *with no standing room*, evening preacher at the Fitzroy Chapel and Foundling Hospital, and teacher of moral philosophy at the Royal Institution in 1804-06. It was replaced by Charles House with its corner turret in 1907.

---

[3] Harry Thompson of Knaresborough, Yorks was a resident of the hotel in 1858-61 and M.P. for Whitby (succeeding Robert Stephenson engineer), and his son Albert Childers Meysey-Thompson went to Eton with Bonsor and Lubbock playing soccer and became a barrister. He then married Mabel Louisa Lascelles and was thus related to the Earls of Harewood.

St. George's Episcopal, Albemarle Street was built on the gardens of *Clarendon House* in the 1740s. Timothy Essex (1765-1847) the composer had a musical academy at 38 Hill Street and was organist, while Rev. William Webb Ellis of rugby fame was chaplain in the 1830s, and the registers date to 1909. The Royal Institution was started by H. Cavendish at No. 21 in 1799 with lectures by Davy and Faraday and a façade by L. Vulliamy; whilst John Murray the famous publishing house was based at No. 50 from 1812.

St Mark's, North Audley Street was built as a chapel of ease on a narrow site by J.P. Gandy in Greek Revival style in 1825-28. At the front was a deep recess, Ionic columns, entablature, small cupola and hall-like entrance whilst it became a parish in 1863. The interior was remodelled by A. Blomfield in Romanesque style in 1878 and improved by J.F. Bentley in 1899, but it was redundant by 1974 and the American Church left. It was then used by the community and subjected to a lengthy planning dispute.

St. Mary's, Bourdon Street - St. Mary's proprietary for Rev. P. Forester of Cosgrove was built by John Spencer and William Timbrell at Park/Green Streets in 1762-63. It was plain with a Doric portico and cost £3,133, but Lord Grosvenor took the lease in 1825 and Thomas Cundy and son added a stucco exterior. Canon Capel Cure asked the Duke of Westminster for a mission thus it was demolished, and Blomfield estate architect built a new Gothic edifice by Bourdon House, Davies Street for 300 at £8,500 in 1880-81. To this was added St. George's Institute and social housing. The Dutch used it when Austin Friars was rebuilt in 1940-54, but it was all replaced by Grosvenor Hill Court.

The Weighhouse Chapel (Congregational) was first at Eastcheap in the 1690s and Fish Street Hill in 1834, its most famous minister Rev. Thomas Binney (Vol. 1). A new building was designed by Alfred Waterhouse on Duke Street in 1891, which became Catholic in 1967 and is now the Ukrainian Cathedral with commemorative streets nearby.

The Grosvenor Chapel

Sir Richard Grosvenor laid the foundation on South Audley Street and it was completed in 1730-31. A syndicate of four undertakers including builder Benjamin Timbrell, one of the first vestrymen at St. George's, did the work at a cost of £4,000. A minimal rent was established whereas the £115 p.a. expense for preachers was covered by pew rents.

Timbrell had worked with Gibbs on St. Martin's and it was easy to follow such designs, thus it was a plain rectangle with two-tiers of arched windows, a portico, bell tower and shallow projection for the altar. Inside was an elegant white interior, unlike the parish church, and a plaster barrel vault. In fact, the nave and galleries retain their box pews, whilst to the west are the arms of George II and an organ case of 1732.

Meanwhile, the Portuguese Embassy removed from Golden Square to 74 South Audley Street in 1747, and a chapel was erected behind. Vincent Novello was organist until 1822 but the embassy departed in 1829 and Portugal Street became Balfour Place.

At this date Grosvenor became a chapel of ease and the pews were lowered in 1877, but the main changes took place under John Ninian Comper who transferred the focus from the pulpit to the altar in 1912. A screen of Ionic columns was inserted before the reredos to create a new Lady Chapel and the communion rails were brought forward.

In addition, Corinthian columns supported a partial altar-canopy, and there was to be an Ionic colonnade instead of gallery pillars but only two were built. The result was a sanctuary in the High Church tradition but encased in a New England exterior.

Grosvenor Chapel was never a parish church and is the only one of its kind still in use today. Regarding its connections there were many and Prince Albert came to a baptism, whilst there were several prominent burials. These included Lady Montagu the traveller and writer, Garrett Wesley and the Countess of Mornington, and William Wellesley Pole 3rd Earl of Mornington d.1845 - with tablet and plaque on the north wall.

The north gallery has a memorial to Col. Mark Wilks of the H.E.I.C.S. late Governor of St. Helena died 1831 who Napoleon is said to have found most affable, and another to John Wilkes with a plain memorial tablet by the sculptor Flaxman. In addition, Florence Nightingale resided at South Street nearby and attended services there. [4]

A plaque outside records links to the U.S. forces in 1939-45 and inside is one to Vincent Massey, the High Commissioner of Canada. In recent times Rev. Dick Sheppard helped to establish a Catholic tradition, whilst Rose Macaulay the writer and Sir John Betjeman (1972-84) worshipped there and helped in its preservation. Adjacent are the Mount Street Gardens, and Church of the Immaculate Conception, Farm Street, an impressive Jesuit building erected by J.J. Scoles in 1844-49 with altar by Pugin (a parish from 1966).

Grosvenor Chapel has a New England façade on Aldford Street which contrasts with its High Church interior of 1912.

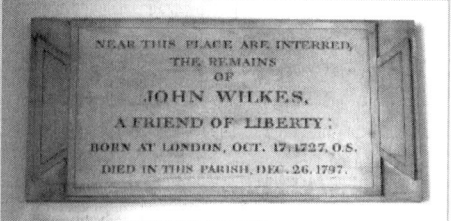

NEAR THIS PLACE ARE INTERRED,
THE REMAINS
OF
JOHN WILKES,
A FRIEND OF LIBERTY;
BORN AT LONDON, OCT. 17, 1727, O.S.
DIED IN THIS PARISH, DEC. 26, 1797.

---

[4] St. Helena, Ascension Island and Tristan da Cunha were in the South Atlantic and the former was controlled by the East India Company from 1658 - Napoleon was a prisoner during 1815-21. It came under Crown control in 1834 and a Governor was then appointed directly.

Hanover Chapel, Regent Street

C.R. Cockerell had just returned from the Continent when he built this *Waterloo Church* near to Oxford Circus from 1823-25. Its dome was modelled on St. Stephen's, Walbrook whilst the Ionic portico echoed the Temple of Minerva Polias at Priene (now in Turkey). It was a major study in neo-Classicism, ornamenting Regent Street, and the twin towers and skylight dome were a great success despite some restrictions on costs.

According to J. Gwilt it was unequalled in design harking back to the time of Palladio, Wren and Hawksmoor, while it operated as a district church. However, there was to be a salutary tale connected with this building. The Duke of Westminster contributed to the income of the incumbent Rev. David Long from 1879, but improvements were needed and the *Board* decided to apply to Parliament to pull it down and relocate.

A site was offered by Grosvenor Market, Davies Street in 1884 but Rev. Long departed which delayed matters - then a second site was found on Weighhouse Street near to the Hanover Schools in 1890. The *Board* backed by the rector of St. George's and the Bishop applied for permission, but R.I.B.A. objected to - "the loss of one of the last monuments to C.R. Cockerell." Despite such objections the bill was passed the next year.

The Duke's surveyor then joined with Thackeray Turner and Walter Holt & Sons of Croydon to build St. Anselm's at a cost of £20,000. It was consecrated as a new parish on 15 February 1896 and Hanover Chapel was demolished, while only its records and a few fittings were transferred. The new building was imbued with the designs of the Arts and Crafts Movement but was found too expensive to maintain by 1923, and was demolished in 1939 - the site being sold back to the Grosvenor Estate at a reduced price.

St. George's Chapel, Mayfair

There were a number of locations around the capital where clandestine marriages took place, the parties often being from out of the area. St. Benet, Paul's Wharf by Doctors' Commons was a good example, but of far greater notoriety were the Fleet Prison, Savoy, Knightsbridge (see later) and of course St. George's Chapel in Mayfair.

George Augustus Curzon, 3rd Viscount Howe owned all of the land east of Park Lane below the Grosvenor Estate and here he founded Curzon Street. Its properties included Chesterfield House for Philip Stanhope, 4th Earl of Chesterfield and just across the road the Mayfair Chapel of 1730 - in the parish of St. George's, Hanover Square.

Like others, it may have shone briefly under a literary vicar or a famous organist - then slowly decayed into relative obscurity. But instead it was brought into the limelight and infamy by a pecuniary incumbent who invited considerable Government scrutiny!

Rev. Alexander Keith was a clergyman from Scotland who purportedly left that country due to his Episcopal leanings. He initially tried to perform marriages at the Fleet, but was ejected, and instead set himself up at the Mayfair Chapel in 1735 where there were far richer pickings. Over some twenty years he performed 7,000 marriages with his assistants, and kept *records* at the chapel until 1744 and then at a nearby house. However, the entries concealed all kinds of irregularities at a price viz. no banns or licence, false dates, unions without names, and convenience marriages for debt or legal reasons.

Such practices were then stopped by Hardwicke's Marriage Act in 1754, and from that time all marriages had to be in an Anglican Church (except Jews and Quakers), while banns or a licence were a legal requirement rather than a religious directive. James Frith senior of the parish of St. George's, Hanover Square also made oath that on the decease of Rev. Alexander Keith he was his deponent. On searching his effects, he found registers to the said chapel annotated "A.B. & C" dating from February 1735.

After the Act the chapel above Hertford Street near to Shepherd Market was operated as an Episcopal institution, within the law, until it was demolished in 1894. Meanwhile several eminent people resided nearby: Henry Holland architect (husband of Bridget d. of Capability Brown), R.B. Sheridan and E.J. Trelawny a friend of Byron at Hertford Street; Beau Brummell at 4 Chesterfield Street and Earl of Rosebery was born at No. 20; William Duke of Clarence at 22 Charles Street; and Robert Berry of South Audley Street whose daughters were the companions of Horace Walpole.

Regarding the marriages these are divided into *regular* and *irregular*, the first including a number of notables such as Edward Rooker the engraver, Bysshe Shelley from Newark in New Jersey the poet's grandfather, and John Hill an actor and physic of Bayswater. The second group are *titled people* who married commoners in unusual circumstances, among them Edward Wortley Montagu the son of Lady Mary the renowned letter writer.

M. 1 May 1746 Mr. Edward Rooker and Mrs. Elizth. Coatham of St. Giles in ye Fields
19 May 1748 Thomas Chippendale and Catherine Redshaw of St. Martin in the Fields
25 June 1749 Charles Burney and Esther Sleep of St. Mary le Bow, London
12 August 1750 Thomas Callcott and Charlotte Urry of Kensington, Middx.
30 June 1752 Bysshe Shelley and Mary Catherine Michell of Horsham, Sussex
27 Sept 1753 John Hill of St. Geo. Bloomsbury and Hen. Wilhelmina Jones of St. Ann's

M. 25 December 1744 His Grace Henry Brydges, Duke of Chandos and Mrs. Ann Jefferys of St. Marylebone, Middx. married by me Alexander Keith (No. 1268)
14 September 1749 William Earl of Kensington and Rachel Hill of Hempstead
21 July 1751 Edward Wortley Montague and Elizabeth Ashe of St. Martin in the Fields
14 February 1751/52 James Duke of Hamilton and Elizth. Gunning of St. Geo. H.S.
20 June 1753 R.H. Ld. George Bentinck Esq. of St. James and Mary Davies of Hanwell

Trinity Chapel, Conduit Street

Conan Doyle might have written *The Strange Case of the Itinerant Chapel*, a curiosity that would certainly fit the bill here. James II decreed that a moving tabernacle or "chapel on wheels" should accompany him to Hounslow in 1688, so his chaplain could say mass, but on his abdication it was brought to a site in Conduit Street below St. George's.

At that time Dr. Tenison was minister of St. Martin's whose parish covered the area, and he begged the King and Queen to make it a chapel of ease which took place in July 1691, with John Evelyn at the first service. It was gradually made brick like the adjacent houses but being leasehold did not receive a district, and was converted to a proprietary chapel in the 1800s. Rev. Beamish then made it quite fashionable, adding galleries, but it was generally unattractive and was demolished for secular building in 1875.

Westminster

Today, it is hard to imagine that Thorney Island, at the end of the Ty Bourne where the seat of power now sits, was once a marshy swamp proving quite inhospitable. Canute may have come and tried to keep back the waters, but it was Edward the Confessor who built the first Royal palace and also began the great cathedral in 1045. The latter replaced a group of Benedictine monks who had been present for some seventy years.

With the arrival of the Normans, Westminster Palace became the principal residence of the monarch and had several important chambers. The oldest surviving part is the main hall dating to the reign of William II, whereas St. Stephen's Chapel (now Hall) was used by the King and St. Mary Undercroft serviced his court and household.

The Royal family held council there and at other palaces thus Edward I summoned his Model Parliament in 1295, but much was changed once Henry VIII moved to Whitehall Palace in 1530. Initially there were no purpose-built rooms hence the opening ceremony was in the King's Painted Chamber, while the Lords used the Queen's Chamber and the Commons utilised St. Stephen's Chapel (a disbanded college) from 1547.

Politically the structure altered after the era of Cromwell and the Commonwealth with the monarch banned from the House, and there were calls for an entirely new building during the 18th century. At this time the complex basically comprised the Old Hall and Exchequer - with the Commons, Court of Requests and Lords to the south.

On the north side was New Palace Yard which was outside the precincts and sat below Westminster Bridge from 1750, whereas Old Palace Yard and St. Margaret's Street were situated towards the cathedral. In fact, a revised Palladian façade was added to the west beside St. Margaret's Street in 1755-70, then James Wyatt did more work in 1799-1801 at which time the Lords moved into the White Chamber (or Court of Requests).

Sir John Soane made alterations with a new south entrance in 1824-27, but it all burnt down in October 1834 except for the hall, jewel-tower, chapel of St. Mary's and cloister. This cleared the way for Charles Barry's Gothic-style palace built mainly in 1840-60 with sumptuous interior by Augustus W.N. Pugin, which retained surviving mediaeval elements and added three towers with a clock by Edward J. Dent. There was extensive damage in the war and the Commons was rebuilt by Sir Giles Gilbert Scott in 1950.

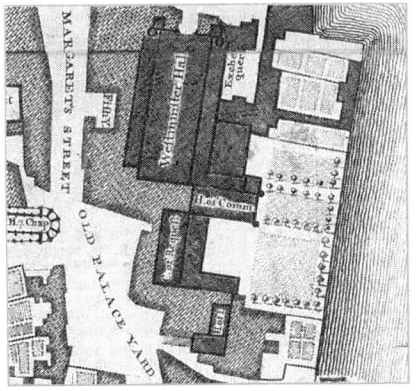

Rocque's Map (1746) reveals the small footprint of the complex.

Westminster Hall depicted by Ackermann in 1808 and **Monet's** "model parliament" of 1903.

Methodist Central Hall

In the 18th century the area north of the Abbey was called the Broad Sanctuary with King Street leading up to Whitehall. To the east were Tothill Street and the Gatehouse then the Broadway, Petty France and Tothill Fields. The adjacent streets consisted of small alleyways and courtyards crowding up against the edge of St. James's Park.

Much had changed by Victorian times and Victoria Street was inserted at an angle right through the existing street pattern in the 1860s, whereas the Sanctuary was occupied by Westminster Hospital, the Guildhall, H.M. Stationery and a school. These were followed by *The Royal Aquarium and Imperial Theatre* a speculative venture in 1876, constructed north of Tothill Street by three businessmen Henry Labouchere, William Whiteley and Arthur Sullivan. Its aim was to attract people like the famous Crystal Palace.

With its palm trees, art gallery, music hall, and restaurants it seemed assured of success, but was a strange accoutrement to the ecclesiastical buildings opposite. In latter years, it received a bad reputation with unaccompanied women visiting its precincts, and rather pointedly the site was closed and sold to the Wesleyan Methodists in 1903.

Its subsequent story began with the centenary of John Wesley's death in 1891, and after many meetings (or so we might suspect), the "Million Guinea Fund" was inaugurated at Wesley's Chapel, City Road on 8 November 1898. A register of one million people who contributed later filled fifty volumes and the Storey's Gate site was purchased. Central Hall was then built in place of the aquarium, the remaining land being sold off.

Henry Lanchester and E.A. Rickards were the architects and a French Gothic edifice was erected at £155,170 from 1905-12. This was to be the centre of world administration and was opened by Rev. Luke Wiseman, president of the Central Methodist Conference, on 3 October 1912. A further sum of £242,206 was then allocated from the funds.

A number of significant events took place there and the Suffragettes used the building in 1914 (as well as nearby Caxton Hall), Gandhi had a rally in 1931, De Gaulle and the Free French used it in 1940 (also Churchill), and the U.N. General Assembly had its first meetings on 10 January - 14 February 1946 (plaque). It was also used for many religious, political and musical events although ceased to be the Methodist H.Q. in 2000.

The Royal Aquarium was not a financial success and George Leybourne soon satirised it in song. The *Million Guinea Fund* then led to the **Methodist Central Hall** a permanent venue with politico-religious agenda.

St. John the Evangelist, Smith Square

Compared to Mayfair and the Strand the two parishes of Westminster covered a relatively small area whilst the Abbey had its own precincts and jurisdiction. In October 1711 the Commissioners suggested that two churches should be built in St. Margaret's parish, and in March 1713 there was a debate regarding Smith's Field at Westminster.

The following month *"The Model of the Church with Four Towers"* proposed by Thomas Archer was selected for the site purchased from Mr. Smith, and in July permission was sought to dig near the Abbey to ascertain the type of foundations. In fact the design was reputedly like the footstool of Queen Anne - and a café there commemorates this.

The land just below the College Garden and above Market Street (part of the route to Lambeth Horse Ferry) received gravel excavated from the Strand and copious numbers of bricks, whereas £2,000 was allocated in December 1714. The church was completed in 1728 and with its distinctive Baroque towers, grand staircases to both north and south, and extensive unspoilt setting - it was notable to say the least. However it suffered from subsidence due to water-logging of the London clay.

St. John's, Smith Square was a fashionable, spacious Baroque church in the 18th century.

The Buxton Memorial designed by S.S. Teulon for Parliament Square in 1835 was moved to Victoria Tower Gardens in 1957. Erected by Charles Buxton M.P. it commemorates Sir T. Fowell Buxton, Wilberforce, Clarkson, Macaulay and the anti-slavery lobby.

A short parish boundary was established running past College and Pye Streets, down Rochester Row and then eastwards along Tachbrook Street back to the river. Just south of Market Street (later Horseferry Road) was a burial ground which in the 19th century had breweries on either side and is now a public open space.

Initially, there was little to the south except for Grosvenor (Peterborough) House which was started by Alexander Davies, heir to the estate of that name. At the boundary of the housing was the road to the horseferry with the open fields of "Tot Hill" laying beyond. The latter then continued into (Great) Peter Street beside the Grey Coat School, and just opposite was an artillery ground and Rochester Row cottages.

St. John's seen from the west and the main façade on Lord North Street. A plaque at 14 Barton Street records that T.E. Lawrence of Arabia lived there.

Badly damaged in the war, it was restored as a classical music venue.

The Grey Coat Hospital was set up by residents in a workhouse owned by the Abbey on St. Andrew's Day in 1698, and aimed to educate poor children from the adjacent precincts and courtyards. A structure with white clock-tower and coat of arms was built on Rochester Row including copious gardens and orchards to the rear. This became a Girls' School in the later 19th century and remains there today (restored in 1955).

David Thompson, its most famous pupil, was born in Marsham Street, Westminster of a Welsh father and attended the school in 1777-84. He received an apprenticeship with the Hudson's Bay Co. and became a surveyor and explorer, his most famous trip being across the Rockies to the Pacific in 1807. Retiring to Montreal he was a national hero but was largely forgotten in Britain. However, Ray Mears unveiled a green plaque outside the school to this luminary "who explored and mapped Canada" in 2007.

In addition three *almshouse charities* were established: one by Rev. James Palmer on the west side of Tothill Fields chapel in 1656, one by Mr. Nicholas Butler nearby for ancient couples in 1675, and a third by Emery Hill on Rochester Row in 1708. The charities were combined as the United Westminster Almshouses at the latter site in 1882, and various plaques record their benefactions - "Christian reader in assurance of thy assistance!"

Later developments in the parish included the Gas Light & Coke Co. established west of Marsham Street below Great Peter Street in 1813-97, and a plaque records: "the first public supply in the world." Vauxhall Bridge was opened to the south in 1816 and at the same time Millbank Prison a six-winged fortress was built under the principles of Jeremy Bentham in 1816-21. Thomas Hardwick, John Harvey and Robert Smirke designed the gaol which was mainly a holding centre for transportation up until 1868, but it closed in 1890. The National Gallery of British Art (The Tate) then replaced it in 1897.

C. 5 July 1753 Frances daughter of Henry Goodwyn by Frances his wife b. 13 June
20 May 1770 David son of David Thompson by Ann his wife born 30 April [5]

---

[5] Henry Goodwyn (1719-1805) was born at Great Massingham, Norfolk and partner in the Red Lion Brewery, L. East Smithfield with his son Henry in the 1760s. He installed the first engine by Boulton and Watt and lived at Maze Hill, Greenwich. Adml. William Henry Smyth son of Joseph and Georgina Caroline was born at 42 Great Peter St. in 1788 and was an astronomer and hydrographer (see Chelsea). His half-brother Augustus Earle was a travel artist.

St. Matthew's, Great Peter Street was beside St. Ann's Street opposite the gas works and was designed in the Gothic style by George Gilbert Scott and G.F. Bodley, a relative by marriage, in 1849-51. It included some early work by Ninian Comper in particular the first-floor Lady Chapel and by C.E. Kempe and Martin Travers. Frank Weston, Bishop of Zanzibar, came there in 1916-18 bringing a Catholic revival, but much was destroyed after a fire in 1977 and it was restored on a smaller scale in 1984 (see picture p. 314).

St. Stephen's, Rochester Row was built opposite the almshouses by Baroness Angela Burdett-Coutts in memory of her father, with encouragement from Dickens, in 1849. Of rough ragstone with an interior of Caen stone it has a memorial bust to William Tennant (first vicar in 1849-79) by a pupil of the Burdett-Coutts school, and an ornate chapel to that minister. There are windows to *St. Stephen* by Wailes (1850) and the *Good Shepherd* by Burne-Jones (1890), also a finely sculpted memorial to Dr. William Brown and his wife Hannah who was governess and companion of Burdett-Coutts (also see p. 314).

St. Margaret's, Westminster

As with other monastic establishments the Benedictine monks of the Abbey started a church to the north for those in the precincts, so they could worship separately. A stone building was erected in the 12th century but this was replaced by a Tudor edifice in 1523 and it became the parish church for the House of Commons from 1614. Strype noted a large pair of organs, antique window, repairs in 1682 and an interesting fact:

Originally there was a second parish church the **Holy Innocents** on the west of King Street with land leading down to the Thames, as recorded in an ancient deed. This served those beyond the Abbey but it was decayed by the 16th century and then became a wine cellar on Thieving Lane. Therefore the two parishes were joined together.

Regarding the numerous historic memorials at St. Margaret's these included a brass to Dame Mary wife of Sir Robert Billing chief justice 1499, Lady Dorothy Stafford g. granddaughter of George Duke of Clarence brother of Edward IV 1604, Edward Reynolds clerk of the Privy Seal register of the Court of Requests 1623, and relatives of Sir John Radcliffe and William Lord Howard of Effingham the Lord High Admiral.

A number of charities pertaining to the parish were recorded on the west wall including James Palmer and Emery Hill for almshouses, John Feckenham the Abbot and William Lord Burghley the Lord Treasurer £10 apiece for the relief of the poor, and Robert Earl of Salisbury the High Steward £100 to many sundry beneficiaries.

However the edifice was transformed after John James rebuilt the tower and encased the nave in Portland stone in 1734-38, resulting in a slightly disproportionate belfry as compared to the main body of the church. John L. Pearson added the western porch in the next century, and the interior was restored with original Tudor features by George Gilbert Scott in 1878 - although the picnic groups outside remain optional.

The eastern window of Flemish stained glass commemorates the betrothal of Henry to Catharine of Aragon (dated c.1520, installed in 1758). The other windows record William Caxton 1491, Sir Walter Raleigh 1618 and John Milton who was a parishioner. A tablet in the porch lists the repairs, while that opposite is to Frederick William Farrar D.D. F.R.S. H.M. of Marlborough (1871), rector (1876) and Dean of Canterbury (1895).

Beating the Bounds - The parish boundary went from Whitehall to St. James's Park, south from Buckingham Palace to Vauxhall Bridge Road, up Rochester Row to Victoria Street and along Old Pye Street to the Abbey - with a detour to parliament. However, it was returned to the Dean and split between St. Matthew's and St. Martin's in 1973.

Webber's *Coat of Many Colours* was once performed at Central Hall and was quite apt given the schools in the area. The Blue Coats were at the end of Little Chapel Street from 1709, Lady Dacre's Almshouses (Brown Coats) were to the west, and the Green Coats were beside the Bridewell to the south - not forgetting the Grey Coats. [6]

Regarding its musical links Fa. Bernard Schmidt the organ maker was organist in 1676-1708, followed by Edward Purcell the son of Henry (also at St. Clement's, Eastcheap) in 1726-40. A number of notable baptisms also took place at the church:

William Talman a pupil of Wren was the architect of Chatsworth and St. Anne's, Soho whilst his son John was an antiquary and art collector. Lavinia Besswick the daughter of a naval officer took the stage name of Fenton, her most famous role as Polly Peachum in *The Beggar's Opera* at Lincoln's Inn Fields. She married lover Charles Powlett, 3rd Duke of Bolton at Aix en Provence, France in 1751 and thereafter lived in Greenwich.

Robert Jenkinson, Lord Liverpool was P.M. from 1812-27 during some turbulent times and William Eden of Beckenham was an ambassador, his son George in the Admiralty and Governor of India. John William Lubbock a banker of Mansion House had a son of that name at Duke Street, Piccadilly; whilst the family purchased High Elms, Downe, in 1808 and in this way came into contact with Charles Darwin (see St. Peter's).

Of the marriages, Samuel Pepys initially worked as a teller at the Exchequer under George Downing near Downing Street, his bride being just fourteen at the time. Another union of note was reference Ignatius Sancho who was born on a slave ship, but came to England where John 2nd Duke of Montagu aided his education. He worked as a grocer and valet but as an actor, composer and writer became something of a celebrity.

David Watson a local upholsterer married Ann Mary Underwood (see St. Luke's) there in 1793 and a daughter Eleanor was baptized in 1804 - then married a doctor of Princes Court. Other links were Edward Grimestone Speaker's assistant who wrote influential histories, Wenceslaus Hollar etcher born in Bohemia who came to Arundel House with Thomas Howard 2nd Earl after a diplomatic trip to Cologne, and Thomas Blood an Irish colonel infamous for trying to steal the Crown Jewels but pardoned.

C. 1 December 1650 William Talman son to William by Sibell
19 July 1677 John Tallman son to William by Elizabeth
22 October 1710 Levinia Besswick to Peter [and] Elizabeth born 7
29 June 1770 Robert Bankes s. of Charles Jenkinson Esq. by Amelia his wife b. 7 June
9 February 1801 Frances Eden d. of R.H. Lord [William] Auckland by Eleanor his wife born 14 Jany baptized by His Grace the Archbishop of Canterbury
19 May 1803 John William Lubbock son of John William by Mary b. 26 March
22 May 1837 Isambard son of Isambard Kingdom and Mary Elizabeth Brunel of Duke St engineer by J.H. Milman inducted 12th [wrote his father's biography in 1870]

---

[6] Anne Sackville, Lady Dacre a granddaughter of Sir John Bridges the Mayor left a benefaction in her will of 1594. With help from her cousin Elizabeth I the hospital and school of Emanuel was built on Buckingham Gate in 1598, but removed to Wandsworth in 1883.

St. Margaret's, Westminster in the shadow of the Abbey had some famous connections including **Brunel and Churchill**.

M. 1 December 1655 Samuell Peps o.t.p. gent and Elizabeth Marchant de Saint Michell of Martins in the Ffields spin pub 19, 22, 29 October 1655 and next married by Richard Sherwyn esq. one of the J.P.'s of the citie and liberties of Westminster [sic]
17 December 1758 [Charles] Ignatius Sancho o.t.p. and Ann Osborne o.t.p. by licence by Thomas Atwood curate "both signed" witness William Dixon, Ann Jones
31 March 1831 Robert Willis M.D. o.t.p. bach and Eleanor Watson of St. Martin in the F lic by J.F. Connell cur pres D. Watson, Frances Jane Watson, John Henry Watson
12 September 1908 Winston Leonard Spencer Churchill 33 president Board of Trade of 7 Whitehall Gardens s. Lord Randolph Churchill MP, sec of state for India & chancellor to Clementine Ogilvy Hosier 23 of 51 Abingdon Villas, Kensington d. Col. Sir Henry lic by A.G. Asaph witness Jennie Cornwallis-West., D. Lloyd George, William Hozier

B. 29 October 1618 Sir Walter Raleigh knight   27 August 1680 Thomas Blood
14 Dec. 1640 Serjeant Grimston midl chancel   17 Dec. 1780 Ignatius Sancho
28 March 1677 Wenceslaus Hollar died 25th

Broadway Chapel (St. Mary Magdalen) was a chantry below the Broadway on Tothill Fields in the 13th century and passed to Westminster after the Dissolution in 1538. Stow noted "it was not wholly ruined" and became a *New Chapel* for St. Margaret's at a cost of over £400 in 1626 - with Chapel Street adjacent and Palmer's Almshouses to the west. It was a stables and prison during the Commonwealth but was rebuilt in 1652.

   The location was used as the burial ground for the parish, while Ambrose Poynter built the parish church of Christchurch on the site in 1841-43. This was in the *Early Pointed Style* with fourteen cast-iron columns supporting a lofty open timber roof, and a flight of steps going up to the chancel and an octagonal apse. The tower at the northwest corner never received a spire and most was destroyed in 1941, leaving it as a garden.

Westminster Chapel, Buckingham Gate was built by Independents in 1840 and under Rev. S. Martin worked with the poor. It was commended by Lord Shaftesbury and Dean Stanley thus it was rebuilt with a 1,500 seat capacity in 1864 and remains today.

Westminster Abbey (St. Peter's)

Mellitus who followed Augustine and Laurence as Archbishop of Canterbury may have settled the site in the 7th century, but the first definite record is when King Edgar and St. Dunstan established a community of Benedictines in c.960. Edward the Confessor built the first stone abbey in 1045 which was consecrated twenty years later, while Henry III began to rebuild the structure in the Gothic style from 1245.

Due to its location by the Palace of Westminster the Abbots became powerful with a seat in the Lords, and the monastery owned large estates around the country. Indeed it was the main employer in the district and the area grew up as a service centre. It became the site of coronations although some Kings were buried in France, but this changed when Henry III developed it with the highest nave as a shrine to his forebear Edward.

Construction of the Gothic masterpiece with its cloisters and passageways was largely finished under mason Henry Yevele, although work continued until 1517. At this time Henry VII added a Lady Chapel at the east end, dedicated to the Virgin Mary, which was a study in Perpendicular perfection with fan-vaults reminiscent of King's College. Its exterior having row upon row of buttresses and gleaming pinnacles above.

At the Dissolution the Abbey's future came under a serious threat, its annual income second only to Glastonbury. However, Henry VIII wanted it preserved and granted the building cathedral status, with a new dedication to St. Peter in 1540. He also established the Diocese of Westminster but this was all abolished under Mary and for nine years the monks returned. Then, Elizabeth I established it as the *Collegiate Church of St. Peter* and a Royal peculiar in 1560 - directly responsible to the monarch rather than a bishop.

The last abbot then became the first dean and during the Commonwealth it was mostly secure due to links with Parliament. Sir Christopher Wren was surveyor to the abbey from 1698-1722 and designed a crossing spire but this feature remains absent; while Nicholas Hawksmoor succeeded him and designed the iconic western towers of Portland stone in 1722-45. Sir George Gilbert Scott also carried out restoration in the 19th century.

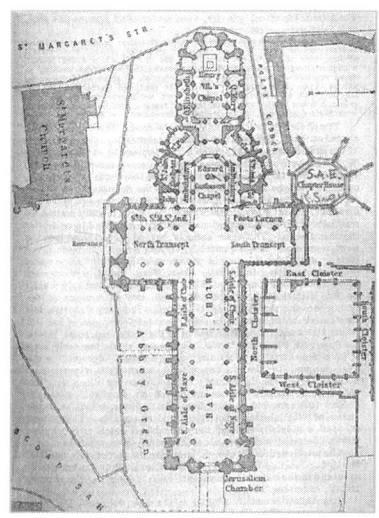

The Abbey with Hawksmoor's west façade and a plan showing St. Margaret's, Henry VII's chapel, the Chapter House and Great Cloister.

The Blue Coat School for poor pupils (1709-1898) contrasts with the intricate opulence of the **Abbey's west door**. The latter was adjacent to Dean's Yard and Westminster School.

On the south side were the cloisters with the adjacent Chapter House built in 1250 and beyond were the little cloister and college gardens. The gatehouse of the abbey was built at the west end in 1370 and was later a prison for political dissenters but was demolished in 1776. At the southeast corner was Dean's Yard with gateway into Great College Street and adjacent was Westminster School on Little Dean's Yard. The latter was present from the mediaeval period but was re-established under Elizabeth I in 1560.

A large number of prominent students attended and it ranked with Charterhouse, Eton, Harrow, Rugby, Winchester &c.; whilst it was separated from the Abbey by the *Public Schools Act* in 1868. The school was a promoter of sporting activity on extensive playing fields at Vincent Square east of Rochester Row, and played early soccer there against the Crusaders (Old Boys) and others. They were advocates of the dribbling game and offside rule which was then incorporated into the first rules of the F.A. in 1863. [7]

M. 1100 Henry I to Matilda of Scotland; 1382 Richard II to Anne of Bohemia
1922 Viscount Lascelles to Princess Mary; 1923 George VI to Elizabeth Bowes-Lyon
1947 Duke of Edinburgh to Queen Elizabeth and other family [8]

Virtual Tour of the Abbey

The Nave - A narthex designed by Sir Edwin Lutyens was never built and given his work at Castle Drogo might have been a suitable Gothic addendum. However, inside the west door one sees the ridge vault of the nave with its many diagonal ribs, reaching into the distance like the uniform canopy of some primaeval forest.

With its Royal connections to France the accentuated height compared to width is more reminiscent of Rheims than the stolid English beauty of Salisbury. Yevele, who rebuilt the Norman nave from c.1376, retained the original *foreign style* of Henry de Reyn; and an ornate gallery and clerestory sits above the towering nave arcade below. In general the lines are perpendicular. However, broken coursing between the levels and the ridge-rib lead the eye towards the crossing and the choir, rather than upwards.

---

[7] Thomas Steward was usher for 46 years and his son Herbert a pupil represented the Crusaders at the first F.A. meeting, proposed Arthur Pember as president, and sat on the committee. A brother G.H. Pember attended the school from 1856-63, as did Robert Walpole Sealy Vidal who was there in 1867-72 and became famous as "The Prince of Dribblers."

[8] William IV mar. at Kew in 1818 and Edward VII at St. George's, Windsor in 1863 (see p. 151).

Returning to more earthly matters the first feature seen on entering has no elevation but is a floor tablet, poppy wreathed, commemorating the "Unknown Warrior." A plaque at Platform 8 on Victoria Station records how the warrior lay there on 10 November 1920, before being laid to rest in the Abbey the next day (erected 1998). Perhaps, it was quite correct that Lutyens narthex never obscured its presence, especially considering his more monumental tribute to the lost soldier at Thiepval in the Somme.

Nearby is a floor tablet to Winston Churchill installed on the 25th anniversary of *The Battle of Britain* and at the door another to Baroness Burdett-Coutts. On the north side standing stately on a drum is Anthony Ashley-Cooper, 7th Earl of Shaftesbury (1801-85) with inscription to his philanthropy. In the corner is a statue to James Montague died on the *Montague* off Brest 1794, a black alabaster to Robert Cecil, Marquess of Salisbury P.M. 1895-1902 erected by Parliament, and one to George, 3rd Viscount Howe who died on the march to Ticonderoga 1758 (at the expense of Massachusetts Province).

In the southwest corner is the *Coronation Chair* of Edward I, displayed in St. George's Chapel during restoration work. Other permanent features are a portrait of Richard I and later memorials to the Earl of Mountbatten, Franklin D. Roosevelt with eagle and Joost de Blank the Bishop of Stepney and Archbishop of Cape Town.

Moving towards the quire screen there are floor memorials to Mr. Thomas Tompion (1713) and George Graham F.R.S. (1751) watchmakers, David Livingstone thirty years an evangelist with the story of Chitambo's Village & Ujiji, Thomas Telford (1757-1834) the engineer, and John "Longitude" Harrison (1693-1776) clockmaker with line *0 degrees 7' 35"*. And perhaps this area should be renamed as time piece crossing.

Dean's Yard near the school with a view of the southwest tower. The organist H. Purcell lived in the precincts.

The Abbey Nave looking to the east in 1784, before Blore's Victorian makeover.

Quire and Screen - Originally the monks worshipped in the quire, an archaic term used to differentiate it from "the singing choir." Henry Keene removed all the mediaeval stalls in the 18th century; however Edward Blore reinstated them as part of a Victorian Gothic quire, with no side partitions and open access to the transepts, in 1831.

The western screen incorporated the organ gallery but the organ was placed to the sides by the columns, such that the view of the interior was not obscured. Four pilasters with decorated finials divided it into three compartments, the centre one framing the gate, and figures of Henry III, Edward Confessor, Edward I and their Queens resided above.

Sir Edward Elgar (1857-1934) showed little pomp or circumstance and was a self-taught musician.

However, the chief glory to the eye, are memorials by the quire entrance. On the left is one to "Isaacus Newton" with globe held above *inscribed in Latin* by J.M. Rysbrack to the designs of William Kent (1731), and to the right Philip Dormer Stanhope, 4th Earl of Chesterfield (1694-1773) a Whig statesman.

Naturally, there were a large number of prominent organists at the Abbey and these included Orlando Gibbons 1623, John Blow 1668, Henry Purcell 1679, John Blow 1696, William Croft 1708, Benjamin Cooke 1762 and Samuel Arnold 1793; most of whom held other significant (and similar) positions at churches within the capital.

North Aisle - Following on from the discussion of the choir we come to the "Musicians Aisle" although first note some memorials found at its western end. These include a large reposing sculpture of Charles J. Fox (1749-1806), those of Attlee, Baldwin and Campbell-Bannerman and one to Sidney and Beatrice Webb the Fabian social reformers.

A short distance to the east is a floor tablet to Charles Lyell author of *The Principles of Geology*, a stone "O rare Ben Jonson," an elaborate memorial to Robert Killigrew page of honour to Charles II and general died Almanza 1707, and below a tablet to Thomas Banks Esq. RA sculptor "whose superior abilities in his profession added a lustre to the arts of this country." Also, nearby, is a brass in granite to John Hunter M.D. 1793.

Moving towards the choir there are floor memorials to scientists William Herschel who discovered Uranus in 1781, his son Joannes Herschel also an astronomer, Charles Robert Darwin naturalist, James Prescott Joule that conserver of energy, John Smeaton with an inlaid *brass lighthouse*, and a more recent one to John Ninian Comper architect.

Along the north wall there are seven or eight bays of ecclesiastical and heraldic finery; plus a window to William, Baron Kelvin of Largs (1824-1907) engineer and philosopher which features Dick Whittington and an enigmatic cat in the corner!

Beside the choir there is a fine sculpture to Almericus de Courcy d.1719 and on the left Sir Thomas Stamford Raffles governor of Java and first president of the Zoological Soc. To the right is a statue to William Wilberforce member of the House for half a century; and on the wall (circular) tablets to Joseph Dalton Hooker of Kew, Lord Joseph Lister and Alfred R. Wallace the geographer with a "Darwin style" beard.

Regarding the Musicians Aisle, whose memorials intermingle with the above, there is a scroll memorial on the north wall to John Blow "doctor in musick, organist, composer, master of the Chapel Royal for 35 years and organist for 15 years... master to the famous Mr. H. Purcell" (whom he put forward for his own position) d.1708. Nearby is a tablet with harp to Charles Burney "unrivalled chief and scientific historian of his tuneful art" of Chelsea College d.1814, and one to Samuel Arnold doctor of musick d.1802.

A floor tablet records "Henricus Purcell organista" who died 21 November 1695. Later memorials are to Edward Elgar of *Hope and Glory* fame, and to Ralph Vaughan Williams the composer - a relative of both Darwin and Wedgwood.

South Aisle - This has fewer monuments and a plainer vault than the nave, whilst the windows below the gallery are closed off due to the proximity of the great cloister.

There is a fine wall memorial with exquisite *Relief of the Abbey* to Josephus Wilcocks d.1756 a bishop and Dean of Westminster. Also nearby is a floor tablet to Lt. General Sir James Outram (1808-63) "The Bayard of India" a hero of the Mutiny.

In addition to this, the space by the choir has a large wall sculpture to Sir Cloudesley Shovell rear admiral and commander of the fleet, which shows him lying in repose with a wig between double Corinthian columns of marble. He was shipwrecked off Scilly on the way from Toulon in 1707 and the tragedy led to the race for Harrison's chronometer. Nearby is a wall tablet to Samuel Augustus Barnett (1844-1913) the social reformer of Toynbee Hall and a canon from 1906, also his wife Henrietta Rowland.

North Transept - Having covered scientists, musicians and timekeepers we come to the "Politicians Corner" with its statues of luminary didactics, who in the dim theatrical lighting may suggest some latter day scenario from a Dr. Who episode.

On the western side are statues to Robert Stewart, 2nd Marquess of Londonderry and Viscount Castlereagh (1769-1822), erected by brother and friend Charles William Vane the 3rd Marquess; Viscount Palmerston who was born nearby at 20 Queen Anne's Gate in 1784; and William Pitt the Earl of Chatham (see St. James's). There is also a bust to George Gordon, 4th Earl of Aberdeen (1784-1860) the Conservative P.M.

Then on the east side are statues to George Canning (1770-1827), Benjamin Disraeli (1804-81) twice P.M. erected by Parliament, his great rival W.E. Gladstone (1809-98) in a cloak who outranked him with four premierships, and Robert Peel (1788-1850) that corn law disciplinarian appearing in a Roman toga with papyrus scroll. Nearby are memorials to two naval heroes Lord Robert Manners and Admiral G. Brydges Rodney.

Regarding the actual fabric the transept has an impressive rose window with rib vault, a finely sculpted gallery and decorated tiles in the arcade spandrels. From here one receives a good view of the crossing with its tall pillars of stone and almost unbroken rib rising to the mediaeval style ceiling. Also a first view of the quire with its azure-blue gilded choir stalls opposite the small sanctuary, altar with apse, and perpendicular vaulting. The choir itself is forward of the crossing unlike at St. Paul's where it is placed behind.

At the rear of the transept is a loosely separated chapel of St. Michael's where there is a wall bust to Sir John Franklin (1786-1847) born Spilsby died off Point Victory, Canada erected by his wife Jane, "O ye frost and cold, O ye ice and snow" (*Benedicite Canticle*). The other significant work is a sculpture to Sir Joseph and Lady Elizabeth Nightingale by Roubiliac carried out in 1761 and inspired by the work of Bernini in Rome. [9]

In addition there are two mediaeval canopied memorials, a statue to Sir William Webb Follett lawyer d.1845 by William Behnes, and one to Admiral Sir George Pocock who served under his uncle Lord Torrington and d.1792 by John Bacon R.A. Just outside the chapel is a fine work by Joseph Wilton commemorating James Wolfe and his expedition against Quebec "who died at the moment of victory" 8 September 1759.

---

[9] Joseph Gascoigne son of a vicar of Enfield married Elizabeth eldest daughter of Washington Shirley, 2nd Earl Ferrers. He changed his name as kinsman and heir of Sir Robert Nightingale whilst his wife's sister was Selina Hastings (née Shirley), the Countess of Huntingdon.

South Transept - One of the most famous areas of the abbey is undoubtedly "Poets Corner" recording the names of literary giants buried there and elsewhere. Approaching from the east there is a chamber of mediaeval tombs and brasses, and in front busts of John Dryden (1632-1700), Longfellow erected by English admirers of American poetry in 1884, and a record of William Spottiswoode (1825-83) president of the R.S.

Beyond on the east side is a Purbeck marble monument to Geoffrey Chaucer d.1400 with Latin inscription, "Of old the bard who struck the noblest strains." It was erected by poet Nicholas Brigham in 1556, and may have come from one of the City churches dissolved by Henry VIII. There was also a floor slab which was removed when one to John Dryden was placed there in 1720 - and in this way Poets Corner was born.

Other memorials are to Matthew Prior (1664-1721) the diplomat and poet and Samuel Butler (1613-80) author of *Hudibras*, plus a cornucopia of commemoratives to: G. Eliot, James, Auden, Lawrence, Carroll, Lear, T.S. Eliot, Tennyson, Browning &c. On the central pier there is a bust to Alfred Lord Tennyson sculpted by Thomas Woolner dated 1857, which was donated by Charles Jenner botanist and merchant in 1893; and nearby a plaque to Adam Lindsay Gordon (1833-70) "the poet of Australia."

In the southwest corner is a memorial to William Shakespeare erected in 1740 showing him leaning upon some books, perhaps musing over Edward Hall's *historical chronicles* to learn more about Richard II. Nearby there is a floor memorial to Samuel Johnson and a bust sculpted by Joseph Nollekens which was presented by G.H. Tite in 1939. A statue had been authorised by the Dean and Chapter in 1790 and may be the one that now sits in St. Paul's Cathedral - perhaps a case of "robbing Peter to pay Paul."

There is also a wall relief to "Olivarii Goldsmith" (1728-74) although the precincts are never deserted, a statue of Joseph Addison by Sir R. Westmacott 1809 and other floor or wall memorials to Brönte, Southey, Wordsworth, Dickens, Hardy, Garrick, Kipling and Macaulay. A wall sculpture to composer Handel (1685-1759) designed by L.F. Roubiliac depicts a life-like figure with his music draped casually across a desk.

The same sculptor produced the memorial to John Campbell, Duke of Argyll in 1745; and others are to architects Robert Adam born Kirkaldie [sic], Chambers and Wyatt. To conclude this rather poetical phase, *"Here in this prodigious space, sleeping below the vaulted dormer; Rest men of famous literary note, This England, this Poets' Corner."*

(Left) - A positive forest of flying buttresses, the ultimate in Gothic design - but where is the spire?

(Below) The diminutive little cloister and Barry's Victoria Tower nestling close behind.

Ambulatory - This was another feature more common in France with its curving lines, narrow walkway and four polygonal chambers, whereas at the heart stood the shrine of Edward the Confessor - now closed for some time due its fragile nature.

Henry III constructed the shrine which stood at the extreme east end from 1269, and a 15th-century screen depicting scenes from his life separated it from the sanctuary. It became a place of pilgrimage, but was dismantled during the Reformation at which time it lost its gold feretory. The design included a Cosmati mosaic floor, while the Purbeck marble base and canopy were rebuilt under Mary - although not exactly as before.

The *Coronation Chair* was made by Edward I in 1300 and enclosed the Stone of Scone from Scotland, being kept in the Chapel of St. Edward except during coronations from 1308. The stone was returned northwards in 1996, whereas the chair was moved to the ambulatory the next year (although, as stated, is now being restored).

On the north side are tombs of Henry III with onyx stone and gilt inlay and Edward I and Eleanor of Castile, while to the south are Edward III and Philippa of Hainault (with brasses) and Richard II and Anne of Bohemia. At the east end is the chantry chapel of Henry V under an elaborate carved vault, although the feet of the effigy protrude above and perhaps are a signal: "Once more unto the breach, dear friends...."

Regarding the side chapels these are all of mediaeval origin comprising delicate tracery, worn stone steps and browning walls - with numerous ancient memorials within. Initially there is a small room on the north side called the Islip Chapel which was restored by the Wilberforce family, followed by Chapels of St. John the Baptist and St. Paul. The former displays a grand memorial to Henry Carey, 1st Baron Hunsdon (1525-96) out of alabaster and marble with fine displays of heraldry, it being the tallest in the Abbey.

On the south side is the Chapel of St. Nicholas with Dukes of Northumberland and George Villiers, Duke of Buckingham, d.1606; followed by the Chapel of St. Edmund with its many heraldic brasses and memorial to Edward G.E.L. Bulwer-Lytton (1803-73) who was "distinguished in all fields of intellectual activity."

However, the chief glory of the cathedral is the Lady Chapel up a flight of steps begun by Henry VII in 1503 with perpendicular windows, ornamental choir stalls and stunning fan vault (almost squared off) with carved pendants. John Leland called it "the wonder of the entire world" with the tomb of the King at the centre, while the *colour of the joust* is recreated by wall banners to Knights of the Bath - installed there since 1725.

On each side of the Lady Chapel are side chapels and to the north are monuments to Elizabeth I (with an orb and sceptre) and Mary I. To the south are Mary Queen of Scots, Catherine Shorter wife of Sir Robert Walpole the first P.M. d.1737, and tablet to empire builder Cecil Rhodes (1853-1902). There are wall paintings in the Islip Chapel, St. Paul's Chapel, St. Faith's Chapel, the ambulatory and south transept.

Henry VII (1457-1509) united the Roses bringing full blossom to Tudor ambition in his chapel.

Philippa of Hainault (1314-69) a Plantagenet beauty was the wife of Edward III.

The Great Cloister with detail - the scalloped ribbed vault, entrance to the chapter house and ancient tombs.

The Cloisters - By the north transept is the Great North Door, while the south one is smaller in width by some degree due to the cloister. Here is the Chapter House built by Henry III in 1246-55 and with its central pillar was one of the largest in England.

A double-vaulted passageway with slim columns leads to the room where monks met to read the rule of Benedict and discuss daily affairs. On the wall are extensive paintings of c.1400 with much detail, experimental pigments and delicate glaze and leaf, also the coat of arms of the King. There were once 96 scenes depicted, whereas the floor has original mediaeval tiles and its pillar rises like a tree trunk to the lierne vaults above.

The King held council there from 1257 and the Commons used it in the 14th century but it became a repository for records in the 1540s. After three hundred years the rolls of parchment and papers crammed against the walls were removed, and George Gilbert Scott restored it to its former glory in 1859-72. Next door is the *Pyx Chamber* a Norman undercroft which stored boxes of gold and silver and later on State documents, while a passageway leads to the Little Cloister and the College Gardens beyond.

Memorials in the cloister include Capt. Edward Tufnell master mason of the College for 22 years d.1719 (s), William Buchan M.D. author of *The Family Physician or Domestic Medicine* d.1805 and William Woollett (1735-85) by T. Banks "whose works of painting, sculpture and architecture are spread over the four corners of the globe" (w).

Westminster Cathedral (Catholic)

The Bridewell, a small workhouse, opened in fields by the Green Coat School just above Rochester Row in 1618 and was later a county jail. As a result the New Bridewell was developed by Robert Abraham to the west in 1834. This was in the Panopticon style with three radiating wings for 900 prisoners but was eventually demolished in 1884.

Meanwhile, Nicholas Wiseman the first R.C. Archbishop was installed in Rome in 1850 and was followed by convert H.E. Manning in 1865. The latter purchased the Bridewell site in memory of his predecessor, and Herbert A. Vaughan (1832-1903) who studied at Stonyhurst, Downside and Belgium was then appointed at The Oratory in 1892.

In fact Archbishop Vaughan is considered the founder of the new cathedral which was built in neo-Byzantine style by John Francis Bentley from 1895-1903. It was inspired by Hagia Sophia and St. Mark's, Venice, while the tower is reminiscent of the campanile of the Palazzo Pubblico in the Piazza del Campo in Siena. The foundations are on the site of the old prison, whilst inside is *a list of arch priests* from the 16th century.

The interior, much larger than expected, has cavernous Romanesque arches with dark brickwork above enclosing a multitude of side chapels. However, this contrasts with the *twenty-four* different marbles from around the world lining the floor and lower levels, creating a striking ambience combined with prayers and incense. Although different in style the interior with its burgeoning crowds reminds one of Notre Dame in Paris.

Further work was done under Francis Bourne the fourth Archbishop (1903-35), and William Brindley colleague of Scott did marble for the columns, chapels and baldachino; Clayton & Bell worked with Salviati of Venice on the mosaics; and Eric Gill sculptor did the Stations of the Cross. The cathedral some 300 feet long was only consecrated when all the debts were paid in 1910 - although it has never been fully completed.

A strong musical tradition persists and the first London performance of Elgar's *Dream of Gerontius*, based on a poem by Newman, took place there in 1903. Sir Richard R. Terry also reintroduced the Tudor music of Byrd and Tallis, utilising the grand-organ in the west gallery and organ and choir in the apse behind the sanctuary. There is a large baptistry and the eastern chapels have relics to St. John Southworth and a marble tomb to Cardinal Vaughan the founder, lying in repose.

With the redevelopment of Victoria Street and the creation of Cathedral Piazza in the 1970s - the cathedral, once a hidden gem, became a highly visible attribute and the Queen made a very symbolic visit there in her Jubilee of 1977. [10]

Westminster Cathedral was built from 1895-1903 in the neo-Byzantine style - with baldachino by Brindley.

---

[10] St. Andrew's, Ashley Place was built in the Gothic style by George Gilbert Scott west of the Bridewell in 1853-55. It was demolished after the war and joined to St. Peter's, Eaton Square.

London West

After spending time in the crowded environs of Central London we now go to pleasurable glades to the west with pensioners, bun houses and gardens. A place to sojourn and rehabilitate with "musick" from Chopin and Mozart, symphonies at the Albert Hall and wonders in the Museums where Trajan's Column and Persian carpets enthralled the *modern* man.

At the centre was Hyde Park with its winding serpentine and palace to the west, spires of churches rising beyond the Royal abode, and squares where merry men resided ministering to amanuensis of renown. Here were canals, grand stations and stucco palaces of the nouveau-riche; the realm of Cubitt and the Victorian elite bringing us respite through *St. Lubbock's Day*.

Nearby was a chapel where Sir Robert Walpole found himself at ease, a place where Catholics and Protestants sat side by side, and also those heroes of our time Baden Powell and Shackleton stirring the imagination of the velded steppes - then again the enduring frozen wastes.

Creativity reigned with Dickens, Hogarth and Wilde but three men in a boat they were not, whilst Brunel built us bridges of gold. Here were sculptors and potters of renown, a singer from that famous Green, and some lesser known evangelists of Knightsbridge "who would valiant be."

Sir Robert Grosvenor (1767-1845) - the creator of Belgravia and Pimlico. The statue was erected by his descendant in 1997 and includes hounds, a wheatsheaf and milestone regarding his Cheshire estates. But in particular there is a quote made by John Ruskin, stating, "When we build let us hope that we build for ever."

Paddington

This was a small country village on the outskirts of London in the late 18th century, but the land between Edgware and Bayswater Roads in the southeast was a prime site for development - similar to the Grosvenor Estate. The area, which was colloquially known as "Tyburnia" aimed for high standards by giving 95-year leases to individuals, but this proved impractical and several speculative builders eventually developed the site.

The Grand Union Canal terminated at Paddington Basin in 1801 and the Regent's Canal branch went from Warwick Road across to Camden Town in 1812-16, which provided the initial impetus for development. But only 36 builders had contracted for 570 houses by 1824 and at the end of the decade only a third of the site was built on.

Despite these teething problems there was a renewal of interest when the G.W.R. built its first terminus at Bishop's (Bridge) Road by the canal in 1838, and many terraces and villas were constructed to rival other developments such as Belgravia. [1]

The parish church of St. Mary's, Paddington Green, became something of a backwater and the focus shifted to the more opulent area by the triangle of Sussex Gardens, villas of Westbourne Terrace and mansions of Lancaster Gate. In addition there was separate development of Bayswater to the west - although on a slightly less dramatic scale.

One of the first undertakings was Connaught Square just east of St. George's Fields in 1828, which was designed by the architect Thomas Allason - who also laid out Ladbroke (Grove) Estate with its large crescents. Indeed, there were great opportunities to those who grasped the nettle, one example of this being William Crake painter &c. of 18 Old Quebec Street and his son John who was an architect.

The Crakes purchased the leases on Hyde Park Gardens in 1837 and built two terraces of stucco mansions, one parallel to the road (1-24) and another at an angle (25-38) with columned porches and further entrances to the rear. Arthur Fitzgerald Kinnaird, the son of Arthur and Mary Jane (Hoare) evangelists, was born at No. 35 on 16 February 1847 and apart from his involvement in soccer was also a churchman of note.

Such developments were very lucrative and William Crake lived nearby at 10 Stanhope Street (Southwick Place), while son W.H. Crake born at Notting Hill and an East India merchant of Old Broad Street resided at 34 Gloucester Square - the latter's estate being valued at £209,820 in 1887. In addition, a plaque erected on No. 35 in 1905 stated, "In memory of Robert Stephenson (1803-59) engineer who died here" (moved 1937).

Other notables included Reginald de Courtney Welch born at 6 Westbourne Place who attended Harrow with William Parry Crake (grandson of the builder). Both played for the Wanderers in the first Cup Final and Welch, who was goalkeeper, was an army tutor at 1 Southwick (Hyde Park) Crescent and principal of the Army College, Heath End near to Farnham in 1895-1939. He was the driving force behind the Aldershot Tattoo and left a number of scholarships to the R.M.A. and R.M.C. in commemoration of his son.

---

[1] Isambard K. Brunel and his associate Matthew D. Wyatt built a new station complex on Praed Street from 1851-54, while the original station became a goods depot. To the front was the Great Western Hotel designed at this time by Philip Charles Hardwick, who was also responsible for the Great Hall at Euston Station in 1849 (son of Philip and grandson of Thomas).

William M. Thackeray the novelist resided at 18 Albion Street whereas Lord Randolph Churchill lived at 2 Connaught Place from 1883-92 and Sir Winston Churchill at Caxton House, Sussex Square in 1921-24. In addition William H. Smith bookseller and statesman occupied 12 Hyde Park Street, and Sir Giles Gilbert Scott designed and lived in "Chester House," Clarendon Place from 1926 (various plaques mark the sites).

Bayswater Chapel

The road above Hyde Park was termed the *Via Trinobantia* by the Romans and in the mediaeval period went west to Ealing and then to Uxbridge. In the vicinity was Bayard's watering place or Bayswater a hamlet by the West Bourne. William Craven, 3rd Baron Craven, purchased a farm of nine acres there and constructed Craven Hill House on the site (also Craven Cottage). To the west was the *Gravel Pits* near to Kensington Gardens whose cognomen was clearly a misnomer since there were many large houses.

Prominent residents in this rural area included John Hill born in Peterborough in 1714 who was apprenticed to a London apothecary and married Susannah Travers, daughter of the steward to the Earl of Burlington, in 1742. In this way he progressed and from the Strand collected specimens for the Duke of Richmond and met with Sir Hans Sloane. He married Henrietta Jones sister of Charles, 4th Viscount Ranelagh at St. George's, Mayfair, in 1753 and lived at Arlington Street with a physic garden in Bayswater.

His numerous works included a dictionary of astronomy, useful family herbal, the flora Britannica (first Linnaean flora), herbal remedies (for the colonies), the family practice of physic, herbarium Britannica and works on fossils. Lord Bute was a benefactor thus he helped him lay out Kew Gardens, and through Richmond attended Goodwood races and met David Garrick - thereby acting at Drury Lane and Covent Garden.

In addition he ran a column called the Inspector in the *Daily Advertiser* and received a knighthood from King Gustavus of Sweden, whilst Hogarth and Churchill satirised him. Although the latter gave a backhanded compliment dubbing him, "The Renaissance Man actor, inspector, doctor and botanist." He died at Golden Square in 1775 and was buried at Denham then his wife wrote his biography but had litigation with Lord Bute.

At this time the physic garden was closed and became Bayswater Tea Gardens "with its springs and salubrious air." Edward Orme (1775-1848), an engraver and print-seller of Bond Street, purchased Elms House and its adjacent gardens in 1809, a lease on Craven Hill including some dwellings near to the old pest house in 1811, and other land further along the main road above the park towards Kensington.

Bayswater Chapel (left) built in 1818 gave spiritual sustenance - but the tea gardens weren't far away.

St. Matthew's was built on the site in 1879-82 by a minister who worked with the Cree Indians.

One of his first buildings was Bayswater Chapel for 1,200 people on St. Petersburgh Place in 1818. The nearby streets were then developed in a piecemeal fashion including Orme Square and Moscow Road (named after a Russian trading venture or visit by Tsar Alexander). Other developments were Lancaster Gate and Porchester Gardens.

This semi-rural area was popular with the artistic community and the poet Sarah Flower Adams moved to 5 Craven Hill in 1834, attracting Thomas Carlyle and a young Robert Browning. Next door at No. 4 were organist Vincent Novello and authors Charles and Mary C. Clarke, whilst John and Jane Loudon botanists lived at 3 Porchester Terrace and their guests included the Landseers, Joseph Bonomi and John Martin. [2]

Edward Orme moved to 6 Fitzroy Square from 1829-48, but should not be confused with Alexander and Cosmo Orme members of the E.I.C. who also resided there. The tea gardens were renamed as "Flora" and "Victoria," but closed in 1854, while the chapel was dedicated to St. Matthew's in 1858 and a baroque façade added. By then the population had swelled to over 75,000 and no doubt the parish proved quite inadequate.

In 1867 Archdeacon Hunter arrived after 23 years working with the Cree in Canada and an unusual four-tier Venetian Gothic campanile was erected in 1871, but by that time the old chapel was quite dilapidated. It was replaced by a new building at the top of St. Petersburgh Place at a cost of £29,050 in 1879-82 - with Chapel Terrace behind.

New West End Synagogue - This was designed by the architect Nathan S. Joseph just below St. Matthew's at a cost of £24,980 in 1879. The foundation was laid by Leopold de Rothschild who was its main benefactor, in the presence of Dr. Nathan Adler the chief rabbi. Indeed, the cosmopolitan nature of the area was confirmed when a Greek Orthodox cathedral was added on Moscow Road in 1882.

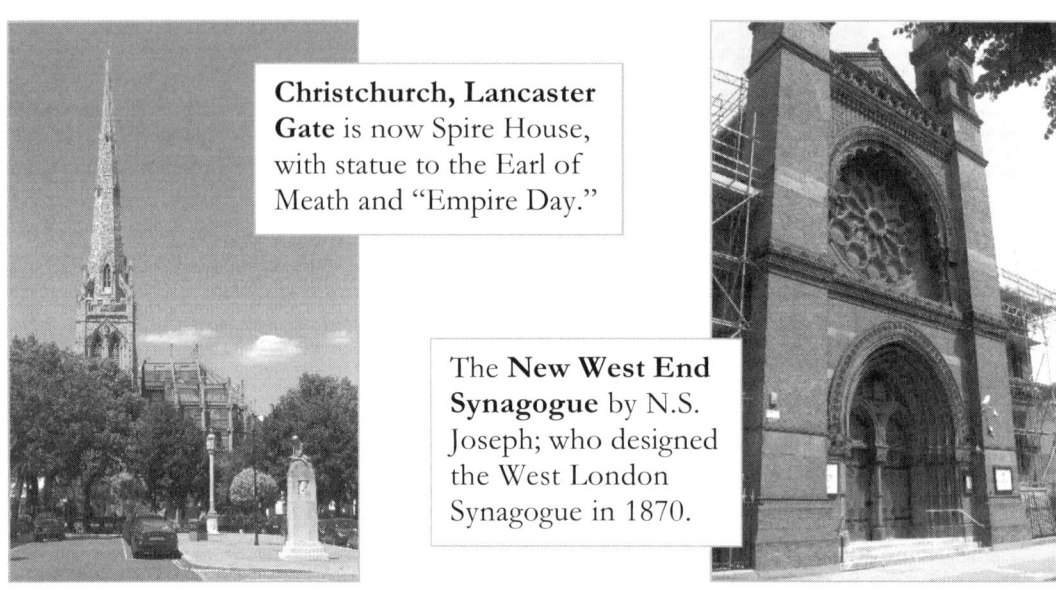

Christchurch, Lancaster Gate is now Spire House, with statue to the Earl of Meath and "Empire Day."

The **New West End Synagogue** by N.S. Joseph; who designed the West London Synagogue in 1870.

---

[2] Other residents were Sir Rowland Hill at 1 Orme Square in 1839-42, Frederic Lord Leighton at 2 Orme Square in 1860-66, J.M. Barrie the novelist at 100 Bayswater Road and Jessie Mitchell daughter of Sir John McGaskill at 87 Kensington Gardens Square (see later), whilst Opus Dei now maintains an office at Orme Square.

Christchurch, Lancaster Gate, a large edifice was built by F. and H. Francis in 1855, and Henry de Bruno Austin developed the adjacent housing in the next decade. The F.A. came to No. 22 a private hotel with stucco façade from Russell Square in 1929, and Sir Frederick Wall secretary and his wife Agnes lived there and were ambassadors for the game. The offices moved to Nos. 16-17 in 1972 before transferring to Soho Square.

The adjacent church was demolished except for the tower in 1977 and was converted to housing, whereas the parish was joined to St. James's, Paddington. In front of the church is a statue to Reginald Brabazon, 12th Earl of Meath (1841-1929) an M.P. patriot and philanthropist responsible for social improvements and Empire Day - erected 1934.

M. 28 December 1865 William Holman Hunt artist of Kensington s. of William manager warehouse and Fanny Waugh of Queensborough Terr d. of George gent by R.G. Maul off min. witness W.M. Rossetti, G. & Emily Waugh, Thomas Combe, R. Home [3]

St. James's, Paddington

After the Regent's Canal had opened Paddington Basin became less significant, and Rev. Archibald Montgomery Campbell vicar (1829-59) suggested a new parish church in 1830. St. Mary's was clearly in the wrong place due to speculative building beside Hyde Park and a foundation stone was laid by Paddington trustees on 12 February 1841.

John Goldicutt and George Gutch architects designed a new structure at £9,000, then Bishop Blomfield consecrated "St. James the Less" at the intersection of Sussex Gardens and Westbourne Terrace on 13 May 1843. The edifice which had seating for only 800 people was then made into the parish church in 1845. However it was of little real merit and eventually Rev. Walter Abbott decided it should be demolished and rebuilt.

George E. Street who had worked on the Law Courts in the Strand was employed and Princess Christian daughter of Victoria laid the foundation in February 1882. The tower, porch and crypt were retained and the sanctuary moved to the west end; whilst a broad nave was built over the top of the existing church, allowing services to continue. All of the work was carried out in less than a year (take note modern developers) and Rev. John Jackson the Bishop of London consecrated it on 22 December 1882.

Gone were the old galleries and cramped spaces and in their place a lofty church faced with flint and Corby stone, leading to an impressive interior of Devonshire marble with its white arcade, wooden vault and gold corbels. The exquisite oak pews were carved on site with no repetition of design and there was seating for 1,320 people. A brass plaque just inside the door commemorates the achievement, while the clergy were also chaplains to St. Mary's Hospital which was near to the station (from 1851).

Meanwhile, there were several significant connections the first being the Kinnaird family who lived at 35 Hyde Park Gardens from 1843-60. They had five children baptized and the father, who was initially named Arthur "Wellesley" after the Duke of Wellington his godfather, became "Fitzgerald" due to an acrimonious political dispute.

---

[3] Holman Hunt married Fanny Waugh but she died on a trip to Florence and has a memorial in the English Cemetery near Elizabeth Barrett Browning (d.1861). He married her sister (Marion) Edith at Neuchâtel, Switzerland in 1875 since this was not permitted in law until 1907, and fell out with Thomas Woolner (see over). Thomas Combe of Oxford Univ. Press was a patron.

190

St. James's, Paddington was a symbol of Christian virtue under Kinnaird and Baden-Powell, but also witnessed the marriage of **Oscar Wilde** who was earnest in other ways.

He was a partner in Ransom & Co. bankers at 1 Pall Mall East and as a Whig Liberal represented Perth as an M.P. from 1852-78. His wife founded the St. John's School for Domestic Servants under the guidance of Rev. Noel of Hornsey before they married and with Lady Canning sent nurses and aid to the wounded in the Crimea.

They moved to 1 & 2 Pall Mall East (Kinnaird House) and were involved in the C.M.S., Malta Protestant College, Lock Hospital, Dr. Barnardo's, L.C.M. and Aged Christian's Society. Kinnaird ranked in zeal with Lord Shaftesbury at the May Meetings and his wife founded the British Ladies' Female Emigration Society and Y.W.C.A. He became 10th Lord in 1878 and owned Rossie Priory near Dundee and Plaistow Lodge, Bromley. His son then followed in his footsteps as a banker, philanthropist and sportsman.

In the second instance, Robert Stephenson S. Powell was the son of a local clergyman and Savilian professor at Oxford, and was named after Robert Stephenson the engineer his godfather who lived nearby. His own father died when he was three and as there were siblings by a former marriage, and out of respect, his mother changed the surname to Baden-Powell. He was educated at Charterhouse and spent much of his time as a soldier in South Africa being involved with the Zulus and during the second Boer War.

After the Siege of Mafeking he became a major general and national hero, whilst he was involved with the Boys Brigade and took a group to Brownsea Island in 1907. The next year he published *Scouting for Boys* based on his army experience, and groups of scouts spontaneously formed around the country with a rally at Crystal Palace in 1909.

Regarding the marriages, Thomas Woolner (1825-92) was born at Hadleigh, Suffolk and as a sculptor and poet founded the Pre-Raphaelites with Holman Hunt, Millais and Rossetti. He went to Australia in 1852 and as a result had several commissions which included a statue of Godley for Christchurch, N.Z. In addition he associated with some leading writers, and proposed to Fanny Waugh prior to marrying her sister.

Oscar Wilde was born in Dublin in 1854, his father a surgeon and mother a writer and nationalist thus he was introduced to Irish folklore and poetry. After attending T.C.D. and Oxford he came to London with an inheritance, and lectured on aesthetics in the U.S. for D'Oyly Carte in 1882. He also lived in Paris on the expected proceeds of *The Duchess of Padua* and proposed to his wife in Dublin, then had a lavish lifestyle at 34 Tite Street, Chelsea. As a journalist he met J.M. Stoddart editor of *Lippincott's* at the Langham Hotel in 1889. It was a significant literary moment and Conan Doyle produced *The Sign of Four* in February 1890, and Wilde wrote *Picture of Dorian Gray* the lead story for July.

At this point all seemed quite favourable and *Lady Windermere's Fan* was performed at St. James's Theatre in 1892, but an affair with Lord Alfred Douglas son of the Marquess of Queensberry was his undoing. *The Importance of Being Earnest* was staged there in 1895 but was followed by high profile court-cases, and he was imprisoned for impropriety in May of that year then served hard labour at Pentonville and Wandsworth.

His wife changed her name to Holland and died in 1898, while his health suffered under the hard regime and on his release he went to the Continent, dying penniless in Paris in 1900. Indeed like Byron and Shelley before him he was persecuted by the authorities for non-conformism, but was greatly honoured in literary circles after his decease.

C. 31 March 1847 Arthur Fitzgerald son of Arthur F. and Mary Jane Kinnaird a banker of 35 Hyde Park Gardens by Joseph J. Parker off min. born 16 February
8 July 1857 Robert Stephenson Smyth son of Baden and Henrietta Powell a clergyman of 6 Stanhope Street by John Buck off. minister born 22 February

M. 6 September 1864 Thomas Woolner sculptor of Marylebone s. of Thomas civil service and Alice Gertrude Waugh minor of Christchurch, Paddington d. of George a chymist [sic] by G. Rhodes off minister presence George Waugh, W. Holman Hunt
29 May 1884 Oscar Finigal O'Flahertie Wilde 28 gent of 9 Charles Street son Sir W.R. Wills Wilde surgeon to Constance Mary Lloyd 26 of 100 Lancaster Gate d. of Horace a Queen's Counsel by special licence Walter Abbott vicar wit Jane 'Speranza' Lady Wilde, L.H. Hempwick, Ced. Swinburn King and William C.K. Wilde MA

St. John's, Hyde Park

Prince William Frederick, otherwise the Duke of Gloucester and Edinburgh and Earl of Connaught, constructed 1 Connaught Place for his brother-in-law the Duke of Sussex in 1807. Once this was completed he also built other properties in the locality. In fact, 7 Connaught Place was later occupied by Princess Caroline who came there after her separation from the Prince Regent with their only daughter Charlotte.

Rev. Dr. Crane then requested a church for these new residents in 1826. Samuel Pepys Cockerell (who was architect to the Bishop of London) produced a design for an edifice called the Connaught Chapel, but died before it could be built. Instead, the Commissioners asked Charles Fowler son-in-law of Dr. Crane for a second design, and he came up with a "13th century" Gothic church with 1,500 seats - half of which were rent free.

Regarding the cost £6,000 came from the Commissioners and the remainder from local donations - the total expenditure £8,735. It was dedicated to St. John the Evangelist and consecrated by Bishop C.J. Blomfield on 26 January 1832. The main features were its central location in an oval, college-style façade to the west, Perpendicular interior with clerestory windows and groin vaults, and chancel with a great east window.

Initially it was a chapel of ease under Rev. James S. Boone and Mendelssohn came there in 1839-40, but became a separate parish in Paddington under Dr. Edward M. Goulburn from 1859 (H.M. of Rugby and of Quebec Chapel). Other local churches were All Saints, Norfolk Square built by Henry Clutton in 1847 but rebuilt by Ralph Nevill in 1895 and closed in 1925; Holy Trinity, Bishop's Road by Thomas Cundy junior erected in 1846 but demolished in 1971; and St. Michael's, Star Street present from 1864-1967.

Today, St. John's has a font donated at the time of Rev. Goulburn in 1862 and an organ dating to 1865. Other features are a marble tablet to Rev. Edmund Hollond of 33 Hyde Park Gardens and Benhall Lodge, Suffolk (1801-84) and his wife Fanny daughter of John Reade of Holbrooke House; memorial to Claud John Hamilton M.P. (1843-1925) son of the 1st Duke of Abercorn; and window to Sir John Aird (1833-1911) churchwarden who rebuilt the Crystal Palace and partnered Lucas (a relative of the Crakes).

As stated a number of prominent people lived nearby viz. Crake, Welch, Churchill and Stephenson, and there were several marriages of importance. Charles Synge Christopher Bowen was born at Woolaston, Gloucester in 1835 the son of Rev. Christopher Bowen a member of the Anglo-Irish gentry. His father was the curate of Bath Abbey in 1838-43 and perpetual curate of St. Mary Magdalen, Bermondsey in 1843-55.

He was educated at Blackheath, Rugby and Oxford and entered Lincoln's Inn in 1861 then married the daughter of James Meadows Rendel C.E. F.R.S. the next year. Whilst at university he met Horace Davey and Edward Pember (also of that Inn) and their lives became entwined in a legal and fraternal sense. The former were Lords of Appeal and the latter parliamentary counsel, while son Francis Pember married Margaret Bowen Davey (named after him). Bowen was also a privy councillor and Baron of Hollymount in 1893 residing at a number of addresses in Kensington and Knightsbridge.

Regarding the Rendel family the father lived at 10 Palace Gardens, Kensington and his daughter Catherine Emily married Clement Francis Wedgwood, great grandson of Josiah founder of *Etruria Works*, at the church in 1866. The latter was in the family business at Barlaston, and son Josiah Clement M.P. married his cousin Ethel Kate Bowen daughter of Charles and Emily (see All Saints, Ennismore Gardens).

M. 7 January 1862 Charles S.C. Bowen bar at law St. Marylebone s. Chris. clerk in holy orders and Emily Frances Rendel of Hyde Park Street d. James Meadows civ eng F.R.S. licence by Christopher Bowen off min pres. J.M. Rendel, Edith Rendel

6 November 1866 Clement Francis Wedgwood potter of Barlaston, Staffs son of Francis potter and Emily Catharine Rendel [sic] o.t.p. daughter of James Meadows civ eng banns by E.M. Goulburn incumbent, W.J. Armstrong pres. A.M., C.J. and Edith Rendel

St. John's, Hyde Park (with interior) was built on Hyde Park Crescent as a Gothic centrepiece in 1832.

St. Mary's, Paddington

The ancient area of Paddington consisted of a small village and mediaeval church by a green on Harrow Road, just west of the Edgware Road. It was first recorded in 1222 and was a chapel for St. Margaret's, Westminster held by the Abbey, whereas John Donne came and preached there in 1615. Sir Joseph Sheldon mayor rented Paddington Manor and the church was rebuilt with a small nave at this time in 1679, while nearby were the manor house, vicarage, an independent chapel, and a few cottages.

However, the area developed in tandem with the city and it was rebuilt again 80 yards to the south by John Plaw, in Georgian style with square nave, in 1788-91 - and had a large churchyard to the north. Charles Greville (1749-1809), Lord Admiral lived by the Green and introduced Emma Hart to his uncle William Hamilton. He took her to Naples as his mistress where she entered society and they married at Marylebone in 1791.

St. Mary's, Paddington

The Georgian church built by John Plaw in 1791, was eventually deemed *too small* for the nouveau-riche residents of the growing parish. Hence it became a chapel for St. James's to the south. It now resides on Paddington Green near the canal, but with ceaseless streams of traffic nearby.

Paddington Green was further enclosed as housing developed reducing its size in 1801 and the church was connected to many prominent people (see below). At the same time the Basin of the Grand Union Canal was built by William Jessop under William Praed resulting in other changes. In fact, the Regent's Canal was to have gone right past the church but was eventually taken to the north and around Regent's Park.

Byron is generally accredited with coining the name *Little Venice* for the junction where the two canals met, and being much travelled clearly knew what he was saying. However, anyone who has been lost in Venice is unlikely to suffer the same fate here! [4]

St. Mary's also lost its parish status as matters transferred south in 1845 and became a chapel of ease, whilst the music-hall performer Harry Clifton (1832-72) wrote the song *Pretty Polly Perkins* in 1863. The church was restored to a parish in 1885 and nearby is the attractive Little Venice, but it suffers from the presence of the Westway flyover.

[4] Robert Browning the poet resided at Warwick Avenue (Road) from 1862-87 and has a plaque. He is sometimes deemed to have originated the name Little Venice - but erroneously.

Paddington (Lost and Found) - The most significant marriage at the church was that of William Hogarth. He was born at Bartholomew Close in the City and began life as an engraver of coats of arms, shop bills and plates for booksellers in 1720.

After preparing a design for Joshua Morris in 1727 he took him to court when it was declined, and also joined the Freemasons at Little Queen Street. Sir James Thornhill the artist/painter had an academy at his house in Covent Garden and Hogarth was a student, then married his daughter Jane and thereafter produced his greatest works.

Of the connections at the old church, John Bushnell the sculptor worked on Temple Bar, the Royal Exchange and owned a property at Tyburn Lane where he built a replica of the Trojan Horse, this being a tavern which blew down in a gale! Others were Joseph F. Nollekens painter of Antwerp sponsored by Richard Child, Earl Tylney of Wanstead who produced work for country houses and lived at 28 Dean Street, Soho; and Matthew Dubourg violinist and composer, a pupil of Geminiani, who led the orchestra in the first performance of Handel's *Messiah* in Dublin.

Later associations were Rev. Alexander Geddes a biblical scholar, Thomas Banks the sculptor who lived at 5 Newman Street, and Joseph Nollekens son of the above who was baptized at the Venetian chapel. The latter trained as a sculptor at Vine Street and copied Roman antiquities for Lord Palmerston and Viscount Spencer; then lived at 9 Mortimer Street, Marylebone and produced three naval memorials for Westminster Abbey.

In addition there was Rev. Basil Woodd (1772-1840) a hymn writer and preacher at St. Peter's Cornhill and the Bentinck Chapel, Marylebone; Sarah Siddons actress who lived at Westbourne Grove during 1805-17; Benjamin Robert Haydon painter and historical writer; and William J.T. Collins landscape painter of 1 Devonport Street who was father of W. Wilkie novelist (opposite) and Charles Alston the Pre-Raphaelite.

St. Mary's was in a quiet rural village in the 1700s; but the arrival of **Little Venice** (so designated by Lord Byron), at the junction of two canals, changed everything.

Sarah Siddons (1755-1831) the most famous actress of her day has a statue on Paddington Green of 1897.

St. Mary's, Paddington parish registers

M. 23 March 1728/29 William Hogarth married Jane Thornhill both of the parish of St. Paul's Covent Garden by licence

B. 15 May 1701 John Bushnel an image maker from St. Martin in the Fields, London a note was sent to the collectors Robt. Talbot curate
24 Jan 1747/48 Joseph Francis Nollekens from St. Anne's, Westminster
7 July 1767 Mathew Dubourg from St. Marylebone

4 March 1802 Rev. Dr. Alexander Geddes from Marylebone
8 February 1805 Thomas Banks of St. Marylebone
1 May 1823 Joseph Nollekens of Mortimer Street, Marylebone, 86
10 April 1831 Rev. Basil Woodd of Paddington Green, 70
15 June 1831 Sarah Siddons of Upper Baker Street, 76
29 June 1846 Benjamin Robert Haydon of Burwood Place, 60
22 February 1847 William John Thos. Collins of Devonport Street, 59

Wilkie Collins
(the novelist)

Other Paddington Churches

St. Augustine's, Kilburn - Richard Carr Kirkpatrick was a friend and disciple of Pusey and curate at St. Mary's, Kilburn but they lacked any High Church doctrines. He formed a new group who worshipped at All Saints, Margaret Street, then erected a "tin shed" on swampy ground near to Carlton Vale in 1870 (see Pember ref. Brixton).

The congregation employed John Loughborough Pearson who had done High Church work at St. Peter's, Vauxhall, and he built a soaring Gothic red brick edifice based on Albi Cathedral and St. Etienne, Caen in France. His primary intention was *to draw people to their knees* and inside was a tall arcade, ornate tiles, furnishings and high altar with lamps. The edifice was consecrated by John Jackson the Bishop of London in 1880.

Following the Ritualist tradition it had sisters under Mother Emily Ayckbowm who went to Ham, whilst the attached St. Peter's Home (started at HT, Brompton in 1861) became a convent in Woking. Rev. Kirkpatrick remained there until 1907 (see picture p. 314).

St. Mary Magdalene, Woodchester Street was one of the best creations by George Edmund Street and was built near to Royal Oak station in 1867-77. It was considered a Gothic masterpiece with polygonal apse, perpendicular nave, red and white banding, and a soaring white stone spire above. Inside was a reredos by Thomas Earp. Today, it is one of the few surviving historic buildings left on the Warwick Estate. St. Saviour's, Warwick Road built by Thomas Little in 1856 was replaced in 1976 (see p. 315).

St. Stephen's, Westbourne Park (Bayswater) was built as an adjunct to properties of wealthy merchants in Crescent Terrace by F. and H. Francis in 1856. It was south of the above church and a focus for the growing area, but being at the intersection of two roads its chancel was at the west end. An apse was added in 1900 and the spire was replaced by pinnacles during the 1950s, while it remains open today (see St. Clement Danes).

M. 6 August 1885 John Raphael Wedgwood 53 wid stationer of Barnes s. Ralph gent to Margaret Strachan 45 wid of St Stephen's d. Edward Swait gent lic Henry J. Heard

Victoria (area)

When the parish of St George's Hanover Square was created in the 1720s it covered the immediate precincts of Mayfair; but also took in fields to the south located around King's Road, Five Fields Road and the hamlet of Pimlico. Across to the east were the extensive Chelsea waterworks and Tothill Fields on the outskirts of Westminster, whilst the area between Sloane Street and Vauxhall Bridge Road became Belgravia and Pimlico.

Robert Grosvenor (1767-1845), 1st Marquess of Westminster the leading developer was the grandson of another Sir Robert, one of three brothers who were all baronets. They were the sons and heirs of Sir Thomas Grosvenor and his wife Mary Davies.

However, the Marquess had a new vision a hundred years after his ancestors and with Thomas Cubitt developed modern stucco mansions for the Victorian nobility and gentry. These opulent houses with their grand porches, classical façades and retiring mews were located near to Belgrave and Eaton Squares in the north, although Pimlico by Belgrave Road and St. George's Drive was constructed on a slightly inferior scale.

The original parish of St. George's Hanover Square was a complete anathema to such residents. Holy Trinity, Knightsbridge (see later) was no more than a chapel of ease, so the urgent need for new churches was clearly apparent. First came St. Peter's followed by a whole network of parishes developed with the poor in mind; while Victoria Station was constructed beyond its Battersea terminus by the Grosvenor Canal in 1860.

St. Barnabas, Pimlico

The locality of Pimlico Road was market gardens and open country in the 18th century and a popular resort for recreation. George II and George III liked to visit *Chelsea Bun House*, whilst Ranelagh Pleasure Gardens with its grand rotunda opened nearby in 1742. It was a top concert venue and Leopold Mozart, wife Maria and their talented son and daughter arrived at Cecil Court, St. Martin's Lane during their tour in April 1764.

Master Mozart, "the prodigy," played the harpsichord at Ranelagh Gardens on 29 June and the family moved to Five Fields Row (Ebury Street) in the July for his father's health. They stayed with Dr. Randall for seven weeks recuperation, and the boy composed his first symphony in the quiet of the house - a plaque at No. 180 records the event.

The area itself had several fashionable venues. Strumbolo House & Gardens were just opposite on Queen Street at the corner with Bloomfield Terrace, and adjacent was the Orange Coffee House which later had a theatre attached. However Ranelagh House and its rotunda were demolished in 1805 and the locality declined from that time.

W.J.E. Bennett then arrived at St. Paul's after wealthy postings in Marylebone, but was greatly perturbed by the Church's neglect of the urban poor and aimed to take action. St. Michael's, Chester Square was built for local residents by Thomas Cundy II in 1844, although the extreme south of St. Paul's parish contained much poorer housing.

What once formed part of the gardens of the Earl of Ranelagh became a foul slum with an open sewer, poverty stricken residents, and much vice and degradation. In particular, the children were without clothes and in ill-health. Bennett imbued with the ideas of the Ritualists and the Catholic tradition of ministering to the needy made an earnest plea.

> **St. Michael's, Chester Square** was built in an affluent part of Belgravia by Thomas Cundy II, who did many other churches in the area....
>
> But the bell cote of **St. Mary Bourne**, a church for servants, was one of its only forms of ornamentation.

He was determined that the Church should be for everyone and not just for those who could pay pew rents, so he talked of the priests' failings in this respect and appealed to the parishioners of St. Paul's by letter to raise £14,000 - as follows:

"This is not an unjust tax upon you for preaching the Gospel to the poor. Belgrave Square, Eaton Place and the like are the cause of Ebury and Queen Streets being filled with populations of poor people. Come with me and visit the dens of infamy, the haunts of vice, filth, ignorance and atheism, then look at your noble houses, the gold that glitters on your sideboards and jewels that glisten in your bosom and say to your conscience as before God at Judgement: What shall I do, if I give not of the one to relieve the other?" Not surprisingly the appeal was a success and £6,500 was collected in just a year.

A school and parsonage was started immediately between Queen Street and Ranelagh Grove, while the plans were enlarged to provide a college for four priests and choristers, and the foundation was laid (on the coffee house site) on St. Barnabas's Day 1847. The architect was again Thomas Cundy II (see below) and his building in the High Church tradition was consecrated by Bishop C.J. Blomfield in 1850.

St. Barnabas, with its school and vestry around a courtyard, was embattled in more than one sense. As a leader in the Ritualist Movement it was satirised in *Punch*, blasphemous graffiti appeared on its walls, the clergy were threatened and insulted and 100 policemen were needed during services to keep the mobs at bay. Bennett refused to yield to such pressure but the Bishop demanded his resignation and despite numerous letters from the parishioners, he resigned in poor health and departed from Pimlico in 1851.

However, his legacy was a High Church edifice, and a cornucopia of top names came to work there. This resulted in a spectacular ceiling, numerous mosaics and much Pre-Raphaelite detail with stained glass by Charles Kempe/Walter Tower, pulpit probably by W. Butterfield, reredos by G.F. Bodley and Lady Chapel and figures by Ninian Comper. Today, the building has a new spire of Portland stone (clearly apparent) which replaced the softer Caen stone, after a serious collapse, in 2006-07.

St. Mary (Bourne), Graham Street was built to the north above the new underground in 1874. Architect R.J. Withers (1823-1904) worked on St. Mary le Strand, but here used cheap brick with windowless aisles, small arcade, an apse, tall clerestory and slate roof at £4,500. The only embellishments were gifts like the reredos, and as *A Church for Servants* it had the same tradition of Catholic style worship and ministering to the poor.

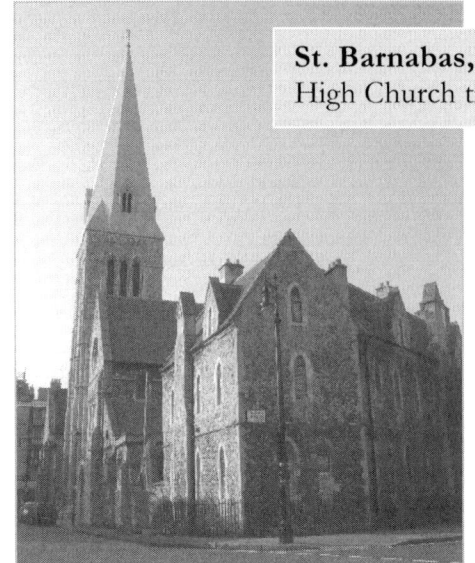

St. Barnabas, Pimlico was built among slums in the High Church tradition but has something of the baronial.

Local Missionaries - One minister of note at St. Barnabas was George R. Adam who was born on the E.I.C. ship *Grenville* in the Channel in 1837 and baptized at Camberwell. His father George Ure Adam was a banker and merchant from Dundee, but his mother Charlotte Clementina Elphinstone was born at Quilon, India, of an elite family. [5]

Adam trained at Cumbrae College attached to a cathedral in the western isles and was ordained by the Bishop of Worcester in 1862. Initially he was a curate at Great Malvern and Dorking but became chaplain to the Earl of Strathmore at Glamis in 1866, no doubt through his family connections. However he then came to St. Barnabas as the assistant curate from 1867-70 and was married there later residing at 23 Chester Terrace. After a period without a cure he went to Yeldham, Essex in 1874-77 and was vicar of Sholden, Kent from 1877-1918, whereas his son Clement attended Sandhurst. [6]

Of the residents, Rev. Charles B. Wollaston married Eleanor Reynolds (see All Souls) and was the vicar of Felpham, Sussex and Amport, Hants during 1847-86. He retired to 35 Westbourne Place (Cliveden Place) near Sloane Square and 8 Bloomfield Terrace by St. Barnabas. In fact, he was related to the academic Wollastons of Charterhouse Square and his son C.H.R. Wollaston also resided in Pimlico (see St. Gabriel's).

Today, Orange Square sits just above the church behind the Chelsea Barracks, and is an improving *Conservation Area* with a statue of a young Mozart and information board about its history. There is also a plaque to H. Nicholson and Vita Sackville West at 182 Ebury Street and artisans dwellings built by the Peabody Trust in 1871-75.

M. 27 June 1870 George Robert Adam priest St. Barnabas College s. of George banker to Montague Marion Mitchell wid of 23 Chester Terrace d. of Richard Wildman Esq. by banns by James Skinner wit. Richard Wildman, G. Adam, Howard Leach

---

[5] Charlotte Clementina was daughter of Charles Elphinstone (1780-1831) a major in the E.I.C. and his wife Primrose Margaret Welsh. The latter descended from the 9th Lord Elphinstone and was thus related to Robert Adam the architect and later on the Royal family.

[6] George and Charlotte Adam had two other children: Charlotte Williamina Ewbank who was born at Weston Super Mare in 1842 the wife of Robert Whyte procurator fiscal of Forfar; and Charles James Elphinstone Adam born at Forfar in 1844 who immigrated to Port Chalmers, New Zealand in 1863, then was a bullock driver and shepherd and later went to Wellington. He is not to be confused with Sir Charles Elphinstone Adam of Blair Adam (of architect fame).

St. Gabriel's, Pimlico

The area of Pimlico "proper" was located east of St. Barnabas and here Thomas Cubitt, main contractor to the Marquess of Westminster, erected a grid of streets comprising of linked parallel roads. The properties were more sedate and affordable than in Belgravia to the north, and a number of churches were built as part of this development.

Thomas Cundy (1790-1867) succeeded his father as surveyor for the Grosvenor Estate and was foreman to Cubitt on the main building project which started in the 1840s. He designed St. Gabriel's at the west end of Warwick Square in Kentish ragstone with spire, as a direct foil to the more classical lines of the stucco villas nearby. The Gothic-style church was completed in 1852 with a rear arch, nave arcade, distinctive double aisles and low fluted columns. Indeed, the area soon attracted "new money" residents.

Charles Rowse a coffee-house keeper resided at 55 Crawford Street, Marylebone (near St. Mary's, Bryanston Square) and had a daughter Catherine Ruth in 1847, whilst of his eight lodgers five were policemen! Coffee was apparently a remunerative commodity and the family eventually departed for Sutherland Place, Pimlico, by vacant ground of the Chelsea Water Works. John F. Alcock who began Forest F.C. later the Wanderers and an F.A. founder then married Catherine at St. Gabriel's in 1867.

However, this apparent respectability hid a whole host of problems and after a year at 5 Sutherland Place they removed to 2 Albert Villas, Amyand Park Road, Twickenham. This was followed by a long legal case with counter-suits revealing a degree of trouble and his final departure in 1873. At this time the respondent sold all the furniture and returned to her 'immoral way of life' at Nassau Street near to Middlesex Hospital.

On one side Catherine was shown to have been drunk and received men in her rooms, whilst her husband was accused of assault and the like at Twickenham. However, there was a High Court case in 1875 and *an all male jury* found in favour of Alcock, his wife being incarcerated in Peckham House Asylum, Banstead and Wandsworth - where she died in 1891. He, meanwhile, remarried to Augusta Lackland White and had a successful career as a shipbroker and ice merchant living in Northchurch (see Hampstead).

Another resident was Charles Henry Reynolds Wollaston who was born at Felpham Vicarage in 1849 and attended Lancing College and Trinity, Oxford. He was a prolific

180 Ebury Street has a plaque to W.A. Mozart and next door were H. Nicholson and Vita Sackville West.

"Strumbolo" at 77-79 Pimlico Road was next to the Orange Coffee House (replaced by St. Barnabas).

player for the Wanderers at Battersea Park and appeared in their five Cup Final victories from 1872-77 and also for England against Scotland. In fact he was referee at the Oval on 5 April 1879 when England won 5-4; then captained the return at 1st Hampden Park in front of 12,000 people on 13 March 1880 when they lost by the same score.

Wollaston was secretary to the Union Bank of London and lived at 14 Coleshill Street (Chester Row), 63 St. George's Road and 46 Belgrave Road where he died in 1926. In his will he left £100 to his two guides of twenty years of Zermatt, Switzerland, while his uncle Rev. William M. Wollaston was chaplain of St. Paul's, Cannes from 1874-1910 and lived at 99 Cambridge Street. There is a statue to Thomas Cubitt with surveyor's tool in Denbigh Street near the site of his offices and works by the river (erected 1995).

M. 27 August 1867 John Forster Alcock 26 ship-agent of Chingford s. Charles ship-agent and Catherine Ruth Rowse 19 of 5 Sutherland Place d. Charles "gentleman" by licence by Henry Thos. Birley witnessed Edward Horne and Betsey Charlton

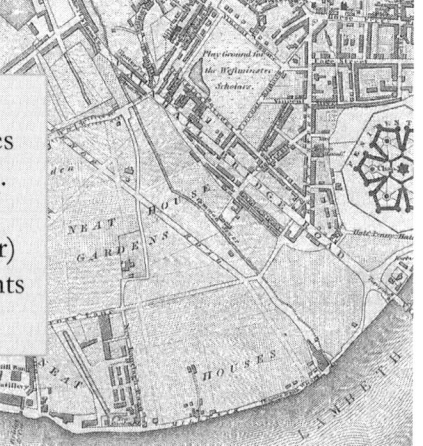

Thomas Cubitt (1788-1855) has his eye on the open spaces of Pimlico below Vincent Sq. on this **Map of 1827**. At the centre is Belgrave (Grosvenor) Road which awaits its regiments of stucco housing.

Holy Trinity, Bessborough Gardens was designed by J.L. Pearson in 1849-52 on land given to the parish by T. Cubitt. It was directly next to Vauxhall Bridge built in 1816, on the other side of which was (New) Spring Gardens (see Lambeth) and Nine Elms Station the London & S.W. Railway terminus in 1838-48. The church was badly damaged in the war and demolished for a garden, being joined with St. James the Less in 1954.

St. James the Less, Moreton Street on Vauxhall Bridge Road was founded by daughters of the late Dr. Monk Bishop of Gloucester and Canon of Westminster. G.E. Street was the architect and he designed an imposing structure of brick, marble and alabaster with a tower and apse for £9,000 at Upper Garden Street in 1862. The nave and aisles had fine detail, and the chancel stone groins, whilst there was an exquisite pulpit by T. Earp and above the altar Our Saviour attended by angels painted by the artist G.F. Watts.

St. Mary the Virgin, Vincent Square was built to the southeast with Gothic steeple by Edward Blore in 1836. Like those above it was separated from St. John's, Smith Square. Rev. Abraham Borrowdaile was vicar until 1873 and a school was attached, but it needed several repairs and with a falling population was demolished in 1923. The land returned to the Dean and Chapter and Vincent House was built on the site.

St. Saviour's
built in 1864.

St. James the Less by G.E. Street - one of several
High Church designs he did in the 19th century.

St. Saviour's, St. George's Square was the twin brother of St. Gabriel's in architectural terms at the top of the square and was built by Thomas Cundy II in 1863-64. The spire was one of the tallest in London and the stained glass was by Romaine-Walker, while the interior had two long galleries and no screen or pulpit. An organ was installed by Hill & Sons in 1871 and a side chapel was added in 1889, whereas the Duke of Westminster and George Cubitt (the son of Thomas) contributed towards the costs.

Gerard Kerr Olivier was the curate there and his son Laurence a choirboy before they moved to St. Mary's, Letchworth in 1918, whilst the son went to the choir school of All Saints, Margaret Street and began his acting there. Outside is a commemoration to Lady Diana Spencer who taught at the kindergarten in the hall, and opposite at No. 33 a plaque to Major Walter Clopton Wingfield (1833-1912) "Father of Lawn Tennis."

St. Paul's, Wilton Place

The locality eventually had a long and interesting history but it was simply fields behind a few houses on Knightsbridge Road in the 1740s. An area of stables was set up there by the east arm of Wilton Place in 1758, and under the guidance of Frederick, Duke of York became barracks for five hundred men of the Coldstream and Grenadier Guards in 1780. However this model barracks was given up and covered by tenements in the 1830s.

The section to the north behind St. George's Place was taken by the *Chinese Collection* of American merchant Nathan Dunn, thus Peto & Grissell built a hall and pagoda at a cost of £800. It closed in 1846 and Sir James Pennethorne moved the pagoda to Victoria Park in Hackney, while the southern parade ground was destined for a church.

St. Paul's was the first church in London to promote the ideals of the Tractarians and the Oxford Movement formulated by J.H. Newman, John Keble and Edward Pusey in 1833-41. The role of this group diminished after the conversion of Newman in 1845, but the seed had been sown, thus a return to Catholic traditions of liturgy and ministering took a hold in the Anglican Church and infiltrated its architecture.

Bishop C.J. Blomfield invited Rev. Bennett to establish a new church at Knightsbridge as perpetual curate in 1840, its aim being to give relief to the large parish of St. George's and to include parts of nearby St. Peter's. An area a mile long had some 12,000 residents but to Bennett's dismay the main support was to be through pew rents.

Thomas Cundy II was the architect of St. Paul's having worked on Belgrave Square to the south and the £10,000 cost was paid by the Commissioners in 1840-43. The exterior had a series of arched windows, shallow buttresses and a Gothic tower with open porch at the front, somewhat provincial in design. Its bells were cast by Mears & Co.

Internally there was a large nave with side galleries, an open roof with wooden beams and ornate bosses, and beyond a tiled chancel incorporating groin vaults. Some of the details of the latter were exquisite, and included a fine east window framed by spiral half columns, carved figures and angels - like those seen on a cathedral façade.

Tiled panels around the wall of the nave depicting the life of Christ were designed by Daniel Bell in the 1870s, and the rood screen and striking reredos with side chapel were added by G.F. Bodley in 1892. All enhancing the High Church aims of the building.

William James Early Bennett (1804-86) was born in Halifax, Nova Scotia, the son of William a major in the Royal Engineers and Mary daughter of James Early another army officer. He attended Westminster in 1816-23 being a keen rower and school captain then matriculated at Christchurch, Oxford the centre of the Tractarian movement with a B.A. in 1827. Initially he was an usher at his school, but was ordained a deacon at the Chapel Royal, St. James's by Bishop W. Howley on 2 March 1828, and married Mary Concetta the daughter of Sir William Franklin an inspector of Army Hospitals.

Bennett was ordained a priest at St. Paul's Cathedral by Bishop Blomfield on 6 June 1830 then was a curate at Oxford Chapel under Rev. John Perceval; but later that year went to Holy Trinity, Marylebone and with an outbreak of cholera did a sermon *God's Visitation*. In 1833 he went to All Souls and in 1836 was minister of St. Paul's, Portman Square holding both posts for two years, then remained at the latter until 1840.

St. Paul's, Knightsbridge another church by Thomas Cundy II on the site of the Old Barrack Yard - with some nave detail. Its first minister Rev. Bennett was embroiled in much controversy.

A letter by his brother G.A. Bennett R.E. noted, "William is very popular with all that know him, whilst his conduct as a clergyman has made him most highly esteemed by his parishioners and congregation. His evenings as well as mornings are all devoted to study or business, and his sermons are certainly the best I ever heard preached - his impressive manner, quite apostolic, lends to his reasonings a powerful effect."

Arriving at St. Paul's, Knightsbridge his first concern was the problem of pew rents. He noted that those who could not pay £15 per annum were unable to obtain a seat to hear the morning prayers. However, many wanted to attend and so his main work there was to build a church for the poor. He also developed an enduring belief in *a real presence* at communion and introduced all kinds of ritual into his services.

These developments were accepted at St. Paul's but there was far more trouble at St. Barnabas, especially after he drew up a type of prayer during a cholera outbreak in 1849. As stated Bennett was forced to resign both livings in 1851. But he soon received some help and Lady Bath a friend of the Tractarians installed him at Frome Selwood, where 56 out of 12,000 signed a petition against him (although 9 of these reneged). [7]

Bennett's work was done but his traditions continued in the architecture, and the church members included Lord John Russell (P.M. 1846-52, 1865-66) of 36 Chesham Place and the Duke of Wellington of Apsley House. Any remnants of the barracks were removed when St. Paul's School was built north of the church in 1857-59 (demolished for a hotel in 1972), whilst there were further ecclesiastical buildings just to the east.

The vicarage was given rent-free to the First Aid Nursing Yeomanry during the First War (including spy Odette) and there is a memorial tablet to this and the school outside. The Festival Choir was begun there to sing Bach's *St. John's Passion* in 1938, and paintings of famous people linked to the church line its walls. George Bentham (1800-84) botanist a nephew of Jeremy Bentham lived at 25 Wilton Place from 1864, and eventually adopted the ideas of Darwin becoming the leading systematic botanist of the century.

M. 4 June 1874 Charles Edward Perugini artist 4 Westbourne Place, Eaton Sq. s. Leonardo musician to Catherine Elizabeth Macready Collins wid 81 Gloucester Terrace d. Charles Dickens author lic by T.W.S. Collis [minister] wit Francis Jeffrey Dickens, Mary Dickens, Georgina Hogarth, John Everett Millais, Henry F. Dickens (see Marylebone)

28 July 1900 George Fredk. M. Cornwallis-West 25 Lt. Scots Guards 50 Park Street s. of William Lord Lt. Denbighshire to Jennie Randolph Spencer Churchill 46 wid 35a Great Cumberland Place d. Leonard Walter Jerome gent lic by Edgar Sheppard sub dean Chapel Royal pres Moreton Frewen, Henry Cecil Elwes, "Marlborough," Winston S. Churchill [8]

---

[7] Bennett wrote a pamphlet *A Plea for Toleration in the Church of England* at Frome which brought a prosecution in 1869; although on appeal the words real (or visible) were deemed to come with the Church Laws, such dogma not being inconsistent. This was a pivotal moment with other enquiries on ritual and he remained at Frome for thirty-five years until he died in 1886.

[8] Jennie Jerome was born in Rochester, N.Y. in 1854 the daughter of financier Leonard who built the Jerome Park racetrack in the Bronx later a reservoir. She married Lord Randolph Spencer-Churchill son of the 7th Duke of Marlborough at the British Embassy in Paris in 1874 and had Winston (1874) and John (1880). Lord Randolph died in 1895 and her second husband was the same age as her son - but they parted in 1912. M. Frewen a writer married Clara Jerome.

St. Peter's, Eaton Square

The first mansions of Belgravia were built under Cubitt's direction in the 1820s and St. Peter's was to be the *Mother Church* of the area. Henry Hakewill was the son of John a landscape artist who worked with Sir William Chambers and John Yenn, thus he trained with his brother under the latter and at the Royal Academy Schools.

He designed the building in the Greek Revival style with a monumental Ionic portico, stepped tower and small domed cupola at £22,427 in 1824-27. It was part of the new Eaton Square and initially was a district church within the parish of St. George's.

This was a very attractive area just behind Buckingham Palace, named for the Belgrave Estate in Cheshire owned by the Grosvenors, and with its spacious boulevards became a magnet to those with wealth and prestige who once resided in the less commodious parts of the city. From the outset the church was found to be inadequate to the needs of the extensive households, thus there were various proprietary chapels nearby:

Eaton Episcopal Chapel - situated at the west end of Eaton Square (c.1836-1901).

Belgrave Chapel, Halkin Street - designed by Robert Smirke with four Ionic columns and portico on the north side in 1812. It was dedicated to St. John and William Horsley was the organist until 1837 but it was demolished in 1910.

Belgrave Presbyterian - built on West Halkin Street in 1846, then joined with Ranelagh Chapel, Chelsea in 1866 and moved to Emperor's Gate, Kensington in 1923.

Another building nearby was the Lock Hospital, Grosvenor Place developed as Lazar institutions for leprosy declined. A charitable society led by William Bromfield began this to treat syphilis in 1746 and Thomas Scott was chaplain from 1785-1803. The latter was a leading figure in the Church Missionary Society (at St. John's, Bedford Row) being the first secretary and wrote his much admired *Commentary on the Whole Bible.* [9]

St. Peter's became a separate parish in 1844, just after St. Paul's was built to the north, whilst a number of prominent people had connections as discussed below.

John Lubbock, Baron Avebury (1834-1913) - His father John William was educated at Eton and Trinity, Cambridge and embarked on *a life of arduous enquiry* with income from his banking firm at Mansion House. He was treasurer of the Royal Society and married Harriet daughter of Lt. Col. George Hotham of Beverley in 1833, then lived at 29 Eaton Place and had six children who were baptized at St. Peter's from 1834-40.

The property had a white stucco ground floor with red brick and pilasters above, whilst the father became vice-president of the Royal Society and vice-chancellor of London University. He inherited High Elms in 1840 and developed it into an Elysian paradise with landscaped grounds around a classical mansion. Six more children were then born at Downe and his other residence 23 St. James's Place - including a son Edgar.

All of his eight sons had prominent roles but the eldest John Lubbock was born at 29 Eaton Place on 30 April 1834 (and has a plaque), being inspired by his father and Charles Darwin at Downe. Receiving a microscope at a young age he joined the Royal Society, Geographical Society, Royal Academy, and was president of the Linnaean Society.

---

[9] The Lock Hospital moved to Harrow Road, Westbourne Green beside the G.W.R. in 1842 and gradually expanded the site, but it was closed down under the N.H.S. in 1952.

St. Peter's, Eaton Square built 1824-27 is similar in style to St. Pancras New Church; whilst **Polesden Lacey** once Sheridan's "run down abode" was home to the Bonsors.

He became Sir John Lubbock the fourth baronet in 1865 and head of Robarts, Lubbock & Co., whilst he received several honorary degrees from universities and wrote many learned papers - especially on plants, evolution and the origins of civilisation.

Sir John was a Liberal Unionist M.P. for West Kent with a manifesto to bring science to the schools, repay the national debt and secure additional holidays! No wonder he got the vote, and he passed the Bank Holidays Act (1871) which established the August Bank Holiday formerly called *St. Lubbock's Day*. He then represented London University from 1880-1900 and passed the Ancient Monuments Act in 1882, meeting General Augustus H.L. Fox-Pitt-Rivers an anthropologist and inspector of monuments.

As a result he married again to his daughter Alice A.L. Lane in 1884 and passed several other Acts including: Shop Hours Regulation, Bankers Books, Open Spaces, Wild Birds Protection and Public Libraries. He was certainly not in the category of "idle rich" and held many senior banking posts being raised to the peerage as Lord Avebury in 1900, but died at Kingsgate Castle, Broadstairs in 1913 leaving an estate worth £362,877.

Henry Cosmo Orme Bonsor (1848-1929) - The Bonsors, formerly stationers, became gentry at Polesden Lacey, while his father Joseph invested £11,000 in Combe, Delafield & Co. and moved to the opulent 1 Belgrave Square in 1872. He increased their assets to £370,000 of which he held £100,000 but died at the house the next year.

His widow Eliza then lived at 51 Eaton Place in 1876-88 and 11 Upper Belgrave Street in 1889-1909, the family being the very model for *Upstairs, Downstairs*. In fact Tennyson resided at No. 9 in the latter street. Henry Cosmo was born at Polesden Lacey and went to Eton with A.F. Kinnaird becoming a partner in Combe, Delafield & Co. with a 7/37th share at his father's decease. The company, a major player, were based at Long Acre but had further premises by the river at numbers 137 and 154-55 Grosvenor Road.

Bonsor married Emily Fellowes in 1872 and lived at 5 Chesham Place and 40 Belgrave Square, but moved to 38 Belgrave Square next to Chapel Street from 1885-1929. He also owned Tandridge Hall, Godstone and through his passion for horse racing purchased Kingswood Warren at Tadworth near Epsom, installing nephew Rev. Wethered as vicar. In terms of business he was a friend of James Watney II who was based at Brewer Street by Victoria Street, Pimlico, and was also a director of the Bank of England.

The company had a share value of £2 million in 1892 with many overseas investments and Henry negotiated a merger as Watney, Combe & Reid in July 1898, whilst he was chairman of the S.E. Railway Co. in 1898-1923 but died at Nice in 1929.

However, his progress was overshadowed by his siblings and Alexander George Bonsor a partner in the company left in acrimonious circumstances and resided in Belgium (see St. Mary, The Boltons), while Herbert Webb Bonsor was married to Evelyn Sarah Moon daughter of the vicar of Fetcham. He was briefly involved in the business, but absconded to live with his lover in Helena, Montana under the sobriquet Mr. and Mrs. Harry Brett; as described in a petition by his wife and witnesses from this gold boomtown.

William Slaney Kenyon-Slaney (1847-1908) - The Kenyons and the Slaneys were noble families with antecedents in Cheshire and Shropshire. William Kenyon was born at Ruyton XI Towns in 1815 - a cognomen which prompted Conan Doyle who worked there as a young doctor to state, "It was not big enough to make one town, far less eleven!"

The former married Frances C. Slaney and their son William Slaney Kenyon was born at Rajkote, Bombay on 24 August 1847 but they soon returned to England. At this time her father Robert Anglionby Slaney who owned Walford Manor, Baschurch and was an M.P. for Shrewsbury made a rather interesting will. He left his farmlands at Ryton and mansion house and pleasure grounds at Hatton Grange, Shifnal, on condition that *any husband of his daughters* took the surname Slaney and bore the family coat of arms.

After he died in 1862 the change of name was granted by Royal Licence at St. James's, whereas the son was educated at Eton with Bonsor, Kinnaird, Lubbock and Thompson. The latter then attended Christchurch, Oxford but did not become a minister and was instead a dashing soldier in the Grenadier Guards. He appeared in Cup Finals at the Oval and played for England in 1873 scoring the first ever international goal, and was a good cricket player appearing for the M.C.C. from 1869-80 scoring 145 runs.

There was a mutiny by Arabi Pasha in 1881 leading to the Egyptian War, thus General Garnet Wolseley occupied the Suez Canal Zone in August the following year. Kenyon-Slaney was despatched with the 2nd Grenadier Guards and fought at the Battle of Tel-el-Kebir (great tumulus) in the September, then received a medal and Khedive's Star.

He retired as a colonel and lived at Hatton Grange being M.P. for Newport, Shropshire from 1886, and married Mabel Selina Bridgeman at Shifnal in 1887 - her father Orlando lived nearby at Weston Hall and was M.P. for Shropshire South with properties at Wilton Crescent and 43 Belgrave Square. They had a daughter at the latter and a son Robert at Lowndes Square. The father died at Hatton Grange in 1908 and his will was proved by brother Francis and relative Hon. William Clive Bridgeman later Home Secretary.

The Church Fabric - Rev. John Fuller was incumbent in 1827-44 and became vicar of the new parish from 1844-69, whilst the organ and choir were at the west end with the focus remaining on the pulpit. Regarding the area, Fryderyk Chopin (1810-49) gave his first London concert at a house in West Eaton Place and a plaque marks the site.

The next incumbent was Rev. George Howard Wilkinson in 1870-83 who was later the Bishop of Truro and St. Andrew's and satirised in *Vanity Fair*. The building was enlarged and restored in 1875 by Sir Arthur Blomfield, who created a more distinctive chancel at the east end and introduced Romanesque features into the interior.

At the entrance are memorials to Harold Wingfield who died in the China Seas during a rescue (1876), and Sir Edward Thornton minister in Latin America and Russia (1906). In addition Austin Thompson was vicar in 1916-41 and a prebend of St. Paul's, but died whilst fire watching during the war. However, the church burnt out in 1987 after being set fire to by someone who believed it to be a Roman Catholic chapel.

The architects John and Nicki Braithwaite lived nearby and witnessed the devastation thus they were approached to redesign the interior and work began in Easter 1990. This was completed in October 1991 and retained the Georgian portico, but moved the organ back to the west end and introduced a vicarage, church hall and offices.

The propylon contains gold-studded doors opening into a creamy white interior. Inside are columns with four detached elements which delineate the aisles, leading to a marble altar and apse with gold mosaics. Several statues and candles create the ambience of an Orthodox church, while there is a side chapel and remains of the old sanctuary.

C. 3 June 1834 John s. John William and Harriet Lubbock Eaton Place banker b. 30 Apr
21 Dec 1880 Robert Cecil s. Henry Cosmo O. and Emily G. Bonsor 40 Belgrave Square
25 Feb 1888 Sybil Agnes d. Col. Wm S. and Mabel S. Kenyon-Slaney 43 Belgrave Square

M. 3 October 1901 Clement George Montague Adam esq. of Coates, Glouc to Violet Ethel Stock of 45 L. Belgrave Street d. Thomas Lt. Col. Essex Reg. banns by G.R. Adam (father) wit W. Prevost, Marg. H. Stock, Arthur and Helen Hill (see St. Barnabas)

Kensington

This had an extremely large parish wrapped around Kensington Gardens. It reached as far as Ladbroke Grove and Kensal Green, down Warwick Road to Chelsea Creek, then up Fulham Road and back across the bottom of Hyde Park. This incorporated the areas of Notting Hill, Kensington Village, South Kensington, and also Old and New Brompton, but Knightsbridge and the Gardens were a peculiar of St. Margaret's, Westminster.

The manor was held by the De Veres or Earls of Oxford hence Earl's Court, whereas the church and lands were granted to Abingdon Abbey resulting in St. Mary Abbots. The opulent Nottingham House was built beside the village by the Earl of Nottingham in the 17th century, but passed to William III in 1689 who wanted a residence away from the smoky capital. A private carriage road was laid out for the King across Hyde Park (later known as Rotten Row), then Sir Christopher Wren extended and improved the building and Sir John Vanbrugh and William Kent also worked there.

It was a favoured residence for the next seventy years although the premier palace was St. James's, and was then used by Edward, Duke of Kent and his wife Victoria who was previously married to Prince Emich of Leiningen. Their daughter Victoria was born there on 24 May 1819 and baptized in the cupola room by Archbishop Charles Manners-Sutton. She was then raised at the house in isolation by her mother and Sir John Conroy.

Kensington remained a very select district, its prominence assured by such Royal links, and its Gardens were redesigned without any parterres by Charles Bridgeman in 1728-38. Preceding the likes of Capability Brown he dammed up the Westbourne Stream to create the Serpentine, and also inserted both the Round Pond and Grand Avenue.

These were combined with Hyde Park in the east to create public gardens, and the area soon witnessed some further Royal developments. Decimus Burton designed the grand entrance to the park beside Apsley House in 1824-25, but it was Prince Albert and other members of the *Royal Society of Arts* who organised the Great Exhibition in 1851. This was then housed in Paxton's "Crystal Palace" on the south side of the park.

Sir William Cubitt was the main contractor for this premier exhibition and the building was 1,848' x 408' with numerous attractions, whereas it held 17,000 exhibitors leading to 6.2 million visitors. Several exhibitions followed on the Continent, whilst the Americans wanted to show their industry had come of age and for ten years planned the Centennial Exposition. This was to coincide with the 100th Anniversary of Independence.

Their exhibition was at Fairmount Park, Philadelphia, on the Schuylkill River and 450-acres housed one of the largest ever seen; providing some relief from the scandals of the Grant administration. It opened on 10 May 1876 and in five months attracted 9 million visitors or 20% of the country, although local people often visited several times. [10]

Back in London, Paxton's creation was moved to Sydenham in 1854 whilst a surplus of £186,000 was used to establish the International Exhibition (Natural History, Geological and Science Museums) and South Kensington Museum (V & A). Other buildings on the Horticultural Society grounds were the Albert Hall by the R.E. and Lucas Bros. 1867-71, Imperial Institute (College), Royal College of Music by A. Blomfield 1894, Royal School of Mines by Sir A. Webb 1909-13, and the Geographical Society which came from Savile Row to Lowther Lodge and added a statue of Shackleton in 1913.

"Arts and Crafts Movement" - Albert Memorial by George Gilbert Scott, frieze in Coade stone at Belgrave Place c.1796 *from Danish-Norwegian Embassy at Wellclose Square*, and the Royal Albert Hall by the Royal Engineers.　　**All Saints, Ennismore Gardens** is based on a basilica in Verona.

---

[10] One of the visitors was reporter Arthur Pember who did an article while the *New York Times* stated, "The American invents as the Greek sculpted, and Italians painted, it is genius!" There were 30,000 exhibitors from 38 states and 50 nations in many large halls, but some used it for propaganda and Krupp's giant guns were an imperialistic display of ominous portent.

All Saints, Ennismore Gardens

The parish covered an exclusive area north of Brompton including Kensington Palace and nearby houses, and was initially part of Knightsbridge but under Westminster. Lewis Vulliamy based his design on the 11th century basilica of San Zeno Maggiore, Verona the west façade an almost exact replica, but with the campanile brought forward to the road. The church was initially east of Princes Terrace and was completed in 1849.

   Meanwhile, a number of prominent residents lived at Ennismore Gardens and Rutland Gate, many of them connected with senior Government positions:

5 Ennismore Gardens - Sir Francis Arthur Marindin married Kathleen Mary Stevenson daughter of the Governor of Mauritius whilst on duty with the Royal Engineers in 1860. Sir William Stevenson was married for a second time to Caroline Octavia Biscoe and had a son Joseph Seymour at Moka in 1862. After his decease his widow married Rev. F.B. Zincke but they lived apart and she resided with Joseph here in the early 1900s.

10 Ennismore Gardens - Samuel Whitbread M.P. and Lady Isabella occupied the house in the 1880s, while son Henry W. a partner in their business lived in apartments with Edgar Lubbock and John Birkbeck Lubbock at 14 Berkeley Street, Mayfair.

8 Rutland Gate - Webster, Wedderburn & Co. had plantations in Jamaica and Andrew Wedderburn-Colvile married Louisa Mary Eden daughter of Lord Auckland in 1806. He resided at Langley Farm, Beckenham and had 13 children, but inherited Craigflower near Dunfermline and Robert Wedderburn a freed slave claimed he was a half-brother.

   Rev. Samuel Marindin married his daughter Isabella in 1834 and her brother Sir James William Colvile inherited the estates in 1856. The latter was a judge of the Bengal Court and a member of the Privy Council, but died at the house in 1880.

9 Rutland Gate - Roland Yorke Bevan married Agneta O. Kinnaird at St. Martin in the Fields in 1874, and was executor to the 10th Lord Kinnaird at this address.

27 Rutland Gate - Hon. William Patrick Adam of Blair Adam M.P. from 1859-80 was secretary to his cousin Lord Elphinstone (governor of Bombay), a lord of the Treasury and a privy councillor. His son Charles Elphinstone Adam was born here on 7 August 1859 and became a baronet when his father died, whilst Blair Adam home to the Scottish architects passed to a nephew Charles Keith Adam who married Barbara Eunice Marindin (her grandfather being a brother of Sir Francis A. Marindin).

   Regarding the church the west front was restored by Harrison Townsend in 1892 but closed in 1955 and soon took a different route. A parish started at the Russian Embassy in 1716 but with the help of Rev. Fynes-Clinton went to St. Philip's, Buckingham Palace Road in 1923-58. On leaving they took over All Saints (purchased 1979) as the Russian Orthodox Cathedral, Diocese of Sourozh in the British Isles under Moscow. In fact the doors on the icon screen were rescued from the embassy after the revolution.

M. 3 July 1894 Josiah Clement Wedgwood 22 naval architect 226 Railton Road, Herne Hill s. Clement F. a potter and Ethel Kate Bowen 24 of 13 Prince's Gardens d. Charles S.C. Bowen Lord of Appeal banns by G.G. Bradley Dean of Westminster in presence of Arthur D. Coleridge, E.E. Bowen, M. Rendel and nine others

Holy Trinity and Brompton Oratory

Following on from these Italianate-Russian connections we come to a church that has remained strictly Church of England. In the 1820s, this was a part of Kensington which was served by St. Mary Abbots over a mile away, and with the growth of population in Brompton a decision was made to buy some land and build a new church.

The Commissioners paid two-thirds of the £10,407 cost and the architect was Thomas Leverton Donaldson (1795-1885), an adventurer who worked in his father's practice. He also designed All Saints, Gordon Square and was involved in the Great Exhibition. The church was erected on a large plot backing onto Kingston House and was consecrated on 6 June 1829. Ennismore Gardens originally on Exhibition Road were rebuilt in the gardens of that house after the 1860s - with a linking passage through the mews.

Regarding design, the church was Gothic in style with a west tower and upper clerestory being somewhat reminiscent of St. Paul's, Knightsbridge; whilst it was well located with a leafy view down to the main road. However, what might seem an unusual decision was then made to sell the front portion of the site to the Catholic Church.

John Henry Newman converted in 1845 and founded St. Philip Neri, Birmingham, this being a brotherhood/oratory begun in Rome in the 16th century. He joined with Frederick William Faber to purchase the 3.5 acre site for £16,000 in November 1852, to start a new London Oratory, and a house and temporary church were built by J.J. Scoles.

An appeal was then launched for a permanent building and architect Herbert Gribble designed a Renaissance Baroque Church of the Immaculate Heart in 1880-84. It was the largest Catholic building before Westminster Cathedral and faced in Portland stone, but the arches and dome were in concrete - the latter by George Sherrin in 1895.

The interior was reminiscent of St. Paul's with opulent Romanesque arches and gilded apse, but it was never a cathedral this role falling to St. George's, Southwark and St. Mary Moorfields (to 1903). The cupola was added and twelve apostles by Guiseppe Mazzuoli were obtained from Siena in 1895, while the funeral of Cardinal Manning took place and marriages of Stéphane Mallarmé (1863) critic, Prince Matila Ghyka of Romania (1918) diplomat/novelist and Alfred Hitchcock (1926) film director.

Holy Trinity, Brompton built in 1829 - the alpha and the omega?

Brompton Oratory built 1880-84.

The Alpha Course swept the nation with searching questions.

Holy Trinity, Knightsbridge by G.F. Bodley had mediaeval origins.

The Oratory became the dominant architectural feature of Holy Trinity - subsumed behind it and accessed down a leafy roadway. However, this was a blessing in modern times as it was sheltered from traffic and it combined with St. Paul's, Onslow Square.

Rev. Nicky Gumbell established a 4,000 congregation in the 1980s initiating the *Alpha Course* which spread around the country and the crypt was redesigned to provide rooms, while a group went to St. Mary's, Bryanston Square. The Oratory was noted for its organ recitals of Bach and Mendelssohn and has a statue to Cardinal Newman at the front.

Holy Trinity - B. 9 February 1856 Andrew Colvile of 11 Eaton Place, 75 R. Liddell

Oratory - M. 8 May 1889 Edward W. Elgar to Caroline Alice Roberts d. of Sir Henry

Holy Trinity, Knightsbridge

To have two churches with the same dedication in such close proximity appears to be confusing, although there is a simple explanation. In fact, such practice was not always uncommon and there was a similar situation at St. George's Hanover Square.

The chapel, as it was deemed, belonged to a brotherhood and leper hospital beside the green in mediaeval times, but was rebuilt as Knightsbridge Chapel just east of Albert Gate by Hyde Park in 1629. It operated under the patronage of Westminster Abbey and this situation still persists today, whilst it was rebuilt in 1699 and renovated in 1789. However such illustrious connections did not secure it from various afflictions.

There was a problem with damp due to the Westbourne Stream, and some informal baptisms and clandestine marriages until *Hardwicke's Act*. The only parishes in 1842 were St. Mary, St. Barnabas and Holy Trinity but fourteen were soon added. The chapel was also rebuilt in *decorated style* with spire by Brandon & Eyton, when the French Embassy was enlarged, in 1861. Being near to St. Paul's, it became redundant, and a new site was found above Prince Consort Road in 1901. A perpendicular design was started by G.F. Bodley and reminds one of the west end in a college chapel, whilst the work was finished by his partner C.G. Hare after 1907 - the first minister being H.B. Coward.

Near to the Albert Hall it remains an impressive building and outside is an information plaque. The interior includes tall slender piers, capacious wooden roof, marble floor and statues in niches flanking the chancel window. It is one of the best examples of Bodley's work and a chalice presented by Bishop Laud in 1629 is now at the V & A.

M. 30 July 1700 Robert Walpole Esq. of Houghton in ye county of Norfolk was married to Katherine Shorter of ye parish of St. James's Westm: Mr. Prevosh [first P.M.]

St. Barnabas, Addison Road

As the area developed several new churches were added and St. Barnabas was built by Lewis Vulliamy in the Tudor-Gothic style west of Little Holland House in 1829 - at the same time as Holy Trinity. Then came St. John's Ladbroke Grove, St. James's Norland Square (by Vulliamy) and St. Mary the Boltons, W. Brompton in the 1840s.

Later ones added nearby were St. Peter's, Notting Hill designed in the Italianate style by Thomas Allom in 1857; All Saints by William White funded by Rev. Samuel Walker in 1861; and St. John the Baptist, Holland Road a stunning Gothic stone edifice with some Cistercian influences by James Brooks and J.S. Adkins from the 1880s.

The parish of St. Barnabas covered an area around the grounds of Holland House (see St. Mary Abbots), and Lord Leighton painter and sculptor built a property at 12 Holland Park Road in 1864 (now a museum). In addition, the Prinseps obtained an adjacent plot from Lord Ilchester in 1871, and G.F. Watts employed Frederick Cockerell to build New Little Holland House, Melbury Road and resided there in 1876-1904.

A host of blue plaques clothe the area like confetti at a wedding including Sir Hamo Thornycroft sculptor 2a Melbury Road, Marcus Stone artist 8 Melbury Road, William Holman Hunt artist 18 Melbury Road (also occupied by Cetshwayo King of the Zulus) and Frederic Lord Leighton artist at Holland Park Road. John Galsworthy novelist and playwright also resided at 14 Addison Road near the church in 1905-13.

St. George's, Campden Hill

During his ministry, Archdeacon Sinclair, vicar of St. Mary Abbots, aimed to separate the large parish in his hands into more manageable units. A site was purchased at the top end of Campden Hill Road for £455 in early 1863 and an iron church was soon erected. This structure had once been used by troops in the Crimea. A new ecclesiastical district was also formed from the aforementioned church and St. John's, Notting Hill.

John Bennett, a builder of Westbourne Park, then put up the funds for a permanent building, although the patronage was eventually transferred from this benefactor to the Bishops of London. The foundation was laid in February 1864 and an *Eclectic Gothic* structure was designed by Enoch Bassett Keeling an architect from Sunderland and Low Church adherent. Its exterior of variegated Bargate stone was *Continental* and included a buttressed cloister entrance, decorative detailing and a sanctuary apse.

Internally there was stock yellow brick on the walls, notched designs and elegant iron columns supporting progressive galleries. The work was carried out by George Myers & Son of Lambeth at a cost of £7,000 and the interior held 1,500 people, while the architect also designed St. Mark's, Notting Hill and St. Paul's, Upper Norwood.

The first incumbent was George Bennett (son) and it flourished with a primary school in Edge Street. It was the main force in the Temperance Society over to Shepherd's Bush and a large rally marched from Portobello Road for a service in 1885. This continued until the war. The organists included G.F. Huntley and Luard-Selby from Salisbury but despite high aspirations there was much poverty. In fact the richer elements near to the church provided a soup kitchen, medical dispensary and working men's club.

St. George's featured in the work of **J.M. Barrie**

Rev. John Robbins arrived in 1900 and took over a newly built vicarage at 25 Campden Hill Square, but after the First War patterns of worship and social interaction changed. Thus there was a move to close the church in the 1930s and this threat persisted for several years. Its future was finally secured when Rt. Rev. Cyril Eastaugh, the Bishop of Kensington and of Peterborough, moved to 19 Campden Hill Square in 1952.

He took a personal interest in the church and Prebendary Eley of St. Mary's (and later of Gibraltar), appointed his curate Rev. Charles Wright as the minister at St. George's. This led to an upturn in the congregation and church activity, but during this period the spire was removed as unsafe and the apse was demolished after a large crack appeared. The latter was then replaced by a flat chancel wall. Other changes included remodelling of the narthex as a community space although the gallery was retained.

Regarding prominent church connections there were two of considerable significance. Gilbert Chesterton was born nearby at 32 Sheffield Terrace, Campden Hill in 1874 and his father was a silent partner in a family of estate agents. Despite being a Unitarian, he had his son baptized at the local parish church. The family went to 11 Warwick Gardens near to Earl's Court in 1881; then Chesterton attended St. Paul's School and University College where he pursued a course at the Slade School of Art.

Embarking on a writing career with a publisher and the *Illustrated London News* he was most prolific, thus he produced plays, poetry, philosophy, literary criticism, biography, fiction and Christian apologetics. This led to his conversion to Catholicism in 1922. In total he wrote 80 books, his most famous works being *The Napoleon of Notting Hill, The Man Who was Thursday* and the ever popular *Father Brown* detective stories.

He had a large circle of literary friends and sparring partners including George Bernard Shaw, P.G. Wodehouse, Jerome K. Jerome, H.G. Wells, Conan Doyle and James Barrie who all played cricket together. In fact, the latter resided at 100 Bayswater Road and St. George's featured in the *Peter Pan* books - the hero flying past Kensington Gardens, the church spire and over the adjacent rooftops.

C. 1 July 1874 Gilbert Keith Chesterton son of Edward and Marie Louise [Grosjean] an estate agent of Campden Hill, Kensington born 29 May

"I am firmly of the opinion that I was baptized, according to the formularies of the Church of England, in the little church of St. George's opposite the large waterworks tower that dominated that ridge" (*The Autobiography of G.K. Chesterton* 1936).

St. Mary Abbots, Kensington

This is one of the oldest sites in the locality and dates back to Saxon times the derivation being *Cynes-ing-ton* or the farmstead belonging to Cynes people. A church was erected by the village, and the De Vere family gave this and 270 acres to the Benedictine Abbey of St. Mary Abingdon in the 12th century - in grateful thanks for their prayers.

A parish was created from these small beginnings in 1260 and the church was dedicated to St. Marie Abbatis, an ecclesiastical term rather than denoting possession. Despite this there was a challenge from the Bishop of London in the Consistory Court, as this was done without permission, and the patronage passed to the latter in perpetuity. The old Norman church was rebuilt in 1370, and at the Dissolution the Abbey lands went to the Crown, whilst it became prominent after William III established court there in 1683.

With this in mind the unstable mediaeval church was pulled down and replaced by a new structure in the late Renaissance style in c.1696. Strype generally passed over the parish although he recorded Thomas Henshaw (see below), John Dickins who left £50 to the school 1694, James Worthington a page to Mary II, and his son Captain John who commanded the King's Army in Flanders and Ireland 1698.

There were many eminent parishioners to follow who included Isaac Newton, Joseph Addison, William Wilberforce, George Canning, W.M. Thackeray and Thomas Macaulay. However as the area became a major urbanised settlement the church with its creeping dry rot and diminutive size was again found to be outdated.

Archdeacon John Sinclair vicar from 1842-75 began a fundraising scheme and George Gilbert Scott was appointed as the architect. Initially it was to be rebuilt just to the north like those at Stoke Newington and Lee in Kent, but Scott recommended the same site "hardly to be surpassed for convenience and grandeur of position." The work was then carried out by Dove Bros. of Islington during 1868-72, and the Victorian Gothic edifice with its towering spire became a prominent landmark from Kensington Gardens.

Hindsight suggests that the previous plan may have been more propitious since traffic and modern developments, crowd in around the site, such that it lacks the more open perspective found at St. Marylebone, the Grosvenor Chapel and elsewhere. The interior, meanwhile, had the dimensions of a cathedral and the unusual vaulted passage leading up from the road certainly creates the atmosphere of monastic precincts.

Entering the nave from the western entrance, there is a lofty arcade with clerestory and barrel-style vault, reaching towards the high altar and sanctuary beneath the east window. The church's main features are marble and Italian mosaics by Salviati of Venice completed by his grandson Giles, oak pulpit from the old church, a reredos of alabaster, font with wrought-iron canopy by Scott (of 1881) and several prominent memorials.

On the south side is a tablet to Thomas Henshaw (1618-1700) the French secretary, envoy to Christian V of Denmark and founder of the Royal Society; an angelic sculpture to Dukes Alfred and Leopold by their sister H.R.H. Princess Louise; and in the side chapel a draped figure to Edward, 7th Earl of Warwick d.1721 and his family. [11]

---

[11] Edward Rich, 6th Earl of Warwick and 3rd Earl of Holland married Charlotte daughter of Sir Thomas Myddleton in 1697 but died in 1701. His widow the dowager Countess of Warwick was married to Joseph Addison tutor to son Edward at St. Edmund's, Lombard Street in 1716.

At the west end by the door is a memorial to James Mill Esq. (1773-1836) economist, critic and historian, "Author of *The History of British India*" published in 1818; and in the northwest corner a monument to Mrs. Joel Boscawen wife of Edward and granddaughter of "the famous" Sydney, Earl of Godolphin, first Lord of the Treasury. In addition she was mother to Anne wife of Sir John Evelyn grandson of the diarist, and to Dorothy the wife of Sir Phillip Meadows d.1730 (with a family coat of arms).

One of the idiosyncrasies of the church is a series of tablets around the walls including several to the Merriman family, and one to Maj. Gen. Sir John McCaskill who fought in the Afghan campaign and Sikh war but fell at Moodkee in 1845. This was erected by his daughter Jessie Mitchell and is on the north side (see St. John's Wood).

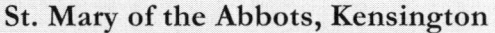

St. Mary of the Abbots, Kensington

The old church dated c.1869 (above); and Gilbert Scott's *Early English Gothic* creation with 278 ft high spire - reminiscent of St. Mary Redcliffe, Bristol.

Local Properties of Note - One of the most significant was Holland House built for Sir Walter Cope in 1605, which passed to his relatives the Rich family who were the Earls of Warwick and Holland. It was used as an army base by Cromwell during the Civil War, whilst Joseph Addison writer and politician spent some time there after his marriage into the Warwick dynasty, and was buried at Westminster Abbey in 1719.

The house then came into the hands of the Fox family, relatives of the politician, and under a new title Baron Holland was a centre for politics and literary associations. Much of this *palace* with its spires, numerous gables, and covered arcade was destroyed in the war and the surviving wing and ruins are now in a park. To the south was Little Holland House (the Dower) and Henry Thoby Prinsep and his wife Sarah Pattle (sister of J.M. Cameron) took a 21-year lease there from Henry Fox, Lord Holland, in 1850.

This became a second centre for artists and writers and in particular a meeting place of the Pre-Raphaelites, including their own son Val Prinsep. Visitors to the house included Tennyson and Thackeray, whilst the artist George Frederick Watts was a resident and his hostess noted, "He came to stay for three days but remained for thirty years!"

William Horsley (1774-1858), organist, was related to Brunel and Callcott.

St. Mary Abbots - font by Scott, statue 7th Earl of Warwick, and south entrance.

There were also links to Leslie Stephen who married Harriet Thackeray and Julia Prinsep Jackson, and to Freshwater Bay where Cameron, Tennyson and Ann Thackeray lived. Meanwhile, the Prinseps left the house on expiry of the lease in 1871 and Lady Holland demolished the building which was replaced by Melbury Road and Ilchester Place. This then became an enclave for further artistry as was discussed under St. Barnabas.

In fact, in the mid-19th century large areas were still covered by fields, the main growth at Kensington, Notting Hill, south of Hyde Park near Brompton, and sporadically along the Old Brompton Road. Cromwell Road by the museums ended in market gardens and Earl's Court had a few houses, a priory and the new West London Cemetery. [12]

Another point of interest was *Kensington Proprietary Grammar* formed by King's College in 1830, with the Bishop of London as patron and vicar as president. Rev. T.S. Evans taught 20 students at 26 Kensington Square, preparing them for E.I.C. military colleges like Haileybury by 1841. The next year Sir Henry Willcock and the E.I.C. began a cadet-ship for Addiscombe Military College which attracted more pupils over 19 years.

The school had a good reputation for university entrants and Rev. W. Haig Brown was principal in 1857-63 before going to Charterhouse. In fact their soccer team was one of twelve at the first meeting of the F.A. at the Freemasons Tavern in 1863. Two years later the playing fields were appropriated by the Metropolitan Railway, and with dwindling numbers it closed down in 1869 - the site being a foundation school until 1896.

Pre-Raphaelite Links - Rev. George B. Macdonald was a Methodist in Birmingham and son Henry introduced his sisters to a group from university. Edward Burne-Jones married Georgiana at Manchester Cathedral in June 1860, and like his son-in-law John William Mackail of Holland Park worked with William Morris. John Lockwood Kipling married Alice at St. Mary Abbots on 18 March 1865 before going to India, and their son Joseph Rudyard Kipling author of *The Jungle Book* was named after a place in Stafford. Whilst Edward John Poynter married Agnes and Alfred Baldwin an industrialist married Louisa (parents of Stanley) at a joint wedding in Wolverhampton in August 1866.

---

[12] Brompton Cemetery opened in 1840 and memorials include Joseph Bonomi y., Fanny Brawne, Francis Buckland, Samuel Cunard (founder), Thomas Cundy II, Charles Fremantle (of Perth), George Godwin, Emmeline Pankhurst (suffragette), Val Prinsep and Dr. John Snow.

Kensington Gravel Pits - This area was on Bayswater Road and Church Street while to the south were some quarries where Edward Orme possibly made his money. There were potteries to the north using local clay, demarked by Pottery Lane and a beehive kiln on Walmer Road. The locality itself became Notting Hill (after an old manor).

Thomas Callcott a builder of some prestige resided at "The Mall" and married Charlotte Urry at St. George's Chapel, Mayfair in 1750 then Charlotte Wall in about 1765. He had two prominent sons whilst there was a further connection to William Horsley.

John Wall Callcott (1766) had a musical education from Henry Whitney organist of St. Mary's from 1778 and at Westminster Abbey, then was deputy at St. George's, Queen Square and joint-organist at St. Paul's, Covent Garden - marrying Elizabeth Mary Hutchins there in 1791. He composed 100 glees, lectured at the Royal Institution, played for the Female Orphan Asylum at Lambeth and wrote *A Musical Grammar* (1806).

Sir Augustus Wall Callcott (1779) was a chorister at Westminster Abbey, then painted refined landscapes and exhibited at the R.A. being Surveyor of the Queen's Pictures. He resided at the Gravel Pits and its rural environs attracted John Linnell, Thomas Webster and William Mulready who painted "The Mall" in 1812 (now at the V & A).

William Horsley was born in 1774 and was encouraged by John Callcott and the Pring Brothers but was articled to Theodore Smith a pianist. He became very successful with glees, rounds, canons, and anthems taking up a position at Ely Chapel, Holborn in 1794, and was then an assistant to Callcott at the Female Orphan Asylum in 1798.

He was chief organist at the asylum during 1802-54 and at the Belgrave Chapel, Halkin Street from 1812-37, whilst he married his mentor's daughter twenty years his junior at St. Mary's. In addition he helped to establish Concentores Sodales and the Philharmonic Society, published *A Collection of Glees, Canons & Catches* by his father-in-law in 1824, and met Mendelssohn at his house 1 High Row (later 128 Church Street).

Horsley exchanged his position at Belgrave Chapel for one at Charterhouse in 1838 and wrote the hymns *Belgrave* and *Horsley* - while of his children John Callcott was a painter, Charles Edward a musician and Mary married Isambard Kingdom Brunel. Meanwhile the area gradually changed and John Whyte established the Hippodrome Racecourse to the north in 1837-42, but it was not a success and was soon covered by housing.

Kensington Square - This is one of the oldest squares in the locality being laid out in 1685 and was home to the Merrimans who came from Marlborough for many years. One of the descendants Frank Boyd, Baron Merriman O.B.E. of Knutsford was a relative of Campbell-Bannerman P.M. and has a seat designated at the Savoy Chapel.

John Merriman was born at Marlborough in 1774 then entered the Royal College of Surgeons and with Thomas Hardwick had a practice in Kensington. He married the niece of his partner in 1800 and his brother James Merriman E.I.C. was a witness. The surgery was at 18 Young Street behind their house 45 Kensington Square and several members of the family entered the profession (E. Burne-Jones lived at No.41 in 1865-67).

Merriman became medical attendant to the Duchess of Kent in 1827 and Princesses Victoria and Sophia in 1828; no doubt recommending more fresh air. His sons John and James Nathaniel joined him as doctors and resided at 11 and 13 Young Street, while they were apothecary extraordinary to the Queen on their father's decease in 1839. There is a memorial window on the north side of the church to John and Jane Merriman.

The next generation also occupied 45 Kensington Square and the first son John married Caroline Jones of Ross in c.1826 then had eight children. Of these John Jones Merriman resided at No.44, and was personal physician to Thackeray who lived at 16 Young Street with his daughters in 1847-54. It was during this period that he published *Vanity Fair, Henry Esmond, Sorrows of Werther* and *The Virginians*. Indeed Thackeray delivered some birds to John J. and his daughter Ann T. Ritchie corresponded with the family.

John senior retired from practice in the 1860s and after travelling died at West Lodge, Putney, in 1881. He has a memorial on the north side of the church "erected by surviving members of Kensington Sunday Class which he founded and taught with self devotion for many years." Nearby is one to his son John Jones Merriman d. Worthing 1896.

Of his other sons, Thomas H. of the Manor House, Barnes was a solicitor at 3 King's Bench Walk (near Morley), and Septimus of Putney was an underwriter at the Exchange but the most notable links were military. Charles James (1831) went to Addiscombe and fought in Persia during 1856-57, then was chief engineer for irrigation in Bombay and achieved the rank of general, sitting on the Legislative Council there.

William Merriman (1838) attended Kensington and Addiscombe then went to Chatham in 1856 and was an instructor under Capt. Marindin R.E. He married Emily daughter of Fitzroy M.H. Somerset head of discipline in 1872 then was goalkeeper in the Cup Final, sat on the F.A. committee, and captained their victory against the Etonians in 1875. He served in the 1st Boer War then joined his brother in Bombay and died in 1917.

C. 8 Dec 1766 John Wall Callcott s. of Thos & Charlotte bricklayer Gravel Pits 20 Nov
12 Feb. 1793 Elizabeth Hutchins Callcott d. John Wall and Elizabeth Mary Gravel Pits
30 January 1801 John Merriman the son of John and Jane of Young Street
19/23 January 1814 Mary Elizabeth daughter of William and Elizabeth Hutchins Horsley of Queen's Buildings, Brompton "Mus. Bac. Oxon"
27 July 1827 John Jones Merriman s. John and Caroline of the Square surgeon 3 July
25 March 1838 William Merriman s. John and Caroline of 13 Young Street 2 April

M. 2 April 1800 John Merriman bach and Jane Hardwick spin b.o.t.p. by licence witness Thomas Hardwick, James Merriman, Olivia Searle and Rebecca Dolbeare
12 January 1813 William Horsley "Mus. Bac." wid and Elizabeth Hutchins Callcott spin b.o.t.p. minor cons of John W. Callcott lic wit Augustus W. Callcott, J. Buckley
5 July 1836 Isambard Kingdom Brunel of St. Margaret, Westminster and Mary Elizabeth Horsley o.t.p. lic wit William Horsley, Eliz H. Horsley, Marc Brunel, Sophia Brand
18 June 1891 Frederick Henry Rich wid ret col R.E. 17 Queen's Gate Terrace to Cecile D'Olier Gowan of 20 Courtfield Gardens lic wit. Leila Gowan, Jno. Rich (see below)
15 October 1913 William Heelis solicitor of Hawkshead s. of John minister and Helen Beatrix Potter of 2 Bolton Gardens spin lic d. of Rupert gentleman (see p.220)

B. 17 September 1796 Thomas Callcott Gravel Pits 66
20 January 1816 Charlotte Callcott Gravel Pits 76
23 May 1821 John Wall Callcott of Bristol M.B. 54
11 August 1825 Elizabeth Mary Callcott Gravel Pits 50
23 June 1839 John Merriman of Kensington Square
6 July 1844 Jane Merriman of Kensington Sq. age 74

South Kensington

St. Augustine's, Queen's Gate - William Butterfield built this interesting church above Old Brompton Road in polychromatic style with coloured brick mosaic and glazed tile murals. The total expenditure was £18,000 and the nave and aisles were completed in 1871 and the chancel and sanctuary in 1876 - the seating for 850 people.

With its banded-tower façade it provided a stark contrast to the stucco housing nearby, while the interior with grand arcades was similar to All Saints. Butterfield also worked on Keble College who were patrons, but after it became a vicarage in the 1960s restoration was needed to remove the old whitewash. John Betjeman gave his support but eventually the brickwork was painted since the damage was too great (see picture p. 315).

St. Cuthbert's, Philbeach Gardens - The Bishop was reticent to start a church here due to a lack of poor people in the vicinity, however a tin shed was erected in 1883 and a new parish was separated from nearby St. Philip's. A plain red brick church with clergy house and hall was then built by H.R. Gough in 1884-87, based on the Cistercian style and Tintern Abbey. In addition it was similar to St. Matthias by J.H. Hakewill.

Its minister Rev. H. Westall entered into the controversy about incense, and over the next thirty years the interior was embellished in the Arts & Crafts style with marble-stone piers and carved pulpit and reredos. Earl's Court exhibition centre was built to the south in 1937 and it took over the parish of St. Matthias, Warwick Road in 1958 (see p. 315).

St. Jude's, Courtfield Gardens - George Godwin wrote a significant work *The Churches of London* in 1838 and with brother Henry built much local housing and three churches, all of which still survive: St. Mary, The Boltons (see below), St. Jude's in Kentish ragstone with gables and spire (1867-70), and St. Luke's at Redcliffe Square (1872).

One connection was Frederick H. Rich R.E. born at Limerick in 1824 who served in Canada and married Elizabeth daughter of R.H. Bayard at St. Stephen's, Philadelphia in 1848. Her family included five senators and her mother Mary was the granddaughter of Charles Carroll. After duty in the West Indies he lived at Dulwich then married Cecile daughter of George Gowan a stockbroker and descendant of Isaac D'Olier of Dublin. He died at Oare, Somerset in 1904 whilst visiting the Doone Valley of R.D. Blackmore.

His son Henry Bayard Rich R.E. was born at Berbice, Guyana in 1849 then attended Dulwich with three brothers and served under Wolseley in Egypt. He married Ada Melvill Simons at South Dulwich in 1881 but died at Roorkee, India in 1884.

M. 16 July 1888 Francis Slater Picot 29 Lt 2nd Wilts of 72 Courtfield Gardens to Ada Melvill Rich wid. same d. H.M. Simons merchant by E.J. Selwyn rector of Pluckley

St. Mary, The Boltons - The site was once a farm below Old Brompton but the area was developed by Robert Gunter, and George Godwin designed a church in Kentish rag with a double-crescent of houses on either side. Hogarth J. Swale the perpetual curate paid most of the £6,000 cost and it was consecrated on 22 October 1850, the spire added four years later. This was the first parish created from Holy Trinity and due to its garden location among London planes was dubbed "the country church in Kensington."

St. Stephen's and **St. Jude's** are "country churches" in Kensington and **Sir F.A. Marindin** (1838-1900) of the Royal Engineers.

Of its various connections Alexander G. Bonsor was born at Polesden Lacey in 1851 and baptized at Great Bookham then went to Eton and played for the Wanderers, scoring the second ever international goal. He owned shares in Combe, Delafield from 1873 but stayed at the Grand Hotel, Charing Cross in 1881 with *wife* Maria a Belgian citizen, then married Jeanne Marie David at the Register Office in Hanover Square in 1893.

They resided at 14 Davies Street and 1 The Boltons but there were serious problems and she took out a petition in 1895 regarding both addresses and a stay in Paris. These involved him arriving home *late*, breaking doors, and adultery thus they were divorced and he married Clara Marie Silvie Kint at Vilvoorde, Belgium in 1897. By then he had left the company and died at Brussels in 1907 his assets in England just £5. [13]

Meanwhile, this affluent development had two important literary links. Beatrix Potter was born at 2 Bolton Gardens in July 1866, her father Rupert a barrister and Unitarian. She wrote many of her stories there for publishers F. Warne & Co. but invested in Hill Top Farm in the Lake District. After marrying William Heelis a solicitor of Hawkshead she left the family home in 1913 (there is a plaque by Old Brompton Road).

In the second instance *Matilda* Winifred Graham was born at 12 Bolton Gardens in 1873. Her family emanated from Hinxton near Cambridge a profitable living whose long term incumbents included: Rev. John Graham (1833-62) her grandfather and Rev. Charles Thornton Forster (1865-91) grandson of Henry Thornton of the Clapham Sect.

Her father Robert George attended Cheltenham and entered the Stock Exchange then lived in Barnes and at St. Alban's Bank, Hampton from 1878 (once home to J.W. Croker author/statesman). Graham was third secretary of the F.A. and his sister Helen married Robert Watson Willis, whereas Rev. Forster's daughter Mabel married W.L. Napier and lived at 1 Temple Sheen, Richmond formerly home to the Willis family.

In fact, the latter's nephew E.M. Forster wrote *A Room with a View, Howard's End* and *A Passage to India* (see Clapham). With such inspiration Winifred Graham became a prolific writer at "St. Alban's" by the Thames, carrying off situations a more sophisticated reader might have found unbelievable. Her work included *Idylls of Suburbia* and an anti *History of the Mormons*, whilst she studied the psychic world and wrote 88 books. Her memorial with book sculpture is at Hampton, as is "Mrs. Thomas" of Jerome's *Three Men in a Boat*.

---

[13] Jeanne Marie Bonsor married Lt. Joseph Ignatius son of Joseph Bonomi and Jessie Martin in 1897. The father, a sculptor, worked with Haliburton and was curator of the Soane Museum.

St. Paul's, Onslow Square - This was designed by James Edmeston in perpendicular style of ragstone in 1859-60, while a hall was added in 1876. Sir Charles J. Freake built the main square and George Basevi was architect of the stucco houses. Rev. Hanmer W. Webb-Peploe made it a centre for evangelism in 1876-1909, and was a prebend of St. Paul's and speaker at Keswick Convention. The church was united with Holy Trinity, Brompton in 1977 and has a memorial to Sir Charles Freake (see picture p. 315). [14]

Its residents included W.M. Thackeray at 36 in 1854-60, Admiral Robert Fitzroy at 38 and William Railton at 65. Charles H.A. Lutyens (1829-1915) was born in Reading then a captain in the Infantry and married Mary Theresa Gallwey at Montreal, Canada in 1852. She was born at Killarney and the sister of Sir Thomas L.J. Gallwey R.E. the Governor of Montreal and Bermuda. The couple came to live at 16 Onslow Square and had a large family, the father a portrait painter being taught by Edwin H. Landseer.

A son Edwin Landseer Lutyens was born there on 29 March 1869 and Dr. J. Merriman was given a painting in payment! He grew up at Thursley, Surrey and trained at South Kensington School of Art in 1885-87, then joined Ernest George and Harold A. Peto (son of Samuel). After starting a practice at 29 Bloomsbury Square he collaborated with Gertrude Jekyll garden designer and did houses in the Arts and Crafts style.

Lutyens married Emily Bulwer-Lytton daughter of Edward Robert son of the novelist and viceroy of India at Knebworth, Herts in August 1897. His later work included Castle Drogo, Lindisfarne, Thiepval, the Cenotaph and the classical buildings for New Delhi in 1912-30. His memorial is located at St. Paul's Cathedral (d.1944).

C. 11 June 1869 Edwin Landseer Lutyens son of Charles Henry Augustus and Mary Theresa of 16 Onslow Square, Kensington gentleman by Capel Molyneux vicar

St. Stephen's, Gloucester Road - Rev. Sinclair established Christchurch, Victoria Road a chapel of ease built by Benjamin Ferrey with G. Myers in 1851. It never received a district, thus an iron mission opened nearby in 1866 and J. Peacock built St. Stephen's parish church the next year. Its first vicar was Rev. John A. Aston (b. Brockley).

A northwest tower with v-shape roof and baronial round was planned for the latter in 1864, but was never built. Instead a distinctive chapel, passage and vestry were added by H.R. Gough at the east end in 1887. Rev. Lord Victor A. Seymour son of the Marquess of Hertford and minister of Carshalton introduced ritual in the 1920s; and the shrine, reredos, screen and font-cover by Bodley and Tapper date from that time. T.S. Eliot was a churchwarden for 25 years under the vicar Eric Cheetham from 1934-59.

Of its links William Merriman married Emily Somerset but as Shakespeare said "what's in a name" as she was descended from the Dukes of Beaufort of Raglan, Monmouth (see over). Another link was George Addison a worsted spinner of Bradford and Paisley who retired to Catherine Place, Bath. His son George W. (1849) attended Cheltenham with Renny-Tailyour of Montrose and joined the R.E. playing in two Cup Finals. He married a daughter of G.R. Stevenson of Hawkhurst, and her sister married Henry A. Brassey M.P. of Preston Hall (home to E.L Betts) son of the railway contractor Thomas.

---

[14] Freake owned the land on which St. Peter's, Cranley Gardens, was built in 1867 and thus held the benefice. It passed to the Armenian Church in 1972 and the parish to St. Mary, The Boltons. Keswick Convention was started in 1875 and later speakers were John Stott and Billy Graham.

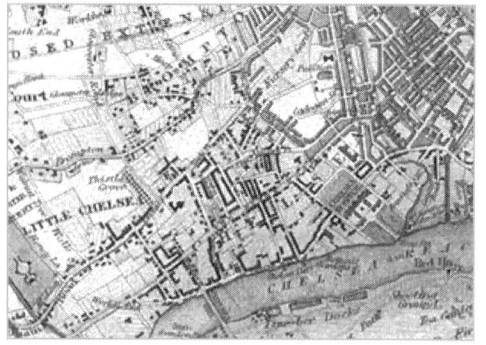

Brompton & Chelsea (1841)

The map reveals the slow development beneath Hyde Park and Kensington, the well-established locality of Belgravia to the east, and first signs of urbanisation within the Chelsea district.

Addison was then seconded to the torpedo service in Malta and his son George was baptized at St. Paul's pro-Cathedral (or Queen Adelaide's). Upon his return he resided at 20 Elm Park Gardens, Fulham Road, and he was aide de camp to Gen. Thomas Gallwey and a private secretary to Hon. W.H. Smith the Secretary of State for War. At this time three of his daughters were baptized at St. Peter's, Cranley Gardens.

He moved to 54 Courtfield Gardens and commanded the Telegraph Battalion then was an inspector of railways at the Board of Trade with Col. F.H. Rich and Maj. F. Marindin. Leaving the army in 1899 he was personal assistant to Edward Guinness, Lord Iveagh until 1927, whilst Renny-Tailyour once A.D.C. to James Hamilton, Lord Lieutenant was the managing director at St. James's Gate, Dublin. Addison died at 16 Ashburn Place and has a memorial at Gunnersbury Cemetery (formerly Kensington).

M. 15 February 1872 William Merriman capt R.E. Old Brompton s. John retired surgeon to Emily Jane Anna Eliz. Somerset 20 spin of 41 Elvaston Place d. Fitzroy M.H. col RE banns by Boscawen T.G.H .Somerset rector of Michel Trywith, Cwmcarren, Monmouth wit Fitzroy Somerset Col R.E., Georgiana Maria Merriman, John Jones Merriman [15]

30 June 1875 George William Addison lieut R.E. of Queen's Gate Terr s. of George gent to Caroline Augusta Stevenson spin of Cromwell House (Road) d. of George gent banns by T.H. Cookes rector of Tadmarton, Oxon witness G.R. and M. Stevenson

South Kensington, Other Residents - These included Hugh Mitchell lieutenant R.E. and solicitor at 6 Douro Place (home of Samuel Palmer artist), Sir Francis A. Marindin nine times Cup Final referee and F.A. president at 22 Sussex Villas (Launceston Pla.) in 1882-96, and William Pember Reeves politician in New Zealand and High Commissioner in England who lived at various local address including 31 Pembroke Square.

Reeves was a journalist on the *Lyttelton Times* and as a radical Liberal was first Minister of Labour in the Empire introducing many social policies, whilst his wife Maud helped win suffrage for women in 1893. They came to London and joined the Webbs and Shaw in the Fabians, and sister Euphemia wife of Cecil H. Lascelles, grandson of the 3rd Earl of Harewood resided with them. After a holiday with H.G. Wells their daughter Amber had a scandalous affair and a child, whereas the father resigned as Commissioner in 1908 to be director of the L.S.E. His wife stayed with the Fabians and with Effie wrote *Round about a Pound a Week* in 1913, a seminal study on poverty in Lambeth.

---

[15] Henry Somerset, 5th Duke of Beaufort, married Elizabeth Boscawen and had seven sons: Robert (1776) who was aide de camp to the Duke of York and King in the Peninsular War and a commander at Waterloo, William (1784) her grandfather who married Elizabeth Molyneux, and Fitzroy James (1788) aide de camp to Wellesley in the Peninsular and at Waterloo and then his secretary. The latter became Lord Raglan in 1852 and wrote down the command at Balaklava which was passed on verbally leading to the *Charge of the Light Brigade*.

Chelsea

This was a relatively small parish compared to those around it viz. Kensington, Hanover Square, and Fulham with its Bishop's Palace. The name derived from a chalk wharf (*cealc hith*) its bounds going down Fulham Road to Kensington Canal and Chelsea Creek, along the river to the Royal Army Hospital and up Sloane Street to Lowndes Square. It was mainly undeveloped and its ancient church was beside the river facing Battersea.

Henry VIII obtained Chelsea Manor or Place (marked by Manor Street) in 1536 thus it was home to Princess Elizabeth, Catharine Parr, Anne of Cleves, and John Dudley Duke of Northumberland. The Crown retained the lease until the 17th century when it passed to Charles Cheyne, Viscount Newhaven with the church advowson. His son William then sold it to Sir Hans Sloane who was a physician and art collector in 1713.

To the south was the Apothecaries Garden by the river (established in 1673). Sloane who was physician to the King, president of the R.S. and governor of the Foundling Hospital asked them for a herbarium which became Chelsea Physic Garden on Swan Walk.

Sloane then bequeathed the manor to his daughters in 1753: Sarah wid. of Sir George Stanley of Paultons and Elizabeth wife of Charles 2nd Lord Cadogan. He asked for his collection to be retained but his trustees moved it to Montagu House (Br. Museum) and the property was replaced by Cheyne Walk. The estate stayed with the Cadogan family who developed the area with roads and housing during the next century.

The second major building was a theological college founded by James I in the east of the parish in 1610. With changing politics it was not a success hence Charles II donated it to the Royal Society in 1667, but they found little use for it and the Royal Hospital for Soldiers was built by Wren on approval in 1682-92. This was located around courtyards with a fine college chapel - its apse painted by Sebastiano Ricci in 1714.

Richard Jones, 1st Earl of Ranelagh was married to Margaret Cecil daughter of the Earl of Salisbury and his uncle was the chemist Robert Boyle. He held senior roles including paymaster and helped to build Chelsea Hospital being its treasurer in 1685-1702. On the fields to the east he built Ranelagh House in 1689, and Solomon Rieti the uncle of Isaac Disraeli's wife created Ranelagh Pleasure Gardens with rotunda in 1742. This was a top venue like Spring Gardens while the section near to Pimlico became housing. [16]

Other Properties - Chelsea was in fact *a village of mansions* by the river and Charles II built a private road through the parish (public in 1830). Of these Beaufort House by the church with its gardens, orchards, and stables was owned by Thomas More from 1521, and there he entertained Erasmus and Holbein. Later owners were Gregory Fiennes, Lord Dacre and Anne in 1575; Sir Robert Cecil, Earl of Salisbury in 1597 (who built Hatfield House at great expense); and Henry Clinton, 2nd Earl of Lincoln in 1599.

It then went to George Villiers, 1st Duke of Buckingham in 1627 and to Henry, Duke of Beaufort in 1682. However, Sir Hans Sloane came into possession in 1737 and by that time the rural nature of the area was changing so he demolished the house.

---

[16] The house and rotunda were demolished in 1805 and the gardens were joined to the hospital. Ranelagh Presbyterian Chapel began in a surviving building at this time but moved just north to Lwr. George Street in 1818 and went to Belgrave Presbyterian, W. Halkin Street in 1866.

By the 20th century all that remained was a Tudor wall and doorway between Beaufort and Danvers Streets - later moved to Chiswick. The Earl of Lincoln built a mansion for his son-in-law Arthur Gorges just by the property, and nearby were Lindsey House, Arch House over Lombard Street, and Danvers House owned by Thomas Wharton.

To the north was Brompton Hall owned by William Cecil, Lord Burghley and there he sheltered under an elm with Queen Elizabeth. His son Robert Cecil the Earl of Salisbury was spymaster to James I (see St. Clement's) and it was later Onslow Square. To the west was Chelsea Park by Fulham Road owned by Thomas Wharton, which was sold in 1727 and replaced by a Lodge and silk farm with mulberry trees. The latter was superseded by flats in 1876 but some of the trees survived in the gardens of Elm Park Road.

Just beyond was Little Chelsea and World's End (a hostelry) on Fulham Lane. Robert Boyle lived there and during a visit Evelyn noted *a chaos of pots, instruments and papers*! Stanley House was built nearby by Sir Arthur Gorges, a friend of Edmund Spenser, and passed to his daughter wife of Sir Robert Stanley son of the Earl of Derby in 1625. It was rebuilt in 1691 then fell to Thomas Arundell in 1728-51 and the Countess of Strathmore in 1777-80 who added conservatories. William Hamilton of Naples came in 1818 and as secretary to Lord Elgin transported the *Elgin Marbles* - some going in the east hall.

The National Society wanted colleges for teachers and purchased it from Hamilton for £9,000 in 1839 then opened St. Mark's Training College. Rev. Derwent Coleridge son of Samuel the poet and cousin of John T. of the Oxford Movement was the first principal and lived in Stanley House. He added a school so his teachers could gain experience and Edward Blore designed an eight-sided octagon by the chapel for 260 students. Coleridge remained there until 1864 and advocated Latin, languages and sacred music. [17]

Royal Hospital - C. 21 May 1734 Walpole s. of Kingsmill and Susannah Eyre [His son Walpole Eyre developed the St. John's Wood estate in Marylebone]

B. 20 April 1814 Dr. Charles Burney of Chelsea College aged 87 [organist from 1783]

Chelsea Chapel, Park Walk - William Sloane leased Wharton's estate to Sir Richard Manningham and he built a chapel before any houses in 1718. The ministers included Dr. Sloane Ellesmere rector of Chelsea (1736-66), Mr. Jacobs from St. Dunstan in the West (pre-1785), and John Owen of the British and Foreign Bible Society (from 1800). There was a school attached and it was enlarged in 1810, but it was replaced by St. Andrew's parish church by A.C. Blomfield in 1913 and combined with St. John's in 1973.

St. Mary's, Cadogan Street - Abbe Jean Voyaux de Franous ministered to the hospital and barracks in 1793-1840 and built a chapel on Cadogan Gardens in 1812. Joseph and Mary Knight then purchased Wellington Cricket Ground below the Prince's Club and built a new convent, school, almshouses and cemetery on Cadogan Street in 1844-45. A permanent church of St. Mary's was designed there by John Francis Bentley, architect of Westminster Cathedral, in 1877-79 and was blessed by Cardinal Manning.

---

[17] Whitelands College for women also started in a school at Turk's Row by the Royal Military Asylum (Duke of York H.Q.) in 1842. St. Mark's merged with St. John's, Battersea in 1923 and moved to Plymouth while F.J. Wall was a pupil. King's College were there until the 1980s then the octagon and chapel became a junior school and it was refurbished as "Kings Chelsea."

Chelsea Congregational - Rev. Ebenezer Morley was minister at Holborn Street, Hull and his son was E.C. Morley solicitor of King's Bench Walk. He came to Albany Chapel, Brentford *a desolate sanctuary* in 1853 and as secretary of the Bible Association preached in the open air. Despite his age he opened a chapel for 300 east of Gunter Grove in early 1858 and lived at 12 Victoria Grove (Netherton) by the St. George's workhouse (later a hospital) d.1862. A new chapel was built at Edith Grove for 1,100 in 1866 but left them in debt and they departed the union in 1902. They had links to the L.C.M. and it became the Chelsea Congregational church in a new building on the site in 1960.

St. Columba's (Presbyterian), Pont Street - This was first built in 1884 but rebuilt by the architect of Guildford Cathedral in the 1950s. Jessie Hardie daughter of Archibald Leitch married there in 1928; her father of 99 Barkston Gardens, Earl's Court designed stands for Craven Cottage and Stamford Bridge which were located nearby.

All Saints, Chelsea

The old church by the river has an interesting history, one that is obscured by its modern façade of red brickwork. A record of All Saints first appears in 1157 and the chancel was built in the 13th century, while chapels were added to north and south in 1325 and a bell-tower was erected in 1393 - all in flint and rough stone. The rector was initially presented by the Abbot of Westminster but this duty passed to the Lord of the Manor in 1536, whereas the north chapel was owned by John Shoreditch local "lord" and later Sir John Lawrence, and the south one by Thomas More and his family viz.

Nave: *North Aisle* - Sir Arthur Gorges 1625 a brass panel and son Arthur last in the line 1668; Charles Cheyne Viscount Newhaven "lord" and Lady Jane Cheyne 1669 poet and playwright by son of Gian Lorenzo Bernini; *South Aisle* - Gregory Fiennes Lord Dacre and Lady Anne Sackville 1595 of the Emanuel Foundation by Nicholas Johnson.

North Chapel: Richard Jervoise 1563 with arched tomb, Thomas Lawrence 1593, Sir John Lawrence 1638 also Sir John Lawrence and Dame Grisel from Iver, Buckingham with members of their family recorded on various tablets.

Chancel: - Edmund Lord Bray 1539 the oldest memorial and Thomas Hungerford 1581 who was present at Musselburgh Fields regarding Edward VI's marriage alliance.

South Chapel: - Remodelled in 1528 by Sir Thomas More with a memorial to his wives Joan and Alice, father Sir John and *Latin* inscriptions with capitals by Holbein; Lady Jane Guilford, Duchess of Northumberland 1555 the wife of John Dudley of Chelsey Manor, warden of the ports and Lord Protector to Edward VI.

The nave and tower were rebuilt in 1670 and Lady Jane Cheyne paid for a new roof; whilst there was an informal change of dedication to St. Luke's at this time and a bell was inscribed with the new *nom de plume*. A number of memorials were recorded by Strype many of which still survive within the restored structure.

The parish applied to the Commissioners for funds to build a new edifice in 1711, but this was rejected, and Sir Hans Sloane gave land at Dovehouse Green on Sydney Street for a new churchyard in 1733. However, a more central church was urgently needed.

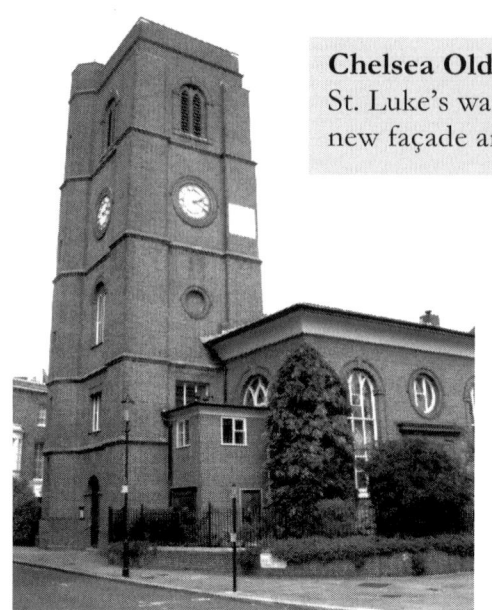

Chelsea Old Church - "White was the colour and St. Luke's was the name," but it was restored with a new façade and dedicated to All Saints once again.

Sir Hans Sloane (1660-1753) was a great collector.

Consequently, an Act was passed moving the *Vestry* to the north in 1819, and Chelsea Old Church was designated *A Chapel without Glebe* - supported only by pew rents and the church rates. Its curates were John Rush in 1824-55 and R.H. Davies for fifty years but all marriages were forbidden and baptisms only by special leave. However it had distinctive white-washed walls and was depicted by Cotman, Turner and Whistler.

Later that century the historic name of All Saints was duly revived, but it was severely damaged in 1941 and worship then took place in the adjacent Cheyne Hospital. Walter H. Godfrey carried out the restoration and a temporary roof was erected above the south chapel in 1950, then the next year it was a parish again. The work involved re-cladding in red brick to create a very different exterior and this was completed in 1954. Apart from the memorials there are several points of interest including a chained library with *Vinegar Bible* &c. (like that at Hereford) donated by Sir Hans Sloane.

On the west side of the church is a garden given to William and Margaret Roper which was later the studio-site of Jacob Epstein. There is a sundial on the tower dated 1692 and memorials to Sir Thomas More by Leslie Cubitt Bevis and to Sir Hans Sloane given by Elizabeth Cadogan and Sarah Stanley. Nearby is a light pedestal from Coalbrookdale of 1874 reference Chelsea Embankment by Bazalgette (also Chelsea and Albert Bridges), and a fountain to George Sparkes of Bromley judge of the Madras E.I.C. 1878.

Regarding the wider area several prominent people lived in Cheyne Walk by the river including George Eliot, Rossetti, Whistler, Vaughan Williams and Henry James (tablet in church). Thomas Carlyle lived at 24 Cheyne Row now a National Trust property, and at 16 Lawrence Street is a plaque: "Chelsea China made here 1745-84 and Tobias Smollett novelist [who criticised Europe] lived in part of the house from 1750-62."

The Chelsea Porcelain Factory was started by Nicholas Sprimont a former silversmith and in particular made tableware and figurines aimed at the aristocratic market. It was bought by William Duesbury of Derby Works in 1769 and moved there in 1784. Other innovations saw Earl Spencer fund Battersea Bridge a toll crossing by Henry Holland in 1772. Later residents were William Wilberforce who died at 44 Cadogan Place in 1833 just after the anti-slavery bill was passed, and Thomas Brassey a railway contractor of 56 Lowndes Square who left a staggering £3.2 million in 1870.

Several new parishes were added: Holy Trinity, Sloane Square (1830) with two towers by J. Savage; Christchurch (1839) by Edward Blore with England organ from St. Michael's, Queenhithe; St. Saviour's, Walton Street (1840) by George Basevi; St. Jude's, Turk's Row (1844) by Basevi demolished 1933; and St. Simon Zelotes (1859) by the Prince's Club. Trinity was rebuilt by J.D. Sedding with windows by Burne-Jones and Morris in 1890, and was called the Cathedral of Arts & Crafts by Betjeman (see pictures p. 316).

B. 24 Nov 1692 Thomas Shadwell Esq. Poet Laureat [between J. Dryden and N. Tate] 18 January 1753 Sir Hans Sloane bart - his collection started the British Museum

St. Luke's, Chelsea

The Hon. Rev. Gerald Valerian Wellesley (1770-1848) brother of the Duke of Wellington married Lady Emily Maud Cadogan the great granddaughter of Sir Hans Sloane in 1802. He was appointed rector of the old church three years later, and under his stewardship plans were implemented to move to a new site on Sydney Street in 1819.

Foundations were laid the next year, but designs by John Nash were turned down in favour of those by James Savage - the foremost expert on mediaeval architecture. His church of St. Luke's was considered the first example of the *Gothic Revival* in London, and sat in a large plot making it a distinctive landmark above the King's Road.

The finished ensemble, with elements like King's College Chapel, Cambridge, had an exterior of Bath stone, flying buttresses and a tower 142 feet high. Inside was a soaring nave arcade with small triforium and the galleries were supported by the arched pillars on either side. Rev. Wellesley moved into his new church on 18 October 1824 and remained there until 1832, when he was succeeded by John William Lockwood A.M.

However, the latter did not remain long and Rev. Charles Kingsley L.L.B. was the rector from 1836-60, his son Charles minister of Eversley and author of *Westward Ho!* and *The Water Babies*. During his time there the church saw the marriage of Charles Dickens to the daughter of George Hogarth, editor of the *Evening Chronicle* who published *Sketches by Boz*. This was two days after the first edition of *Pickwick Papers*.

St. Luke's with its Gothic buttresses and fan vaults, and the original **Rev. Baden Powell** who married his third wife there.

Another marriage was of Rev. Baden Powell who had a mathematics degree at Oriel and was ordained in 1820. He was curate of Midhurst and vicar of Plumstead in 1820-27, but as a fellow of the R.S. became Savilian Professor of Geometry at Oxford at the latter date. He was sympathetic to evolution and argued that important teachings in the Bible came from the New Testament. After contributing to *Essays & Reviews* any hope of advancement was ended and he died at 6 Stanhope Street, Paddington in 1860.

Of the residents Walter Greaves was born at Cheyne Walk the son of a waterman (who rowed Turner) on 4 July 1846, whilst James Whistler moved to Lindsey Row in 1863 and Walter took him on the river. As a result he became his studio assistant and did work for Carlyle, Mr. Leyland a ship-owner, and painted river scenes at Streatham Town Hall. But he was later turned away by Whistler when asking for help, and accused of plagiarism after exhibiting in 1911. Despite this he was an honorary member of Chelsea Arts Club and retired to Charterhouse being buried at Little Hallingbury in 1930.

Regarding the church, the next minister was Rev. Abel G.W. Blunt M.A. in 1860-1902 who retired to 91 Cheyne Walk. During this period Jerome K. Jerome the author was married there. The latter worked for the London & North Western Railway but inspired by his sister tried acting, and wrote *Three Men in a Boat* after a honeymoon with his wife Ettie in a small boat on the Thames. This was a great financial success which meant he could devote all his time to writing - although he never surpassed this.

C. 29 July 1846 Walter the son of Charles and Elizabeth Greaves of Cheyne Walk boat builder baptized by E. Rudge born on 4 July

M. 2 April 1836 Charles John Huffam Dickens of Furnival's Inn and Catherine Thomson Hogarth o.t.p. a minor lic with consent of father by R.W. Morice cur pres Geo. Hogarth [father], Elizth. Dickens, Georgina Hogarth, Thomas Beard, John Dickens

10 March 1846 Baden Powell wid in Holy Orders St. Peter in the East, Oxford s. Baden Esq. to Henrietta Grace Smyth spin o.t.p. d. Capt. William Henry R.N. licence by Charles Kingsley rector pres W.H. Smyth, G.B. Airy, Josephine B. Smyth, Richard Airy &c. [18]

21 June 1888 Jerome Klapka Jerome 29 dramatic author of St. Martin son Jerome Clapp Jerome nonconformist minister and Georgina Elizabeth Henrietta Stanley Marris 29 div High Ct of Justice 12 June on her petition of 88 Chelsea Gardens d. George Nesza soldier by Fred Relton curate wit G. Wingrave, C.J.F. Banister, Gretchen Hentschel

B. 12 May 1852 James Savage of North Place, Hampstead Road, 73 T.H. Kent

---

[18] William Henry Smyth (1788-1865) the son of Joseph an American was born at Westminster and an admiral R.N., astronomer, hydrographer, R.S. fellow and R.G.S. founder. He resided at 3 Cheyne Walk in 1840-51 whilst his son Charles Piazzi was Astronomer Royal in Scotland and put forward theories on the pyramids. Through links in The Cape they knew William Petrie an electrical engineer who became attached to Henrietta, but married Anne daughter of Matthew Flinders whom he met at Cheyne Walk (see Hampstead). Baden-Powell was born at Stanhope Street in 1857 and served in the Army from 1876-1910, writing *Scouting for Boys* in 1908.

London
South

In the early 19th century most housing was located at Southwark with its cathedral, winding mediaeval streets, courtyard-coaching inns and prisons such as the Marshalsea. To the west was the Archbishop's Palace and nearby were those pleasure grounds - Paris, Vauxhall and Surrey Gardens.

Leisure was always prominent in the area with sport at Battersea, Clapham and the Oval - that eponymous agrarian field, while nearby was the famous Astley's Emporium with its menagerie to amaze. Bridges there were few but artistes there were many including Fletcher, Shakespeare, Massinger, Blake and Tate although for pathos none could better *The Little Tramp*.

This was an area of evangelists, philanthropists and reformers - the Clapham Sect leading the way through residents Thornton and Venn with other links to churchmen of note Andrewes, Booth, Jowett and Newman. It was a place where a man might retire to classify plants, reconsider his bounty, discover a room with a view, or just enjoy some light relief at the opera.

Others sojourners in the vicinity included Pugin that co-creator of Gothic palaces, Peto the architect of columns and beyond, and Pember the man of disguise who Holmes owed a very significant debt to. But mostly it was the land of "Four Gospels" with large crowds waiting on every word.

"London, Chatham & Dover"
(south side of Blackfriars Bridge)

Peto, Betts and Crampton began the project through to Holborn in 1860, but were bankrupted during the financial crisis of 1866.

Clapham

William Makepeace Thackeray wrote in the mid-19th century, "Of all the pretty suburbs that still adorn our metropolis there are few that exceed in charm Clapham Common." At this time there were grand houses delineating its periphery mostly with fields beyond, except on the east side where the mediaeval village was located.

Market gardens and pastures separated it from Battersea to the north, Wandsworth to the west, and Tooting Graveney and Streatham to the south. In fact at Stockwell, and Brixton in Lambeth, it was still possible to witness swathes of growing crops.

The Roman road known as Stane Street was contiguous with Clapham Road, and the village to the north was the homestead of the *Cloppa* people. At the Domesday Book the manor was held by Geoffrey de Mandeville. It passed to Dr. Henry Atkins physician to James I for £6,000 in 1617, and to Sir Richard Atkins d.1689 (memorial in old church). After the latter's descendant died in 1756 it passed to his sister Penelope wife of George Pitt, Baron Rivers, then to Richard Bowyer who assumed the name of Atkins.

There was poor soil in much of the district and the first villas were built beside the common for wealthy Londoners in the late-17th and 18th centuries. One of the early residents was Samuel Pepys, who lived there with his servant William Hewer until 1703. Another was Elizabeth the widow of Captain James Cook the explorer.

However, it was not long before the developers changed this, and one of the earliest examples was Clapham Park laid out by the ubiquitous Thomas Cubitt. Unlike his other schemes this was a *Garden Suburb* to the southeast on the border with Streatham, and he purchased 229 acres from William Atkins, Lord of the Manor, in 1824. He then built large detached villas with extensive grounds on wide tree-lined avenues.

Cubitt purchased some additional land to the south, and a plot by King's Road which served as a brickfield. This had a dual purpose, dividing the estate from less desirable parts of Lyham Road and Brixton. But development was slow and he still held 179 acres of land in 1842. He lived at Cubitt House a mansion on Clarence Road, and his brother Sir William a partner in the project resided at Bedford Hill House to the south.

Clapham was a relatively small parish - its boundary running above Wandsworth Road, across the common by Cedars Road, eastwards around Clapham Park estate, and north in a line along what is now King's Avenue. In fact, this enclave was developed before most of the land around it, and the common was spared the railway lines that carved a swathe through those of Tooting Bec and Wandsworth.

Regarding this the London & S.W. and West London & Crystal Palace railways plus the West London Extension were located to the north, and the London, Chatham & Dover with its large railway works was to the east. Clapham Junction station opened in 1863 and despite being firmly set in Battersea was given this cognomen to raise its status.

Another development was Clapham Grammar School on Clapham High Street, below Manor Street. Charles Pritchard was educated at the Merchant Taylors, Christ's Hospital and St. John's, Cambridge where he studied science, and was appointed headmaster of Stockwell, a feeder for King's College, in 1832. But his liberal ideas on education meant he was moved to the new school at Clapham two years later. He was very successful and Herschel, Airy, Hamilton and Darwin all sent their sons to be educated there.

However, he transferred his interests including an observatory to Dr. Alfred Wrigley in 1862 and moved to Freshwater where he was a prominent astronomer. His successor was also educated at St. John's and had been at Addiscombe College from 1842 (which disbanded at this time). Thus he turned Clapham into a training college for the Army and Civil Service - which it remained until it was closed down in 1882.

The school had a tradition in sport and their pupil Charles C. Dacre was an expert at the dribbling game, thus he appeared in an important test match between Middlesex and Kent & Surrey at Beaufort House beside Lillie Bridge, Fulham in November 1867. At a latter date he took the game to New Zealand. Clapham Rovers amateurs (1869-86) who played on all three local commons also won the F.A. Cup in 1879-80.

Local Churches - Henry Wilkinson of the *Westminster Assembly* had a Presbyterian congregation in Clapham in 1672 and there were 350 independents in 1715. A meeting house was located in the Old Town and moved to a site in Grafton Square in 1852, while the Baptist Chapel in New Park Road (built in 1842) still remains. This is one of the last surviving historic buildings with houses in King's Avenue and Thornton Road.

However this was generally the domain of the Anglicans and St. James's, Park Hill was built above the estate by Lewis Vulliamy in 1829 and became a parish in 1854. It was in the Gothic style with clock tower, pinnacles, 14th century transepts and three galleries but was rebuilt after the war. In contrast St. John the Evangelist, Clapham Rise a chapel of ease was designed by Thomas Marsh Nelson in the Greek Revival style in 1840-42. It had a portico of six Ionic columns, three galleries, Ionic pillars and chancel with small reredos, whereas Rev. William Jowett was the minister from 1851-55.

Other developments were Christchurch on Union Grove below the Wandsworth Road with five bays, south chapel and bell-cote in 1860; and St. Clement Danes Almshouses on Garratt Lane which fell just within Streatham parish. However, Cubitt was slow to provide churches and All Saints for the poorer people of Lyham Road was built in 1873 (although little remains), and St. Stephen's on Grove Road came as late as 1880.

St. Mary's, Battersea

The settlement by the river was recorded in a charter of Ethelred of Mercia in 693, and there was an Anglo-Saxon church there by c.800. This makes it the first consecrated site south of the Thames. It was listed as "Patricsey" in the Domesday Book, being held by Westminster Abbey with 45 villeins and 16 smallholders. The nave was extended with an east window in 1380, a south chapel was added in 1489, and a steeple in 1639.

The Archbishop of York built York House nearby during the 15th century, whilst Sir Oliver St. John owned the manor and resided in a large mansion by the river with forty rooms. William Batten colleague of Pepys also had a property in the area. The manor passed down to Sir Walter St. John who added a church-gallery for boys of his school in 1705 (later the National School), and also to Henry Lord Bolingbroke (1678-1751) his grandson, who became a senior Tory statesman and rival of Walpole.

It was then conveyed to John, Earl Spencer in 1762 who rebuilt the nave and the nearby bridge - making Battersea a fashionable area for rich merchants. However, "the ruinous church" was pulled down in 1771 and most of Bolingbroke House soon afterwards.

St. Mary's, Battersea was by a local architect in 1776 and **Henry St. John, Lord Bolingbroke**.

A new edifice was built by local architect Joseph Dixon for £4,000 by November 1776 with some of the monuments transferred and the bells recast; but later on the organ was removed and box pews taken out. The most prominent memorials were to Sir Oliver St. John, Sir John Fleet the mayor d.1693, Sir Walter St. John and Henry St. John Lord Bolingbroke - who had a grey and white marble by Roubiliac with long epitaph.

The parish boundary reached down to Wandsworth and Clapham Common then went across from Lavender Hill to Nine Elms (with its railway terminus in 1838-48). Indeed, the church had an attractive view and Turner painted the scene from the vestry window, whereas Sir Arthur Blomfield the architect spoke at the centenary in 1876.

Regarding the local environs, housing was initially by the church then developed on a piecemeal basis with a grid of roads south of Battersea Rise. There was an industrial base by the river including a starch works, silk factory, Price's Patent Candle Co., the West London Extension, National Society Training College, St. Mary's, flour mills, chemical works, turpentine works, a timber yard and an iron foundry to name but a few.

Nearby Battersea Fields was reclaimed from the marshes in the 16th century and was a major venue for fairs, pigeon shooting and donkey racing but was designated under H.M. Office of Works in 1846. It was then drained and levelled using soil from the Victoria Docks (by Peto & Betts), and the new park covered 200 acres with another 120 acres for housing. Its main features were a boating lake, cascades, Italian gardens and some sports grounds to the north which were used by the Wanderers F.C. in 1864-70.

Local churches included St George's, Sleaford Street built by Edward Blore in 1827 and enlarged with a chancel in 1874 (demolished 1960), and Christchurch at the west end of Battersea Park Road built in 1849. The Royal Freemasons Female School was formed at St. George's Fields (128 Westminster Bridge Road) in 1788, but moved to Battersea Rise by the railway in 1853 and went to Rickmansworth in 1926 (Royal Masonic). In its place came Emanuel School founded by Lady Dacre which first arrived nearby in 1883.

Other Local Celebrities - William Blake (1757-1827) painter, poet and printmaker spent most off his life in London except for three years in Felpham. He was apprenticed to an engraver and John Flaxman was his patron from 1782, whilst his wife Catherine worked with him and he produced "Jerusalem" as part of *Milton: A Poem* in 1804-08. His family were dissenters, possibly Moravians, and he has a memorial at Bunhill Fields.

Another link was Benedict Arnold who was born at Norwich, Connecticut in 1741, his ancestor of the same name being the Governor of Rhode Island. He was a commander at Philadelphia and West Point under Washington, but changed sides through dealings with William Franklin and was a British general from 1781. After going to New Brunswick he came back to London in 1791 and died at Gloucester Place, Portman Square.

Of the residents the Wall family were labourers at Rainham, Essex and William Wall a servant married Elizabeth Mansfield at St. Botolph's Bishopsgate in 1850, but was then a coachman at 2 St. John's Road soon afterwards. He had three sons, and the youngest Frederick attended St. Mark's College being a solicitor's clerk and manager. The father himself was a cab proprietor at Clifton Villa, 118 Northcote Road.

Frederick was a member of Rangers F.C. who played at Balham Cricket Ground located on Bedford Hill Road in 1875-88, and with his wife had addresses nearby. Consequently he represented Middlesex at the F.A., was vice president of London F.A. and secretary of the Amateur Cup - replacing Alcock as F.A. secretary in 1895. It was a full time position and he moved to St. Julian's Farm Road and Casewick House, West Norwood, but after his wife died married Agnes Frances Hall at West Ham Register Office in 1918.

He helped negotiate the move to Wembley and in latter years resided with his wife at Lancaster Gate as ambassadors for the F.A., whilst he was knighted in 1930 and retired from the game in 1934. He received many accolades and a cheque for £10,000 then lived in Sutton until he died in 1944 - his memorial at Wandsworth Cemetery. At his marriage his father was listed as a landed proprietor. In fact, an entry in *Kelly's Titled, Landed & Official Classes* stated, he was, "The son of William Wall of Wormley."

C. 10 October 1678 Henry son of Henry St. John Esq. was baptized
26 December 1858 Frederick Joseph son of William & Eliz. Wall of Battersea coachman
b. 14 April *also* Arthur Alfred b. 6 November 1856 both by Robt Graves curate

M. 18 August 1782 William Blake and Catherine Butcher b.o.t.p. by licence by J. Gardner vicar witness Thomas Monger, James Blake, Robert Munday (parish clerk)
2 September 1880 Frederick Joseph Wall 22 sol. clerk of Clifton Villa, Northcote Road s. William coachman to Marie Louise White 21 of Clapham Parish d. Charles gent banns by H. Hodgson cur wit Augustus G.H. Toulyan, Henrietta Raven, Wm. Geo. Wall

B. 12 January 1630/31 The Lord Oliver St. John bur.
9 July 1708 Sir Walter St. John bart aged 87
31 January 1731 Charles Williams from London [1]
18 Dec 1751 Henry St. John late L. Viscount Bolingbroke
17 April 1787 Joseph Dixon [architect - in the church]
14 June 1801 Bendick Arnold [sic] aged 59

General Benedict Arnold (1741-1801) fought for both sides in the American War of Independence.

---

[1] Charles Williams acted at Drury Lane thus Colley and Theophilus Cibber and Robert Wilks were present.

St. Paul's, Clapham

The first church dedicated to St. Mary's was recorded in the 12th century, but this was soon changed to Holy Trinity. It sat on a bluff beyond Old Town at the end of Rectory Grove, beside the aptly named Matrimony Hill and manor house. Here the parishioners could gaze out across the marshes towards the Thames and London, their backs firmly exercised against the stony, unprofitable acres of common land behind them.

However, as the circumstances changed during the 18th century, the focus was moved southwards and what pertained before was no longer relevant. This clearly compared to the situation in Chelsea, Paddington and St. Pancras where a small country church in a poor location, no longer suited the needs of its wealthy modern residents. Instead, they demanded an edifice that would not put their social position to shame!

This was certainly true in Clapham where the church was built in a haphazard fashion down the years, and by the middle of the century was in a dilapidated state of repair with cramped accommodation. At this time a village suburb developed and a new edifice was built by the common in 1776. The old church was then just a chapel but was demolished, and St. Paul's was built in its place with a Georgian nave in 1815.

The latter had a low gabled roof with slates and galleries on three sides and became a parish itself in 1861. An apsidal chancel was added later that century, while the east end became a community centre in the 1970s. It now sits in seclusion on Iveley Road by Matrimony Place near to the Clapham Parish Schools (of 1809 rebuilt 1887).

"The Clapham Sect"

John Thornton was born in Clapham in 1720 son of Robert and Hannah who emanated from Hull, and became a wealthy Russian merchant and director of the Bank of England. He used his wealth to promote a *Gospel Ministry* and made several anonymous donations viz. a College and 1,000 hymn books from St. George's, Southwark for the Countess of Huntingdon, money for Thomas Scott at Lock Hospital to distribute Bibles, and funds for St. Edmund Hall home of Calvinistic Methodism. He also sponsored Rev. Newton to take up positions at Olney, Buckingham and at St. Mary, Woolnoth in London.

Thornton married Lucy Watson of Hull on 28 November 1753 and had children Henry a banker and political economist, Samuel a Russia merchant, Robert an M.P. and Jane who was wife of the Earl of Leven. From this prominent position the family invested in both a new church for the parish and also initiated the influential Clapham Sect.

St. Paul's, Clapham on the site of the mediaeval church is now hidden away.

His son Henry was educated in the classics at Wandsworth School then joined *Down, Thornton & Free* bankers and became M.P. for Southwark in 1782. William Wilberforce made his first speech in 1789 and visited the Thorntons, thus the two who were second cousins occupied Battersea Rise House, west of the common, in 1792. The former was also chairman of the Sierra Leone Co. at the same time as Macaulay was governor.

The scene was set when Henry Venn came to Clapham as a curate in 1754 and married Eling Bishop in 1757, writing devotional books in the fashion of Whitefield. He was the vicar of Huddersfield in 1759-70 and made a financial loss, but provided 8-10 sermons a week and drew large crowds then transferred to Yelling, Hunts in 1771-91. [2]

His son John was educated at Hipperholme School, Yorkshire and at this time met the Jowetts who were in Leeds. He became curate to his father at Yelling, rector of Little Dunham, Norfolk in 1783-92, and significantly rector of Clapham in 1792-1813. [3]

At this point everything intersected and Venn set about improving social conditions of the poor and abolished skittles and gaming. A group was also started to campaign against slavery led by John Venn, Henry Thornton, William Wilberforce, James Stephen lawyer and Zachary Macaulay meeting in the oval library of Henry Thornton's house. Through their other links they also helped start the Church Missionary Society in 1799 with Venn as the first chairman, and the British and Foreign Bible Society in 1804.

C. 30 March 1759 John Venn son of Henry and Eling Venn
18 April 1760 Henry Thornton son of John Thornton Esq. and Lucy his wife

M. 10 May 1757 Henry Venn o.t.p. and Eling Bishop of St. Mary's, Lambeth by licence by W. Romains witness John Lefever, Wm. Daw junior
11 July 1758 William Thornton o.t.p. and Elizabeth Thornton o.t.p. by licence by me Henry Venn curate witness John and Jane Thornton

B. 15 November 1790 John Thornton Esq.
30 June 1797 The Rev. Henry Venn clerk, widower rector of Yelling, Hunts son of the Rev. Richard Venn rector of St. Antholin, London and Ann Maria Margaretta Elizabetha Beatrix his wife late *surnamed* Ashton [sic] aged 72 years
9 July 1813 The Revd. Mr John Venn A.M. more than 21 years the beloved and highly venerated rector of this parish aged 54 years
24 January 1815 Henry Thornton Esq. a married man, banker M.P. for the Borough of Southwark of Battersea Rise aged 55 years, decline - in family vault

---

[2] Henry Venn (1725-97) was curate at St. Matthew's, Friday Street in 1750 and at West Horsley whilst after arriving at Clapham lectured at St. Alban's, Wood Street and St. Swithin's, London Stone. His wife was a daughter of the minister of the Tower Church, Ipswich.

[3] John Venn (1759-1813) married Katherine King 1789 and Frances Turton 1812 his children: Jane Catherine (1793-1875) who m. Sir James Stephen 1814 and had son Leslie; and Henry Venn (1796-1873) friend of Charles Simeon, curate St. Dunstan in the West 1821-24, lecturer Cambs., rector Drypool Hull 1827-34, St. John Holloway 1834-47, prebend St. Paul's, Hon. Sec. C.M.S. and grandfather's biographer. His own son John Venn (1834-1923) was educated at Highgate and the fifth generation to graduate at Cambridge - he was curate at Cheshunt & Mortlake, a college lecturer (re. Venn Diagram) and collaborated with son John A. Venn on *Cambridge Alumni*.

Holy Trinity, Clapham

John Thornton retained a life interest in Clapham Manor and was the leading trustee in releasing a plot by Act of Parliament on the northeast of the common in 1774. The grant devolved from Mrs. Penelope Pitt lord of the manor, a descendant of Atkins.

Kenton Couse, a student of Flitcroft who designed Government buildings for *The Office of Works* including the façade of 10 Downing Street, provided a new church which had a relatively simple, but grand design. There was a basic rectangle with a short chancel and galleries, three main doors to the west, a stubby clock tower and four bells from Thwaites of Clerkenwell. It was opened in 1776 and John Venn became rector in 1792 with a large congregation, such that those left outside had to listen to him via an iron pipe!

A new porch was added and an organ, while the high box pews were rented and plain benches in the middle were for the poor. Communion took place once a month and the mahogany table used in those days is still there, as is the reredos. A.W. Blomfield made several changes in 1875 and the "horse boxes" were removed, the three-decker pulpit was reduced in size, and a new font was inserted - see baptism of E.M. Forster.

In the late 19th century there was a move to demolish the church and replace it with a Gothic Revival edifice. However, Prof. A. Beresford Pite introduced a rich Edwardian interior and reconstructed the chancel in 1903, all in sympathy with the old. Battersea Rise House was sold by the Thornton family in 1907, whereas the church was restored after the war in 1952 and incorporates the "William Wilberforce Centre."

Pember Family - St. John Pember was born at Ledbury in 1769 a tailor's son and with his brother Edward ran a draper's store at Crescent Place, New Bridge St., Blackfriars, from 1797 until about 1828. After marrying Mary Carless he resided at Vauxhall Walk next to New Spring Gardens and witnessed many of their incandescent events.

His son John Edward Ross Pember (1801) a prosperous stockbroker initially lived at Stockwell and 4 New Park Road, but moved to "Langlands" a mansion on the east side of King's Road in 1848. His own sons included Edward H. a barrister and parliamentary counsel, Arthur a founder of soccer and reporter in New York, and Frederick a minister in New Zealand and America. In addition, his daughter Ellen married William Reeves a newspaper proprietor and provincial M.P of Christchurch, New Zealand.

William Gilbert - Although born at Bishopstoke, Hampshire in 1804 he was raised in Blackfriars and spent time with the E.I.C and as a naval surgeon. He married twice first to Mary Ann Skelton in 1832, then left the Strand and with an annuity travelled around France and Italy. After returning home in 1849 he became a writer of distinction and his son W.S. Gilbert illustrated his works. His daughter Jane Morris married Alfred Weigall a miniature painter and he lived with her at The Close, Salisbury until he died in 1890.

Henrietta O.W. Rowland - She was the daughter of Alexander a wealthy businessman of Clapham Park, and worked with Octavia Hill the social reformer and campaigner for open spaces. As a result she met her husband Samuel Barnett of St. Mary's, Bryanston Square. After moving to Whitechapel she helped start Toynbee Hall, wrote on Christian Socialist beliefs and initiated the Hampstead Garden Suburb receiving a D.B.E. for her work. However, one of the most interesting connections here brings us full circle.

Holy Trinity, Clapham "the church on the common" built by Kenton Couse in 1776 was the scene of an evangelical social revolution.

E.M. Forster (writer) - Henry Thornton married Marianne Sykes daughter of Joseph a Hull merchant in 1796. They had nine children including Henry S. (1800) who succeeded his father, and Laura (1808) who married Charles Forster a Welsh clergyman.

Of their sons: Charles Thornton Forster was born at Ash, Kent in 1836 and was the vicar of Hinxton with links to both Graham and Willis; and Edward Morgan Llewellyn Forster born in 1848 became an architect and married Alice Clara Whichelo at Clapham in 1877. Their own son Edward Morgan Forster was born at 6 Melcombe Place, Dorset Square, Marylebone, on 1 January 1879, but his father died soon afterwards and he was raised by his mother 'Lily' then came into a most opportune inheritance.

Marianne Thornton (1797), his great aunt, continued her father's work as an evangelist, reformer and author and through the Clapham Sect was friends with the writer Thomas Babington Macaulay. She lived at The Sweep, Clapham with other family members and five servants leaving £8,000 in trust for E.M. Forster in her will dated 1887. Due to such fine generosity the Forster family removed to Rooks Nest, Stevenage, and the son was educated at Tonbridge School and King's College, Cambridge.

After graduating he travelled with his mother to Greece and Italy providing inspiration for his books, while he inherited Abinger Harvest in 1924. He gave the Clark Lectures at Cambridge based on his book *Aspects of the Novel* (1927), which was similar in content to *The Craft of Fiction* written by Percy Lubbock two years earlier. In addition he had links to the Bloomsbury Group and did a biography of Marianne Thornton later in life.

C. 29 Oct 1851 Henrietta Octavia Weston d. Alex Wm. and Henrietta Margeretta Monica Rowland of Clapham Park merchant W.H. Wentworth, A. Bowyer rector 4 May [4]
10 January 1855 Amabel Ellen daughter of William and Ellen Reeves of [12 The Grove] Clapham gentleman by John T. Manley b. 25 November 1854 [5]
15 February 1879 Edward Morgan s. of Edward Morgan Llewellyn and Alice Clara Forster of 6 Melcombe Place, Dorset Square N.W. architect by R.B. Lewis Exton

---

[4] Rev. Fitzwilliam Atkins Bowyer was both the rector and lord of the manor of Clapham.

[5] William Reeves had a financial setback at the Stock Exchange and sailed with Ellen and Amabel to Lyttelton, New Zealand on the *Rose of Sharon* arriving in January 1857, after three months at sea. He rebuilt his fortune and lived in a mansion "Risingholme" in the south of Christchurch.

M. 29 January 1801 John Pember bach o.t.p. and Mary Carless of St. Ann Blackfriars spin licence A. Bishop of Canterbury by John Sharpe wit. John Taylor, J. Comley

31 August 1833 Charles Forster clerk of Wandsworth bach and Laura Thornton o.t.p. spin married by licence by C.J. London pres. Saml. Thornton, Richd. Jebb, Esther Marie Thornton, Robert Harry Inglis, Robt. Grant [6]

12 February 1836 William Gilbert o.t.p. a widr and Anne Mary Bye Morris of St. Paul's Covent Garden spin lic by A. Murray curate witness Jno. Saml Schwenck, Jane Gilbert, Thomas Morris, J.H. Edwards and J.M. Gilbert

21 April 1853 William Reeves of Portland Place, Lambeth and Ellen Pember minor lic by Charlton Lane incumb of Kennington John E./Fanny Pember, Coleridge J. Kennard

Regarding memorials there is one to Henry and Marianne Thornton outside St. Paul's, Rectory Grove and a plaque/damaged tablet to the Clapham Sect at Holy Trinity. Inside are those to John Venn rector of 20 years, Marianne Thornton (brass), John Thornton missionary d.1861 a nephew, and relief of John Jebb Bishop of Limerick d.1833 who lived with them. At the east end of the north and south galleries are columns to John Castell d.1804, and John Thornton d.1790 (erected 1816) by J. Bacon junior.

Lambeth

Compared to Clapham this was a historic parish of almost ridiculously large proportions. It went from Blackfriars Road around the river to Nine Elms, south past Clapham Park to the far edge of Streatham Common, east across to Anerley Hill, north to Herne Hill and the centre of Camberwell, then around to Kennington Road and back to the start. Without doubt beating the bounds was an event of marathon undertaking!

The area on the south bank of the river was mainly marshy and inhospitable, thus the name Lambeth may relate to an access point - a hythe for landing sheep. An area of 24 acres was obtained by the Archbishop of Canterbury in 1190, and Lambeth Palace was started opposite to Westminster. Its oldest surviving parts are the Early English chapel, a prison tower, and the gatehouse built by Cardinal John Morton in 1495. [7]

To the north there was boat building, glass making, pottery, reclaimed market gardens and St. George's Fields. To the south there were further commons, dense woodland and some scattered hamlets at Kennington, Stockwell, Brixton and West Norwood.

Such isolation began to change with the building of a series of bridges: Westminster in 1750, Blackfriars in 1768, Vauxhall in 1816, Waterloo in 1817, and Lambeth in 1862. A series of roads then radiated from St. George's Circus at the centre of the fields to each bridge, and Kennington Road led south to Brixton and Clapham. With the infrastructure in place Georgian and Victorian terraces and grand villas promptly followed.

Regarding the churches in the area St. Mary's, Lambeth beside the Archbishop's Palace was clearly inadequate to the demands, and a petition was made to the *Commissioners for*

---

[6] Henry Sykes Thornton of Battersea married Harriet Maria Dealtry o.t.p. at the same time.

[7] Lambeth Palace received a new great hall with hammer-beam roof under William Juxon in 1663 after Cromwell's troops had destroyed the old one. Edward Blore did a neo-Gothic restoration on buildings by the quadrangle in 1834, and there are some spacious gardens behind.

Fifty Churches by the people of Stockwell in 1711 but a proposed church never came to fruition (see below). In fact, it took another hundred years before anything changed and the Commissioners built *Waterloo Churches* in Brixton, Kennington, Waterloo Road and West Norwood which were dedicated to the four gospel writers.

"Recreation" - The area was a centre for leisure and New Spring Gardens, Vauxhall opened in 1661. Evelyn and Pepys were visitors and Dr. Jonathan Swift wrote in 1711, "The gardens are exquisitely pleasant; the fragrancy of its walks and bowers, the choirs of birds in the trees." Frederick Prince of Wales was a patron and Handel its musician, while a loggia (1735) and rotunda (1743) were added and large crowds blocked up the roads!

Its success continued under George III with further innovation including masked balls in 1792, fireworks in 1798, and balloon ascents in 1802, reaching a zenith in the Regency era. After being sold for £30,000 in 1821 it became the Royal Gardens and 20,000 came for music, illuminations, fountains, fireworks, and refreshments - including Victoria and Wellington. But arrival of the railway and the Crystal Palace saw it closed in 1859.

Another notable Phillip Astley was born at Newcastle under Lyme in 1742, and after leaving the army became a showman near St. John's in 1768. A year later he purchased land by Westminster Bridge for a ring and stage with roof but it burnt down many times. Astley's Royal Amphitheatre passed to his son John then to Andrew Ducrow (memorial at St. Mary's) and was recorded in *Sketches by Boz* written by Dickens in 1836.

Lords John and George Sanger purchased the site for £11,000 in 1871 and modernised the arena, then *Howes Great London Circus & Sanger's Menagerie* toured New England and Ontario in 1871-73 under proprietors Egbert and Elbert Howes. This famous circus was previously started by Seth and Nathan Howes in New York State.

However, there were problems with the ecclesiastical landlords and the amphitheatre was demolished in 1893. A more enduring venue was Canterbury Hall on Upper Marsh just below Westminster Bridge Road. This was the first purpose built music hall erected by Charles Morton in 1852 and remained in operation until 1943.

Regarding sport the Montpelier Club was started at Walworth in 1796 and took land at Lorrimore Square below the Surrey Gardens, but this was built over in 1844. They then considered a site leased by the Otter family from the Duchy of Cornwall, "A nursery and garden ground in extent about 10 acres called the Oval with buildings thereon."

William Baker the treasurer negotiated a lease to play cricket there in 1845 and Surrey C.C.C. was formed at this time. The club received considerable help from Prince Albert and John and William Burrup were secretaries from 1848 - but handed over to Charles Alcock, the journalist and writer, in 1872-1907. The latter brought the Cup Final there during 1872-92, as well as the first international soccer and some Rugby Union.

St. Peter's, Vauxhall - Spring Gardens were soon covered by roads and a church was built beside Tyers Street on Kennington Lane in 1864. Its architect John Loughborough Pearson (1817-97) came from Durham and trained under Ignatius Bonomi (brother of Joseph), whilst he moved to London where he was tutored by Philip Hardwick.

He was a leading Gothic Revival architect and the church had a tower, round-headed/rose windows, and his first groined-vaults, but was more limited than his work at Bristol, Kilburn, Truro, and overseas. St. Anne's R.C. by F.A. Walters provided a foil from 1907, and the "gardens" became an open space again after the war (see picture p. 316).

St. Mary's, Lambeth

Lambeth was most eloquently *A Parish of Manors* with a large number in its bounds, and Goda wife of the Count of Boulogne and sister of Edward the Confessor first held that of North Lambeth. It passed to the monks of St. Andrew's, Rochester, but after some opposition was bestowed on the Archbishop in exchange for Darenth, Kent in 1196.

Subsidiary manors included: Lambeth Wick or Loughborough, South Lambeth given by Harold to Waltham Abbey and joined to Vauxhall, Stockwell owned by William de Redvers, Kennington (or King's Town) owned by the Duchy of Cornwall from the reign of Edward III, Levehurst at West Norwood, Bodley held by St. Thomas's Hospital and Sir Henry Tulse, and the reputed Heathrow or Knights manor near to Streatham.

Clearly the area generated considerable wealth, prestige and court intrigue but the main centre of power was at Lambeth Palace home to the Archbishops of Canterbury. Such centralised focus was reflected in the appointment of ministers at St. Mary's, many of the rectors being chaplains or household officers from the adjoining palace.

It was a unique position, although ultimately this did not protect the church from the ravages of time, the changing vicissitudes of fortune. The living of St. Mary's was held by Countess Goda in Saxon times and passed to the monks of St. Andrew's with the manor, then was rebuilt by the Archbishop in flint and stone with a tower in 1374-78. The north and south aisles were added in 1504-05, and chapels of Howard and Leigh twenty years later. There was also a fraternity of St. Christopher's linked to the church.

Regarding the fittings, the rood loft was taken down in 1570 and John Hart gentleman paid for an elaborate marble font in 1615 which was eventually moved to Holy Trinity, Carlisle Street. In fact, Rev. Daniel Featley *a man for all seasons* was rector in 1618-43 but was accused of placing the communion table altar-like at the east end. In his defence he stated: he gave no order to move it away from the centre; that it stood there since his arrival by agreement with the parish, this being the most convenient place to allow access to the Howard Chapel and "for the hearing of the preacher."

St. Mary's, Lambeth from the south east; with detail showing its position by Lambeth Palace and the river.

From a distance it has the appearance of a mediaeval church but only the tower is original. Both nave and aisles were rebuilt by P.C. Hardwick in 1851-52.

In addition he argued that the steps up could not be lowered without damage to the structure. Despite this he aroused much animosity from the Puritans and the church was raided, then he was deprived of his living - being buried there in 1645. In a similar vein the King's Arms were installed in 1660, and Ralph Snowe treasurer to the Archbishop gave a chandelier and pulpit in 1698. The next year a south and west gallery were added and an organ from Renatus Harris at a cost of £50 - whose case still survives.

The original mediaeval church included a paved stone floor, raised chancel, octagonal pillars with Gothic arches, a plaster roof in the nave, and to the east: Howard's Chapel in the north aisle and Leigh's (or Pelham's) Chapel in the south aisle. Later developments included a handsome Gothic portal at the west end, for those who arrived by carriage, erected in 1778 and a further gallery provided for the charity children.

Extensive repairs were carried out on the tower in 1834-35, but this was the only part to survive a rebuilding by Philip C. Hardwick (son of Philip and Julia née Shaw) in 1851-52. A new church was built on the old foundations in Kentish ragstone and *Decorated Style* whilst the nave, aisles and vestry received a slate roof with gable ends. From the river it still has the appearance of a mediaeval church, but closer inspection shows the clean cut lines of the nave - which are clearly not of such great antiquity.

Dr. Sumner Bishop of Winchester re-opened the church in February 1852, but under Rev. J.F. Lingham (1854-84) the galleries restored by Hardwick were taken down and the organ was moved to the east end chapel. In addition, communion rails were installed which came from the Archbishop's chapel at Addington - once at All Saints, Maidstone. Canon F.G. Pelham who followed also removed the box pews (saved by Hardwick), and used their wood to wainscot the aisle-walls with a continuous dado effect. [8]

The pulpit was brought there from St. James's, Kennington Park Road in 1924, but as the parish population declined the church was nearly demolished and was deconsecrated, despite its prominent associations, in 1972. For a time it was used by the charity *Crisis at Xmas*, however after Tradescant the plant hunter and Royal gardener was traced there in 1976 it was converted into a Museum of Garden History.

"Doing the Lambeth Walk"

A large number of prominent people were connected to St. Mary's church and ancient memorials include two altar tombs in the chancel: *north* Hugh Pentwyn 1504 and *south* John Mompesson 1524 - although the latter inscription is now undecipherable.

The north chapel has ones to the family of Thomas Howard, 2nd Duke of Norfolk of Flodden including sons of the 3rd Duke, Anne daughter of Edward IV, and Katherine wife of William Howard 1535. The south chapel has a marble monument to Sir John Leigh knight of the Bath, lord of the manor of Stockwell and Levehurst 1524.

On the north wall are tablets to Ralphe Snowe registrar to four archbishops 1707, James Morris by Flaxman 1781, Peter Dollond optician 1821 (see *South Lambeth Chapel*), Rev. George D'Oyly 1846 and Archbishops M. Hutton 1758 and F. Cornwallis 1783. In the north quire is a memorial to Robert Scot of Sweden and Denmark 1631, and flat tablets to Bishop Cuthbert Tunstall 1559, Archbishop Tenison 1715 and the two above.

---

[8] A similar arrangement occurred at St. Mary Woolnoth - William Butterfield took down the old galleries and attached the front panels to the nave walls in 1875 (still present).

In the south porch are tablets to Elias Ashmole the founder of the Ashmolean 1692, Judith Raleigh wife of Capt. George Raleigh Governor of Jersey 1701 (nephew), and those to comptrollers and secretaries of the ecclesiastical household. However the role of the church is best highlighted by the list of rectors in the 18th and 19th centuries:

1703-17	Edmund Gibson an antiquary, bishop and librarian to Tenison
1717-31	Richard Ibbetson the chaplain to Archbishops Tenison and Wake
1731-67	John Denne antiquary and vicar of St. Leonard's, Shoreditch whose son Samuel published a history of Lambeth and its Palace
1767-77	Beilby Porteus later the Bishop of Chester and London
1820-46	George D'Oyly a theologian, biographer, chaplain to Archbishop Manners-Sutton and founder of King's College in the Strand
1884-94	Francis Godolpin Pelham who was 5th Earl of Chichester in 1902

Archbishop Tenison donated land to the south on Paradise Row by the High Street for a new churchyard in 1704 (now a park). There were also further significant memorials outside the church. St. John Pember and his wife Mary of Vauxhall Terrace had a large family but only their children John and Mary Jane survived. A lengthy memorial was then erected north of the church and remains by the tower but is now faded and worn.

Meanwhile, a building boom resulted in a great demand for new materials. Mrs. Eleanor Coade (1733-1821) from Lyme Regis set up a factory on the *Festival Hall* site to make a vitrified ceramic, known as Coade stone, in 1769. Although unmarried she followed the convention of the day by calling herself "Mrs" and took on her cousin John Sealy as a partner. To the south there is a memorial to John Sealy 1813, his wife Elizabeth daughter of John Crolyn of the Pump House, Bromsgrove 1817 and their family. [9]

However, the most notable monuments are located in the garden at the east end. John Tradescant of Suffolk married Elizabeth Day daughter of the vicar of Meopham in 1607, and then worked for Robert Cecil, 1st Earl of Salisbury at Hatfield House. As a result he visited Flushing and Paris to collect plants, bulbs, and vines, travelled with the fleet to Algiers and Archangel, and went with Lord Buckingham to Flanders in 1625.

His main achievement was to establish Tradescant's Ark museum and garden near the road of that name. As custodian of the Oxford Physic Garden he also met Lord Wotton and was buried at St. Mary's in 1638 (although no entry exists). His son John was born at Meopham and made two trips to Virginia to collect plants then ran the museum, whilst he married Hester Pooks in 1638 and donated the collection to Ashmole in 1659. After his death his wife claimed a life interest hence a dispute ensued until 1678. [10]

Regarding nautical matters Capt. William Bligh first rose to prominence as master of the *Resolution* during Cook's third and final voyage to the Pacific in 1776-80. However it was his exploits on the *Bounty* with Fletcher Christian that brought him to notoriety in 1787, although he was acquitted of any wrong doing. He was made Governor of New South Wales by Sir Joseph Banks from 1806-08 but this sojourn ended in rebellion.

---

[9] Coade stone was hard wearing and used for buildings and sculptures in Britain and around the world. However it was replaced by the cheaper, artificial Portland cement in the 1840s.

[10] A memorial to John Tradescant jun. with arms was erected in 1662, restored in 1773, and again by G.P. White in 1853. The latter also provided a new font and worked on York Minster.

After retiring to the Manor House at Farningham, Kent beside the old church and mill house, he died at Bond Street in 1817. His memorial of Coade stone in Grecian style with an urn is by that of Tradescant: "He was vice admiral of the blue, the celebrated navigator who first transplanted the bread fruit tree from Otaheite to the West Indies, bravely fought the battles of his country and died beloved, respected and lamented."

Other celebrities appearing in the records were Thomas Banks (1735-1805) the sculptor whose father was a surveyor and land steward to the Duke of Beaufort, Arthur Sullivan (1842-1900) who attended the Royal Academy of Music son of a military bandmaster, John Newman a banker possibly of Jewish descent father of Cardinal Newman, and Sir Samuel Morton Peto (1809-89) the entrepreneur and railway contractor.

C. 18 January 1735/36 Thomas s. of Thomas Banks and Mary his wife
20 September 1801 John Edw. Ross s. Saint John and Mary Pember
31 July 1842 Arthur Seymour son of Thomas and Mary Clementina Sullivan of Bolwell Terrace [Lambeth Walk] musician by A. Peat

M. 29 October 1799 John Newman batch of St. Bennet Fink and Jemima Fourdrinier o.t.p. spin licence by W. Battell curate presence of Henry and Elizabeth Fourdrinier
18 May 1831 Samuel Morton Peto Esq. and Mary Grissell by lic by me William Borrows minister of St. Paul's, Clapham witness Sophia Peto and six others

B. 25 April 1662 Mr. John Tredeskin from South Lambeth
17 December 1701 Judeth the wife of Capt. George Rawly [sic]
28 October 1813 John Sealey of Pedlars Acre, 63 J.T. Barrett
15 December 1817 V. Admiral William Bligh St Geo. H. Sq., 63
1 February 1825 Mary Pember of Vauxhall Walk, 48
13 January 1835 John Pember of St. Anne, Blackfriars, 63

William Bligh (1754-1817) had a successful naval career, but will always be associated with mutiny on the *Bounty*.

St. Andrew's, Stockwell

As stated, Lambeth had a scarcity of Anglican churches, but there might have been a different story near to Stockwell Manor and its Green. A humble petition was submitted and Sir John Thornycroft, lord of the manor, offered two acres of waste ground in the liberty, with consent from freeholders who would retain rights on the common.

A scheme was agreed by the Commissioners in November 1711, and six months later the surveyors were told to contact Sir John about laying out the site. They discussed title to the manor and land issues thus conveyance took place in February 1713. But matters dragged on, until the surveyors were directed to mark out the church-ground and notify Sir John, Mr. Angel, and other parishioners in March 1715. Nothing was done after this and the new Commission met at St. Paul's, Chapter House in the January with renewed financial constraints - hence the whole project fell by the wayside.

In fact, it was not until 1767 that a chapel was erected on land owned by the Duke of Bedford just west of Stockwell Green, and this passed to the Archbishop and rector of Lambeth for a chapel of ease in 1788. Such was the provision of Episcopal churches in the area despite its prominent ecclesiastical patrons. St. Michael's was built in Park Road as the first parish church by W. Rogers in 1840 (and later restored by Thomas F. Ford), even though Stockwell Chapel contained pews to seat 800 people by that time.

The chapel was then remodelled in Romanesque style with a western extension, south-west tower, new galleries and seating for 1,043 in 1867. It was consecrated as the parish of St. Andrew's the next year, and the only later changes were the rendering of the grey brick during the 1880s and the removal of the galleries in 1924.

M. 29 November 1879 Edmund Henry Niemann 38 artist of 3 York Villas s. Edmund J. artist and Emma Harriet Blythe 23 of 50 Park Terrace d. Colin silk mercer lic by Rev. S.S. Maguth [later a healer] presence Edward Gibbon Blythe, Kate Alma Niemann

Stockwell New Chapel - This was built just south of the green for the Congregational Church in 1798, and might be compared to St. Andrew's which is now generally found in poor condition. Its early baptisms included twins John and William Burrup who worked as stationers and printers but became consecutive secretaries of Surrey C.C.C.

The chapel was rebuilt with three galleries in 1850 and a tablet recorded the marriage of William Booth who worked for a pawnbroker, but became a minister connected to the short-lived *Methodist Reform Church* at Clapham in 1852. He met his wife Catherine, who lived in Brixton, when preaching at her church and eventually left the Methodists and founded the Salvation Army in the East End in 1865. The chapel itself was sold by the U.R.C. in 1987 and has since been used by the Islamic faith and restored. [11]

C. 22 September 1820 John & William sons of John Burrup and Mary Maynard b.17 May

M. 16 June 1855 William Booth church minister 26 s. of Samuel builder and Catherine Mumford 26 d. of John coach-builder of Stockwell

St. John's, Waterloo Road
by Francis Bedford (1824)

This Anglican church looked back to the Greek era, but **William Booth (1829-1912)** looked forward to Salvation for the poor.

---

[11] The Salvation Army Training College at Denmark Hill was by Sir Giles Gilbert Scott in 1932.

St. John's, Waterloo Road

Regarding the building of the Waterloo Churches one of the most significant architects was without doubt Francis Octavius Bedford (1784-1858). Initially he was engaged by the Society of Dilettanti to tour Greece and Asia Minor with J.P. Gandy and William Wilkins under Sir William Gell. The result was a publication *The Antiquities of Attica* in 1817. After this he designed four major churches in the Greek Revival style in South London.

The first to consider is St. John's which was begun on Waterloo Road by the approaches to the new bridge in 1817. Some land was purchased from the Archbishop of Canterbury but this was unpromising with a swampy-pond on site, and John Rennie was consulted on the matter, recommending piling of the foundations. This proved a most propitious decision with respect to the subsequent history of the church.

A sum of £64,000 was designated by the Commissioners for the Lambeth Churches but that at Waterloo Road was somewhat grander due to its prominent location. The façade with its well-proportioned Doric propylon blends imperceptibly with the nave, as in times of antiquity. However, the three-tiered tower sits awkwardly above, and is more suited to the Baroque of Wren than the simplistic dictates of Palladio and Vitruvius.

It was consecrated by the Bishop of Winchester on 3rd November 1824, and whatever these concerns, the interior was definitely in the category of *preaching box*. An entrance lobby led up to three galleries which were supported on short Doric columns, but there was little decoration except for rose motifs on the flat panelled roof.

A school costing £2,000 was built to the south and several churches were added: Holy Trinity Carlisle Street by E. Blore on the palace gardens (1839); All Saints Lower Marsh by W. Rogers (1845), removed for the railway 1899; St. Andrew's Coin Street (1854) and St Thomas's Westminster Bridge Road (1856) both by S.S. Teulon, joined after the war. Later changes saw A. Blomfield renovate St. John's in 1885, and Ninian Comper erected a baldachino (canopy) before the altar and a Lady Chapel behind in 1924.

Rev. Charles Hutchinson (vicar 1925-43) recorded a direct hit with 150 people inside on 8 December 1940, yet it was so stoutly built everyone survived. The roof remained open for eleven years with services in the crypt, but Thomas F. Ford restored it in 1950-51 and the Bishop of Southwark rededicated it before Princess Elizabeth and the Archbishop. It was then used for the Festival of Britain and now hosts concerts and exhibitions.

St. Luke's, West Norwood

The locality was named after the great *North Wood* and the first signs of development came with the enclosure of the manor in 1806. However, there were just some country lanes, a few cottages, an independent chapel and house of industry by the 1820s. In the mould of Limehouse the church's arrival owed something to Nostradamus, and a site was chosen at the extreme south of the parish on an ascending hill. Francis Bedford was appointed architect and Elizabeth Broomfield of Walworth was the builder.

The foundation was laid by the Archbishop of Canterbury in April 1823 and the church was consecrated by the Bishop of Winchester on 15 July 1825. Its façade was similar to Bedford's other churches but the columns were thin and nondescript; while the interior was rectangular with box pews, galleries and triple-decker pulpit. It seated 1,800 people and cost £12,947. Such a design clearly satisfied the remit of the Commissioners who demanded large churches for many parishioners, but at relatively low prices.

Other developments saw West Norwood Cemetery opened nearby in 1837 and Lower Norwood Station introduced just behind the church in 1856 (but renamed in 1886). The result of this was the introduction of numerous villas and these included a Royal circus no less. However, as in North Lambeth, there was a problem keeping pace with events and Holy Trinity, Norwood Road was built as a separate parish in 1855-56.

St. Luke's, meanwhile, was extensively remodelled by George E. Street during 1871-72. After removing the galleries he re-designed the nave and aisles introducing arcades in the Italianate-Roman style. Then in the 1970s a floor was inserted in the chancel to create a hall and the churchyard in front was made into gardens. Its location at the intersection of busy roads remains detrimental - although it is called "The Light on the Hill."

St. Mark's, Kennington (below) was designed by D.R. Roper in 1824. It was beside the common where Whitefield and Wesley preached.

St. Luke's, W. Norwood (above) built in 1825 was one of four by F. Bedford.

Field M. Montgomery "Monty" of El Alamein, son of the vicar, was baptized there in 1888.

The adjacent cemetery has an arched entrance-gate designed by Sir William Tite and a number of prominent people have memorials there. At the intersection of the paths is one to James William Gilbart of the London & Westminster "engaged in the science of banking," and to the south a restored memorial to Charles William Alcock with F.A. Cup relief. Just beyond is the family vault of John and Fanny Pember stockbroker of Clapham Park and Sir William Cubitt president of the Institution of Civil Engineers.

Other significant memorials by the entrance are to Sir Hiram Maxim, Baron Julius de Reuter and Sir Horace Jones; and towards the centre Dr. William Marsden, Rev. Charles H. Spurgeon, Sir Henry Bessemer, John George Appold, Sir Henry Doulton, Sir Henry Tate, Thomas de la Garde Grissell and Ann (née Peto), and near the latter a modern one to Isabella Beeton and her husband of cook book culinary fame.

St. Mark's, Kennington

Kennington Common sat at the intersection of Stane Street to Chichester and a second Roman road leading to Newhaven. It had a variety of public purposes including grazing and cricket but was best known for oration. Whitefield preached twice in 1739, Wesley expounded to 50,000 in 1789 and R. Wedderburn the black preacher also came.

This growing evangelical area was clearly in need of a permanent church but the Duchy of Cornwall had no power to convey the site. Despite this D.R. Roper, architect of the Shot Tower, Lambeth, designed one at £15,224 in 1822-24, being more solid in concept than the nearby churches constructed by F. Bedford. In fact, an Act of Parliament only released the common-land six days before consecration by the Archbishop!

The façade had four Doric columns and two outer piers, a tall entablature and shallow pediment, surmounted by a squat tower with extended open cupola above. The interior was typical of a Commissioners' church and cast-iron Doric columns supported galleries on three sides. There were two tiers of windows in five bays with a frieze around the top, and the upper level was adorned with pilasters and moulded capitals. The altar recess was framed by two Ionic columns and there was seating for 2,000 people.

Rev. William Otter the first minister became principal of King's College and Bishop of Chichester, whilst half the pews were rented and any surplus less the minister's stipend helped build a parsonage. At this time the residents included William and Elizabeth Jane Reeves at 4 U. Kennington Green, whose son William was a stockbroker with Denison, Heywood & Kennard and married into the Pember family (see Clapham).

After the Reform Act (1832), Lambeth became a parliamentary constituency, however this brought political activity and the Chartists held a mass demonstration there on 10 April 1848 - highlighting social unrest in the area. The incumbent, Rev. Charlton Lane, was quite alarmed by its proximity to the church and led a deputation. This resulted in an Act which allowed enclosure as a park at a cost of £3,650 in 1852.

The church had three curates and 250 workers but there were 16,000 parishioners and 1,500 children attended three Sunday schools, thus several other edifices were soon built. St. Mary the Less in Gothic style on Princes Road by F. Bedford in 1827, demolished in the 1960s; St. Barnabas, Guildford Road with foundation by the Duke of Cambridge and design by Isaac Clarke and James Humphrys at £4,800 in 1848, with Vaughan Williams as organist (now flats); and St. Stephen's by John Barnett promoted by Rev. C. Kemble of St. Michael's in 1861. The latter two were constructed by G. Myers & Sons.

One of the most significant events was the appointment of Rev. Henry H. Montgomery (1847-1932) as the vicar of St. Mark's in 1879, who was formerly curate at Hurstpierpoint and St. Margaret's, Westminster. He married Maud Farrar daughter of the Archdeacon of Westminster at the Abbey on 28 July 1881, but left to become Bishop of Tasmania in 1889 then returned as secretary of the S.P.G. in 1901 and was also a historian. His son Bernard was born in the parish and was later Field Marshall of El Alamein.

Two restorations were carried out neither of them in keeping with its Greek origins. The first involved replacement of the pews, new choir-stalls and transfer of the organ to the east end - all with Gothic pretensions, in the 1870s. The second went in the direction of Wren and included plaster motifs over the windows in the 1900s. In fact after being restored yet again in 1931 it was bombed out and rebuilt during 1949-60.

Its main features include an oak pulpit brought from the demolished St. Michael's, Wood Street in 1898, a brass lectern presented by Charlotte Darlington, and a reredos which went to St. George's, Southwark from Wood Street but also came there in 1923. This filled the void at the west end caused by the transferral of the organ. Outside there is an information board recording the districts chief historical moments.

C. 18 May 1832 Mary d. of Samuel Morton & Mary Peto of York Road, Lambeth builder according to the cert. of Rev. W. Borrows, min of St. Paul's Clapham (also 3 others)
15 January 1888 Bernard Law s. of Henry Hutchinson and Maud Montgomery of The Vicarage clerk in Holy Orders by F.W. Farrar archdeacon of Westminster b. 17 Nov

South Lambeth Chapel - John and Sarah Bond took out a lease for a proprietary chapel on Miles Street by South Lambeth Road in 1793, although clearly the opportunities were not as great as in Marylebone and Mayfair. A committee was set up including Sir Charles Blicke (master R.C.S.), Philip Buckley, Peter Dollond (optical maker), and James Gubbins who limited the costs to £3,000 and raised shares to facilitate the building work.

The minister was to be chosen by the rector of St. Mary's, and the proprietors were to reimburse him £40 per annum salary. However, in latter years the arrival of Nine Elms Station and the Phoenix Gas Works drove out these wealthy patrons, and a serious fire took place there in 1856. The committee persuaded the Commissioners to take it for a parish and it was consecrated as St. Anne's on 3 February 1869, but on the strict understanding that it would be enlarged. In fact, R. Parkinson designed a new edifice in quasi-Romanesque style with an apse in 1876 - but the tower was never completed.

St. Matthew's, Brixton

The last of the four new Lambeth churches was a variation on a theme and was built at the upper end of Rushey Green (or Rush Common). This area of heath formed a triangle above Water Lane and was enclosed in 1806, with the north section divided into three plots - owned by the Archbishop, the rector of Lambeth, and Robert Stone.

Clearly it was a good site for a church and when the Commission convened in 1818 the archbishop and rector donated their land, and £88 was paid to Stone to release him. Due to restraints on building an Act was passed to allow construction in 1821, and C.F. Porden designed an imposing façade the next year. The Archbishop laid the foundation and it was consecrated by the Bishop of Winchester on 21 June 1824, the total cost £16,150. Half of this came from the Commission and the remainder from Lambeth parish.

Like the other *Gospel Churches* it was rectangular and of grey brick faced with Bath stone but came closer to the Greek-temple ideal than any plagiarised church amalgam. It had four Doric columns of pristine white Portland stone framed by solid piers and pedestals, supporting a plain entablature with triglyphs and pediment. Shallow steps led up to three entrance doors, whereas the pillars glowed in the corpulent portico recess.

However, the main innovation was to move the steeple, which usually sat incongruous above the pediment, to the east end and thereby provide a façade of interest on both Brixton Hill and Effra Road. This was the aim but the three-tiered tower at the extremity appeared anomalous without a doorway, and the church seems unsure where it begins

St. Matthew's, Brixton (1822-24) has an anomalous tower sited at the east end.

and where it ends. Porden had produced an authentic temple reproduction but the tower looked like it had slipped backwards, and whatever the aesthetics of the Greek art, this appeared an uneasy solution to the problem of uniting the two elements.

Inside the grand doorway there was a large vestibule and stairs led up to three galleries, whilst beyond was a plain interior with flat roof. In the west gallery there was an organ and in the nave some box pews. The plainness was broken only by a shallow chancel framed by tall Doric columns and pilasters beneath a rectangular window, plus several later memorials. Meanwhile in recent times it was adapted for multiple uses.

This was a growing area with many new villas on Brixton Hill, Coldharbour Lane and nearby roads. The first minister Edwin Prodgers attended Trinity, Oxford and married Caroline daughter of John Blades of Brockwell Hall there in 1828. The marriage was by Rev. George D'Oyly of Lambeth and a son Edwin was baptized in 1833. Prodgers' name appears on many entries in the registers, as in the examples shown below. [12]

For the first nine months the burials were recorded at Lambeth. One notable memorial outside was that of Richard Budd (1748-1824) who was born in Brixton - erected to the north by his son Henry and designed by R. Day in c.1826. This still remains and is a multi-tiered structure built of Portland stone on a granite base. Its Greek and Egyptian features are undoubtedly reminiscent of Soane's work at nearby Dulwich.

Opposite the church was Brixton Oval (Grammar) School and Tate Library Gardens where sheep were grazed until the early 1900s. In addition, several new churches were added including: Trinity Congregational built just to the south in the Doric style in 1828; St. John's, Angell Road built by Benjamin Ferrey who trained with Pugin in 1853; and Christchurch, North Brixton constructed in Byzantine style in 1856. Both of these were established as separate districts from the original parish of St. Matthew's.

C. 29 June 1832 Edward Henry s. John Edward and Fanny Pember of Stockwell gent
9 July 1835 Arthur s. John E. and Fanny Pember of Brixton Hill gent E. Prodgers

B. 9 September 1826 Richard Budd of Russell Square, 75 Edwin Prodgers [sic]

---

[12] Rev. Prodgers purchased the advowson of Ayot St. Peter's, Herts from Lady Mexborough in 1852 and a new church was built there by J.L. Pearson. The living passed to his son Edwin who was rector from 1861 although he relinquished Holy Orders and it burnt down in 1874. It was replaced with a design by J.P. Seddon and the family held the parish until 1906.

Arthur Pember (1835-86) climbed "Mont Blanc" but was later an undercover reporter in New York and "Amateur Beggar."

Edward H. Pember attended Charterhouse, Christchurch and Lincoln's Inn then for 30 years was a parliamentary speaker viz. the Manchester Ship Canal and Jameson Raid. He trained in music under Perugini and was secretary of the Society of Dilettanti whilst he lived at Vicars Hill, Lymington, until 1911 - his brother George was at Fair Oak. His son Francis was vice-chancellor of Oxford and his granddaughter Katharine married Charles Galton Darwin later donating their home Newnham Grange for Darwin College.

Arthur Pember was born at 4 New Park Road at the junction with Brixton Hill in 1835 and was raised at Clapham Park. Unlike his brothers Edward, Frederick and George he did not attend public school and was educated at home by aunts Kate and Jane Robson. His family moved to "Langlands," King's Road, one of Cubitt's mansions, in 1848 and he went to France, Italy and Switzerland making a perilous ascent of Mont Blanc.

Initially Pember joined his father as a stockbroker and married Elizabeth Hoghton in 1860 and Alice Mary Grieve in 1862. He then resided at 30 Carlton Road, Kilburn where he inaugurated the *No Names Club*, possibly a take on his fellow insurers, and became first president of the F.A. in 1863-67. As a result he helped to establish the rules and in particular banned practices such as hacking and handling of the ball.

Meanwhile, he was something of a polymath and wrote political articles predicting the demise of the House of Lords due to the liberal revolution, and supported the religious practice of Ritualism which he believed was spreading around the world.

Due to such beliefs he immigrated with his wife and two children to New York in 1868 and then resided at 1233, 3rd Avenue in the Upper East Side. He abandoned his previous life and became a journalist with the New York Press working with Louis Jennings at the *Times*, Whitelaw Reid at the *Tribune* and John Russell Young at the *Standard*. Having barely settled in, he reported on the notorious Water Street Revival behind Newspaper Row and met infamous characters such as Kit Burns and Tommy Hadden.

Amongst his writings were *Our State Institutions* with English flavour, political poetry for *Punchinello*, and undercover work on keno joints, panel houses and bogus doctors. In fact he posed as a beggar, tramped to Philadelphia, and worked on the Erie Canal often at some risk. These were recorded in, "The Mysteries & Miseries of the Great Metropolis, with some adventures in the country: being the disguises and surprises of a New York journalist," by 'A.P.' the Amateur Vagabond, Appleton & Co. and Gurney (1874).

Two main factors came from this. Firstly, he coined the phrase "How the Other Half Lives" through his attempts to expose people's unusual modes of earning a living, later used by Jacob Riis and others. Secondly, his *Amateur Beggar* which first appeared in the *N.Y. Times* on 21 April 1872 had almost identical plot and lines to *The Man with the Twisted Lip*, a Sherlock Holmes story by Conan Doyle which appeared a few years later.

However, this was his greatest work and after his wife Alice died in 1881 he spent time at the Natural History Museum classifying genera and species; then turned his attentions to his five sons. He purchased a three-quarter section of land at La Moure, North Dakota from the railroad in 1884 and planned to build a fine dwelling with crops and livestock, then entertained the local settlers with stories of his exploits. However, he died there on 3 April 1886 and his obituary stated, "He was an Englishman by birth," whilst his sons returned to New York with Cyril an artist and Gilbert a minister in Philadelphia.

Southwark

Generally the City was north of the river however this area became Bridge Without or the 26th Ward, and like Farringdon Extra and Portsoken was totally outside the walls. As part of the Roman settlement it may have had a bridge joining it to Stane and Watling Streets. The cognomen itself was derived from the *South Works* or defences.

However, the proximity of this large inhabited area was an inconvenience, and all kinds of malefactors and felons escaped there outside the jurisdiction of the London officials. Thus a charter was passed by Edward III and the Barons in Parliament in the first of his reign (1327), and the "village" was then incorporated within the *City Edicts*.

After the Dissolution the Mayor and Communality applied to create a ward to help the administration, but this only came about under Edward VI when £647 2s 1d was paid on 23 April 1550. The manor of Southwark Place and its associated tenements were once owned by Charles, Duke of Suffolk but then passed into the hands of the King.

The main inhabited area by the bridge dated to late Saxon times and to the south was Long Southwark with its many lanes and alleys, leading to St. George's church and on to Newington. To the west was the priory of St. Mary Overie which was later St. Saviour's and Winchester House home to the Bishops of Winchester. A number of ancient inns pertaining to various ecclesiastics were also situated by the river.

However these became subdivided and the liberties of Paris (Parish) Garden and Clink Street (the Stews) with its dingy tenements were quite a problem. Due to a lack of civil authority several theatres were built including: *The Rose* (1587) home to Henslowe and Alleyn, and *The Globe* (1599) home to Shakespeare and the Lord Chamberlain's Men. To the east was Tooley Street, St. Thomas's hospital founded by St. Mary Overie priory in the 12th century, Bermondsey Street, St. Saviour's monastery (or Abbey), Long Lane and back to the High Street to complete the ward boundary. Today, there is a tablet at no. 49 Bankside stating Wren lived there, but his house was probably nearby.

The ancient area of Southwark took the name Borough in the 16th century and within its bounds were six archaic parishes: St. Margaret on the Hill in the middle High Street later a court room; St. Mary Magdalene chapel of St. Mary Overie which joined with the former as St. Saviour's in the monastery grounds; St. George's owned by Bermondsey

Abbey; St. Thomas's situated in the hospital precincts; St. Olave's on the banks of the river; and at a latter date Christchurch in the locality of Paris Garden.

Other buildings in the area were the Clink by the river, the Compter by St. Margaret's, the Old Marshalsea, King's Bench and White Lion or Borough Jail near to St. George's; and houses of the Bishop of Rochester, Abbot of Hyde, Prior of Lewes, and Abbot of Battle. Later developments included Southwark Bridge by John Rennie in 1819.

Christchurch, Blackfriars Road

This was a small parish covering an area analogous with the manor of Paris Garden and was created by a legacy contained in the will of John Marshall gent in 1631. The latter left £700 to establish a church and yard - the money to be raised from his lands, and the last trustee Sir Samuel Brown took out a cause regarding this in 1663. William Angel who was lord of the manor (in the liberty) then provided a suitable parcel of land.

The minister received £40 per annum and the property endowed a sum of £60, while the first church was erected among the fields by Bennet Street and Green Walk in 1670. Nearby were market gardens and tenter grounds for cloth but much was marshland until it was embanked, and the building sank into the riverside mud in just 30 years!

Most inhabitants were shipwrights and watermen who were grateful not to walk to St. Saviour's, thus a second mighty edifice was built in 1730. Gradually a warren of streets evolved and Charles Hopton (1654-1731) merchant fishmonger provided almshouses to the east, with pediment and wings, built in 1749-52 (modernised 1988). Meanwhile, the church became more prominent after Blackfriars Bridge was built in 1768, and by the mid-19th century a parish of just 45-acres contained 17,000 people.

A station opened to the south, part of the Charing Cross Railway, in 1864-69 but was then replaced by Waterloo East (and has a plaque). The church was destroyed in the war and rebuilt in red-brick on a smaller scale in 1959. Today, a series of windows depict its history and activities. The residents included Joseph Gwilt a prominent local architect whose son Charles was an antiquarian writer; and Samuel Joseph Addis (1811-71) a skilled tool maker with family at Bermondsey for several generations. [13]

C. 10 March 1809 Charles Perkins s. of Joseph Gwilt architect and Louisa b. 4 January

Surrey Chapel - Rowland Hill (1744-1833) a Calvinistic Methodist was refused priests orders and built a distinctive circular chapel, above Little Charlotte Street, in 1783. With funds from the Countess of Huntingdon it was also open to Congregational members. Hill was buried beneath the pulpit, and Sir Rowland Hill father of the postal system was named after him. His successors were Rev. James Sherman and C. Newman Hall in 1854 but the latter relocated to Christchurch, Westminster Bridge Road in 1876.

---

[13] S.J. Addis traded at 2/20 Gravel Lane (Suffolk St.) and his brother James at Little Charlotte Street, both exhibiting in the tool section of the Great Exhibition. Two daughters married at St. George's but he remarried as "George White" at All Saints, Poplar in 1863 and had children Pheasant and White. Once the railway was built he removed to 49-50 Worship Street, Finsbury and his brother to Sheffield (the Prince of Wales a patron), whilst Ward & Payne purchased the trademark "S.J. Addis London" in 1875 - his work now collectable examples.

St. George the Martyr, Borough

The first reference is to a Norman church held by Bermondsey Abbey in 1122, this being a gift from Thomas de Ardern with tithes from a manor at Horndon, Essex. In fact, its dedication relates to the Crusades. A new structure was erected in the 14th century close to Suffolk Place, and a noble history then followed. Henry V was greeted by Aldermen on the steps of the church when returning from Agincourt in 1415.

Meanwhile, Charles Brandon was raised in the court of Henry VII holding senior posts in his household, and was created Duke of Suffolk in 1514 - then married Mary Tudor, Dowager Queen of France the next year. He resided in Brandon or Suffolk Place which his family had held for some three generations, but exchanged it with the King for the old residence of the Bishop of Norwich at Cannon Row, Westminster, in 1536. For a time it was a minor Royal residence and then a mint in 1545-51, but was demolished in 1562 and from that time the estate was covered by small tenements. [14]

Likewise the church became a separate parish after the Dissolution and was repaired at the expense of 21 livery companies in 1629. This included the nave, steeple, galleries, pews and an enlargement of the south aisle into the churchyard at £166 12s, whilst in the north aisle a window depicted the arms of all the companies who contributed.

The mediaeval church appears in *Southwark Fair* by Hogarth in 1733, but it was rebuilt in Classical style with red brick, white quoins, Portland stone and large galleries by John Price in 1734-36. The Commission for Fifty Churches gave £6,000 and other funds came from a livery company and Bridge House Estate whose arms decorate the ceiling.

Several changes occurred after Westminster Bridge was built in 1750 and St. George's Fields were settled, Church Lane and Kent (or Tabard) Street were realigned, and Great Dover Street was inserted through the parish. There was a rather idiosyncratic boundary above the Fields with Newington lying below, and a strip to the southeast along Kent Street where St. Stephen's, Manciple Street was added by S.S. Teulon in 1850.

The church retained its Georgian exterior up until the present day but Basil Champneys designed a stunning new ceiling in Italianate parlour-style in 1897. Some restoration took place after the war, but it was found to be unsafe in 2000 and was underpinned, at which time Roman and mediaeval parts were uncovered. Services resumed in 2007 and it has many original features including bells, font, organ pipes by Smith, clocks by George Clarke of Whitechapel, and 18th century Dutch fireplace in the "Little Dorrit Vestry."

St. George the Martyr built in 1734-36 appeared in *Little Dorrit* by Charles Dickens who lived nearby.

---

[14] A tablet records the site of Suffolk Place in Marshalsea Road (Mint St.), and nearby are Suffolk Street and Mint Square. Due to its Royal associations it was a liberty and place of ill-repute with coiners and thieves living there.

Local Residents - Nahum Tate was born in Ireland in c.1652 and educated at Trinity College then as a schoolmaster entered literary circles as poet, playwright and translator. He collaborated with Dryden, wrote the libretto for Purcell's *Dido & Aeneas*, adapted King Lear and composed *While Shepherd's Watched*. With Royal patronage he was made poet laureate in 1692, but moved to the Liberty of the Mint to escape his creditors.

George Gwilt (1746-1809) the son of Richard a peruke maker was born in Southwark and married there - then had two architect sons. He was made Surrey Co. Surveyor and built the Bridewell at St. George's Fields (below Bethlem) in 1781, Newington Sessions in 1791-99, and several bridges. His main work was North Quay Warehouse, West India Dock with son George in 1800-03 - at a salary of 1,000 guineas per annum each!

Charles Dickens lived at Lant Street and worked in the blacking factory by Hungerford Market in 1824, when his father John was in the New Marshalsea. His experiences of the prison feature in *Little Dorrit* who married at St. George's, while part of the wall remains in gardens above the churchyard with plaque. Bob Sawyer also lived at The Mint in *The Pickwick Papers*. Joseph N. Lyons (1847-1917) was born at 50 Lant Street and went to school in Kennington but began Lyons Corner Houses in 1894.

M. 6 September 1773 George Gwilt and Hannah Tristed by licence

B. 1 August 1715 Nahum Tate [from] next to Prince Eugene ye mint

---

Thomas Wallis (1853-1902) "A Local Hero"

The Wallis family emanated from North Stoneham, Hampshire and they ran Home Farm there for over 200 years. They were connected to several prominent residents and their relatives the Smiths of Otterbourne were churchwardens at the time of John Keble and Charlotte Yonge.

John Wallis married Mary Deane of Farningham, Kent in 1846 but lost any inheritance due to this, and his nephew William built an *Inland Bournemouth* at Chandlers Ford living at "King's Court." They moved to London Bridge as a guard and waitress and son Thomas was born nearby at John Street on 13 April 1853. After the father died at Bishopstoke they came to St. Olave's, and the son attended the Grammar School and was a compositor for Johnson & Hogg, Fleet Street.

Entering into political and social issues he joined the Bermondsey Working Men's Institute and met accomplished debaters, then joined the Hearts of Oak Benefit Society at Greek Street, Soho in 1874. Being interested in their growth he attended meetings at Exeter Hall, and on being refused admittance on 25 November 1876 joined a demonstration in Trafalgar Square. An angry meeting followed at the Agricultural Hall on 17 February 1877 but a democratic system was adopted.

That year, he married Eliza Dyus daughter of a Shoreditch silversmith, who trained with Edward Smith of Birmingham, and moved to Ethnard Road by Christchurch O.K.R. Attending meetings in Bermondsey he associated with Dixon and Knight - pioneers of the electoral movement, and transferred from the Rotherhithe Association to the *Central Committee* in 1887.

He abolished systematic overtime in the office and founded the Convalescent Homes Aid Society in 1890, thus he was elected the president in 1894-95. At this time he encouraged work with firms complying with Trade Union regulations and was a member of the Peckham Liberal & Radical Council, but after a long illness died in 1902 and was buried at Camberwell Old Cemetery.

St. Olave's, Southwark

The dedication refers to Olaf ally of King Ethelred II the Unready against the Danes, including at the *Battle of London Bridge* in 1014. Godwin, Earl of Wessex then established a private chapel nearby which passed to King Harold, and there was a church present in Norman times although it was damaged by flooding of the marshes in 1327.

Ownership was transferred to Lewes Priory, and it served as a parish for the strangers and poor people living in the narrow streets by the river. It was just east of the bridge facing St. Magnus, and Stow described it as "*a fair and metely large church*" repaired and beautified in 1617. It also received a gallery for boys of the free school in 1697.

There were a few memorials and a benefaction from Bridge House, and to the south a large residence of the Prior of Lewes later a hostelry with a sign in Walnut Tree Court. To the east was a quay built in 1330, the Abbot of Augustine's inn (later tenements), the Bridge House with granaries, ovens and storage, the Abbot of Battle's inn with gardens later Fleur de Lis Court, and "Battle Bridge" over a stream beside a mill.

In fact the edifice had several aisles and a maze of pillars thus digging caused the north side to collapse in 1736. Henry Flitcroft then designed a new church of Portland stone with Ionic columns and a chancel-apse in 1740. Henry Gauntlett was organist in 1827-46 his father being minister at Olney. He wrote "Irby" for *Once in Royal David's City* and worked with W. Hill to perfect a new organ (then went to the Union Chapel). Only the tower and walls survived the Tooley Street fire on 19 August 1843, and it was rebuilt in similar style, but it soon became redundant and was demolished in 1926-28.

The parish established a Free School of Queen Elizabeth in a nearby lane in 1571 which had many pupils. It relocated to Bermondsey Street in 1829 and Tooley Street in 1855, being rebuilt by Edward W. Mountford in 1894 (the building still remains). After joining with St. Saviour's, a girls' school of the same foundation moved to New Kent Road in 1903, while St. Olave's Boys School was relocated to Orpington in 1968.

Other buildings in the area included the London & Greenwich Railway who opened a terminus in 1836. A line from Croydon ended at the Bricklayers Arms and a new station was built with the old roads beneath in 1847-50. Alexander Hay acquired Bridge House itself in 1651 and it passed to John Humphrey during the mid-19th century.

He employed William Cubitt to construct Hay's Wharf and large amounts of produce passed through, especially tea, therefore it was dubbed *The Larder of London*. When it was restored in 1987 the offices were located in St. Olave's House on the site of the church. In fact, the funds from the sale of the latter paid for St. Olave's, Mitcham which was consecrated by the Rt. Rev. Cyril Garbett, Bishop of Southwark in 1931.

C. 7 Nov 1858 Thomas s. John and Mary Wallis of Marble Court railway guard by J.P. Spenell rector b. 13 Apr 1853 (with John H. 3 Oct. 1848 and Alice M. 24 Dec. 1856)

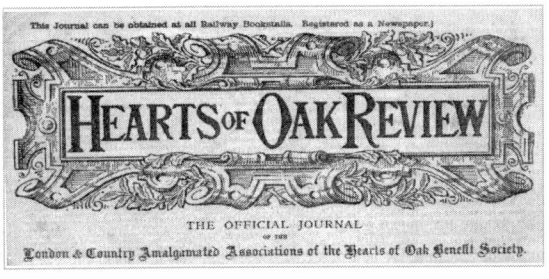

Hearts of Oak Benefit Society

The name referred to the protection given by naval ships. It started at Long Acre in 1842 but went to Greek Street in 1863, Charlotte Street in 1875, and Euston Road (opened by the King) in 1906. A board took over in 1877 with private schemes from 1948.

St. Saviour's Cathedral

A Saxon convent of sisters established St. Mary Overie "over the river" and nearby was a ferry, but St. Swithin replaced it with a college of priests in 852-67. It then fell to Bishop Odo of Bayeux as a minster, but was converted to an Augustinian priory by Henry I in 1106. William Gifford, Bishop of Winchester was a benefactor thus he built Winchester House on a plot of land, owned by the Abbey of Bermondsey, just to the west.

This became a substantial monastery with a chapter house, dormitories and refectory to the north, and chapel of St. Mary Magdalene which was a parish church for the precincts to the south. In addition, Henry I gave them the nearby church of St. Margaret's. The main priory burnt down in 1206, and a new Gothic structure with vaulted nave, transepts, quire, chapels and tower was erected over the next two hundred years.

After a serious fire Henry Beaufort, Bishop of Winchester rebuilt the south transept and tower in 1412 and had grand feasts at the house, but the Dissolution changed everything in 1536. The monastery was repressed and the two parishes were combined in the main church as St. Saviour's, whilst the house was forfeited to the Crown, then reverted to the see of Winchester under Queen Mary. Hollar drew a panorama showing the church by the great house with its gallery in 1638 - but the latter's days were numbered.

Many of the bishops of the see also held high positions, eight of them chancellors, and large social events took place. However, the abode was used less and less and Lancelot Andrewes was the last such occupant, it being promptly divided into fifteen apartments. During the time of the Commonwealth it was requisitioned for a prison and in 1649 was sold to Thomas Walker of Camberwell for £4,380. He immediately knocked down some of the building and laid out Stoney Street in the centre by Winchester Yard.

At the Restoration the property was returned to the bishop, but the process had gone too far and he applied to lease out the tenements on the site of the mansion. Despite this some parts survived, in particular the great hall with its rose window and undercroft on Clink Street by St. Mary Overie Dock (the latter has a replica of the *Golden Hind*).

St. Saviour's Cathedral dated to Saxon times and was a monastery and a parish church - The east-end with its 13th century chapels… and a view from the river showing the low choir.

Lancelot Andrewes (1555-1626) by Hollar was Dean of Westminster, Bishop of Chichester, Ely and Winchester and oversaw the translation of the *King James Bible.*

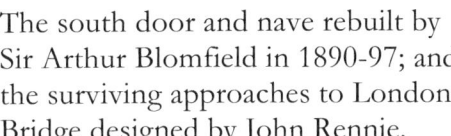

The south door and nave rebuilt by Sir Arthur Blomfield in 1890-97; and the surviving approaches to London Bridge designed by John Rennie.

St. Saviour's continued as a parish church although the monastic buildings to the north were demolished and properties replaced them. There was a certain incongruity between the palace with its gardens reaching to Gravel Lane, the inns of religious houses, and the great church, sited among the liberty of the Clink with its dungeon-like prison and near to "The Stews" of Bankside with its brothels permitted by Parliament.

However, the church remained steadfast in a changing area and received two galleries, one above St. Peter's chapel and another over the middle aisle. Some repairs were carried out in 1621. This was followed by a major restoration, including new pavement, galleries, pulpit, altar, communion rails, marble fittings, south and west windows, bells and a coat of whitewash in 1703-04. An organ was also installed, the total cost £2,600.

Local connections included Henry Thrale proprietor of the Anchor Brewery which was near Park Street, who was a friend of Johnson and had a large estate in Streatham. It was sold to David Barclay for £135,000, with the manager Mr. Perkins as a partner, in 1781. Thrale was a patron of George Gwilt the architect who lived nearby at Union Street and had two sons who joined him: George (1775-1856) baptized at Globe Alley Independent and Joseph (1784-1863) baptized at Collier's Rents Chapel.

London Bridge and its approaches were built on the east side to a John Rennie design in 1824-31, leading to the demolition of Andrewes Chapel; while Borough Market dating to the 13th century was added in the 1850s, and the Railway and Southwark Street came close by soon afterwards. Other events were the building of St. Peter's, Sumner Street by the Potts Vinegar Co. in 1839 (lost in the war), and the arrival of C.H. Spurgeon who first preached at New Park Street in 1853 attracting large congregations (see later). [15]

---

[15] Two alcoves from the ancient bridge were removed to Victoria Park, Hackney in 1860; while Rennie's bridge was replaced in 1967-72 and transferred to Lake Havasu City, Arizona. There are still some remnants on Montague Close (once an old house) and just north of the river.

A massive programme of restoration was then implemented at the church by George Gwilt the younger, who replaced the choir ceiling and tower pinnacles from 1822-25 and renovated the Lady Chapel or retro-choir in 1832-33. Further work was done on the nave and transepts, the former being remodelled at this time. However, the nave was totally rebuilt in the 13th-century style by Sir Arthur Blomfield during 1890-97.

The result was a grand Gothic building at a major transport intersection known as the collegiate church of St. Saviour under Rochester (in 1897). It was a cathedral for the new Diocese of Southwark in 1905 and the first bishop was Edward Talbot until 1911, then it became the cathedral of St. Saviour and college of St. Mary Overie in 1937. Matters had gone full circle and inside is a fascinating record of its history - as detailed below.

Virtual Tour of St. Saviour's Cathedral

The Nave - Entering by the south door into Blomfield's creation there are a number of reminders from the past. Just inside the entrance is arcading dating back to 1206, near a section of the 13th century west wall. To the rear are bosses from the 15th century, and a later font and cover in memory of Robert Philipson Barrow (dated 1904).

On the north side is a Norman arch from the priory of 1106 but demolished 1206 - its floor some two feet below, also a tablet recording priors in 1106-1539, history of the site and bishops since 1905. To the east is the tomb of John Gower poet to Richard II and Henry IV who first wrote in English rather than French and Latin. He occupied a house and chantry chapel just to the north and was buried there in 1408, but was moved when it was demolished. The memorial has a canopy with pendants, some deep colours with gold embellishments, and Gower resting on some books in the three languages.

Above is a series of stained-glass windows to literary figures by C.E. Kempe done in 1900 - from left to right: Oliver Goldsmith, Samuel Johnson, Henry Sacheverell church chaplain, Alexander Cruden *Bible Concordance*, John Bunyan a Baptist, John Gower and G. Chaucer 1340-1400 given by A.W. Piggott to celebrate his 500th anniversary.

On the south side near the crossing is the Shakespeare memorial of 1911 with a relief behind depicting the Cathedral, Bridge, Globe and Winchester House, whilst the window above has characters from his plays. The decorated nave has a double-bay vault with the ribs leading up from the arcade and a blank triforium below the clerestory.

Transepts - The lower walls to the north are 12th century and have memorials to the Austin family restored in 1706, and to Dr. Lionel Lockyer d.1672 - "His virtues and his pills are soe well known." Nearby are a Jacobean communion table and sideboard. On the east side is the Harvard (St. John the Evangelist) Chapel dating to the 12th century, with its golden tabernacle by A.W. Pugin - all restored by Harvard University.

The crossing has four piers dating to the 14th century which are flattened on the inside while the ceiling is adorned with green, red and gold bosses and a chandelier 1680. Here there is a stilted arch to accommodate a spiral staircase. On the southwest pier is a tablet to Wenceslaus Hollar an exile from Bohemia, artist in England, with a quote by George Vertue dated 1745, "The works of nature and of men by thee preserved."

In the south transept is an organ by T.F. Lewis of 1897, and coat of arms to Cardinal Beaufort - who restored this area and a chapel to the east. Nearby is a memorial tablet to Isabella Gilmore who was a nurse at Guy's Hospital and sister of William Morris.

WENCESLAUS HOLLAR

Wenceslaus Hollar (1607-77), etcher, was brought to England by Thomas, Earl of Arundel. He did a famous "Long View" of London from the cathedral in 1638/47 b. St. Margaret's, Westminster.

The Choir - This is raised with a low ceiling and has a screen by Bishop Fox of 1520, but the figures and throne are of 1905. It has a model of the priory by T. Keane headmaster of St. Saviour's 1928 and an east window by Ninian Comper in 1950. On turning from the high altar there is a view of the nave with its multi-layered vault, like Exeter Cathedral, restored in 13th-century decorated style to match the choir and chancel.

Regarding the north ambulatory which leads to the Harvard Chapel there are a number of monuments including John Treherne gentleman porter to James I (brightly restored), a tablet to Thomas Cure Esq. 1588 with effigy below, and an impressive wood effigy of a knight dated 1280-1300. Opposite is a canopied tomb to Richard Humble alderman 1616 and Margaret Pierson his wife by son Peter with kneeling figures in ruffs.

The south ambulatory has a memorial to Edward S. Talbot the first bishop in gold, and to Lancelot Andrewes, Bishop of Winchester who died at the palace in 1626 with canopy of blue/gold. It was originally in a chapel at the east end (demolished for the bridge in 1830 - its foundation outside) and behind the altar until 1919. Nearby is a prayer by him reminiscent of *St. Francis*. On the wall is a tablet to Abraham Newland cashier of The Bank from 1747-1807 who was born in the parish in 1730 and lived at Highbury.

Lady Chapel - This is generally called the retro-choir and squared off with four chapels dated 1215-60. It has delicate columns, blind tracery and arches on the west wall dating to the 14th century and housed the Consistory Court of the Bishop of Winchester. A model of the cathedral in 1600 is found here and tablets to George Gwilt y. *eminent architect and scientific man* and his nephew Charles Perkins Gwilt with family coat of arms.

Outside on the south wall is a memorial to the former, "who restored the choir, tower and Ladye Chapel." To the north are the Millennium Rooms opened by Nelson Mandela with names of diocesan churches in the pavement - and impressive Norman arch/apse, unique delft oven and road tiles found during the building work. Opposite is the Glaziers Hall in Montague Close which came there in 1977 having shared since the fire.

C. 29 November 1607 John Harvye [sic] p. ob. Robert a butcher [16]
21 July 1717 Richard son of John Gwilt a barber and Sarah [father of George sen.]

B. 31 December 1607 Edmond Shakespeare a player in the church [brother]
29 August 1625 Mr. John Ffletcher a man in the church - playwright with Massinger
22 November 1626 Lancelott Andrewes the Lord Bishop of Winton
18 March 1639/40 Philip Massenger a stranger - wrote for the King's Men

---

[16] John Harvard (1607-38) was educated at St. Saviour's School and Emmanuel, Cambridge then went to Charleston with his wife Ann Sadler in 1637. He became a minister but died of T.B. and bequeathed £779 and 400 books to a new college at nearby Cambridge which took his name.

St. Thomas's, Southwark

This was the infirmary for St. Mary Overie and after a fire Peter des Roches, Bishop of Winchester moved the buildings to the east of Borough High Street in 1215. The chapel was dedicated to Thomas à Becket and it was run by Augustinians, whilst Whittington endowed a ward and it was made into a parish in 1496. The site saw the first printing of the English Bible in 1537, but according to Stow the Abbot of Bermondsey charged a large rent of £340 and at the Dissolution it was duly surrendered in 1538.

However, the citizens of London purchased the hospital and Edward VI gave beds and furniture to both Bridewell and St. Thomas's in 1553, whereas the chapel was rededicated to St. Thomas the Apostle. There were some ancient memorials including those to Sir Robert Chambers, William Fiennes Lord Saye, Robert son of Sir Thomas Fleming, and Agnes wife of Sir Walter Dennis and heir of Sir Robert Danvers.

The buildings covered a large site above St. Thomas's Street while a gallery was added to the church in 1618, and the tower was rough-cast with a fair turret in 1633, then the entrance and east window were improved. Sir Robert Clayton president (1692-1707) and former mayor paid to rebuild it in 1703, the work done by architect Thomas Cartwright with red brick, white quoins and a terrace of fine houses attached.

Meanwhile, Thomas Guy a governor who published Bibles and made a fortune in the South Sea Bubble established a new hospital to treat those discharged as being hopeless. This was built to the south around a quadrangle on land owned by St. Thomas's in 1721 and by agreement there was only a minimal rent (and has his statue).

An Act was passed to build Charing Cross Railway through the garden and new north wing in 1859. The governors realised it was pointless to contest this or to take the small compensation and instead briefly relocated to Surrey Gardens. A site was then negotiated on the Albert Embankment in Lambeth with Florence Nightingale consulted on design, and architect Henry Currey built the new St. Thomas's from 1868-71.

Only a few fittings were moved including a marble statue of Clayton by Gibbons and two of Edward VI. The church was redundant by 1899 and merged with St. Saviour's as its chapter house, but is now a museum with herb garret. The adjacent area was gradually altered by the development of Guy's Hospital, approaches to London Bridge station, and is now undergoing further changes under Italian architect Renzo Piano.

B. 7 January 1724/25 Thomas Guy Esq.

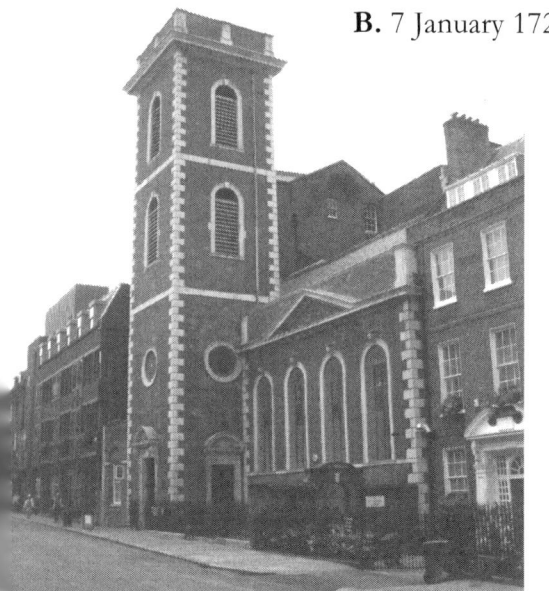

St. Thomas's built in 1703 has the look of a Wren City church.

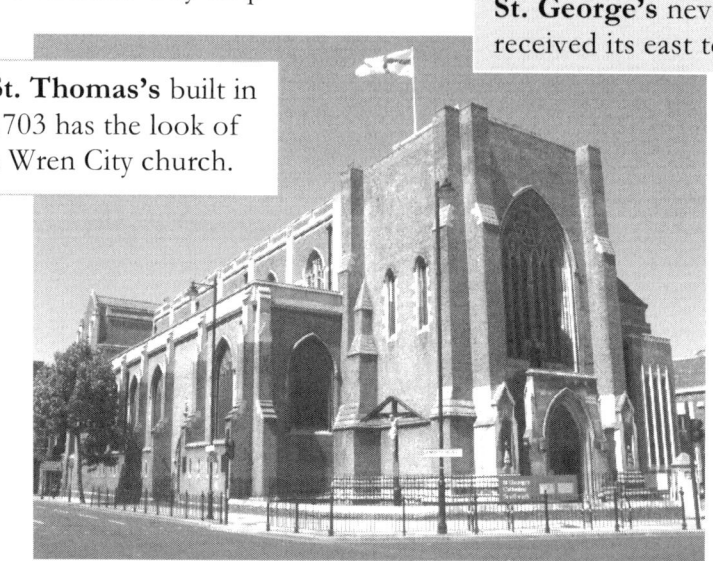

St. George's never received its east tower.

St. George's R.C. Cathedral

St. George's Fields was a large open space above the road from Lambeth Palace across to Newington, and beside Newington Causeway which led up to Borough High Street. On its western side were fields, but to the north was Gravel Lane reaching to the river, and a veritable warren of alleys and houses including The Mint above Dirty Lane.

After the Catholic Relief Act 1779, Lord George Gordon of the Protestant Association arranged a protest meeting at St. George's Fields in June 1780 and 50,000 attended. They marched towards Westminster with anti-Catholic sentiment and after being refused entry a week of riots ensued with many chapels and properties destroyed.

Several new bridges were then built and London Road was extended from Newington to connect with them, and nearby a Catholic chapel of St. George's was erected in 1793. It was at this church where the first mass was heard outside an *Ambassador's Chapel*, and this became a centre of worship for French exiles, and also a growing number of Irish Catholics. Following the Emancipation Act of 1829 there was more equality and further churches were added. Likewise, Fr. Thomas Doyle established a large congregation in the vicinity of the chapel, which by then proved to be grossly inadequate.

He had to minister to a parish population of 15,000 which had doubled in a few years and thereby envisaged a great church in the area. There was still considerable opposition but an area above St. George's Road was chosen in 1839, and Augustus W.N. Pugin was informed of the scheme by his patron Lord Shrewsbury. He then submitted a design with cathedral, chapter house and cloisters - but walked out when asked for a price? [17]

No price was too much in his eyes! However, the committee then laid down a limit of £20,000 to include a church for 2,500 and school for 500 mixed pupils, all in the *Pointed Style* prevalent at the time. A number of tenders were received and a triangle of land was provided for £3,200 on condition that: it would take six years, no ecclesiastical ornament would go outside, and Pugin was the architect. This was all agreed in December 1839 and the foundation was laid in secret at 7 a.m. in the morning on 26 May 1841.

Pugin was heavily committed at the time as he began work on the Houses of Parliament with Charles Barry, but designed a lofty parochial church without galleries like those at the time of Edward III. In particular it was based on Austin Friars in the City, with three parallel aisles, gabled roof and no triforium or clerestory. Its dimensions were 240' x 72' whilst walls eight feet thick were built to take a large tower and spire at the west end. But financial constraints meant this was never built above a height of 64 feet.

The contract went to Myers & Wilson with concrete foundations and Bath stone for the walls, and the school and clergy house were completed in two years. Bishop Wiseman opened the church on 4 July 1848 and in honour of this Pope Pius IX presented a golden chalice and a paten. Wiseman was inducted as the Archbishop of Westminster there in December 1850, and it became the first Catholic cathedral since the Reformation.

---

[17] Augustus Welby N. Pugin (1812-52) was educated at Christ's Hospital, Newgate, then worked with his father Augustus a French draughtsman (trained by Nash), and together they wrote books on Gothic architecture in particular the Continental style. After his marriage to Louisa Burton in 1833 he became a Catholic and lived in Salisbury, whilst he worked with John Talbot, Earl of Shrewsbury especially in the north of England and did designs for Australian churches.

St. George's showing transverse vaults and detail from the Petre Chantry and Lady Chapel.

When the building opened it was criticised for its lack of ornamentation, slim arches, and shortened chancel for a cathedral, but Pugin countered saying the constraints of the committee had ruined the architecture. He was the first to marry there and his bride Jane was daughter of Thomas Knill of Typtree Hall, Herefordshire but was raised by her uncle John Knill a prominent Catholic of Blackheath. However, due to the strain he spent time in Bethlem Hospital opposite then died at The Grange, Ramsgate in 1852.

St. George's became the centre of Catholic life in London thus the Notre Dame School was opened nearby by sisters from Namur in 1855. Meanwhile the parish school moved in 1887, Frederick A. Walters designed a new clergy house in 1889, and the controversial rood screen was removed and a south chapel was added. Once all the debts were finally cleared it was consecrated by Bishop J.B. Butt on 7 November 1894.

The cathedral's role was reduced after the opening of Westminster in 1903 and it was destroyed except for the walls during the bombing on 16 April 1941. From that time the adjacent Amigo Hall was occupied as the pro-cathedral. Romilly B. Craze then designed a new building using what remained of the old; and combined Arts and Crafts with various Gothic styles to replicate the effects of age discerned in older cathedrals.

In particular he looked to the French church at Brou for inspiration and it re-opened in 1958, while the Lady Chapel on the north side was completed in 1966. However, as was perhaps destined, the intended spire was never built due to a lack of money, and the east end retains a rather awkward appearance with its stolid base. One of the main internal changes was to raise the inner walls and introduce a clerestory to let in more light.

The outcome was a Gothic nave, Perpendicular baptistry, Tudor chapel and chantries to: Edward R. Petre a benefactor (whose relatives settled New Zealand), and to Knill in the Blessed Sacrament Chapel by Edward Pugin. One to George Talbot was unfinished. Other features are a memorial to Thomas Doyle provost d.1879, Flemish statue (1725) in the Lady Chapel, bronze crucifix from Napoleon given by the Emperor of Austria *south aisle*, and statues and Stations of the Cross by H.J. Youngman *north aisle*.

Nearby buildings included the Bethlem Hospital which came there from Moorfields in 1815 and had a central dome with wings designed by Sydney Smirke. It departed in 1930 and was then occupied by the Imperial War Museum - but without its wings.

M. 10 August 1848 Augustus Welby Northmore Pugin and Jane Knill
23 January 1850 Stuart Knill s. of John and Mary Anne Rosa Parker [mayor 1892]

Christchurch, Westminster Bridge Road - The Female Orphan Asylum was west of the cathedral from 1758, but Rev. C. Newman Hall purchased the site as a successor to Surrey Chapel, Blackfriars Road, in 1873. A memorial tablet was laid by Samuel Morley M.P. and foundation by the American Ambassador since Hall supported Lincoln in the war. The new Congregational chapel by E.C. Robins included the lofty *Lincoln Tower* with spire and opened on 4 July 1876, but it was destroyed in the war and joined with Upton Baptist in a new office-style building by the tower. Inside is a plaque of 1894 from the Surrey Chapel pulpit noting how Rowland Hill, Henry Venn, Thomas Scott et al preached there, and nearby is Morley College which relocated from the Old Vic in the 1920s.

Newington

This parish just east of St. George's Fields ran from Kennington Park to Albany Road, then up the Old Kent Road to Great Dover Street and St. George's church. It comprised the Manor of Walworth but a *new* settlement was established on Stane Street to the west, and there were 100 residents at the time of the Domesday Book. Its importance then increased due to Lambeth Palace and the main occupation was farming or light industry, whilst the appendage of butts came from mounds used for archery practice.

St. Mary's, Newington

A church was built west of Newington Butts in c.1200 and again in the 14th century then a south aisle was added at the expense of Sir Hugh Brawne in c.1600 - his memorial with knight in armour being located there. Just north of the church were the fishmongers' almshouses or hospital and a theatre at the time of Shakespeare in 1580-99.

Thomas Middleton was baptized at St. Lawrence Jewry in 1580 the son of William, but his mother remarried Thomas Harvey a grocer who lost money in the Roanoke scheme. Despite this he went to Oxford and wrote *The Wisdom of Solomon* dedicated to Essex and plays for the Admiral's Men at the Rose Theatre. He resided at Newington Butts near the theatres and worked with Dekker, leading to a conflict with Jonson. His titles included satirical pamphlets and plays, in particular *The Puritan Widow* and *A Game at Chess*.

The church, meanwhile, was repaired and a new altar erected at great cost in 1704, but ten years later the wall cracked during a service and the congregation made a hasty exit. On inspection the foundations, walls, pillars, beams and roof were in severe decay, thus it was demolished and rebuilt at £926 in 1720 - with mediaeval tower retained.

The area remained a village until the late 18th century when Henry Penton a landowner and M.P. for Winchester sold the adjacent farmland for housing. John Horsley and his son Samuel were rectors at this time, the latter a writer and bishop, whereas the church in its large churchyard was rebuilt with a portico and double pediment in 1793.

As the adjacent properties were erected there were a number of significant parishioners and Charles Babbage was born at 44 Crosby Row on the Walworth Road in December 1791. His father a partner in the banking firm of Praeds had a home in Teignmouth and he was educated at Totnes, by tutors, and at Cambridge. He then became a significant mathematician and mechanical inventor and had a property in Marylebone.

However, several residents did not appear in the registers including Michael Faraday who was born at Newington Butts on 22 September 1791. His father was a member of the Glasite or Sandemanian sect and they attended the chapel near Cripplegate, thus the son became an elder. Faraday had a great interest in science and attended lectures given by Humphrey Davy at the Royal Institution, but after writing a 300-page discourse which was well received he became Davy's laboratory assistant and valet.

A second example was William Jowett born there in 1787 but baptized at St. John's Horsleydown. He was educated at Little Dunham by his uncle Henry then a missionary for the C.M.S., church lecturer and vicar of St. John's, Clapham Rise. His father John was an evangelist and his sister married Rev. J. Pratt of St. John's, Bedford Row - while at the wedding his uncle was minister and his brothers were witnesses. Thirdly Samuel Palmer was born in Surrey Square on 27 January 1805, his father a Baptist minister and book-seller - and he became a landscape painter of Kensington and Shoreham.

Another resident Robert Rogers was born at Dunbarton, N.H. in 1731 and became famous for *Rogers Rangers* who held off the French, and commanded a New Hampshire regiment in 1755-60. He wrote journals of his exploits and a play favoured by the King then took charge in Michigan, but returned to England due to debts/irregularities. After another spell in America in the War of Independence he returned home again.

Rev. William D. Maclagan was minister in 1869 and Archbishop of York but the church was demolished for road-widening in 1876, and a new one was built east of Kennington Park Road. This was designed by James Fowler in the Early English style of Bath stone and the nave had a hammer-beam roof although the spire was never added. It burnt down in 1941 and was replaced by a building behind the surviving entrance-façade and tower. Meanwhile, a clock-tower was erected on the church site by R.S. Faulconer in 1877 but was demolished in 1971, and today there is a park (with information board).

C. 6 January 1792 Charles son of Benjamin and Betty Plumleigh Babbage

M. 7 September 1797 Josiah Pratt of St. George's, Bloomsbury batch and Elizabeth Jowett o.t.p. spin by licence by Joseph Jowett clerk presence of Henry Jowett, W. Terrington, Joshua Jowett and John Jowett junior

B. 4 July 1627 Mr. Thomas Middleton was buryed
20 May 1795 Richard [sic] Rogers male

> **St. Mary's, Newington** behind the surviving façade of 1876.

The Tabernacle was built for a young **Spurgeon** in 1861.

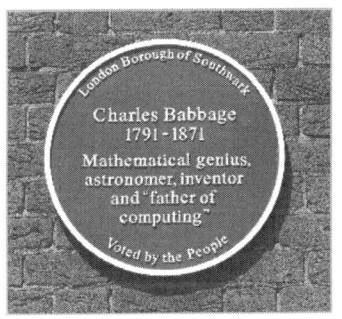

The Tabernacle interior held 6,000 people but it burnt down in 1898, and plaque in Larcom Street.

Metropolitan Tabernacle

Continuing on a theme, Charles H. Spurgeon was born at Kelvedon, Essex in 1834 and during a snowstorm stopped at a Methodist chapel in Colchester and heard Isaiah 45:22 "Look unto me and be saved, for I am God and there is nothing else." He was converted and became pastor at New Park Street, Baptist chapel at Southwark in 1854. [18]

Upon his arrival the congregation numbered just 232, but during his ministry there and at the Tabernacle some 14,000 were baptized. These included Susannah Thompson who he baptized in 1855 and married at the chapel on 8 January 1856. The following year he established The Pastor's College - which became Spurgeon's College when it moved to South Norwood Hill (in 1923). He soon outgrew the premises and preached to audiences of over 10,000 people at Exeter Hall and the Surrey Music Hall. [19]

The Metropolitan Tabernacle was designed by W.W. Pocock for £31,000 on the site of the old almshouses - with 5,000 seated and 1,000 standing, and they moved there on 18 March 1861. Spurgeon never called people forward after his sermons, but asked them to visit him the next day at the vestry - in fact, there were *always* callers. He continued to preach for 31 years and died at Mentone, France but was buried at West Norwood.

The original tabernacle by the Elephant and Castle was burnt down in 1898 leaving just the grand portico and basement, while the same occurred during the war. However, it was rebuilt on a smaller scale but retaining the original façade in 1957.

Holy Trinity, Newington

The square of land below Borough High Street and Great Dover Street had a number of ecclesiastical owners but was owned by the Bostock family at the time of Elizabeth I. It went to Christopher Merrick in 1605; then to his son Christopher a merchant/brother of Trinity House who conveyed it to them for the support of sick seamen in 1661.

The land was generally used for grazing, market gardens and tenter grounds, and a bill to create Great Dover Street in 1809 was opposed in Parliament without result. Indeed, the Corporation arranged to build Trinity Street on the site with the Dean and Chapter of Canterbury (who were owners of the manor), and also purchased some land at the west end from St. Thomas's Hospital to facilitate this scheme.

---

[18] The fellowship dated back to the 1650s, whilst Rev. John Gill and Rev. John Rippon were the consecutive pastors for one hundred years until 1836, but it declined in the next 20 years.

[19] Royal Surrey Gardens were established in the grounds of Walworth Manor by Edward Cross in 1831 and had a zoo and conservatory, but after competition from the Crystal Palace a music hall was built there for 12,000 spectators in 1856. It was destroyed by a fire in 1861 and St. Thomas's were the temporary occupants, but it was closed and replaced by housing in 1877.

St. Peter's (1823-25) by Sir John Soane may be compared to Trinity at Marylebone.

Holy Trinity now a music venue.

Initially there were problems with road maintenance, regarding responsibility. However Trinity (Church) Square an exclusive development was built in the north of the parish in the 1820s, with most of the houses being erected by William Chadwick.

The same Act that authorised St. Peter's, Walworth permitted the building of a church on the Trinity Estate and Francis Bedford was employed as architect, while the builders were Chadwick and Elizabeth Broomfield. The foundation stone was laid by Archbishop Manners-Sutton on a former tenter ground on 2 June 1823 and it was consecrated on 16 December 1824. A parish was then created from St. Mary's and C.V. Holme Sumner was the first minister in 1824-27; whereas St. Mary Magdalene, Massinger Street was added by B. Ferrey above Surrey Square in 1842 (although it was lost in the war).

Designed as a long rectangle with north porch Holy Trinity was unlike Bedford's two churches in Lambeth, and had plain façades with a pediment facing the three adjacent roads. In general, it seemed low compared to its size and the main Corinthian portico, with grand pediment and blanked-out windows, faced onto the garden. The tower above had two lower stages - one of them being open, all surmounted by a cupola.

Regarding the interior, it was mainly plain with three galleries raised on Doric columns in the west half, and an organ by Hugh Russell & Son positioned to the rear of them. The eastern sanctuary had altar rails and was framed by a pediment, whereas the walls were detailed with a frieze and also had shallow pilasters. The latter supported beams which separated the simple roof into fifteen coffered bays.

The main aisle was damaged in the war and the side chapel and crypt were used until it was closed as unsafe in 1961. Due to its acoustics it was considered for music and tested by the Philharmonic & Symphony Orchestra in December 1972, but as the scheme was underway a serious fire occurred. However, it was repaired as the *Henry Wood Hall* for rehearsing and recording with the first concert taking place on 16 June 1975.

Trinity House restored the square which is now a conservation area and original pillars are at the church entrance. A statue of Alfred at the centre of the garden may be one of a pair by Rysbrack made for Carlton House in 1735, and brought there by the builder. In the edifice there were a number of memorials including to William Chadwick, builder of Grove Park, Camberwell (1797-1852), and also to some former ministers.

St. Peter's, Walworth

The population of Newington was 14,000 in 1800 but twenty years later had grown to 44,000, and since St. Mary's held a fraction of that number - "with no room for servants except in the aisles," something had to be done. There were many Nonconformist chapels hence an Act was passed for two Anglican churches in 1820, and a house and orchards were purchased from the Clutton family, east of Walworth Road, for £2,197.

A Gothic design by Simeon Thomas Bull was turned down and Rev. Arthur C. Onslow of St. Mary's complained about the delay. As a result they asked Soane to prepare plans and the foundation was laid by the Archbishop on 2 June 1823 (with Holy Trinity), while this Waterloo Church was consecrated slightly later on 28 February 1825.

The main façade had four Ionic columns in a recess with entablature and, instead of a pediment, a small cornice/balcony with narrow tower and cupola above. One of its hallmarks was tall arched windows similar to Trinity, Marylebone, but in this instance there was yellow brick rather than a stone dressing. The side walls were plain and the east end had three round-headed windows with a gable and slate roof above. Middle-class houses sat on Liverpool Grove to the south but there were backs of terraces to the north.

Regarding the interior, the vestibule had arches at the lower level and Ionic columns dividing the bell-ringing chamber above. However, there was a *reverse tardis effect* since the lobby at the west end, and vestries to the east, shortened the nave by some degree. As was common there were galleries on three sides. A new altar and choir stalls were added at the east end in 1886. But serious cracks appeared in 1919, and the timber foundations which had rotted were replaced with concrete and the sanctuary underpinned.

The church was badly damaged during the war and restored by Thomas F. Ford then re-dedicated by the Bishop of Southwark in 1953. At this time the choir stalls were shifted back, and the east bays enclosed to form a Lady Chapel and choir vestry. Further repairs were done in 1982 and features include a Soane altar piece, organ by H.C. Lincoln, and a columned font made locally and presented by the Misses Boyman in 1839.

C. 11 September 1836 Louis John son of John and Sarah Jennings b. 19 May [20]

York Street Independent - Lock's Field Congregational was built south of the street in 1790 with a plain façade, round-headed windows and pediment. Rev. George Clayton was the minister for over 50 years whilst Capt. James Wilson, son-in-law of Richard Holbert a founder, sailed the first missionary ship and had a memorial. Other links were Robert Moffat a pioneer missionary in Africa whose daughter Mary married David Livingstone of the L.M.S. In addition, H.H. Asquith spoke there for social change in 1895, and Rev. Francis Stead campaigned from 1898 with W. Booth leading to the Pensions Act (1908). The chapel was renamed Browning Hall (and Street) but was demolished in 1950.

C. 14 June 1812 Robert s. of Rob and Sara Anna Browning b. 7 May - poet, playwright
30 September 1821 Henry s. of John and Jane Doulton b. 24 July - inventor, potter

---

[20] Jennings was foreign correspondent for the *Times* and married actress Madeline Henriques then was editor of the *N.Y. Times* in 1870-76 exposing the Tweed "Ring." He was M.P. for Stockport and wrote *The Millionaire* based on Jay Gould also material on Croker, Gladstone and Churchill.

St. John's, Walworth

The area between Browning and Heygate Streets was still undeveloped in the 1860s, and Larcom Street was built on fields there with St. John's church. The Dean and Chapter of Canterbury were patrons and it was designed by Henry Jarvis, in the decorated style, for £5,000 in 1865. St. Paul's, Lorrimore Square opened below Surrey Gardens in 1856, and was rebuilt in modern fashion after the war.

Walworth was generally a built-up area of terraced housing from this time, and the two churches took some of the burden from St. Peter's erected some thirty years earlier. A library for St. Mary's Newington parish was opened at the entrance to Larcom Street by Rev. Canon Parker in 1892. This has plaques to both Babbage and Faraday, the latter "a scientific genius and discoverer of electromagnetism."

However the most interesting plaque on the wall of East Street to the south records the birth of Charlie Chaplin. His father Charles of Ipswich a barman resided with a brother Spencer at Northcote House, Battersea Rise; while mother Hannah Harriet Pedlingham Hill was born at Camden Street, Walworth, on 6 August 1865. She was the daughter of a boot-maker and later on a mantle machinist at 132 Southwark Bridge Road.

Under the name Lily Harley she became a singer and actress and son Sydney Hill was born on 16 March 1885, thus she married fellow entertainer Charles Chaplin soon after. Their son Charles was born on 16 April 1889 but the marriage failed and the mother and children moved to 94 Barlow Street. A third child George Dryden was born in 1892 and Chaplin followed his mother onto the stage, whilst his father died in 1901, and he then entered a troupe called the *Lancashire Lads* and resided in Lambeth.

His mother spent time in mental asylums at Coulsdon and Peckham and he joined Fred Karno on tours of the States from 1910, then joined Mack Sennett at Keystone Studios and created his famous character *The Tramp*. He formed United Artists with Pickford, Fairbanks and Griffiths from 1919-39, whereas his mother died in 1928.

C. 1 April 1885 Sidney John s. of Hannah Harriet Hill, 57 Brandon St. by H. Colbor cur

M. 22 June 1885 Charles Chaplin 22 bach professional singer of 57 Brandon Street s. of Spencer butcher and Hannah Harriet Hill 19 spin same d. Charles boot-maker by banns by G.J. Cotham vicar witness George Bailey, Mary Ann Hill

London
South East

The final area to consider was historically not in London at all and straddled the northern climes of the counties of Kent and Surrey. Here were abbeys, dockyards, Royal palaces, naval hospitals, school foundations and forsooth the strange story of the brotherhood of Trinity House.

This was indeed the domain of the Royal Navy with its regal sponsors. Thus renowned architects designed buildings of great moment, and pioneers and settlers tarried forth to America, the Southern Oceans, South Africa and the Antipodes. Not forgetting several missionaries and Wolfe of Quebec.

Longitude was the question on everyone's minds and with the chronometer ticking at treble time everything came in threes; three churches built by the Commissioners, three canals facilitating trade links, and three Astronomer Royals burning the midnight oil to observe the stars.

Nearby were visionaries of note John Ruskin and Ebenezer Howard looking for a utopian future, as others strived on a practical level including Boulton, Savery, Brady and Harrison. Meanwhile, Evelyn and Cleverley recorded the scene - one that included parks, retreats and Elysian chapels from whence to contemplate heroes of the Empire and beyond.

Greenwich - the Maritime Museum was once a school and nearby were a Royal palace, hospital and naval college.

Bermondsey

This district just east of Southwark was settled at an early date, and a letter from the monastery at Peterborough talked of a related foundation at *Bermond's Eye* (or Island) in 715 A.D. A settlement was listed in the Domesday Book, while in confusing fashion a priory of St. Saviour's was established there by Elwin Childe a citizen in 1082. This was soon taken over by the Cluniacs and as a result became accountable to France.

Bermondsey Manor was held by the Norman Kings and William II gave the manor to the monks with appurtenances, and built a great new church, by 1094. In addition they received the manors of Charlton and Southwark and nearby St. George's from Thomas of Arderne in 1122. However, most alien priories were seized in 1378 and Richard II converted it to an abbey in 1399 with John Attleborough as the first abbot.

The Abbey was valued at £474 14s 4d and surrendered to the King in 1539, whereas Sir Thomas Pope (founder of Trinity, Oxford) pulled it down and replaced it with a large house of stone and timber, later owned by the Earls of Sussex. A few persons of note were buried in the abbey according to their wills: Sir William and Elizabeth Bowes, Dame Anne wife of Lord Audley, and John Holgrave baron of the exchequer. A plaque can be observed in Abbey Street and foundations were excavated at Bermondsey Square.

Another place of note nearby was the horse down or "horsey down" owned by the Abbey and Manor of Southwark, used by the local inhabitants to pasture their horses and cattle. This passed over to Christopher Eglisfeild gent of Gray's Inn and he conveyed it to the governors of St. Olave's Grammar in 1581 with whom it remained. The changing nature of the area was revealed by its rents, which for pasture earned just £6 per annum but by the late 19th century produced £3,000 income for the school.

The east section of Horsleydown was initially in the hands of the Knights Templar, and was adjacent to St. Saviour's Dock built by the Cluniacs at the outlet of the Neckinger River. The site passed to the order of St. John of Jerusalem in 1313 and was a liberty with three water mills, whilst at the Dissolution it went to the Eglisfeild family.

In fact, the name Shad Thames derived from *St. John by the Thames* and on the site was erected the Courage Brewery. Also in the vicinity were numerous warehouses and the notorious Jacob's Island shanty town - parodied in the writings of Dickens. Names such as dock-head and pickle herring signified features in the locality, and Shad Thames became a favourite film location until it was recently gentrified.

Several rich merchants lived on Grange Road among the fields, and "Jamaica House" was found to the east on Cherry Garden Street in Jacobean times. Pepys was one of the visitors to the *cherry garden*, a place of leisure with bowling greens, and the house was only demolished in the 1860s. Other features were the Lock Hospital a Lazar house by a milestone in Kent Street, a spa/health resort, and Spa Road Station the first terminus on the Deptford line. This was open from 1836-1915 and remains can still be seen.

Meanwhile, Bermondsey Street and Long Lane ran into Southwark and had numerous courtyards and alleys for artisans, including the Leather Market with related industry such as silk hatting. In addition to the three main churches St. Paul's, Kipling Street was built by S.S. Teulon, and Christchurch, Parker's Row in the Romanesque style by W.B. Hays both in 1848. The latter was a colonial architect in Adelaide, Aust. soon afterwards.

St. Mary Magdalen a college style church has two unusual tablets outside regarding baptisms and marriages, and the times of services at 11.00, 3.00 and 6.30. Nearby *The Road to Morocco* points the way to the Leather Market buildings some of which still survive.

St. Mary Magdalen

Bermondsey Priory was located just south of the church site and St. Mary's was built for its lay workers in 1290; however the two separated when the priory was converted into a Benedictine abbey in 1399. The wives of Henry V and Edward IV stayed in the precincts of the monastic buildings, and engravings on the church silver showed it was a wealthy living (now at the V & A). Strype recorded that £860 was spent on a new south aisle in 1608-10 and also £33 16s to repair the steeple with a fair turret in 1619.

Despite such lavish endowment the decayed mediaeval building was demolished in 1680 except for the tower with its Gothic window and four arches. Ten years were then spent rebuilding, whilst there were two organs installed and a north gallery was added in 1705. No old monuments survived except ones to Rev. Edward Elton 1604-05, Rev. Jeremiah Whitaker 1654 and William Castel J.P., shipwright of Redriff (Rotherhithe) and major in the Surrey Militia 1681 (which is now the oldest memorial).

A south gallery was erected with cast-iron Ionic columns in 1794 and there were several Victorian restorations. The first involved the rebuilding of the upper tower and a stucco west façade in 1830 (giving today's appearance). Later ones were a Gothic enhancement in 1852, enlargement of the chancel and vestry and replacement of the Tuscan columns of the nave in 1883, and an additional vestry in the northeast corner in 1898.

The result was five bays and an elliptical plaster ceiling with a coffered chancel roof, whereas the western bays formed a vestibule. In fact, the central bay was actually wider and the aisles (which were flat-roofed) joined it with a matching groined vault. A small transept to the south was later converted into a quire vestry.

Only the tower and west wall of the north aisle are mediaeval but many of the fittings are 18th century - box pews in the galleries, organ case and Royal arms, octagonal pulpit and chancel panels. A font and cover were donated by James Hardwidge churchwarden in 1808 and capitals from the abbey are also found there. Little damage occurred in the blitz but there was a serious fire in 1971 and the walls were rendered in 1994.

Rectors and Residents - There were several rectors of note and a board with pediment on the north wall records them. Of these, Rev. Thomas Paske was appointed in 1624 but was regularly absent, failed to give his curate a home, and was of Arminian persuasion thus the parish applied to the Lords and he was promptly ejected in 1642.

He was succeeded by Jeremiah Whitaker an eminent Orientalist and member of the Westminster Assembly who was buried in the chancel. The latter was followed by his son William Whitaker who was ejected at the Restoration, and by Rev. Richard Parr a theologian and vicar of Camberwell who remained there until 1682.

William Browning was presented by his father in 1726-40 and his successor John Paget came there under the same advowson, but when this arrangement expired the latter was removed. W. Browning sen. has a memorial on the south wall d.1758. Other ministers were Rev. John Edgar Gibson rector in 1827-59 at the same time as Christopher Bowen was perpetual curate in 1843-55 (see St. Margaret's, Lee), whilst Lewin Tugwell followed from 1865-79 and his name appears on two tablets outside the west door.

Regarding the early parishioners, John Rogers a writer was born at Messing, Essex and as a Puritan lectured at St. Thomas Apostle and also preached in Dublin, but opposed Cromwell and a burial of July 1670 may be him. There are many entries to Joseph Addis and son Benjamin weavers and grandson Thomas cordwainer, near Bermondsey Square from the 1700s, their descendants becoming noted toolmakers in Deptford.

In addition the parish had a number of notables in Victorian times. Alfred Marshall was born there, but grew up in Clapham, and attended the Merchant Taylors and St. John's, Cambridge. He was a leading economist and his seminal work *Principles of Economics* in 1881 was the leading textbook on supply, demand, capital and labour for many years. His residence Balliol Croft later became part of Lucy Cavendish College.

Joseph Watson was the nephew of Thomas Braidwood who established the first school for the deaf in Edinburgh in 1760. He joined the staff when it came to Hackney in 1783 and was headmaster of the Asylum for the Deaf and Dumb, Surrey Square, in 1792. This moved to a larger site on Townsend Street, Kent Road in 1809 and Watson wrote a book, part of the controversy around oral teaching, which formed a guide for many years. He has a memorial on the north chancel wall stating "he worked there for 37 years."

Other tablets nearby are to Henry Gaitskell of the Paragon, O.K.R. and Abbey Road, St. John's Wood; his brother Thomas Gaitskell Esq. a deputy lieutenant for Surrey; and William Nottidge merchant of the staple of Wandsworth, treasurer of the deaf asylum and of Bacon's Free Grammar School, and a member of several public bodies. [1]

C. 7 September 1842 Alfred s. of William & Rebecca Marshall, Long Lane clerk J.E.G.

B. 1 Dec 1829 Joseph Watson of St George Southwark, 64
12 March 1836 Henry Gaitskell of St. Mary le Bowe, 68
21 September 1839 Thomas Gaitskell of Streatham, 81
23 March 1853 William Nottidge of Wandsworth, 85   (all by John E. Gibson)

---

[1] Josiah Bacon a leather merchant was born in the parish and left a legacy to start a school for poor children in 1703. This taught English and arithmetic to prepare them for a trade and was in Grange Road near the church in the 1860s, but is now a college at Rotherhithe. There is also a memorial on the south side to Edward William Wilson head of the school for 25 years.

St. James's, Bermondsey

A workhouse was established in 1710, later situated on Russell Street, whilst a *Bishop's Visitation* revealed that Bermondsey parish already had 9,000 people in 1724. Areas along the river and around the abbey once occupied by merchants became tenements, and new housing was built on former country lanes, with Abbey Street and Spa Road laid out in 1825-30. However environs to the south by Blue Anchor Lane still had market gardens reaching to the parish boundary - the latter delineated by Lynton Road.

Land for a new church was purchased in the fields just below Bermondsey Lower Road in 1821 and the chairman of the committee was William Nottidge a wool stapler. James Savage had considerable success with his Gothic masterpiece St. Luke's, Chelsea, but was a strange choice to design the new church at Bermondsey. This was strictly Classical and included a taste of the Baroque interspersed from the time of Wren.

There was some delay in starting, but eventually sufficient funds were raised from a loan, the Commissioners, and local parishioners to pay the bill of £21,412 - thus building went ahead in February 1827. This was to be a substantial church and the nave was in the style of a Greek temple, although had galleries on three sides and an organ at the west end. The result was seating for 2,000 people - with over half the pews rent free.

Bishop Sumner of Winchester consecrated the grand edifice on 7 May 1829; however the spire based on St. Stephen's Walbrook cost an extra £2,300. As a result a further loan had to be raised from Parliament in 1831. Indeed, in true Wren tradition a lack of funds delayed the final completion and all the debts were only paid off in 1840.

Despite this the outcome was a stunning landmark among the fields as observed from both land and water. In fact, later generations travelling to London Bridge by train could not fail to observe it. The nave was generally plain, but the façade had a portico of four Ionic columns, pediment and temple doors; whilst the three-stage tower sat on a roof plinth above, challenging the notion that "spire and temple" do not mix.

St. James's provided a testament to faith of those in the parish who wanted a church for the growing populace, but also to the architect who had proved himself in both the Classical and Gothic arenas to great merit. However, its aspect was altered by St. James's Road to the east and the railway to the south, leaving just a glimpse of the façade through the unimaginative West Street North.

St. James's spire was based on St. Stephen's, Walbrook.

Often referred to as *Bermondsey New Church* it is the sole survivor from the days when Grange Court and Jamaica House graced the area. Its main features include a cast of ten bells from Mears of Whitechapel, a four-faced clock in the tower at £160, an organ by J.C. Bishop of 1829 (restored in 1879), silver communion vessels and clock in the west gallery from the original committee, and a font given by Samuel H. Sterry in 1841.

Regarding the interior there is a shallow-arched sanctuary, low galleries supported on piers, Ionic columns leading up to the clerestory windows and a flat ceiling with square recesses above. The aisles were later converted and include a local doctor's surgery, while a distinctive wooden slide that stood outside for many years was removed in the 1970s. Today the church is unchanged, but some modern flats on Old Jamaica Road with little relation to the past provide a striking frame to the former (as no doubt intended).

St. John's was similar to St. Luke's, Old Street, but was replaced by the L.C.M. on its Grade II listed plinth.

St. John's, Horsleydown

The original St. Olave's parish reached to the inlet of St. Saviour's Dock at a time when Tower Bridge was just a figment of an architect's imagination. As the grazing land was developed a new parish was formed beyond Bermondsey Street, incorporating the manor of Horsleydown and was dedicated to St. John after the nearby Templars Hospital. This took place in about 1640 but it was some years before a proper church was built.

At the time Benjamin Keach operated a celebrated Baptist meeting house at Goat Yard from 1668-1704 and introduced their first hymns. It moved to Carter Lane in 1757 and New Park Street in 1830, making it the forerunner of Spurgeon's Tabernacle.

The school governors erected the Artillery Hall for the militia by St. Olave's or Tooley Street (a corruption) in 1639, and to the east were Free School Street named after the school and Fair Street. However, Southwark Fair was generally held on St. Margaret's Hill in Borough High Street. The hall was used for elections and a burial ground was laid out beside the martial ground, with a 500-year lease, in 1665. Thomas Guy (1645-1724) "who built and endowed a hospital" lived just to the east in Pritchard's Alley.

After a severe delay the parish approached the Commission for Fifty Churches and a part of the martial ground was set aside for a parsonage by 1718. Likewise the Artillery Hall was converted into a workhouse in 1725 (as seen in the picture opposite).

Designs for a substantial church were put forward by Nicholas Hawksmoor and John James, who were thus employed to build one of the last Commissioners' schemes from 1727-33. By that time the main dictate was a low price, but the broken pediment and tall obelisk clearly had the stamp of Hawksmoor's more extravagant creations. In particular it was similar to St. Luke's at Old Street as well as his churches in the East End.

During the 19th century the population reached some 10,000 and the church, with its narrow nave and corner wings, sat beyond a labyrinth of alleyways. These disappeared under the station approaches as if into caverns. St. Olave's School was to the north from 1855-1967 and the district then became a civil association. The *Illustrated London News* complimented the church "recreation ground" as one of the largest in July 1882.

Other developments saw the area transformed with the building of Tower Bridge and its approaches from 1886-92. Sir Horace Jones, one of the judges, was employed by the City and worked with Sir John Wolfe Barry (son of Charles) who was the chief engineer. In addition the Bermondsey Union covered most of the area from 1904.

However, the church which was close to Docklands was badly damaged in the blitz in 1940 and a scheme was prepared to rebuild it in 1956. For the next four years baptisms were carried out there, but any lifeline was eventually rescinded and it closed in 1968 and was demolished soon after. The London City Mission acquired the site from the Church Commissioners for £37,811 on 26 November 1971 and opened Nasmith House in 1975. This now sits on the original foundations and plinth which are grade II listed. [2]

The Jowetts - This family came second only to Thornton and Venn in the missionary world, and Henry Jowett (1685-1747) a yeoman had land at Bradford, then came to East Smithfield with his wife Elizabeth and both were buried at St. Botolph's, Aldgate.

Their son Henry (1719-1801) was a skinner at Cow Lane, West Smithfield and had eight offspring with his wife Sarah, baptized at St. Sepulchre's, in 1744-56. He returned to Leeds in 1757 and his children attended school there, whilst son John married Betty Bankes and removed to Newington in 1771. The latter was a founder of the C.M.S. and his brothers were: Henry minister of Little Dunham after John Venn in 1792-1830, and Joseph tutor at Cambridge who originated the chimes of Great St. Mary's used for Big Ben.

William Jowett son of John had the most significant role and was their first missionary to Malta and the Holy Land in 1813. His sister Elizabeth married Josiah Pratt who was secretary at Salisbury Square in 1802-23 and William held this post in 1832-41, also being a lecturer at Holy Trinity, Clapham and minister of nearby St. John's. Benjamin a cousin and furrier married at Camberwell and his son Benjamin is discussed later.

C. 24 October 1787 Willm s. of John & Betty Jowett skinner New Berm. b. 23 Sept

B. 28 February 1800 John Jowett from Newington age 55 years
18 June 1835 Betty Jowett from Finsbury age 87 [residence of Josiah Pratt]

---

[2] The L.C.M. was started by David Nasmith at Hoxton in 1835 and they also began charities such as the Ragged Schools. James Braidwood of Edinburgh a fire chief arranged for his members to see their missionaries, but died at Tooley Street in June 1861 (see St. Mary Aldermary Vol. I).

St. Mary's, Rotherhithe

On John Rocque's map the street in front of the church is described as Rotherhithe or Redriff, the latter being an archaic corruption in a district with many sailors. For much of its history the main settlement was centred upon the church with ribbon development, warehouses, and wharves by the river. The bulk of the parish from Jamaica Level (Southwark Park Road) across to what was later South Dock remained as fields.

The manor stayed in the hands of Bermondsey Abbey until the Dissolution, and several records exist of great breaches in the embankments which flooded the low-lying parish. In addition Edward III built a moated manor-house west of the church in 1370, and this became known as "King John's House" with its hall, courtyard, stables and orchards. It was later a pottery and farm then covered by warehouses, and the walls are now visible at the junction of Bermondsey Wall and Cathay Street - by the King's Stairs.

Regarding the church, a building was present from late Saxon times although Roman bricks were also found on the site. Like others it was replaced by a Norman edifice in the 12th century, and at the Dissolution vestments were sold off to help pay for its repair. In fact the building often became flooded, rotting its foundations, and the parishioners were in great danger from it falling down during divine service!

Thomas Gatacre arrived there as rector in 1611. In his *Discours Apologetical* he noted that the main residence was completely neglected by the late incumbent, and its wharf was falling down. As a result he replaced the thatched-roof with tiling, and doubled the size of the property to include a library. Later, he added rooms for scribes and students who came there from university to prepare themselves for the ministry.

Repairs were carried out and new pews fitted in 1687; but the mediaeval building was rather small, and the area had much poverty due to so many seafaring families. Such a fact was witnessed by the various memorials including: Richard Hills 1614 a mariner of Trinity House and benefactor, Capt. Anthony Wood 1625 (see below), Roger Tweedy Esq. 1655 who left money for poor seamen - and several other naval men.

Not surprisingly the parish applied to pull the decaying structure down in 1710. It was rebuilt by John James, architect and associate of Wren, at a cost of £4,361 in 1714-15. The design included a rectangular nave with two tiers of windows, the upper ones being round-headed with a top stone, and a tower of distinct red brick with white quoins and balustrade. Although due to a lack of funds its open cupola-drum and pinnacle were only completed by Lancelot Dowbiggin (architect of St. Mary's, Islington) in 1747.

The interior repeatedly echoes its maritime associations and four Ionic pillars in the nave, with golden capitals, support a barrel roof with thin plaster-shell. Underneath is a wooden frame and massive beams, which bear all the hallmarks of a skilled shipwright. A small chancel at the east end behind a curved arch repeats the styling of the nave roof, whereas the delicate reredos includes work by Grinling Gibbons.

At the west end is the vestibule and gallery, its crowning glory an organ designed by John Byfield in 1764 which despite additions is basically as he built it. In the Epiphany Chapel there stands a communion table made from the timbers of the *Fighting Temeraire*, immortalised by Turner when it was broken up in 1838. A few parts of the old building survive in the crypt; while the wood-panelling records how it was rebuilt under Rev. Lovell in 1715, then re-seated and restored under Rev. E.J. Beck in 1876.

The church is a hidden gem sequestered among its narrow lanes of antiquity with the rectory, watch-house (1821), and free school (started 1613, combined 1797) nearby. But despite these improvements the population soon outstripped the church and three were added in 1838-40: Christchurch below Paradise Street by Lewis Vulliamy, All Saints on Lower Road, and Holy Trinity east of the docks - the latter two by S. Kempthorne.

In addition, the Great Wet Dock (or Greenland) was dug out above Deptford back in 1696, and was owned by the South Sea Company; the Surrey Canal and its basin were added in 1807; and then other docks until 1870. Nearby was the Thames Tunnel built by Marc Brunel in 1825-42 and sold to the East London Railway in 1865 (part is now a museum), and Southwark Park which was laid out on market gardens in 1864.

Other changes occurred when the Rotherhithe Tunnel was built in 1908 and St. Olav's Norwegian church was constructed on Albion Street in 1927 - with those of Finland and Sweden coming later. By the early 1980s the area was run down, but changed when the docks were filled in and new housing was built. This left remnants at Canada Water and Surrey (Canal) Basin linked by a channel - plus two surviving docks to the south.

"Old Salts of Rotherhithe"

The church is a major landmark when sailing down the river and it was from here that *The Mayflower* departed to collect the Pilgrim Fathers at Southampton in July 1620. Capt. Jones was first in Harwich but was registered at London in 1611, and was master of the ship from that time. His second in command John Clarke was baptized in the parish and Richard Gardner and John Moore the part-owners resided there, whilst there were a few false starts and she finally sailed from Plymouth in the September.

Of the marriages Matthew Boulton was sole owner of a family business in Birmingham by 1759, and came there the next year. His bride was the sister of his deceased wife and such a union could be voided if anyone objected to the banns, hence the location. Two years later he started the Soho Works, Handsworth and there formed the Lunar Society with Erasmus Darwin, John Whitehurst, Josiah Wedgwood, Joseph Priestley and others. But, it was with his partner James Watt, that he produced the first steam engines.

St. Mary's, Rotherhithe with anniversary plaque, organ dated 1764 and barrel vaulted nave.

THE MAYFLOWER
Christopher Jones, Master and part owner was buried in this churchyard, 5th March 1622
This Tablet was erected on the occasion of the 250th Anniversary of the Consecration of this Church

Another interesting character was Prince Lee Boo son of the ruler of the Pelew Islands who aided the crew of *The Antelope* when it was shipwrecked in 1783. Captain Wilson of Rotherhithe was master and brought the prince back to live with him at Paradise Row, and he became a celebrity but died of smallpox five months later. *The Interesting History of Prince Lee Boo* was published by George Keate in 1788 and was a best-seller until 1850. As a result the Secretary of State for India erected a grand memorial tablet on the north side of the church to commemorate such events in 1892.

The manor passed down to Robert, Earl of Salisbury and then to Philip Goldsworthy an equerry to George III in 1777. He left it to his sister Martha governess to the princess in 1801 and she in turn bequeathed it to her companion Miss Gomm in 1816. In this way it came to William Maynard Gomm six years later, and he rose up to be Commander of Jamaica in 1839-42 and Governor of Mauritius in 1850-55 (died 1875).

During his ownership much of the land was sold to the Surrey Commercial Docks and it went to his niece Emily Carr who took the name Gomm; and then to her son Hubert William Carr-Gomm M.P. for Rotherhithe in 1909 who restored the tower in 1913. On the church wall there is tablet recording this fact and also a blue plaque to the "Sailing of the Mayflower" which was erected on Thanksgiving Day in 2004.

C. XXVI of March 1574 John Clarke was baptized

M. 25 June 1760 Matthew Boulton and Ann Robinson b.o.t.p. banns by me James Penfold curate presence Mary Boulton, Stephen Ogee

B. 5 March 1621/22 Christopher Jones
29 Dec 1784 Prince Lee Boo from Capt. Williams [sic], Paradise Row

Capt. Wood memorial

Camberwell

This parish below Bermondsey and Southwark across to the border with Kent covered a large area from the village itself down to Herne Hill and Crystal Palace. It then continued along Sydenham Hill over to Nunhead and back above the Old Kent Road to Albany Road. The church was in the west of the parish and the main hamlets included Peckham with its "New Town" and Dulwich in the countryside to the south.

The original settlement was separated from London by fields, and its derivation may be from a spring on Denmark Hill. A fair was held on the green at the feast of St. Giles from 1279-1855 and it remained a rural village until the 19th century, whilst there were a number of manors in the district viz. Buckingham, Friern, Uvedale and others.

Having a pleasant location away from the less wholesome air of London, several large houses were built, and John Scott then Edmund Bowyer held *Camberwell and Peckham* once home to the Duke of Buckingham from 1583. On the west side of the main road was Bowyer House with the manor of *Camberwell Buckingham*, which was demolished for the railway and station in 1861 and replaced by Friern then Wyndham Road.

Claude de Crespigny a Huguenot built Champion Lodge at the foot of Denmark Hill in 1717, and ninety years later the Prince of Wales visited this family home; but it was covered by the houses of Champion and De Crespigny Parks in the 1860s. Just beyond was Grove Lane which had several fine properties; and Dr. John C. Lettsom son of a planter (b. 1744) a Quaker physician lived at "Grove Hill" a large and elegant villa. Other residents included George Tierney M.P. for Southwark (1802) and friend of Fox who was satirised as "the friend of humanity" by Gilray; and Thomas Hood the poet and humorist who resided at 8 South Place, 181 Camberwell New Road, in 1840.

There was a proliferation of grammar schools nearby and Rev. Edward Wilson the vicar started a free school under James I in 1615. But this declined into a poor financial state and closed in 1845, being superseded by Denmark Hill Grammar - a large building in fine grounds founded by Joseph Payne in 1838. Despite such ample provision, a Council of Queen Victoria re-instated Wilson's on Church Street in 1883, and it combined with the ancient Green Coat School in 1958, then removed to Carshalton in 1975.

Meanwhile, the fair was a major attraction but it caused much rowdiness and there were attempts to close it from the 1820s. This finally took place in 1855 when the manorial rights were purchased and the green was enclosed. Other entertainments remained such as the Camberwell/Flora Tea Gardens, medicinal springs, and several music halls.

However, the area was changing rapidly and the Grand Surrey Canal reached a terminus beside Addington Square in 1810, and a branch to Peckham was completed by 1826. The scheme originally involved a route to Mitcham but the cost of locks was prohibitive, thus the idea was abandoned and they concentrated on the far more profitable docks instead. This fact was borne out when Croydon Canal, built at the same time, closed in 1836 and was sold to the railway for £40,250. Indeed, the population rose from 7,059 in 1801 to a staggering 111,306 in 1871 resulting in many new churches in the vicinity:

Christchurch, Old Kent Road - This was built at the end of Church Street by the canal in 1838. But due to new gasworks was replaced with a design by E.B. Keeling south of the main road in 1868. Nearby was Old Kent Road Station which closed in 1917.

Emmanuel, Camberwell Rd. was designed by Thomas Bellamy in 1842 probably due to the fire at St. Giles. It had twin-towers at the east end, north and south porches, and yellow brick with white stone at the entrance-ways - but was demolished in 1968.

St. Chrysostom, Hill Street was a chapel in Peckham from 1813 and a parish in 1864. It had an impressive façade with turrets but was demolished in 1963 and relocated to the site of St. Jude's. Nearby was St. Luke's rebuilt by Romilly Craze after the war.

St. Mary Magdalene, Nunhead - This was built in 12th-century style in a square below Queen's Road by local architect R.P. Browne in 1840. It was near to the cemetery built at that time and initially amongst fields, but was lost in the war and rebuilt in 1962.

St. Matthew's, Denmark Hill - A proprietary chapel existed here from 1793 but this was taken over and a new building erected nearby, inside the Lambeth district, in 1848. It had a tower in the 14th century style but was destroyed in 1940.

St. John's, East Dulwich was built on Goose Green in the Gothic style in 1865, an area which up until then was simply fields.

Surrey Canal - A lime kiln in Burgess Park once by the canal, but more likely seen by the rias of Devon than in Camberwell.

A postcard dated 1907.

Marlborough Chapel (left) was built on the Old Kent Road above the canal with fields behind in 1827 and had a large congregation. **Christchurch** a short distance to the east was relocated to accommodate the new gas works in 1868.

Camberwell Green (Congregational) constructed in 1780 was one of a proliferation of independent chapels in the area followed by Albany Road (1830), New Road (1853) and Loughborough Park (1860). It was given an impressive mid-19th century Gothic façade but was demolished for road improvements, *which never took place*, in 1966.

The Camden Chapel in Peckham Road was opened by some unhappy parishioners as an independent chapel in 1797, but converted to the Episcopal faith in 1829. Rev. Henry Melvill reputedly "the most popular preacher in London" was minister from 1829-43, and spoke so quickly that he covered as much as others did in twice the time!

A north transept was added to accommodate his large congregations and he was then a lecturer at St. Margaret Lothbury, chaplain at Haileybury E.I.C., chaplain to the Queen, rector of Barnes (1863-71), and a canon of St. Paul's where he was buried. It was built in the Renaissance style with a parapet at the main entrance and remained until c.1937.

Grove Chapel (Independent) was located west of Camberwell Grove and designed by David R. Roper in late Georgian style in 1819. It had a plain front with three doorways, round-headed windows and the main nave behind, plus galleries on slim iron columns. In fact it was barely distinguishable from the classical houses built nearby.

The first minister Rev. Joseph Irons was a popular preacher until his death in 1852 and his son William Josiah was at St. Mary's Newington, St Peter's Walworth and St Mary Woolnoth. Rev. Thomas Bradbury (1831-1905) a wool-carder in Manchester was minister for 31 years and lived near the church at 4 Love Walk, 12 De Crespigny Terrace and 178 Camberwell Grove. He was buried at Forest Hill but has a memorial at the church with a prayer of thanks he wrote, whilst his daughter Polly published his life and letters:

"All fullness dwells in Thee, Lord, Thy rich and glorious Grace; Thou hast bestowed on me Lord, A sinner vile and base. All fullness of affection, Thou hast so sweetly shown, for sovereign free election, has made me Thine alone."

Asylum Road (Congregational) - The Old Kent Road despite being a main route into Kent had a shortage of Anglican churches, but the void was filled by dissenting chapels. This was founded below the Licensed Victuallers Asylum in 1852 and was renamed as the Clifton Chapel. Regarding this Aaron Buzacott senior entered Hoxton Academy in 1820 and attended Whitefield's chapels at Moorfields and Tottenham Court Road, then joined the L.M.S. (non-denominational) and sailed for Tahiti and Rarotonga in 1827.

With his wife he spent most of his life there and was a colleague of John Williams while their son Aaron Buzacott junior was born at Tahiti in 1829. The latter became secretary of the Anti-Slavery Society and was minister of the church during the 1860s. [3]

Marlborough Chapel (Congregational) sat on Marlborough Place, which was named for a mansion near the site, once a home to the family of the Duke of Marlborough. It was established just west of Christchurch in 1827, in an area euphemistically known as Peckham New Town centred in the vicinity of the canal bridge.

Thomas Wilson (1764-1843) who funded many chapels in the city laid the foundation, and was also the treasurer of Hoxton Academy and Highbury College, a director of the London Missionary Society, and a founder of University College. Rev. Thomas Hughes was appointed the first minister and soon paid off all the loans, thus he utilised a surplus to establish the British School between Oakley Place and Trafalgar Road.

Henry Richards who attended Highbury College followed as second pastor in 1835, but resigned to become secretary of the Peace Society in 1850 - an organisation created just after the Battle of Waterloo. He was a leading nonconformist in Parliament as Liberal M.P. for Merthyr and was chairman of the Congregational Union in 1877. The church was destroyed in the war but continued in other premises until 1982.

St. George's, Wells Way

Regarding its original setting this church suffered one of the greatest transformations in London, since it was initially in fields by an attractive canal with some windmills nearby. However, within a few decades the area was overrun with a maze of streets and terraced houses, leaving the building a sole reminder of its more gentrified past.

The architect was Francis O. Bedford who produced another Waterloo Church straight from the pages of *The Standard Guidebook for Classical Design in the Victorian era*. The foundation was laid on 23 April 1822 and it was then consecrated by George P. Tomline, the Bishop of Winchester, on 24 March 1824.

As with those at Waterloo Road and West Norwood there was a plain rectangular nave and many other similar features: A grand portico of six Doric columns, entranceway with five doors and matching windows above, entablature with myrtle wreaths, monumental pediment, and to finish off a two stage 'open' square tower sitting on a solid base.

---

[3] John Thomas Pocock (1814-76) was an affluent pharmacist at Rondebosch, Cape Town and married Grace Vernon Buzacott sister of the missionary in 1841. Their nephew Aaron lived at Lime Villas, Harder's Road, Peckham and she died nearby during a visit in November 1868. Pocock then married Parthenia Martin at the Congregational Chapel in Maple Road, Surbiton who was an assistant from his wife's school in Cape Town (see Deptford).

St. George's, Wells Way

Built in 1822-24, it was once by a canal with long boats sailing past creating shades of Amsterdam and Venice. But the modern building survives as flats.

The tower was quite similar to his other designs whilst the interior was very plain with a flat, panelled ceiling and galleries supported on Doric columns. The only ornamentation present involved some pilasters situated between the windows.

For many years the church remained by the canal-side surrounded by market gardens, but the Camberwell Bridge was built to the front in 1862 and, as stated, the area became urbanised with industry nearby. However, it was found to be structurally unsafe in 1970 and the congregation met in a school before moving to new premises in 1982.

In the meantime it was used by the Celestial Church of Christ but after a fire which left just the walls standing, it was transferred to the G.L.C in 1984. Ten years later it was sold to developers who converted it into thirty flats - part of a Housing Co-operative. Matters then went full circle as the canal was filled-in and derelict properties were removed to create Burgess Park. As a result the church once again sits in leafy surrounds.

St. Giles, Camberwell

Stow began his discourse on the area by stating, "Where the ancient worshipful families of Scott and Bowyer now (or lately) inhabited, with divers other fair seats; it taketh in Peckham and Dulwich, famed for its purging waters, and the College."

Regarding the church it is thought to have been present from the mid-7th century or sixty years after the arrival of Augustine, while the Domesday Book recorded the district in some detail. A new edifice was built by William FitzRobert, Earl of Gloucester lord of the manor in 1152, at which time it passed to St. Saviour's Priory, Bermondsey. It was then reconstructed early in Henry VIII's reign - either, altered so greatly that the previous structure was literally erased, or, completely rebuilt on the same site. [4]

Generally the church was developed in a piecemeal fashion over the centuries and was a large edifice with Lady Chapel, painted windows and several monuments. In the chancel

---

[4] Daniel Lyson who wrote *Environs of London* and *Magna Britannia* recorded its longevity, while Mr. Blanch who laid foundations in the 1840s said two mediaeval churches were present.

was a brass to John Scot Esq. 1532 baron of the escheker, brass plate to John Bowyer Esq. 1570 and Elizabeth daughter of Robert Draper, a memorial to Dame Anne wife of Sir Robert Vernon clerk of the green cloth 1629, and to Sir Edmund Bowyer 1681 and his wife Dame Hester. In the south aisle was an effigy and brass to Edward Scot 1537 and family, and outside one to Rev. Richard Parr D.D. vicar for 38 years d.1691.

According to the vestry minutes the building was usually *under repair* and £130 was spent on pews, windows, bells, a clock, prayer books and surplues from 1675-79. Other work included a new gallery in 1688, a pavement and three further galleries in 1708, some beautification during the 1790s, and an enlargement of the building in 1825.

However, all this mighty effort was eventually in vain! The great cluster of columns with their pointed arches, the sedilia in the south chancel concealed by Bowyer's wainscoting of 1715, the ancient stained glass, the box pews lodged in the rambling nave and side aisles, were all consumed in a terrible conflagration on 7 February 1841.

George Gilbert Scott then won a competition ahead of fifty applicants and created his first major Gothic building, the foundation being laid in September 1842. Working with partner W.B. Moffatt he produced a cruciform design in the *Early English* and *Decorated* styles of the 13th century. The total cost was eventually £24,000 and Charles Sumner, Bishop of Winchester, consecrated the building on 21 November 1844.

The main features were the nave in Kentish rag and Caen stone dressing, clerestory and transepts, soaring steeple at 240 feet, and peal of bells by Mears & Co. of Whitechapel all in a large churchyard. The scene was only spoilt by the chancel which sat at a lower level as if a kind of afterthought, rather like at St. Saviour's. However, much effort was expended and John Ruskin visited Chartres and other French cathedrals to find some inspiration for the east window, which he created with Edmund Oldfield. Likewise, the generous organ by J.C. Bishop was designed by Samuel Sebastian Wesley the organist and grandson of Charles the hymn-writer.

During the reconstruction a small outhouse was erected in the gardens of the vicarage opposite, to shelter the 14th century sedilia and piscina. This was a poor set-up, since it was open at the front, and they were moved to the south chancel by William Isaac Shard in December 1916 - in memory of his ancestors buried there. The outhouse went to the Church Hall in Benhill Road and has a plaque recording these events.

Thomas Savery (1650-1715) was partner to Newcomen and generated considerable steam.

St. Giles and architect **George G. Scott** whose grandson Giles worked nearby.

One link to the parish was Thomas Savery born at Modbury, Devon in 1650. As a mine owner and military engineer he invented a patented vacuum steam-pump, worked with Newcomen and created a capstan favoured by William III in 1696. He lived at Salisbury Court marrying at St. Bride's and died at Marsham Street, Westminster.

Regarding the residents, Benjamin Jowett attended St. Paul's and Balliol, Oxford and as tutor to Swinburne *criticised* his Latin translations, then worked on educational reform. He was Chair of Greek from 1855 editing Plato but treated *The Bible* as a classic and as a college preacher met Browning, Tennyson, Stanley (Dean of Westminster), Nightingale and George Eliot. He was master of Balliol and vice chancellor from 1882-86.

Clement le Neve Foster, son of the secretary of the Society of Arts, attended the Royal School of Mines and studied erosion of the Weald for the Geological Survey in 1860-65. He then worked in the mining industry and was a fellow of the Royal Society.

C. 16 May 1817 Benjamin s. Benj. and Isabella Jowett of Peckham furrier Robt. Roe
12 July 1837 George Robert s. George Ure and Charlotte Clementina Adam, 9 Grove Lane merchant by H.W.C. Hyde curate "born at sea" 30 May (see St. Barnabas)
21 April 1841 Clement le Neve s. Peter le Neve and Georgiana Elizabeth Foster of Champion Grove barrister born 23 March by H.W.C. Hyde curate

M. 22 September 1814 Benjamin Jowett jun o.t.p. and Isabella Langhorn lic by Robt. P. Crane A.M. cur. wit. Benj Jowett sen., Hy Jowett, J.H. Courthope, Josiah Jowett [5]

B. 22 May 1715 Mr. Tho: Savory buryed
13 Oct 1781 Mary Wesley buried [the wife of Rev. John]

St. Saviour's, Ruskin Park

The west side of Denmark Hill came within Lambeth and a temporary structure was built north of Coldharbour Lane in 1864. A site on the corner of Flaxman Road was offered by the Commissioners but the design was rejected, and James Lewis Minet provided an acre in Herne Hill Road with £50 towards costs which was accepted. The Commission added £500 and Millicent wife of W.H. Stone M.P. laid the foundation in June 1866.

A.D. Gough designed the church in the Norman style of Bath stone with four bays, double transepts, an apse, tower and pinnacles to seat 850 plus a school, and the Bishop of Winchester consecrated it a year later. The chancel and south transept were added by W.G. Bartleet in 1870 the architect of St. George's, Beckenham, but it was demolished in 1981. The parish became part of St. Paul's, Herne Hill (1845) which itself was rebuilt by George Edmund Street in 1858 and displays a tablet to John Ruskin.

Local residents included Sir Henry Bessemer who resided in "Bessemer House" a large mansion with lake on Denmark Hill from 1863-98. It was previously part of the Dulwich College Estate and Charles Barry jun., estate surveyor, extended the house and added an observatory. John Ruskin (1819-1900) artist, critic, and visionary came to 28 Herne Hill with his family in 1824, and attended Beresford Independent Chapel (1826-1923) "a barn with galleries on iron pipes" - the site is now on John Ruskin Street, Walworth.

---

[5] Isabella was a relative of Rev. John Langhorne the poet who translated *Plutarch's Lives*; whilst *Cambridge Alumni* later recorded her husband as a printer of Bolt Court, Fleet Street.

He then lived at 163 Denmark Hill from 1842 and married Effie Gray in 1848, but this was annulled and she then remarried John Everett Millais once his protégé. However the arrival of the nearby railway and urbanization of the area *spoilt his view and peace*, thus he departed in 1872 and spent the rest of his life at Brantwood by Lake Coniston.

Perhaps he should have consulted with Sir Ebenezer Howard who was born at 62 Fore Street by Moorgate on 29 January 1850 (plaque). His father was a confectioner but as a clerk he learnt shorthand, and became private secretary to Dr. Joseph Parker who was a renowned Congregational preacher at City Temple, Holborn. After a change of direction he tried farming in Nebraska, but when this failed he was a law stenographer in Chicago and after a disastrous fire witnessed the city's rebuilding with extensive parks.

Returning to Britain in 1876 he was a writer for parliamentary reporters working in the law courts and lived at Dulwich, Stoke Newington and Stamford Hill. He also invented a typewriter device and joined a debating group with Bernard Shaw and Sidney Webb. But most significantly he was inspired by the concepts of Edward G. Wakefield and Edward Bellamy's *Looking Backward*, then wrote the reforming *Garden Cities of Tomorrow* (1898) and formed an association with conferences at Bournville and Port Sunlight.

Indeed, a site at Letchworth was purchased in 1903-04 and he became a resident, then he was also involved in the development of Welwyn Garden City where he died in 1928. Today, he has memorials in both towns and a plaque at Welwyn records, "His vision and practical idealism profoundly affected town planning throughout the world."

M. 30 August 1879 Ebenezer Howard full bach shorthand writer of 44 Kemerton Road s. Ebenezer confectioner and Eliza Ann Bills spin of same d. Thomas gent by banns by Hamilton Smyth Cobb cur of St. Saviour wit Tamar Ann Howard, Willoughby Bills

St. Stephen's, Dulwich

In the 1860s the area below Dulwich Village had just a few villas and dairy farms, whilst the Penge Road rose up towards Dulwich Woods past a toll gate which is still present. At this time both a new railway and college were being built nearby, and Charles Barry jun. designed an edifice on the west side of the road beside a rise in the hill.

This was a church of considerable beauty decorated in the Victorian Gothic style with a slender spire and interior of arcades, open wooden roof and apsidal sanctuary. Soon after its completion in 1868, Sir Edward Poynter painted a *mediaeval style* fresco of St. Stephen for a recess in the south wall of the chancel. Indeed, its fame spread, and impressionist Camille Pissarro, who moved to Upper Norwood in the Franco-Prussian War, painted the church among the woods with the Crystal Palace just behind in 1870.

Lord Vestey owner of Kingswood House commissioned C.E. Kempe to design the east window in 1924. A bomb blast in the war then damaged the walls, but they were jacked back up and secured with tie-beams. St. Stephen's was restored on its centenary and today remains among the fields of the Dulwich Estate - its most impressive features being the sanctuary with panelled ceiling, and a new organ located at the west end.

M. 3 May 1881 Henry Bayard Rich 31 bach lieut RE of St. Giles Colchester s. F.H. Rich col RE to Ada Melvill Simons 21 spin of Tyersall, Sydenham Hill d. Henry M. merchant banns E.J. Selwyn rector of Pluckley, Kent wit H.M. Simons, F.H. Rich (see over)

Dulwich College Chapel

One might say that Dulwich owes its existence to Edward Alleyn and its College, or at least the level of importance to which it rose. Alleyn was born at Bishopsgate, son of an innkeeper, in 1566 and became an actor on the same level as Richard Burbage. He took the lead role in plays by Marlowe and during a tour headed the Admiral's Men, but like a latter day sportsman retired at the height of his career to enter management.

With his father-in-law Philip Henslowe he was involved in The Rose at Bankside and together they started The Fortune at Finsbury Fields for the Admiral's Men in 1600. In addition, Alleyn was appointed master of the King's games of baiting, and as a result had significant interests at Paris Garden including both brothels and bear-baiting.

However, he became aware of the temporal nature of things and the kind of life he led and purchased the Manor of Dulwich for £35,000 from Sir Francis Calton in 1605. After lengthy negotiations the entire estate passed into his hands in 1614, and reached from Denmark Hill in the north to Sydenham Hill in the south, thus the future of the area was determined. By this stage his projected *College of God's Gift* had been built in the small hamlet, although the letters patent were not approved until 21 June 1619.

College of   God's Gift

The Grammar School designed by Barry in 1842 - at the same time as Westminster.

Alleyn, despite his associations, was a churchwarden of St. Saviour's and a governor of its grammar school, then after moving to Dulwich endowed his college and almshouses with his manor. The college with its tower, porch and treasury had mostly fallen down by 1703 and only Christ's Chapel, a chaplain's house and south library remained. There was also a west wing of the almshouses dated 1667 and the east one was rebuilt in 1740. The chapel itself was used by the village folk and there was a churchyard nearby.

The family retained its connection with the school and provided masters; while James Allen came there as a teacher and left a bequest for "a reading school for poor children" in the village in 1746. A new aisle was added to the chapel in 1823, then Sir Charles Barry introduced the stucco perpendicular style in the 1830s with new dwellings, and after its status was questioned a grammar school for boys was built opposite in 1842. Barry was again the architect and at this point the girls of the reading school departed.

Further questions were asked and the foundation was re-organised in 1857 whereas the college-house and hall were enlarged. Rev. Alfred Carver the master established an upper school of a public nature, and the lower school was left for poorer students, whilst the adjacent almshouses received a rather incongruous tower and cloister in 1864.

The greatest changes occurred after the College Estates sold large areas of land to the London, Chatham & Dover Railway in 1863, and with the money Charles Barry junior built Dulwich College in 1866-70. The lower school remained in the village, but under the influence of William Rogers this became Alleyn's at Townley Road in 1882, and a third foundation James Allen's Girls School was located nearby from 1895.

Above the north door of the almshouses is a tablet commemorating the founding of the college. Other features are an organ by G. England 1759, communion plate with the Alleyn family name, and a modern statue located outside. Old Alleynians include C.F.A. Voysey (1872-73), Ernest Shackleton (1887-90) and C.S. Forester (1915-16).

Meanwhile, several large houses followed the foundation including Belair perhaps by Robert Adam in 1785, whereas Sir J. Soane built Dulwich Picture Gallery by the college to house the Bourgeois and Desenfans Collection in 1811-14. After the common was enclosed more houses were developed in the vicinity and residents included Frederick H. Rich R.E. inspector of railways at Woodlands, Dulwich Common, from 1861.

The property was named after his birthplace in Limerick and four of his sons including Henry attended the college; whilst Philip Gowan and wife Cecilia D'Olier from Ireland moved there in 1815 and a son George D'Olier Gowan stockbroker lived at Woodlawn. This connection is discussed under South Kensington. In addition, Charles Voysey was later a resident at Woodlawn and at Camden House in the High Street. [6]

C. 17 March 1824 Louisa Emily d. Phillip and Cecilia Gowan b. 18 February
11 June 1839 Phillip Hamilton s. George D'Olier and Sarah Clementina Gowan b. 9 May

B. 21 November 1626 Edward Alleyn Esq. founder of this church and college, 61

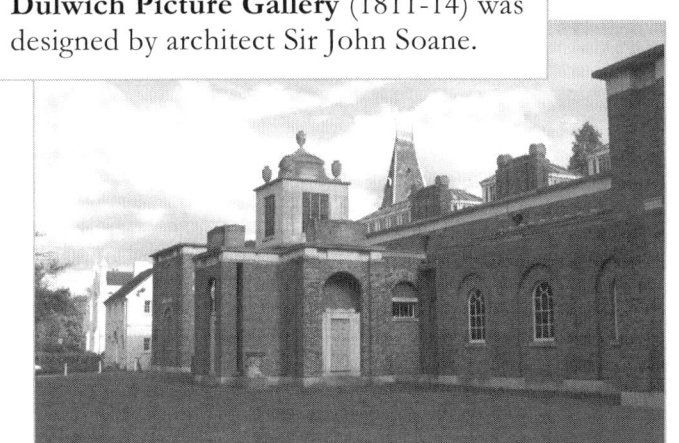

Dulwich Picture Gallery (1811-14) was designed by architect Sir John Soane.

Edward Alleyn (1566-1626) actor, theatre manager and school founder.

---

[6] Charles Voysey (1828-1912) descendant of a sister of Wesley was expelled from the Church in 1871 and founded the Theistic Church, Piccadilly. His son Charles F.A. Voysey (1857-1941) was an architect and designer who was influenced by the Arts and Crafts Movement.

Deptford

The River Ravensbourne emerged at Deptford Creek by a sweeping bend of the Thames, a geographical feature that would destine the future of the area for centuries. Originally the name referred to a *Deep Ford* in the locality of Broadway and Deptford Bridge on an ancient Celtic route-way, however a separate fishing village developed to the north and was denoted as Deptford Strond (Strand) or West Greenwich.

Regarding the early parish boundary this included an extensive area below the docks down to New Cross and Hatcham (with part in Surrey), across the rural spaces around Telegraph Hill, and back from Loampit Hill up the Ravensbourne. The manor came into the hands of Geoffrey de Saye in the 12th century and his family held it until 1383, thus the manor house on Broomfield was known by the name "Sayes Court."

The main developments were of a maritime nature and the village was by the river with a church green, three watergates to the west, and two routes to the south viz. Butt Lane and a road to Gravel Pitts. Much of the surrounding area was market gardens, but this changed after Henry VIII established the King's Yard in 1513 and it became a significant dockyard. The latter was rumoured to be the site of a monastery and it was here that Elizabeth I knighted Sir Francis Drake on the *Golden Hind* in April 1581. [7]

An area of meadow covering 250 acres was purchased for harbours and provisioning in 1656, and a Victualling Yard was built with quadrangle, warehouses and a rigging loft. It was the main Navy storehouse on 30 acres from 1742 including two wet docks, three slips, basins, smiths with 20 forges for anchors, mast houses, timber sheds, workshops and officers quarters. Deptford Ware was made there and the Royal Yacht was docked, whereas the number of artificers and labourers totalled over 1,300 men. [8]

One of the most significant institutions was Trinity House begun by Sir Thomas Spert Comptroller of the Navy to Henry VIII, after concerns about seafaring on the Thames, in 1514. This began as a chantry connected to the church and its charter specified, "The master, wardens and assistants of the guild or fraternity of the glorious and undivided Trinity and of St. Clement in the parish church of Deptford Stronde, Kent."

The society had a master, deputy, 31 elder brethren and other members including great Officers of State, Navy personnel and merchantmen. Its initial aim was the defence and pilotage of the Thames but this expanded to navigation, seamen, merchant ships, duties, lighthouses and maths exams at Christ's Hospital. Other premises were built at Stepney in 1618 but were too far out and they moved to Lower Thames Street in 1660, although came to Deptford for services on Trinity Monday. They moved to Tower Hill in 1796 and masters of the Corporation included Adm. Penn, Pepys and later Wellington.

---

[7] A number of prominent people came to the docks and Pepys was a frequent visitor as Clerk to the Navy, moving his belongings there during the fire. Ben Jonson in his comedy *Eastward Ho* mentioned the ship, which was later broken up and a chair made for Oxford University.

[8] The Dockyard was closed in 1869 and the Royal Victoria Victualling Yard gradually took over the site, which also housed a cattle market. This was closed in 1961 and became part of Pepys Estate whilst the main entrance gates on Grove Road were designed by Samuel Wyatt (in 1788). Some warehouses survive by the river and Convoys Wharf is on the site of the dockyard.

The ancient hall at Deptford where their meetings were held was pulled down just prior to this, but two almshouses or hospitals remained. One just east of the church dating to the formation was rebuilt with 25 apartments in 1788. The second in Church Street was on land donated by Sir Richard Browne of Sayes Court in 1672, and Capt. William Maples gave £1,300 to build 56 apartments on a square with his statue, chapel and hall in 1680. Single men received £18 and married men £28 per annum (demolished 1877).

Apart from such royal maritime links, the other main developments were regarding the manor at Sayes Court, located just north of Prince Street. The site was initially given by William I to Geoffrey de Saye in 1181 and he conveyed it to the Knights Templar, but his son recovered it in exchange for Saddlescombe, Sussex. The family lost it for a time when they took arms against King John and it then had several prominent owners.

Sir Richard Browne purchased much of the manor in the 1590s and was a supporter of the Earl of Leicester. As a result he was a privy councillor and clerk of the green cloth to Elizabeth I, then master of the household to James I. His grandson also Sir Richard was clerk to the council of Charles I and an ambassador to France from 1641-60.

John Evelyn (1620-1706) emanated from a rich family of Wotton, Surrey, who made their money in gunpowder and was educated at The Grange, Lewes and Balliol, Oxford. He then travelled in Europe and married Mary daughter of Sir Richard Browne jun. in Paris in 1647, and took out a lease on the house in 1651. He was a founder of the Royal Society and writer of books and diaries, whilst he developed gardens of great distinction there with a beautiful holly hedge and Pepys amongst others was a visitor.

A great flood occurred in 1671 carrying away much livestock and the family &c. retired to the Upper Town by boat, but the house survived and his father-in law died there in 1683. Sir John Evelyn retired to Wotton in the 1690s and Peter the Great was then his tenant for three months, when he came to study naval architecture and amused himself by riding around in a wheelbarrow! A statue above Stowage records this significant visit in 1698. The manor went to Francis, Earl of Godolphin in trust for the family, but the house was pulled down and replaced by a workhouse in 1728-29. The estate itself had passed over to the Crown by then and became part of the dockyards.

Local Churches and Chapels - Today the parish church of St. Nicholas is secluded by Deptford Green away from the noisy traffic of Creek Road, but this was a historic site of some antiquity originally serving the entire parish. The small lanes and alleyways of the Upper Town became inadequate to its inhabitants in the 18th century, and new houses were built to the south shifting the focus to Butt Lane (later the High Street).

The Commissioners built St. Paul's there with Church Street just behind in 1713-30 and at this point St. Nicholas was reduced to a small parish. As the area was developed other new churches followed including St James's, Hatcham by New Cross separated from St. Paul's in 1845, although the building was erected in 14th-century style in 1854. This was followed by St. John's on Lewisham Way and Loampit Hill a year later, which was beside the Stone House and served New Town one of the first Victorian developments.

At this stage Brockley was mostly rural and St. Peter's, Brockley was built in 1866-70, whilst St. Luke's on Deptford Lower Road (Evelyn Street) came in 1870-72. This had a tower and eastern apse and was paid for by William J. Evelyn of Wotton. In addition the Hatcham area was divided into All Saints, St. Katherine's and St Michael's.

The provision of these new Anglican churches began in the mid-19th century but there were a large number of dissenting chapels present from an early date. These included the Congregational in Butt Lane 1660, Baptist in Church Street 1679, Wesleyan in Loving Edwards Lane 1783 and Mary Ann's Buildings 1793, an Independent at New Cross 1805, Ebenezer Chapel King Street and Jireh Chapel Victory Street 1811, and Zion Baptist at New Cross Road 1841. Due to the large number of Irish workers in the docklands area the Catholic, Church of the Assumption was built on the High Street in 1844.

Regarding other developments the most significant was the first "city railway" and a line from Deptford to Spa Road opened on 8 February 1836. This was immediately extended to London Bridge and then to Greenwich in 1838, whilst two branch lines were added: one to St. John's, Catford and Lewisham and the other for the London & Brighton down to Croydon. As a result there were initially two stations called "New Cross."

In terms of education, John Addey shipbuilder founded a charity in 1606 resulting in a school in 1821, and Dean Stanhope the vicar established the Stanhope School in 1715. These combined on New Cross Road in 1894-99. The Royal Naval School a boarding school for sons of officers was built nearby on Lewisham Way by John Shaw jun. in 1844. It moved to Mottingham in 1889 (later Eltham College) and the site was taken over by the Goldsmiths Company who established an institute which still remains.

Sports and Pastimes - Deptford with its narrow streets and docks appeared to provide little opportunity for leisure, however both soccer and cricket came there. Reveley's plan to divert the Thames via the Isle of Dogs in 1796 almost scuppered proceedings, but workers at the Morton & Co. jam factory began Millwall Rovers on some waste ground beside Glengall Road in 1885. With the lion emblem and blue and white of their Scottish antecedents they had two temporary sites then went to East Ferry Road in 1890.

The enclosure was capable of holding 15,000 spectators and with the West India and Millwall Docks nearby - masts, sails, and rigging formed a nautical backdrop. Prominent teams such as Preston North End otherwise *The Invincibles* and Sunderland's *Team of All Talents* came to play there, whereas Millwall led the way in establishing a professional Southern League in 1894 and were champions during its first two seasons.

They also made two appearances in the F.A. Cup semi-final but the land reverted to the dock company and they moved to North Greenwich in 1901. However, they wanted to attract more support despite the arrival of a foot tunnel a year later, and moved to a site on Cold Blow Lane (once a farm of that name), near to New Cross, in 1910. Archibald Leitch who had worked on Fulham, Chelsea, Arsenal and Tottenham designed a basic ground amongst the numerous railway lines below the Surrey Canal, and the club joined the new Third Division (South) and the Football League in 1920.

Some success followed the best moments a Cup semi-final against Sunderland at Leeds Road, Huddersfield with 67,000 in 1937, and promotion to the First Division in 1987-88 with goals from leading striker Teddy Sheringham (later of Man United and England). At this time they were unique in being sponsored by Lewisham Council, who helped them relocate to the New Den among the railway lines of South Bermondsey in 1993. They also continued to progress and beat Sunderland to reach the Cup Final itself in 2004.

Regarding cricket there was even less opportunity to play the sport, except perhaps at Southwark Park or in the nearby parish of Greenwich. In this respect James Blyth came from a family of cordwainers in Edinburgh but joined the Royal Navy and after passing the relevant exams became a gunner in 1790. He saw action on the *Prince Edward* and *Dryad* then served under Captain Browell on the Royal yacht *Princess Augusta*, in particular when she brought Princess Caroline to Greenwich in April 1795.

Despite his age Blyth remained active, and whilst on service attended the Princes Street Independent Chapel, Devonport - the minister Rev. Andrew Kinsman being a coadjutor of Whitefield. He married Margaret Phillips at nearby Stoke Damerel under the existing legislation on 22 February 1797, and spent time at Portsmouth and Deptford, but retired to Chatham in 1813. The couple had children Margaret (1800) see below, James Turner (1801) who attended the Hospital School and was master of a convict ship to Tasmania, and Colin (1808) who went to the Naval Asylum and became a silk merchant.

Colin Blythe senior had warehouses at Gresham Street by the Guildhall and as a result lived in the first properties on Upper Brockley Road, while his brother-in-law was Samuel Joseph Addis the toolmaker. Of his family a son Edward Gibbon was an artist and his daughter married Edmund H. Niemann, but after a separation his youngest son Walter was an engineer at the Woolwich Arsenal. The latter had a large family of twelve children in 1879-1902 and the eldest Colin Blythe was a cricketer for Kent and England.

Blythe was born at 78 Evelyn Street on 30 May 1879 and baptized with his sister Jessie at St. Luke's, then attended Duke Street Schools and worked with his father at the Arsenal. He was discovered in the nets at Rectory Field, Blackheath (a Kent ground) in 1897 and was one of the finest slow bowlers of the era. After training at the Tonbridge Nursery he watched the records tumble and went on the first England tours of Australia and South Africa, his best bowling figures being 17 for 48 against Northampton.

Kent won four championships at this time and played Surrey at Rectory Field in 1906. On the first two days 10,000 spectators turned up and with the match balanced on the third morning 5,000 arrived early. Large numbers were then seen climbing Westcombe Hill, but on their arrival were shocked to find the game almost over due to the superior bowling of Blythe. Despite top batsmen Hayward and Hobbs he took 5 for 25 and they were all out for 80 - leaving Kent with a crucial victory by 164 runs.

Such statistics continued throughout his career and at the outset of war he joined the Kent Fortress Engineers in Chatham. His brother Sidney was killed on the Somme in 1916 and the next year he asked to be transferred, joining the K.O.Y.L.I., but died after a blast whilst laying rail tracks at Ypres, Belgium. Memorials were erected at Oxford Road Cemetery, in Tonbridge Church and at the St. Lawrence Ground, Canterbury.

St. Luke's, Deptford was built by the Evelyn family during 1870-72.

Colin Blythe (1879-1917) was baptized there on 30 January 1881 - his parents of 206 Evelyn Street.

St. Nicholas, Deptford

Stow described Deptford as "the first town in Kent" where many good ships were built and at a latter date it became a centre for provisioning. But in earlier times, Gilbert de Magminot held the manor from William I and had a castle near the site of Sayes Court. The widow of his grandson Wakelin gave the church itself to a convent in Brockley, and this was confirmed by his sister Alice the wife of Geoffrey de Saye.

The foundation then moved to Begham, Sussex and the church passed to the Knights Templar, but the Bishop of Rochester appropriated it in 1183 and it was transferred back to the abbot and convent. Being a smaller monastery, Begham was dissolved in 1526, and the advowson passed to Cardinal Wolsey for his colleges, but was held by the Crown in 1529-1648. It then devolved to various families including Wickham, Drake-Tyrwhitt and Windham - although the part of the parish in Surrey fell to the Bowyer family.

The old church with its chancel, nave and aisles was repaired and enlarged at the costs of the E.I.C. (who had premises in the dockyard) and Sir William Russell in 1630. Apart from Sayes Court, other residents were Sir Thomas Smith an ambassador to Russia for James I, Abraham Cowley the poet, and the Earl of Nottingham lord admiral.

Indeed, due to the upsurge in population and need for repairs, the church was pulled down except for the tower of flint and stone in 1697. Isaac Loader Esq. then contributed £900 to rebuild it on a far larger scale; however the job was done so badly a major repair was needed costing £400 in 1716. A fact recorded by a tablet on the external south wall. The work included an organ at the expense of Robert Castle, an altar piece with reredos by Grinling Gibbons at £293, and a new marble floor costing £161.

Regarding the vicars Samuel Page D.D. came in 1603 and published sermons and tracts and was buried there on 8 August 1630, while Thomas Mallory was appointed minister in 1644 but resigned to become lecturer at St. Michael's, Crooked Lane. He was ejected from there for nonconformity in 1662. Later ministers were Richard Holden (1692-1700) who published a sermon preached before Trinity House, and George Stanhope also the Dean of Canterbury who was vicar from 1700 until he died in 1728.

St. Nicholas with its mediaeval tower is in a secluded location.

Sir John Evelyn (1620-1706) kept an important diary at Sayes Court near the church and corresponded with Pepys.

Significant memorials included: *Chancel* - William Hawkyns 1589 brother of Sir John commissioner of the Navy, Captain Edward Fenton 1603 a Latin inscription who went with Frobisher to find the N.W. Passage; *South* - Sir Richard Browne of Hitchin 1604, his son Christopher Esq. 1645 and grandson Sir Richard bart 1682; *North* - Peter Pett master shipwright 1652 with a frigate emblem, two sons of John Evelyn 1658, and Capt. George Shelvocke who navigated the globe 1742. A tablet on the west wall records Christopher Marlowe poet and playwright who died in a brawl in a Deptford tavern in 1593.

The number of baptisms was about 42 per year in 1600 but by the end of the century had reached over 200, thus the parish petitioned the Commissioners for another church and St. Paul's was consecrated in 1730. However, there were lengthy deliberations over matters of tithes and funding, thus the parish of St. Nicholas ended up covering a small parcel of land in the vicinity of Deptford Green and the Old Town.

Repairs were carried out in 1780 with new bells cast, and the resulting structure was a mixture of red-brick nave and stone tower from different periods, although the interior with its galleries, transept-style aisles, and small chancel was more uniform. St. Nicholas found itself in a backwater by Deptford Green and Stowage, with social housing nearby, but was restored in 1940-58 and again more recently. In addition the area by the river was developed and modernized including the advent of the Thames Footpath.

C. 26 January 1654/55 John son of Mr. John Evelyn [and Mary] was baptized
2 March 1681/82 Jno son of Jno Evelyn Esq. grandson of Jno Evelyn Esq. and great grandson of Sir Richard Browne kt and baronet [9]

B. 1 of June 1593 Christopher Marlowe slaine by Francis Freziri sept. –
26 Janue 1653/54 John Standsfield Evelyn son of Mr. Joh Evelyn [sic]

St. Paul's, Deptford

George Stanhope, the Dean of Canterbury and vicar of Deptford and Lewisham, was one of the Commissioners for Fifty Churches. So it was no surprise that "with the steeple falling down" this was the first place chosen for a new church in October 1711.

The following year a sum of £400 was agreed to pay Richard Wise for 2.5 acres on the east side of Butt Lane, with a further £240 for four houses which had to be removed to create an avenue to the site. In addition, £70 was paid in compensation for lost crops, and Thomas Archer who travelled in Europe in 1691-93 was chosen as the architect. He also worked on edifices at St. John's Smith Square and Birmingham Cathedral.

Archer was inspired by the creations of Bernini and Borromini and adopted a strictly Baroque style, whilst the new church was begun in Portland stone in 1713. The masons were Edward Tufnell and Edward Strong jun. and 100,000 bricks were ordered for this site and Westminster. In fact work continued apace and Hawksmoor arranged for gates and walling at the east end in May 1715. However, there were problems over the adjacent rectory to the south which had to be triangular due to the shape of the site.

---

[9] John Evelyn (1655-99) inherited his father's literature and love of science translating Plutarch whilst his poems appeared in *Dryden's Miscellanies*. He married Martha Spencer at St. Andrew's, Holborn on 24 February 1679/80 and his own son John became a baronet in 1713.

By the time the Queen Anne Commission concluded business in September 1715 the roof was already going on, and George Osmond plumber was inserting pipes at 9d per foot and cisterns at 15s each. Due to the new constraints imposed, the services of Archer were dispensed with in 1720, and the building was finished four years later. In fact the imposing portico was only completed as contractors were leaving the site.

The parish boundaries were discussed by the Diocese of Rochester but problems soon arose. St. Paul's received most of the 2,000 acres in the original parish, and St. Nicholas which only retained land by the church and river - received the tithes for the *whole* area and thereby paid a good poor rate. The new parish to the south had a large population consisting mainly of poor residents who could not support a church, therefore St. Paul's which was completed in 1724 was not utilised for another six years.

A petition was then taken to the House of Commons by the new parish, and an Act was passed stating money from the Commission should be invested in South Sea Stock - for the support of a minister. Edmund Gibson, Bishop of London consecrated the church on 30 June 1730 and the first rector was William Norton D.D. (also of St. Nicholas) soon followed by James Bate B.D. in 1731-75. The King made the first presentation but this duty then fell to the patrons of the old church and initially to Mrs. Wickham.

The building sat in an irregular piece of land with Crossfield Lane at an oblique angle to the south, whereas a long footpath led up to the entrance and the semi-circular portico. The latter had four Doric columns reminiscent of Santa Maria della Pace, Rome designed by Pietro de Cortona in 1667, and with its semi-circular balustrade wrapped around the circular tower, lantern and spire - it provided a most assured sequence.

Archer, at St. Paul's, had come closest to solving the problem of combining a classical temple with a steeple, one that caused so much criticism regarding design elsewhere. At the entrance is a tablet recording the date of the consecration, with names of the rector and churchwardens inscribed. The church is raised up with steps on three sides, and some of the work was done by Thomas Lucas a local man including the vaulted crypt.

Regarding the interior the nave is a Greek cross, but the corners are filled-in with stairs up to the gallery in the west and warming rooms for gentry to the east. The columns that support the side galleries and pilasters on the walls are Corinthian, while the impressive chancel has a crescent of Doric columns with entablature around the altar. In addition the apse has a Venetian window with elongated openings. There is no clerestory and an elaborate cornice sits below the flat ceiling, "moulded" as in a stately home.

On entering the nave there is an extensive space in line with the High Church aims of the Commissioners, echoing Palladio's El Redentore in Venice. But there is a significant absentee. A picture of Queen Anne painted by Sir Godfrey Kneller for the church prior to its opening, was kept at St. Nicholas and has remained there ever since!

Benjamin Ffinch installed an organ in memory of his brother Matthew at the west end in 1748 - by Richard Bridge a probable pupil of Renatus Harris, whilst other fittings were a mural by Henry Turner (of 1725) and the pulpit part of a three-decker. Dr. Burney also gave a painting by Benjamin West (since gone) and two chairs. Such opulence, however, came at a price and the church was in decay by the 1850s, thus £930 was raised and the box pews were removed and heating installed. There were more repairs in 1883, although the rectory was then demolished and a new font came in 1897. The roof and spire were restored in the 1930s and the steps and balustrades reinstated outside in 2003-04.

St. Paul's one of the Fifty Churches was in the Baroque style of Rome - and completely different to St. Nicholas…

… With its elegant spire, grand portico and chancel apse it was rightly dubbed *"The Jewel of Deptford."*

Ministers and Parishioners

A number of families had ongoing links apart from the dockworkers, shopkeepers and tradesmen who came there for services, baptisms, marriages and the like. Of the ministers John Thornton of Clapham was a patron and presented the living to Richard Conyers his brother in law in 1775, and Mrs. Wickham gave it to Rev. John Eaton in 1786. However, the most significant appointment was Rev. Charles Burney (1757-1817) son of the music historian and brother of Admiral James and novelist Fanny, Madame d'Arblay.

Rev. Burney was educated at Charterhouse and Cambridge then was tutor at a private school in Chiswick under Dr. William Rose. He married Sarah his daughter in 1783 and when the doctor died took over the school, bringing it to Greenwich ten years later.

A large number of naval and military officers were educated at this private academy and he collected a library of 13,000 rare books and manuscripts. After being ordained in 1808 he was appointed to St. Paul's in 1811, and a Royal chaplain and prebend of Lincoln, whilst he kept his collection of books in the polygonal rectory. A memorial was erected to him in the south chancel in 1818, whereas his son Charles Parr Burney (1785-1864) ran the school until 1833 and his books formed a core of the British Museum.

According to the records, Benjamin Ffinch Esq. resided at the Gravel Pitts found at the south end of Church Street, and his brother Matthew was variously a wine merchant and a brick manufacturer of Back Lane (New King Street). The family memorial below that of Burney is in the Baroque style by Thomas Green of Camberwell, and their descendant Rev. Benjamin Sanderson Ffinch was the rector in 1834-73 during the renovations. There is also a memorial to John David Rolt son of *the clerk of cheques* in the docks, and later a gentleman. He is believed to be a descendant of the Pett family of shipbuilders, and a relative of the Ffinches, whereas his son Peter was an M.P. for Greenwich.

On the north side of the chancel is one of the best works to James Sayer vice admiral of the white (and his family) who was first to plant a British flag on Tobago in 1739. With its anchor, flag and cannon it was quite good enough for a cathedral and was the work of Joseph Nollekens, the renowned sculptor. In fact, a plaster bust of C. Burney presented by his son is nearby, the work of Lewis A. Goblet an assistant to Nollekens.

Naval Associations - A battle scene by R. Cleveley, and memorials to Admiral Sayer and "Dr. Charles Burney M.A."

With regard to the parishioners Robert Cleveley may have had some training with Paul Sandby, but initially worked in the docks and spent time as a purser on ships of the Royal Navy. He specialised in painting maritime scenes especially of battles and first exhibited at the Royal Academy in 1780, whilst his father and brother were also artists. Another connection at this time was John Harrison who established the London Hospital for the poor in 1740, which later moved to Whitechapel Road (memorial in south aisle).

Not surprisingly, given the nature of docks and their environs, there were also social reformers who came from the area. Anthony Brady was storekeeper of the Royal William Yard in Plymouth and married Marianne Perigal at Berry Pomeroy in 1810, her father Francis a master of the clockmakers (see St. Botolph's, Bishopsgate). He transferred to the Victualling Yard, Deptford and a son Antonio was born there soon after.

Antonio Brady was educated at Colfe's in Lewisham then a clerk in the yard with his father. After a series of promotions he was first superintendent of Admiralty contracts and retired with a good pension and a knighthood in 1870. He then devoted himself to social, educational and religious reform and investigated local geological deposits making many finds for the Natural History Museum. He was buried near his home at St. John's, Stratford in 1881, whereas his son Nicholas was a minister in Essex.

However another resident, who was born just after him, was far more radical regarding social issues. George Harney entered the Naval School at Greenwich, but took work with Henry Hetherington editor of a socialist paper and became involved with the Chartists meeting Karl Marx and Friedrich Engels. He edited the *Northern Star* and persuaded them to write articles, whilst he advocated socialism in Trade Unions and stood as a Chartist against Lord Palmerston at Tiverton in 1848. After this he immigrated to Massachusetts in 1863 but later returned to Newcastle, England and died there in 1897.

Another interesting link was Arthur Martin son of a smith born at St. Agnes, Truro in 1798 who married Margaret Blyth (daughter of the gunner) at Frindsbury, Kent in 1823. The couple initially lived in Poplar, but then moved to Church Street, Deptford where they attended the Wesleyan chapel at Mary Ann's Buildings and St. Paul's parish church. Martin was employed as the chief blacksmith for William J.A. Ive a shipbuilder and wood merchant on the Green, but there were soon some serious developments.

One of their customers was accused of stealing wood from *the frame* in July 1840 and the case went to the Old Bailey, but Martin and his employer were cross-examined and the verdict was not guilty. The main issue was whether there were five or six feet of wood taken, a matter that was hard to prove in retrospect. In addition his wife Margaret died in February 1842 and was buried at St. Paul's, whilst he married Elizabeth Kennedy soon after and immigrated to Cape Town which was then part of Cape Colony.

This was a good decision, and he established a house and shop at Loop Street in the central district. His son Cyrus became a successful bookseller and daughter Octavia was a governess to Rev. R. Birt of the London Missionary Society at Peelton. However, his other daughter Parthenia assisted Grace Pocock (née Buzacott) at her girls' school, and after she died married husband John Pocock a successful pharmacist in 1874. [10]

C. 7 January 1747/48 Robert and John *tweens* of John and Sarah Cleveley shipwright
26 March 1769 John David Rolt s. of John and Mary clerk in ye yard Broomfields
9 Dec 1811 Antonio Brady s. Anthony & Marianne Victualling Yd. storekeeper 10 Nov
16 Mar. 1817 George s. George & Sarah Harney Back Lane rigger J.F. Walker cur 17 Feb
25 Dec 1828 Cyrus James s. Arthur and Mgt. Martin Giffin St. smith B.S. Ffinch 28 Sept
4 October 1835 Parthenia Mary d. Arthur and Mgt. Martin Church St. smith 9 Sept

M. 29 September 1766 Henry Goodwyn junior bach and Elizabeth Gray spin b.o.t.p. by licence by Jas. Bate rector pres Henry Goodwyn, Mary Gray (see Greenwich)
29 August 1822 William Hunt and Sarah Hobman b.o.t.p. banns by William McGuire rector pres. Wm and Eliza Ann Hobman [parents W. Holman Hunt bapt. St. Giles]

B. 26 March 1746 Mathew Finch Esq. from Mr. Benjamin Finch's near ye Gravel
3 May 1753 John Harrison surgeon at ye London Hospital
5 November 1776 James Sayer Esq. vice admiral of the white
3 January 1818 Rev. Charles Burney DD FRS rector of parish, 61 J.F. Walker cur.

Deptford Congregational Church

The Congregational or Independent faith was established in the town in 1660, and Butt Lane Meeting House was built just east of the High Street in 1756. However there was an unexpected connection in Hampshire. John Purkis of Hounsdown in the New Forest claimed descent from "Purkis" who took the King's body to Winchester, as is recorded on the Rufus Stone. The family were charcoal burners, but raised horses on their farm and operated a stage coach from Southampton to London by the 18th century.

Huguenots were still being persecuted in France and the family adopted two children of the name Dubois, who were later entitled to a large inheritance. However, the elder son John Purkis married Mary Dubois (or Boyes) at Eling on 2 June 1773, and had fourteen children, many of whom worked in the locality as carriers and auctioneers. The mother gave up any plans to return to France or her fortune, and died at the almshouses of All Saints, Southampton in 1841 - "leaving over 100 descendants to lament the loss."

---

[10] William F.H. Pocock (a nephew) ran the business and was mayor of Rondebosch, whilst his children were noted academics: Mary Agard was a botanist at Cambridge and Rhodes Univ. and Lewis was a classical scholar at U.C.L. moving to Canterbury Univ., Christchurch N.Z., in 1927. The latter's son Prof. J.G.A. Pocock became a renowned historian at Baltimore University.

During her sojourn at Eling the minister was of lax faith thus they left the Anglican fold and then joined the Independents. A son Isaac was born at Eling in 1784 and on reading Richard Baxter's *Call to the Unconverted* entered the theological seminary at Gosport under Rev. David Bogue, and was ordained in 1809. The London Missionary Society sent him to Kingston, Jamaica but he became ill and was cared for by the Governor's son.

Returning home, he married Mary Johnson daughter of a naval officer at Alverstoke on 15 March 1811, who he had been engaged to whilst studying at the seminary. His young bride was a *Ward of Chancery* which caused delays in the marriage and in the meantime he preached the Gospel around Gloucestershire and Somerset.

The next year he received a call to become the pastor of the Congregational church in Deptford, and when there wrote books, poems and a treatise on *Observance of the Lord's Day*. His wife also taught French and music from their home at 1 Poitiers Place. [11]

Meanwhile, his dreams were fulfilled when he was asked by St. John's, Quebec, to do missionary work, and he sailed from Southampton in 1821 - then after two years went to La Prairie on the St. Lawrence River. Apart from Catholic churches there was no place of worship except in Montreal, thus he set up a residence in the barracks. Due to the fact there were so many Scottish he established a church linked to the Presbyterians.

After failing to pay homage to the Archbishop of Montreal in c.1831, his family had to retire to New York and he toured the Catskill Mountains, but could not settle and went to Toronto soon afterwards. He established several pioneer churches and spent time at Guelph and Osnabrück but returned to see his mother in 1840, and preached a sermon to his family at Totton before his departure. This referred to their long history in the area and a copy was then passed around his relatives for those who had missed it.

He spent the last twelve years of his life at Osnabrück forming a church with Scotch Presbyterians and German Lutherans, but died there on 16 October 1852. Returning to events in Deptford the original chapel was replaced by a larger edifice in 1862, but lost considerable land to the railway and was closed down in 1969.

C. 15 October 1811 William s. of Thomas and Mary Smart of New Row b. 15 Sept.
11 April 1815 Elizabeth d. of Thomas and Elizabeth Smart, Bethel Place b. 16 Mch.

The Rufus Stone, New Forest

"My very dear relatives and friends; Although your names were never obscured by titles or had a reputation for literary degrees, yet they were both ancient and honourable, no less than the Norman usurper who sent them to the depths of the forest... After travelling thousands of miles I have found just a few of that name and it is remarkable that a family should stay in one place 800 years... I trust this sermon is of use and return to a land where despotism shall never plant its feet."

Isaac Purkis on the eve of his departure 26 June 1840 (extract)

---

[11] Elizabeth the sister of Rev. Purkis met Thomas Smart a shipwright at the church and they were married at Eling in 1814 then lived at Bethel Place by the canal. A step-son William Smart built a chandlers shop in Bridge Street, Greenwich and his son George Cloke Smart was a blacksmith at the corner of Lamb Lane occupying a fine property in Hyde Vale.

Greenwich

Although the parish never had a single dock within its precincts, it became a centre for naval manoeuvres quite as important as those of its illustrious neighbour. In fact, it was known as East Greenwich until the 19th century. Sitting beside a prominent rise above the river it was occupied from the earliest days and had evidence of Bronze Age tumuli, Roman villas and Watling Street running across Blackheath just to the north.

The Danes were camped there for three years during their conflicts with Kent and at this time captured Alfege, Archbishop of Canterbury. However, it was also a settlement of the Saxons and the name *Grene Wich* referred to a village by the green, but in general the inhabitants were occupied with fishing for much of the mediaeval period. The area had two manors, and one with Lewisham was in the hands of St. Peter's, Ghent but after the suppression of alien priories it passed to a Carthusian monastery at Shene.

The Palace of Placentia, Greenwich (17th century)

Home to the Tudors it was demolished in 1660, being replaced by the Royal Naval Hospital and its school.

The second nearer the river was held by Odo, Bishop of Bayeux but was seized by the Crown on his disgrace in 1080, thus determining its later history. Edward I resided there in 1300 confirmed by an offering made in the chapel of the Virgin Mary, and Henry IV signed his will at the residence. But Henry V granted it to his uncle Humphrey, Duke of Gloucester in c.1417 who embattled the house, enclosed a park of 200 acres, and built a tower on the site of the observatory. He then renamed it Placentia Palace in 1433.

The connotations of the name were pleasaunce or pleasurable and after his death King Edward IV lavished much money on completing it, and it became a principal residence of Henry VII. Consequently his son Henry VIII was born there as were granddaughters Mary and Elizabeth - today a tablet in the pavement by the river records this. Indeed the latter neglected Eltham Palace home of his forebears, and his marriage to Catherine of Aragon was solemnized in the *friary church* at Greenwich on 11 June 1509.

This continued to be a Royal Palace and was the summer residence of Elizabeth I, while James I settled the manor on Anne of Denmark who started her "house of delight" to the rear. This was completed by Inigo Jones in Palladian style in 1635. Underneath was the cobbled roadway into Greenwich which had formerly been on the north side of the palace. During the Civil War the complex was occupied by troops and was home to the Lord Protector, but when it was returned to the Crown in 1660 was found to be in poor repair and was scheduled for rebuilding.

Charles II then employed the architect John Webb, a nephew by marriage to Jones, who designed some rooms by the river on the west side. However little more was done and after Queen Mary put forward plans for a new Royal Naval Hospital, Sir Christopher Wren recommended the site and the old buildings were demolished in 1694. The only one retained was that designed by Webb, and this formed part of the King Charles range near to the river in the west - the Queen Anne range being to the east.

The whole composition was cleverly planned with Wren, Vanbrugh and Hawksmoor all having input. Designed in four quadrants the buildings included a central avenue, which looked south towards the Queen's House and Greenwich Park beyond.

This ensured the view from the former was not obscured, whilst the principal buildings behind were set closer and included two blocks: King William to the west with its painted hall by Sir James Thornhill in 1727, and Queen Mary to the east with chapel of St. Peter and St. Paul finished by Thomas Ripley in 1752. The whole ensemble with its colonnades and two domed-towers, looking towards the park and Ranger's House, was one of the finest architectural compositions in the country - if not in the entire world.

The first forty-two pensioners were admitted there in January 1705 but this number had risen to over 2,000 by the end of the century. A plot of land to the east on the Woolwich Road was used for a burial ground from 1749, and Nicholas Tindal one of its chaplains produced his famous *A History of England* and was buried there in 1774.

However, there was a serious fire in 1779 which destroyed much of the chapel and it was rebuilt by James Stuart the antiquarian. Its main features were elegant Greek designs by the door, an ornamented ceiling, painting of the shipwreck of St. Paul, and galleries for officers on each side. In the quadrangle was a statue of George II by Rysbrack 1735, and at the chapel entrance memorials to Thomas M. Hardy, Admiral R.G. Keats colleague of William IV, and a large relief to the ill-fated Sir John Franklin expedition.

The Hospital School for the sons of sailors was started in 1731 and a separate building was erected to the rear. A larger one was added for 200 boys with support from Lloyd's in 1782-84. The Royal Naval Asylum founded in 1798 was then given the Queen's House by George III in 1806, and colonnades and wings were added. In fact, some 800 children were resident and received an education by 1815 (with a ship at the centre).

The two were amalgamated as an upper and lower school in January 1821 and the old buildings became an infirmary, whilst the Admiralty took over in 1829. It had a tough naval regime but good scientific attainment, and several of its pupils became admirals or distinguished navigators. The west wing was later enlarged and the upper school took 400 boys already educated and nominated by patrons. In fact, a similar number attended the lower school (including some girls) - all being aged from 9-15 years. [12]

Meanwhile, the Royal Naval Hospital closed to pensioners in 1869 and the site was then used by the Royal Naval College from 1873-1998, but when this closed the only similar college was Britannia at Dartmouth. Greenwich Park housed the Royal Observatory on the site of the old tower from 1675 and was first open to the public in the 18th century. The hospital site was then made a public space in 2002, and includes accommodation for the University of Greenwich and a College of Music.

---

[12] Several buildings were demolished when the Royal Hospital School removed to Holbrook in 1933, and those that remained became the National Maritime Museum in 1937.

St. Alphege's, Greenwich

The manor of Greenwich with its appendage of a church was with the Abbey of Ghent from the 10th century, and this was confirmed by Edward the Confessor and William I. This situation pertained for many years but at the start of the reign of Henry V in 1414 all alien priories were suppressed, and both *Est Grenwych* and *Levesham* passed to the new priory at Shene. However under Henry VIII the advowson of the vicarage came into the hands of the Crown and there it has remained ever since.

A second church was built in 1290 and from the 15th century there was a major palace nearby, thus Henry VIII was born there on 28 June 1491, and baptized at the church by the Bishop of Exeter with the Earl of Oxford and Bishop of Winchester as godparents. As stated before, other members of the Royal family were born in the palace but they were baptized in its own chapel. The area gradually developed and in the reign of James I the park received a wall, but there were just a few properties by the church and along the road to Lewisham on Samuel Travers map (of 1695).

Further changes occurred in the 18th century with building on Church Street down to the river and at the foot of Blackheath Hill, but there was a disaster at the church due to the practice of burying within its walls. The whole structure was weakened and during a storm the roof and walls collapsed into the nave on 28 November 1710, whilst only the tower remained and very few memorials were retrieved from the rubble.

Prior to the collapse there were numerous tablets and brasses, most of them relating to members of the Royal household: *North Aisle* Robert Adams architect and surveyor of the Queen's works 1595, Mary wife of Richard Ward sergeant at arms 1628; *Chancel* Richard Bowyer gentleman of the chapel and the master of the Royal children 1561, Anthony Lyle usher to Queen Elizabeth 1579, Henry Trafford clerk of the green cloth 1585; *South Aisle (east)* Sir William Hooker mayor 1674 fine marble d.1697; and *Outside* Richard Warner master of the barges 1612, Thomas Sheffield keeper of the manor 1613 and by the doorway William Boreman senior armiger 1646.

Regarding the latter there were two school foundations the first of these started by Sir William Boreman who endowed the Green Coat School with an income of £700 in 1672. The other foundation was established by John Roan under his will in 1643 and left a sum of £95 per annum to the vicar and vestry to educate 20 poor boys. Dr. Thomas Plume the vicar in 1658-1704 was governor of the Grey Coats from 1672, and they owned all of the properties in Roan Street (but removed to Maze Hill in the 1920s).

R.N. Hospital Chapel by James Stuart 1779-89 has intricate mouldings on its walls and ceiling.

Thomas Tallis (1505-85), "father of church music." His work was revived by Vaughan Williams and at Westminster Cathedral.

Meanwhile, the most notable memorials were to a musician and perambulator. Thomas Tallis (1505-85) was a composer of church music at St. Mary at Hill, Waltham Abbey and Canterbury, but became musician in the Chapel Royal from 1543. Elizabeth I then gave him permission to print music with William Byrd. After writing Latin masses he made a transition to hymnal compositions - although his memorial in the chancel was lost.

On the south wall was an inscription, "William Lambarde of Lincoln's Inn sometimes master in chancery, keeper of the rolls and records within the tower, endowed a college of the poor and died at Westcombe 19 Auguste 1601; also his son and heir Sir Moulton Lambard 1634." The former was born at St. Nicholas Acon in 1536 and entered the legal profession but produced his *Perambulation of Kent*, the first work of its kind, in 1570. His memorial was salvaged from the rubble and removed to Sevenoaks Church.

Regarding local almshouses the Queen Elizabeth College was started by Lambarde on Greenwich Road and run by the Drapers; whilst Henry Howard, Earl of Northampton established another college by the river in 1613. This was endowed by his brother the Duke of Norfolk for twenty pensioners - twelve being local and eight from Norfolk. The foundation of Trinity Hospital with its chapel was run by the Mercers, and a monument to the Earl was removed there from a ruined edifice at Dover Castle in 1696.

Hawksmoor's Church - However, this was a time to look forward and not backwards. With impeccable timing the parish approached the Commission for Fifty Churches, and asked that money from the coal levy used for St. Paul's and the Hospital, be applied to the church. Hawksmoor submitted a plan in June 1712 although initially each church was of a general model with low pews, raised chancel and grand portico. Matters moved on when agreements were made with the mason and bricklayers in January 1713.

The development of the design was then apparently piecemeal. It was decided to accept some arcades suggested by the architect in the March, and the finishing touches were made in September 1714. Indeed, "a notice for pewing" was sent out to the parishioners in March 1715 to make it ready. The building had a prominent location on Church Street with a new churchyard above Roan Street to the west, and it was consecrated by Dr. Francis Atterbury the Bishop of Rochester on 29 September 1718.

The ancient tower was incorporated in the design and the main features were the west end displaying a broken-arched pediment, Tuscan columns, pilasters, and an entablature with cornice and triglyphs extending all around the building. In fact, the ceiling was the largest unsupported church span to be found anywhere in the country.

As the concept of a more general design was abandoned, Hawksmoor put forward a monolithic tower to adorn the church. But there was a lack of funds at this time and his scheme was eventually used at Limehouse. However, the original retained-steeple was to be a poor substitute. John James, who assisted Hawksmoor on the project, encased it in Portland stone and added a domed cupola with finial in 1730.

The spire was destroyed again a hundred years later when it was struck by lightning, and a number of prominent people were connected with the church (see below). Meanwhile the area experienced many changes. A bridge was built over the creek in 1804 and Bridge Street developed to the north, then a station opened in 1836 and George Smith designed the building in 1840. Plans to construct a viaduct across Greenwich Park were contested for many years, and eventually a tunnel went through to Maze Hill in 1878.

The church was designed by Hawksmoor in 1712-18 and the tower by James in 1730 but the interior was restored in the 1950s. It has stained-glass to Wolfe (above), Gordon and Tallis.

The roof was burnt down in March 1941 destroying most of the nave, although the walls and tower survived, and it was restored by Sir Albert Richardson in 1953. The main features are: the light brown woodwork of the pews and balconies (which are on slender supports), the large wooden pulpit, the chancel in a recess with panelled arch, and oval ceiling with mouldings and chandelier - like that seen in a livery company hall.

Entering beneath the tower at the west end there are steps up into the vestibule; and on the left is a memorial to Sir George Biddle Airy (1801-92) who started the Greenwich Meridian in 1851/84. On the right is a tablet to John Julius Angerstein of "Woodlands" a merchant, Lloyd's underwriter, art collector and churchwarden died 1823.

In the northwest corner are a plaque, tablet and window to Major General James Wolfe who died during the taking of Quebec in 1759, and nearby a window to General Gordon of Woolwich who was baptized in the church. He was a relative of Enderby, Governor of the Sudan and hero at the siege of Khartoum died 1885. Further along the north wall is a memorial to Samuel Enderby himself and his wife of Crooms Hill (see inset), and in the southwest corner a brass plaque to Thomas Tallis (1876) and a window. Adjacent to this is a part-Tudor organ with 18th century keyboard - rebuilt in 1910.

Other worthies recorded in the parish included Henry Kelsey who was born at East Greenwich the son of a mariner in c.1667. He was apprenticed to the Hudson's Bay Co. for four years in 1684 and worked as a fur trader having contact with the Cree, whilst he explored virgin areas and was one of the first white men to see the prairies. Kelsey was also a ship-master and married in Greenwich, then was in charge of York Fort and other company lands up until his retirement to England in 1722 (there is a plaque).

Lavinia Besswick was baptized at St. Margaret's, Westminster in October 1710 and her father may have been a naval officer. She took the name of Fenton after the husband of her mother, and first went on the stage at the Haymarket Theatre in 1726. However, it was at Lincoln's Inn Fields that she made her name especially as Polly Peachum in *The Beggar's Opera*. She married her lover Charles Powlett, 3rd Duke of Bolton in France in 1851 and they resided at Westcombe House, Greenwich (an ancient manor).

Goodwyn - Enderby - Gordon

Henry Goodwyn (1719-1801) purchased shares in the Red Lion Brewery at East Smithfield in the 1760s and his son Henry was married at Deptford at this time. They built the business up as Goodwyn & Co. and installed the first engine by Boulton & Watt in 1784, while the father lived at Maze Hill and died in 1805. Henry junior of Blackheath continued the business but it passed to Hoare & Co. in 1823, and son Thomas W. married Elizabeth daughter of Charles Flower the mayor, then ran a soap and starch company at Goodman's Fields.

There were a number of local connections and Samuel Enderby (1756-1829) married Mary Goodwyn, elder sister of Thomas, and had addresses at Crooms Hill and Vansittart Terrace. His father founded a whaling firm which explored the Southern Oceans and was immortalised in Melville's *Moby Dick*, whilst they helped take convicts to Botany Bay corresponding with Sir Joseph Banks and discovered the ill-fated Auckland Islands.

Charles Enderby (1798-1876), his son, ran the operation from Paul's Wharf and Greenwich Marsh where he established a factory and house with viewpoint - still situated at Enderby's Wharf. However, after the factory burnt down he was governor of a new settlement on the aforementioned islands - which only lasted from 1849-53 due to the hostile climate.

Meanwhile, Henry William Gordon born 1786 joined the Royal Artillery and fought at Naples then married Elizabeth Enderby the sister of Charles. They had six sons three achieving senior ranks in the army and all fought in the Crimea: Sir Henry William KCB, Gen. Samuel Enderby and Gen. Charles George who made his name in China but was sent to evacuate Khartoum, and died before the relief expedition under Wolseley and Kitchener arrived.

St. Alphege's, Greenwich parish registers

C. 29 July 1788 Thomas Wildman s. of Henry Goodwyn gent. and Elizabeth b. 26 Apr
28 February 1833 Charles George the son of Henry William and Elizabeth Gordon of Woolwich Common major R.A. born 28 January by Thomas Singer

M. 7 April 1698 Henry Kelsey of this parish and Eliz: [abeth] Dix of ye same by licence of ye Lord Bishop of Rochester
31 May 1817 Henry William Gordon captain R.A. of Woolwich and Elizabeth Enderby o.t.p. licence by G. Mathus vicar pres. Saml. Enderby, M. Enderby, Jn. Enderby

B. 2 November 1724 Henry Kelsey [gap from 1713-48]
2 April 1759 Lieut. General Edward Wolf [his father]
20 November 1759 General James Wolfe in the chancel
3 February 1760 Lavinia, Dutchess Dowager of Bolton
5 February 1823 John Julius Angerstein Esq. of Woodlands, 91
30 October 1829 Samuel Enderby of Crooms Hill age 74
3 March 1846 Mary Enderby of Charlton, Kent, 78

General Charles "Chinese" Gordon (1833-85) was baptized at Greenwich, and was related to both Goodwyn and Enderby who had links there.

Greenwich Chapels - Apart from St. Alphege's there were a number of nonconformist chapels including the Independents at Devonshire Road and Park Street, the Providence Baptist in Bridge Street and the Methodist Hall in King George Street. One of the oldest places of worship was Our Lady Star of the Sea built on Crooms Hill for Catholic sailors who lived at the Hospital in 1793. This was rebuilt in impressive style by W.W. Wardell in 1851 with an interior by Pugin and still remains a landmark from the river.

The original parish became inadequate and St. Mary's, King William Walk was built by George Basevi beside the park and St. Mary's Gate in 1824. However it was closed in 1919 and demolished in 1936. Others were Holy Trinity, Blackheath Hill 1837-1950 by the Blue Coats School, Christchurch Trafalgar Road 1847-1989, St Paul's Devonshire Road 1865-1984 (still active), and St Peter's Bridge Street 1866-1955. The impressive St. John's, Blackheath in Gothic style was designed by Arthur Ashpitel in 1854.

St. Margaret's, Lee

Greenwich was bordered by Deptford to the west and by Charlton and Woolwich to the east, whereas across the common to the south were Lee and Lewisham. Regarding Lee the upper parish boundary was below the heath in the area of the railway, however on its western side it was demarked by a winding watercourse, the Kid Brook or Quaggy. The manor dated back to the time of Edward the Confessor and passed to Odo the Bishop of Bayeux, but came into the hands of Lewis Monson, Earl of Rockingham in the 18th century. However, the "Manor House" built on the land was unconnected.

A mediaeval church of flint and stone with plain nave and chancel sat on the hill above Lee Lane, and at the western end was a low tower, whose upper parts were rebuilt with brick and red tiles. But, due to the ongoing "ruinous state of the building" and need for repairs, there was "agitation" to replace it on more than one occasion. The rectory came under the Diocese of Rochester and the patronage passed to the Crown in 1641.

This was a popular area high above the environs of London and the resort of wealthy merchants from the metropolis during the 17th century. In addition, there were many burials of those from other areas. However, the church itself was not wealthy and had only a few monuments viz. Nicholas Annesley a brass 1593, Bryan Annesley gentleman pensioner to Elizabeth I alabaster and marble with Corinthian columns 1604, and tablet to Rev. Abraham Sherman rector who rebuilt the parsonage 1654.

Those outside were more numerous and some are now listed monuments: Hon. Joseph Pilgrim chief judge of Barbados 1733, Edmond Halley L.L.D. Astronomer Royal 1742, Thomas Negus D.D. rector of Rotherhithe 1765, Sir Samuel Fludyer a merchant 1768, William James the rector of Ash, Kent 1779, Thomas Lucas Esq. 1784, Trevor Charles Roper Lord Dacre 1794, and Sir John Call M.P. and military engineer 1801.

Regarding earlier residents, Samuel Purchas the travel writer was reputed to have lived in Lee but may have just "passed through," and Christopher Boone a Spanish merchant built Lee Place to the south in the 17th century. He was a good friend of John Evelyn and appears in his diaries, but must not be confused with Rev. Ralph Bohun who was the tutor to Evelyn's sons. In his will he left money for almshouses, a chapel and school which were built nearby on Lee Road, and extended under the Merchant Taylors. In fact several notable people lived in the parish and developed adjacent properties.

Sir Samuel Fludyer clothworker, director of the Bank, M.P. for Chippenham and mayor (in 1762) resided at Lee Place, but his brother Sir Thomas who worked with him built a modern villa above on the site of the moated manor house. The latter's daughter Mary Jane married R.H. Trevor Roper, Baron Dacre in 1773 and the property called Dacre House was her home until 1808. The former was demolished in 1825 and the latter in the 1900s, while their location is now denoted by Boone Street and Dacre Park.

Thomas Lucas a West India merchant and treasurer of Guy's was the next owner of Lee Place, but employed Richard Jupp to build a new residence on a mediaeval farmhouse site by Old Road in 1772. His widow Eliza married John Julius Angerstein after he died in 1784, and she sold it to Sir Francis Baring who bought the manorial rights and named it the Manor House in 1796. Thomas G. Baring, Earl Northbrook a philanthropist then sold the estate to the L.C.C. in 1898 and it became a library and gardens in 1902.

The New Church - There were a number of prominent rectors appointed including John Ovington D.D. chaplain to Queen Anne who published his sermons d.1731. Rev. Henry Reginald Courtenay came there in 1773 and was minister of St. George's Hanover Square and Bishop of Bristol and Exeter. He was buried at Grosvenor Chapel in 1803. Meanwhile, his successor Rev. George Lock (1770-1864) who resided in the Old Rectory was to preach and hold services in no less than "three churches."

Initially he struggled on in the damp mediaeval building which had 150 seats, but then commissioned Joseph Gwilt to build a new edifice on the site in 1813-14. This was by all accounts a beautiful structure of 500 seats and worshippers included Princess Sophia of Gloucester, Lord Bexley and other nobility. However, being built on the old foundations it was found unsafe and demolished except for the mediaeval tower, whilst land to the south was purchased from Thomas Brandram for £1,000 in 1839. [13]

St. Margaret's, Lee was built in Gothic style from 1839-41. The ornamental lych gate is dated 1882.

---

[13] Joseph Gwilt (1784-1863) married Louisa the daughter of Samuel Brandram merchant of Lee Grove in 1808, while his brother George restored Southwark Cathedral. The former did a survey of the churchyard with his son Charles Perkins Gwilt, the famous antiquarian, in 1830.

Sir Thomas Baring laid the foundation stone and a new Gothic structure was built by John Brown & Sons the surveyors to Norwich Cathedral, and it was consecrated by the Bishop of Rochester in 1841. The first wedding was that of daughter Julia Lock to Rev. Hanson. However, James Brooks soon carried out a major transformation introducing the Gothic Revival style in 1875-1900. The interior then had Minton tiles in the nave, a rood screen by Cox & Buckley, and Pre-Raphaelite murals and stained glass.

Royal Observatory, Greenwich (1824) before the time ball was added in 1833; and **Sir George Biddell Airy** Astronomer Royal from 1835-81.

Parish Matters - John Flamsteed (1646-1719) was the first Astronomer Royal in 1675 and occupied the new Royal Observatory, Greenwich, worshipping at St. Alphege's for forty years. He made some early sightings of Uranus, but came into dispute with Newton who published parts of his work with Halley whilst failing to credit him. He also held the parish of Burstow, Surrey from 1684 and was buried at the latter church.

Edmond Halley (1656-1742) was born at Shoreditch but attended St. Paul's and Oxford and went on an expedition to St. Helena to study the southern hemisphere. He identified a short period comet in 1705 and after some senior appointments was Astronomer Royal in 1720. He was followed by Nathaniel Bliss in 1762-64 and also John Pond who carried out modernization of the observatory in 1811-35 (all three being buried at Lee).

Other developments saw Lady Gertrude Proby start a school in 1834 with support from Arthur Witherby of Dacre House and Lady Baring of the Manor House, followed by a national school. In addition, Rev. Christopher Bowen perpetual curate of St. Mary's lived at Priory Lane, Blackheath Park and Hon. Crosbie Ward, Viscount Bangor's son, was a house guest - later editor of the *Lyttelton Times*. His brother Charles Bowen and his wife Georgiana moved to Lee Park in 1845, but sailed on the *Charlotte Jane* to Lyttelton, N.Z. on 7 September 1850. Their party included sons Charles C. J.P., secretary to Godley and editor of the paper, and also Croasdaile the first minister at Riccarton. [14]

---

[14] Charles C. Bowen (1830-1917) was the brother-in-law of Clements Markham president of the R.G.S. in 1893-1905; thus Bowen entertained both Scott and Shackleton at his home *Middleton Grange*, Christchurch prior to their expeditions to the Antarctic.

Further to this Rev. Edward J. Selwyn a relative of Bishop Selwyn N.Z. was headmaster of Blackheath Proprietary School by the station in 1847-64, and Rev. Bowen's two sons Charles Synge and Edward Ernest (a pioneer of soccer) were pupils there. To complete this antipodean link, the parishioners established a new edifice Christchurch on Lee Park from 1853-1940 and named it after Rev. Lock's own college at Oxford.

C. 1 Sept 1850 Letitia Ann Hannah d. of Charles and Georgiana Bowen of Milverton, Leamington, Warwick, gentleman by Geo. Lock rector "received" b. 4 March 1840

B. 22 July 1686 Christopher Boon [sic] merchant
20 January 1741/42 Dr. Edmond Halley of Greenwich; "He was a doctor of law, Savilian professor of geometry at Oxford, Astronomer Royal at Greenwich, honorary master of ye academy of science and the vice president of ye Royal Society"
4 September 1764 Revd. Mr. Nathaniel Bliss of East Greenwich *he was Astronomer Royal*
24 January 1768 Sir Samuel Fludyer bart and alderman of the City o.t.p. in linen
15 February 1795 Mr. William Parsons from St. Mary's, Lambeth [Drury La. comedian]
13 September 1836 John Pond F.R.S. lately the Astronomer Royal at Greenwich abode Greenwich by George Lock aged 68 [with Halley]

St. Mary's, Lewisham

The final parish to consider was on the extreme edge of London peering into the garden of Kent with its blossoming orchards, oast houses, and towering downs climbing above the plains below. In most ancient records it was called *Levesham*, or a homestead by the meadow, and its historic church sat beside the meandering River Ravensbourne.

Originally there was a priory owned by the abbots of St. Peter's, Ghent and the manor and parish church were included in its charter dating back to the 10th century. However, this all changed after the suppression of alien priories in 1414, and they were transferred to Shene Priory who presented several vicars. At the time of Henry VIII both likewise passed to the Crown who then appointed John Glyn as minister from 1545-68.

The parish covered a most extensive region reaching from Blackheath down to Rushey Green and Catford, then across to Sydenham, and fell within the Diocese of Rochester. In fact the main village was strung out along the high road for about a mile.

Rev. Abraham Colfe (1580-1657) arrived as curate in 1604 and was vicar from 1610, then laboured for the welfare of the parish and founded Colfe's School at Lewisham Hill in 1652. This was a reincarnation of an earlier foundation by Rev. Glyn and he entrusted its operation to the Leathersellers Co. In addition he enclosed the local common, started a library and reading rooms, and built some almshouses south of the church. [15]

There was then a considerable change and the manor and advowson fell to Admiral George Legge, son of Col. William Legge Royalist and Elizabeth Washington, in 1677. The son evacuated Tangier, held some senior Royal appointments and was a relative of Washington, then 1st Baron Dartmouth in 1682. The family estate was Sandwell Hall near West Bromwich but he built a large property on Dartmouth Row in 1690.

---

[15] Colfe's School on Lewisham Hill was originally under a proprietor but became a grammar school in 1794, and was transferred to Horn Park Lane in nearby Lee in 1958.

His personal chaplain Rev. George Stanhope became vicar in 1689-1728 and Dean of Canterbury while his son William Legge a politician was Earl of Dartmouth in 1711. The next two vicars were John Inglis in 1728-39 and William Lowth in 1739-95, whose niece Mary Eden was the wife of Ebenezer Blackwell of The Limes in the High Street. Their friend John Wesley was a regular visitor and used this as a retreat from 1746-82 (a plaque marks the site). Blackwell was also a major contributor to the renovations.

In fact the church was in a poor state by 1774 and the parishioners applied to rebuild it. George Gibson a local architect designed an oblong nave with portico of four Corinthian columns and an apse, although retained the west tower except the upper levels. He also designed "Woodlands" at Westcombe Hill for J. Angerstein. The work was finished on 7 September 1777 and Wesley preached there on 23 October, but the east end collapsed soon after and was replaced. An organ installed to the west had memorials on each side to John and William Petrie and family - the south one (of 1791) by Banks.

Other memorials on the north wall were to: Margaret Colfe 1643, Rev. Geo. Stanhope vicar for 38 years founder of Stanhope School 1728, and John Pery of Blackheath M.P. for Shoreham 1732. Outside was a tablet regarding Rev. Abraham Colfe and memorials to Rev. John Inglis vicar 1739, James Purcell Esq. Gov. of the Virgin Islands 1759, and Rev. William Lowth M.A. vicar for 55 years brother of the Bishop of London 1795.

Rev. Hugh Jones was curate and briefly vicar but resigned in favour of Edward Legge son of William 2nd Earl in 1797, although stayed there under him and when he was made the Bishop of Oxford was vicar again in 1825-31. He was succeeded by Henry Legge son of George 3rd Earl in 1831-79 and by Augustus son of William 5th Earl in 1879-91. The latter was at Handsworth, St. Mary's Bryanston Square and St. Bartholomew's Sydenham then became Bishop of Lichfield and has a memorial at St. Bartholomew's.

There were several Nonconformist chapels viz. a Wesleyan in Avenue Road near to the Limes, a Baptist in Dartmouth Place, and a Congregational on Courthill Road, also some early Anglican edifices. A converted Presbyterian was used at Sydenham until St. Bartholomew's was built by L. Vulliamy in 1827-32 - the latter appearing in a painting by Pissarro. Others were St. John Southend proprietary 1824, Church of the Ascension Dartmouth Hill 1838 a former Episcopal chapel, Christchurch Forest Hill built 1852-54, and the dramatic All Saints Blackheath by Benjamin Ferrey dated 1857-67.

St. Mary's, Lewisham has the look of a country church, but the portico by Gibson reflects the aspirations of city merchants.

There were some large mansions towards Blackheath and the main areas developed in the 1860s were the High Street, Loampit Vale, Blackheath and Sydenham. To the east there were mostly fields with some new roads at East Down Park, although nearby Lee already had many villas. Much of the parish remained rural, but from that time there was extensive development and a proliferation of churches in tandem with this.

The interior of St. Mary's itself was redesigned by A. Blomfield pupil of P.C. Hardwick in 1881, but today sits on a busy main road with only a few old buildings nearby. The residence of the Earls of Dartmouth passed to the Bishop of Southwark in 1905.

Regarding the parishioners Brian Duppa was baptized at the church and educated at Westminster and Christchurch, Oxford. He received wealthy patronage and became vice chancellor of the university and also the Bishop of Chichester, Salisbury and Winchester, despite his Royalist leanings. Another resident was Benjamin Martyn son of Richard an agent for the South Sea Co. in Buenos Aires. He helped establish Georgia in 1733 and as a playwright promoted the monument to Shakespeare in Westminster Abbey.

Other local connections were Benjamin Disraeli who attended the school of Rev. John Potticary at Elliott Place, Blackheath; and Rev. Joseph Prendergast the headmaster of Colfe's School from 1831-57. He left a bequest of £5,000 to establish a Girls Grammar which opened at Hilly Fields in 1890 and is still present there today.

C. 18 March 1588/89 Brian son of Jeffrey Duppa baptized
26 Oct 1755 George *Legge*, Lord Viscount Lewisham s. William and Frances Catherine the Earl and Countess of Dartmouth [M.P., Privy Councillor &c.]

M. 11 November 1818 Charles Samuel Goodwyn bach of Greenwich to Letitia Young spin o.t.p. licence by Charles Parr Burney M.A. of Greenwich, presence Geo. Young, Sophia Warner, Anne Goodwyn [the brother of T.W. Goodwyn]

B. 31 October 1763 Benjamin Martin Esq. buried [sic]
13 June 1792 David Henry for many years editor of the Gentleman's Magazine
27 February 1855 William Jowett of Clapham, 67 by Joseph Fenn & H. Legge vicar [16]

---

[16] William Jowett was a member of the C.M.S., while his wife Martha Whiting was a missionary on Malta for eleven years and has a memorial at the church (see St. John's, Horsleydown). Rev. Joseph Fenn (1790-1878) was also a missionary at Kottayam, India but returned to be vicar of Blackheath Park Chapel (St. Michael's) and helped establish the Proprietary School in 1830.

Additional Photos

St. George's, German Lutheran Church

Diedrich Beckman, a wealthy sugar refiner, established this at Alie Street, Aldgate in 1762, and most of the congregation were immigrants in that industry. The organ-case was by John England in 1794, and there was a new organ in 1886. But it closed and became H.Q. of the *Historic Chapels Trust* in 1996 (ref. page 14).

St. Mark's, Myddelton Square (right) was built by W.C. Mylne, surveyor for the New River Co., at Clerkenwell in 1825-28. This was due to a shortage of churches locally (ref. page 53).

St. Mary's or Somers Town Chapel

There was a chapel on Seymour Street in 1787, later taken by the Baptists, but this was built by W. & H. Inwood with a grant of over £15,000 in 1824-27. However the design and cost were much criticised. Rev. T.J. Judkin was minister until 1868, and it was the scene of Catholic conversions to the Anglican faith (ref. page 68).

Christchurch, Albany Street was built by James Pennethorne in 1837. The main features were the entablature, corner towers and columned spire. But today it is in need of repair, and a sign records it was "Antiochian Orthodox" from 1989 (ref. page 69).

Cumberland Hay Market

Regent's Canal Basin was built on a cutting in 1813, and the Cumberland Hay Market in 1819. This was used by merchants from Haymarket, Piccadilly, and had a large ice store. William Leftwich was first to bring ice from Norway to Limehouse and up by barge in 1822. It was later a centre for artists of the Camden Town Group i.e. R.P. Bevan, L. Pissarro and W.R. Sickert. The market closed in 1926, and after being bombed the basin was replaced by Windsor House and Regent's Park estate. A tablet records the visit of Duke of Edinburgh in 1955, and there are cobbles and historical information.

The Church of the Annunciation (below) was designed by W. Tapper in the High Church style in 1914. It is on the site of the old Quebec Chapel near to Marble Arch (ref. page 97).

St. Mary Magdalene, Munster Square

Rev. Edward Stuart an assistant at Christchurch built this and was first vicar in 1852. The architect R.C. Carpenter did churches in Brighton, and with its wide aisles equal to the nave it was based on the monastic Austin Friars. The east window was by A.W. Pugin, north aisle by son R.H. Carpenter in 1884, and a Clergy House was added in 1894 (but the tower was never built). The latter has a tablet to Frederick J. Ponsonby the second vicar (ref. page 69).

The Churches of Hampstead - from left to right (ref. pages 106 and 110).

Christchurch designed by S.W. Daukes in 1852 has work by George Gilbert Scott and Ewan Christian. Rev. C. Newman Hall lived at Vine House opposite and left almshouses, while Attlee married in 1922.

St. Saviour's by E.M. Barry was built on land of Eton College in 1856, and has a reredos/pulpit by T. Earp and windows by Clayton & Bell and William Wailes.

St. Stephen's was designed by S. Teulon in 1869 with a large tower, ornate arcade, and apsidal end on a sloping site. It is now an events venue on Hampstead Green.

Orange Street Chapel

This is situated just behind the National Gallery, and started out as a Huguenot Temple in 1693. Sir Isaac Newton and Charles Burney lived in the house next door. It was briefly Anglican but became Congregational in 1787, and was rebuilt last century. A plaque above the door records 1693-1929 (ref. page 147).

St. Matthew's, Great Peter Street (left) was built by George Gilbert Scott in 1852, but there were no funds available for the intended spire. It was located in an area of poor lodgings and a school, Peabody flats, and a Church House were then added. After the fire in 1977, the only parts remaining were from the crossing to the chancel, and Lady Chapel upstairs.

St. Stephen's, Rochester Row (right) was built by Benjamin Ferrey for Baroness A.G. Burdett-Coutts in 1847-50. It was constructed in the 14th century Gothic style with a High Church interior, and just opposite are some ancient almshouses (ref. page 173).

St. Augustine's, Kilburn

This stunning edifice by John Loughborough Pearson was built in 1871-80, with the spire added in 1898, and was based on the French Gothic so admired by Pugin. It was one of the architect's major works with Truro Cathedral, the towers of Bristol, and those in Auckland and Brisbane. Today, it sits above Carlton Vale near to Kilburn Park underground and its stucco villas, and the opulent interior is still used for high mass (ref. page 195)

St. Mary Magdalene, Woodchester Street

The first houses were built by the canal in the 1850s in a poor area. Rev. R. West grandson of H. Walpole then established a mission from All Saints, Margaret Street (as with St. Augustine) in 1865, and G.E. Street built the church on a restricted sloping site in 1867-72. Thus there was a false aisle on the north side. Ninian Comper built a south chapel and memorial to Father West in 1885, a school was erected at the end in 1914, and Martin Travers added a Lady Chapel in the 1920s. The old slum housing was cleared by 1962, and it now sits on Westbourne Green beside the canal, near to Little Venice and Warwick Avenue (ref. page 195)

South Kensington Churches
(ref. pages 219 and 221)

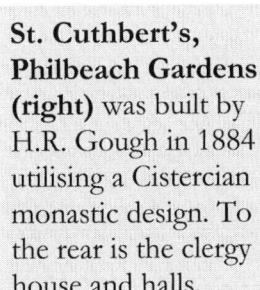

St. Paul's, Onslow Square (far left) was built by James Edmeston in 1860 with leafy gardens behind. The architect Edwin L. Lutyens was baptized there soon afterwards, and his father a friend of Landseer resided nearby.

St. Augustine's, Queen's Gate (left) was a mission for Holy Trinity in 1865, and Butterfield designed a church in 1869-76. It is one of his most important works with All Saints, St. Alban's and Melbourne and was recently re-united with Holy Trinity.

St. Cuthbert's, Philbeach Gardens (right) was built by H.R. Gough in 1884 utilising a Cistercian monastic design. To the rear is the clergy house and halls.

Chelsea Churches (ref. page 227)

Holy Trinity, Sloane Square the Cathedral of Arts and Crafts was built by J.D. Sedding in 1890. Its main feature is the east window by Burne-Jones and Morris (similar to that shown), whilst there is a baldachino and grand canopied pulpit. In the north aisle are memorials to the first two ministers: Henry Blunt 1832-36, also of Streatham, and Richard Burgess 1836-70.

Christchurch (below) was designed by Edward Blore in 1839, and is well set off by Robinson Street with its school buildings of 1872. Nearby is the Physic Garden the oldest after Oxford with a statue of Hans Sloane by Rysbrack, and Chelsea Hospital which has memorials to: Sir Thomas Ogle first governor, Sir David Dundas, Sir Thomas Renton royal physician, Samuel Wyatt the architect and Charles Burney musician.

St. Peter's, Vauxhall (left) was another designed by J.L. Pearson in 1863-64 - with an apsidal end, a Lady Chapel to the north and clergy buildings on each side. It is located by Spring Gardens and has a city farm on Tyers Street just behind (ref. page 239).

Bibliography, Sources

GENERAL RESEARCH

The Metropolitan Archives, Northampton Road, Clerkenwell
Westminster Archives, St. Ann's Street, Westminster
The Genealogical Society, Charterhouse Buildings, London

The Family Record Centre, Myddelton Street (former)
First Avenue House, High Holborn ref. wills after 1858
The National Archives, Kew ref. Army and Navy records
Scottish General Register Office, New Register House, Edinburgh
The Football Association Archives, 25 Soho Square, London

Burke's Gentry Baronetcy & Peerage; Butterworth's Business Biography; Crockford's
Clerical Directory; Hart's Army Lists; Law Society Records; National Biography; Navy
Lists; Oxbridge and Cambridge Alumni; Who's Who
Charterhouse, Eton, Harrow, Westminster, Winchester; Times Newspaper & Index

History of the Football Association for the F.A., Green G. (Naldrett 1953)
Association Football, Fabian A.H. and Green, Geoffrey (Caxton 1960)
Assoc. Football and The Men Who Made It, Gibson A. & Pickford W. (Caxton)
The Wow Factor, Smart J.B. (Blythe Smart 2005)
The Founders of Soccer, Smart J.B. (Blythe Smart 2008)

I.G.I., Free B.M.D., G.R.O. online (cert.), P.R.O. census-wills, Scotland's people,
peerage.com, American census, 19th century Street Directories

SPECIFIC RESEARCH

John Rocque Map of London 1746 (online ref. MOTCO)
Historical Map of London by Stanford 1862 (ref. mappalondon)
Commission for 50 new churches, Minute Books 1711-27 - British History online
reference the London Record Society compiled by M.H. Port (1986)
Individual Churches from Strype, church pamphlets/sites, and Wikipedia

St. Katharine's by the Tower: Royall Family and East London
Stratford le Bow: Environs of London, Lysons, Daniel 1796 (Br. History online)
Wesley's Chapel and Leysian Mission at City Road (online)
Charterhouse its History and Records, Collins, Francis (Harleian Soc. Vol. 18, 1892)
Clerkenwell: Old and New London, Thornbury W. 1878 (Br. History online)
Parish Church of St. Alban's, Holborn - church history

St. Pancras & Neighbourhood, Roberts J.R. and Godfrey W.H. 1949 (online)
St. Mark's Hamilton Terrace church site (brief history)
Highgate school and church, Victoria County History 1969
Great Queen St. Chapel, Survey of London, Riley W. and Gomme L. 1914
Mary Davies and The Manor of Ebury, Gatty, Charles T. (Cassell & Co. 1921)
Spring Gardens & Orange St., Survey of London, Gater G.H. & Hiorns F.R. 1940

Craven Chapel, Survey of London by Sheppard F.H.W. 1963 (History online)
Trinity Chapel, Conduit Street, Old and New London, Walford E. 1878
J. Wilkes - Arch & Historical I of Wight, Boucher Rev. E. (H. Frowde 1896)
Bayswater Chapel, Victoria County History of Middlesex 1989 (online)
W.J.E. Bennett ref the Catholic Literature Assoc. 1933 project Canterbury
Chelsea, Survey of London by Sheppard F.H.W. 1983 (Br. History online)

Clapham, Lambeth, Victoria County History by Malden H.E. 1912
Stockwell & Kennington, Old and New London by Walford E. 1878
Arthur Pember's Great Adventures, Smart J.B. (Blythe Smart 2007)
Municipal Archive, National Archive, Public Library in New York
Southwark, Newington, Victoria County History by Malden H.E. 1912

Bermondsey, Rotherhithe, Old and New London by Walford E. 1878
Camberwell, Victoria County History by Malden H.E. 1912
Deptford, Greenwich, Environs of London, Lysons, Daniel 1796 (online)
The Real Colin Blythe, Smart J.B. (Blythe Smart 2009)
Isaac Purkis "The Fire Kindlers" by Purkis, Leslie S. (1930s)
Lewisham Record Office, High Street, Lewisham ref. Blythe
Lee and Lewisham, Old and New London by Walford E. 1878

PHOTOGRAPHS

All church drawings and photographs are by J.B. Smart, whilst any other pictures are out of copyright and fall in the public domain due to their age or description as such. E.C. Morley is reference Barnes & Mortlake Historical Society.

Drawings - Spalatro Palace, St. Mary's Whitechapel, St Mary's Haggerston, St. John's Wapping, Bayswater Chapel façade and St. Mary's Paddington.

Churches Index

General Index

Blythe Smart Publications